NATIVE PEOPLE IN CANADA

CONTEMPORARY CONFLICTS

JAMES S. FRIDERES
PROFESSOR OF SOCIOLOGY
UNIVERSITY OF CALGARY

D1264042

PRENTICE-HALL CANADA INC., SCARBOROUGH, ONTARIO

To three important people in my life:
Carol, Steffani and Jereme

Canadian Cataloguing in Publication Data

Frideries, James S., 1943-
  Native people in Canada: contemporary conflicts

ISBN 0-13-114058-2

1. Indians of North America — Canada — Social
conditions. I. Title.

E78.C2F74   971'.00497   C82-095307-5

Prentice-Hall, Inc., Englewood Cliffs, New Jersey
Prentice-Hall International, Inc., London
Prentice-Hall of Australia, Pty. Ltd., Sydney
Prentice-Hall of India Private Limited, New Delhi
Prentice-Hall of Japan, Inc., Tokyo
Prentice-Hall of Southeast Asia (Pte.) Ltd., Singapore
Editora Prentice-Hall do Brazil, Ltda., Rio de Janeiro

ISBN 0-13-114058-2

Production Editors: Heather Strongitharm/
                      Janet MacLean
Design: Joe Chin
Cover: Kok-Kwan Shum
Production: Monika Heike
Compositor: Linotext Inc.

Printed and bound in Canada by Hunter Rose Co. Ltd.
1 2 3 4 5 HR 87 86 85 84 83

Contents

PART II

PART III

Preface

The revision of this book is a response to the changes in Canadian society that have taken place in the past eight years, both on the part of government and on the part of Native peoples. The federal government has, in the recent past, begun to promote Native control over Native affairs, and has met with both acceptance and resistance. As a result, reforms have been introduced that are not entirely acceptable either to government officials or to Native people.

This revision also reflects the increasing amount of research on Native affairs that has been carried out both by government and by academics. This research reflects a variety of theoretical stances as well as modes of analysis. All of it, however, points to the need for more co-operation between all concerned if solutions to the problems encountered by Natives are to be implemented.

It is clear that, traditionally, Native-White relations have reflected a one-way communication process emanating from the federal government. Today, because of the increased politicization of Natives, communication has, to a certain extent, become a two-way process. Moreover, Native-White relations are no longer the exclusive concern of the federal government. However unwillingly, provincial governments, municipal governments, and private industry are now forced to confront Native issues. As a result, a new dimension has been added to the already complex interactions of Native and White cultures. Intergroup relations have become increasingly dynamic, though they continue to revolve around many of the old, familiar problems.

A number of new chapters have been added to update my analysis of the contemporary problems facing Native Canadians. A short overview of the *Indian Act* has been provided, along with some information on the historical development of the administration of the Department of Indian Affairs. A section on treaties and Native claims also has been introduced. These materials will provide the reader with a comprehensive overview of current Native issues as well as some of the problems that hinder solutions to these issues.

The sections on socio-demographic attributes, urbanization, and Native organizations have been updated and extended, once again demonstrating the remarkable advance in research on these issues.

Finally, I have added a new chapter on a neglected subgroup of Natives – the Métis. This chapter, by A. Olmsted, traces the emergence of the Métis and examines them within their contemporary socio-political context.

Acknowledgements

I have been helped by many individuals in the production of this book and I express my apologies for not being able to mention them all. Various scholars have been good enough to read parts of the manuscript and to offer criticisms and suggestions.

However, I must express my appreciation to certain persons and organizations. I owe a special debt of gratitude to Dr. Roy Bowles. I have drawn upon his ideas for stimulation and I have incorporated much of his research and thinking into this work.

I am grateful for the help of Katie Cook and the Department of Indian Affairs and Northern Development who continually honoured my request for more information. Without their help, this volume could not have been finished.

I would like to thank two people with whom I have spoken, worked, and corresponded, but never met: Janet MacLean, who did a thorough and professional job of copy-editing the manuscript, and Heather Strongitharm, who managed to put it all together in a relatively painless fashion.

Finally, I wish to extend my thanks to Special Projects Editor Marta Tomins, Acquisitions Editor Cliff Newman, and all those other individuals working for Prentice-Hall who helped in the final production of the book. It has been a pleasure working with them.

James S. Frideres
Calgary, Alberta

PART I

The first section of the book provides the historical context essential to an understanding of the contemporary issues now facing Native people in Canada. The section also provides documentation concerning the establishment of treaties and outlines some of the provisions within those treaties.

1

Natives
and History

Introduction

The economic and social status of the Canadian Native is characterized by abject poverty. The assistance that has been provided to Native peoples by empowered groups has usually been so minimal that its impact has been negligible. In general, the treatment of Native Canadians has been based on a single ideology – racism.

Although some people may object to this claim, racism is undeniably the underlying ideology of the manifest policies regarding Native-White relations throughout the history of Canada. To choose just one indicator, the proceedings of the federal parliament with regard to Native issues are shot through with racist dogma. As another example, Dosman (1972) has shown that the Agents' Reports of Native life have historically been inundated with racist comments. The following is an example from Alexander Morris, who arranged the initial treaties with Native peoples:

> Let us have Christianity and civilization to leaven the masses of heathanism and paganism among the Indian Tribes; let us have a wise and paternal government faithfully carrying out the provisions of our treaties . . . . They (Native people) are wards of Canada, let us do our duty by them . . . . (1880: 296-97)

And here is a statement by the Minister of the Interior, in 1902:

> Our position with reference to the Indian is this: We have them with us, and we have to deal with them as wards of the country. There is no question

2

that the method we have adopted (will bring) these people to an improved state . . . . There is a difference between the savage and a person who has become civilized, though perhaps not of a high type. (*Debate of the House of Commons, 2nd sess., 9th Parl., 1902: 3046.*)

The reader may claim that these are isolated examples from a different era. However, these statements are representative of the widely prevailing legal, academic, and literary attitudes of the time. The reader might also claim that people are far more enlightened today. Although the contemporary examples could be presented to refute this claim, discussion of this issue will be deferred until later in the text.

Although it may never be possible to quantify the degree of racism that exists in a given society, the evidence unmistakably reveals that racism widely distorts the attitudes of White Canadians toward Native peoples. Whether blatantly or covertly, most Canadians still believe that Natives are biologically and socially inferior; as a result, these people believe that there is a sound rational basis for discrimination against Natives at both the individual and institutional level.

Confrontations between Natives and Whites tend to focus on specific complaints and overlook broader issues. Hence, Natives are labelled as malcontents, troublemakers, and opportunists, labels that can only be defended through a distorted and abbreviated view of history. The stage for clashes between Natives and Whites has generally been set by historical facts and existing structural relations, though few people are interested in examining these.

For example, the Indians who protested at Cold Lake in the early 1970s were presented as irresponsible troublemakers. Yet surely the reasons for their protest were linked to the fact that hundreds of Native children die before their first birthday, that thousands of Native people are unable to get jobs, and that few Natives are able to secure adequate housing. When confrontations erupt, the suggestion that the fault lies largely with Native people reveals a short-term perspective and, often, a racist bias. Such a suggestion ignores the subtle violence that has been perpetrated against Natives since the arrival of the White explorers. It also serves those who want to remain in power and maintain the status quo that excludes Native Canadians from a share in their country's bounty, and that allows them to remain hungry, uneducated, and inadequately housed in the midst of plenty.

Some readers will be angered by these statements, and indignant that their society should be labelled racist. They will say that other history books do not make such claims. But history is humanity's way of recording past behaviour; historians are extremely susceptible to the political and social forces that govern while their histories are actually being written. What Natives have been encouraged to write histories?

And when Native histories have been written, why have they been dismissed as fabrications?

An author's explanation of social events depends on an individual point of view. Because overt social behaviour can be interpreted in many different ways, the historian must always infer the actors' motives. For example, if you saw your professor sitting in a pub late at night with a beautiful female student, you might assume many motives for his behaviour which may, or may not, be accurate. Historians infer motives for groups as well as for individuals. Unfortunately, until recently, our historians have largely been Euro-Canadians; largely, they have based their inferences on the same primary assumptions and have presented similar views of social reality.

Throughout recorded time, empowered groups have been able to define history and provide an explanation of the present. A good example is the portrayal of wars between Indians and Whites by Canadian historians. White historians have concentrated on these wars partly because of the "enemy concept": as Pelletier (1970) has pointed out, White endeavours are continually described in terms of fighting an enemy, whether the war is waged against crime, inflation, or cancer.

In the history books, when Indians attacked a White village or fort and won, the result was called a massacre. If Whites attacked an Indian village and won, it was described as a victory. Because the dominant group was able to make these interpretations and definitions, it was also able to keep others from initiating alternative explanations or definitions. History gives credence and legitimacy to a society's normative structure; to legitimize its power, the dominant group must reconstruct social history whenever necessary. The early reconstructions of Canadian history were effective: today, most Canadians continue to associate "savage" and "heinous" behaviour with Canadian Natives.

An example of the reconstruction of history can be found in the comparison by Trudel and Jain (1970) of French-Canadian and English-Canadian history textbooks. Anyone who reads, for example, about the battle of the Plains of Abraham in both an English and a French text, comes away feeling that the two books are not discussing the same event. As Patterson (1972) points out, alien history is pulled down and discredited, and national history replaces it. Continuity of tradition for any group is truncated when the communication channels are taken over by others who wish to transmit different information (Lindesmith and Strauss, 1968). How often have we known something to be true only to find out many years later that the government, or some other group, distorted information that might have led us to believe something quite different? Brown (1971) and Andrist (1964) have vividly portrayed American-Indian history from an alternative point of view. Their information concerning Indian-White relations is quite dissimilar to that provided by "established" historians.

Readers have reacted quite differently to books by Cardinal (1969), Pelletier (1970), and Waubageshig (1970) than they have to books by Morton (1963), McInnes (1959), and Lower (1957). The layperson typically rejects the conclusions of the first three authors as the products of bias. But the same layperson tends to accept the explanations provided by the second group of "established academic" authors. I am not suggesting that the first are right or the second wrong. But both groups deserve to be read and judged fairly.

It is essential to realize that the history of Canada that is taught from grade five through university has been written mainly by English-speaking Euro-Canadians, specifically of British ethnicity. The Ontario Education Commission, in a study of elementary Canadian history books, has discovered that many historical events involving Native people have not even been recorded. In fact, the commission found that many history books did not discuss the role of Indians in Canadian history at all. In a preliminary study, I have found the same omission from university history texts.

Walter (1971) characterized Canadian historians in their analysis of Indians in Canada as ignorant, prejudiced, and, in some cases, dishonest. But we do not have to attribute deliberate falsification to historians. In any reconstruction of the past, the author shapes an interpretation of events according to individual perceptions, memories, analytical preferences, and social background. Whether deliberately or unconsciously a reshaping of the past occurs. No historian is free of bias, no history is capable of presenting only the facts.

Native peoples in Canada are using the legal system at present in an attempt either to get back or to be compensated for the land they claim is theirs. They regard as a precedent the legal battle in Alaska between Natives and the United States Government in which Aleuts, Inuit, and Indians received $942 million and 40 million acres of land in compensation for lands taken away (Harrison, 1972).

Canadian Natives believe that, regardless of the legal outcome, their position will be strengthened by a court battle. If the courts rule in their favour, Native peoples will be in an excellent position to become an economically independent and competitive force in Canadian society. They will be able to shake loose the "wardship" policy that has plagued them since the coming of the White man. If they lose, they will have a clearcut instance of discrimination by White culture around which to mobilize. Stronger feelings of anger and hatred will emerge, and a tighter internal cohesion will form among Native people. An evil image of Whites will crystallize, leading to a bipolarized ideology in which all

Natives are seen as good and all Whites are bad. Radical and militant leaders will emerge.

Indian leaders in British Columbia have discussed the possibility of these developments in a National Film Board documentary called *This Land*. The film, dealing with the land issue in BC during the 1960s, clearly demonstrates the growing determination of Canadian Natives as they become increasingly angered by unfairness and lose all faith in the existing establishment procedures. Eventually, these Natives will rise to the call of their militant leaders, and a guerrilla-style war may result.

This text aims to give the student of Native-White relations a new perspective on the problem. Usually these relations are defined as a Native problem, and issues are addressed individually. Conventional solutions are then based on this perspective. In my view, however, Native-White relations are largely a White problem, although this does not absolve Natives from the need for a certain amount of house-cleaning. And no view of Native-White relations based on an individualistic perspective will provide solutions for large-scale problems, such as how to integrate Native people into the larger Canadian society.

Indian: A Legal Concept

Before we can present any historical data, we must first make a distinction between several different legal and quasi-legal categories of Canadian Natives. It is not easy to determine who is an Indian and who is not in Canada. Definitions are complicated by historical factors as well as by operational distinctions.

Initially, Whites defined Natives as Indian if they exhibited a certain way of life. However, after miscegenation had occurred for some time between Indians and Whites (specifically the French), a distinct ethnic group called the Métis emerged. For some time, a distinction was made between Indians and Métis. Both groups were legally recognized in Canada as ethnically separate and distinct. Later, more importance was given to Indians, and the label of Métis was downgraded as a symbol for a distinct ethnic group.

In the consensus before 1941, ethnic origin was traced through the mother. Since eastern Indian tribes were matrilocal, this seemed a satisfactory means of distinguishing Indians from other ethnic groups. Before 1941, children whose mother was Indian were also defined as Indian. However, this was only true for those people who had been previously defined as Indian under the *British North America Act*. Before 1941 Statistics Canada still made a distinction between Indian and "mixed origin".

In 1941, the definition was changed so that, for off-reserve Indians, the father's ethnic status determined that of his children. For those who lived on the reserve, both the mother's and father's lineages were used to classify a person as Indian (Romanuik and Piché, 1972).

In 1951 a more complex legal definition was introduced, stating that only those individuals who fell under the *Indian Act* would be classified as Indians.[1] Today, while the federal government only recognizes any legal obligation to registered Indians, it nominally recognizes the ethnic group referred to as Métis. On the other hand, certain provinces, such as Alberta, have formally recognized the Métis and have established Métis colonies.

Culture and race no longer affect the definition of an Indian: today's definition is a legal one. If someone who exhibits all the racial and cultural attributes traditionally associated with "Indianness" does not come under the terms of the *Indian Act*, that person is not an Indian in the eyes of the federal and provincial governments. The following categories explain the government typology.

REGISTERED INDIAN

The terms "legal", "registered", and "status" are generally used interchangeably to denote a registered Indian. Registered Indians are defined in a legal manner, as opposed to other Indians who lack special legal status. Because the original *Indian Act* (1876) has continually been changed by the federal government since Confederation, the legal definition of an Indian has been continually revised. In short, "Indian" refers to a person who, pursuant to the *Indian Act*, is registered as an Indian or is entitled to be registered as an Indian. Because of the complexity of such a definition, we reproduce Sections 11, 12, and 13 of the most recent *Indian Act* in their entirety:

11. (1) Subject to Section 12, a person is entitled to be registered if that person

(a) on the 26th day of May 1874 was, for the purposes of *An Act providing for the organization of the Department of the Secretary of State of Canada, and for the management of Indian and Ordnance Lands,* being chapter 42 of the Statutes of Canada, 1868, as amended by section 6 of the Statutes of Canada, 1869, and section 8 of chapter 21 of the Statutes of Canada, 1874, considered to be entitled to hold, use, or enjoy the lands and other immovable property belonging to or appropriated to the use of the various tribes, bands, or bodies of Indians in Canada;

(b) is a member of a band
    (i) for whose use and benefit, in common, lands have been set apart or, since the 26th day of May 1874, have been agreed by treaty to be set apart, or
    (ii) that has been declared by the Governor in Council to be a band for the purpose of this Act;
(c) is a male person who is a direct descendant in the male line of a male person described in paragraph (a) or (b);
(d) is the legitimate child of
    (i) a male person described in paragraph (a) or (b), or
    (ii) a male person described in paragraph (c);
(e) is the illegitimate child of a female person described in paragraph (a), (b), or (d); or
(f) is the wife or widow of a person who is entitled to be registered by virtue of paragraph (a), (b), (c), (d), or (e).

(2) Paragraph (1) (e) applies only to persons born after the 13th day of August 1956. R.S., c. 149, s. 11; 1956, c. 40, s. 3.

12. (1) The following persons are not entitled to be registered, namely,
  (a) a person who
    (i) has received or has been allotted half-breed lands or money scrip,
    (ii) is a descendant of a person described in sub-paragraph (i)
    (iii) is enfranchised, or
    (iv) is a person born of a marriage entered into after the 4th day of September 1951 and has attained the age of twenty-one years, whose mother and whose father's mother are not persons described in paragraph 11 (1) (a), (b), or (d) or entitled to be registered by virtue of paragraph 11 (1) (e), unless, being a woman, that person is the wife or widow of a person described in Section 11, and
  (b) a woman who married a person who is not an Indian, unless that woman is subsequently the wife or widow of a person described in Section 11.

(2) The addition to a Band List of the name of an illegitimate child described in paragraph 11 (1) (e) may be protested at any time within twelve months after the addition, and if upon the protest it is decided that the father of the child was not an Indian, the child is not entitled to be registered under that paragraph.

(3) The Minister may issue to any Indian to whom this Act ceases to apply, a certificate to that effect.

(4) Subparagraphs (1) (a) (i) and (ii) do not apply to a person who
  (a) pursuant to this Act is registered as an Indian on the 13th day of August 1958, or

(b) Is a descendant of a person described in paragraph (a) of this subsection.

(5) Subsection (2) applies only to persons born after the 13th day of August 1956. R.S., c. 149, s. 12; 1956, c. 40, ss. 3, 4; 1958, c. 19, s. 1.

13. Subject to the approval of the Minister and, if the Minister so directs, to the consent of the admitting band,
    (a) a person whose name appears on a General List may be admitted into membership of a band with the consent of the council of the band, and
    (b) a member of a band may be admitted into membership of another band with the consent of the council of the latter band. (1956, c. 40, s. 5.)

Registered Indians are under the legislative and administrative competence of the federal government, as spelled out in the *British North America* (BNA) *Act*, and are regulated by the contents of the *Indian Act*. Slightly more than 30 000 Canadians are considered registered Indians. Being registered means that, with some exceptions, a Native is attached to a band and on the "roll" in Ottawa. Over the years, a number of different criteria have been used by the federal government to decide who is and who isn't Indian. For example, at one time in history, an Indian who achieved a certain educational attainment was automatically taken off the roll and was no longer a registered Indian.

As identified in Figure 1.1, there are sub-types of legal Indians. First of all, legal Indians can be categorized according to whether or not they have "taken treaty"; that is, whether or not their ancestors signed a treaty with the federal government. As Figure 1.2 shows, Indians in British Columbia, the Yukon, Quebec, and the Atlantic provinces did not sign any treaties. Other groups, like the Iroquois of Brantford and Tyendingaga, who emigrated from the United States, are also considered non-treaty registered Indians.

Regardless of whether or not their ancestors signed a treaty, Indians are further subdivided into reserve and non-reserve, according to whether or not their ancestors were provided with reserve lands. For example, although a treaty (No. 11) was signed by Indians in the Northwest Territories, virtually no reserves exist. On the other hand, although British Columbian Indians have not taken treaty most of them live on reserves.

In summary, the classification of a group of people as Indian arises from a legal definition. The concept "Indian" today does not reflect social, cultural, or racial attributes. The distinction between an Indian and a non-Indian is strictly a legal one.

FIGURE 1.1   *Social-legal categories of Natives residing in Canada*

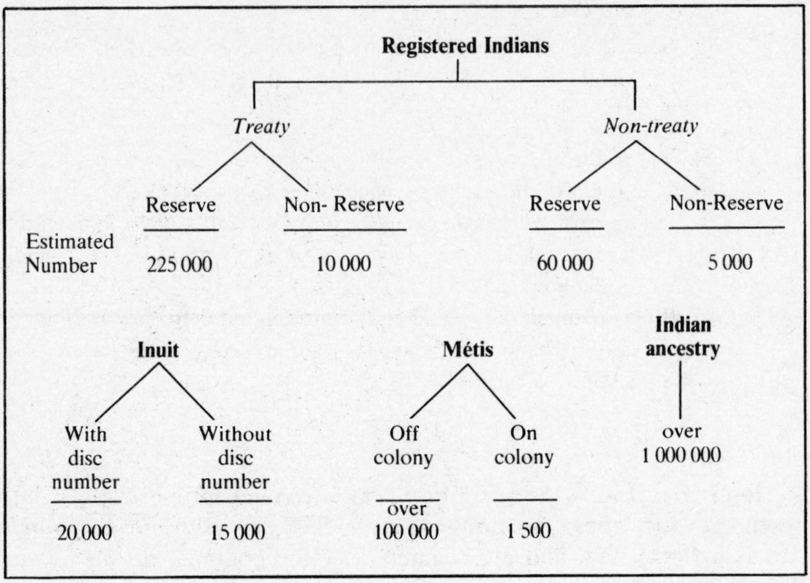

					Registered Indians					

Registered Indians

Treaty   Non-treaty

	Reserve	Non- Reserve		Reserve	Non-Reserve
Estimated Number	225 000	10 000		60 000	5 000

Inuit   Métis   **Indian ancestry**

With disc number	Without disc number	Off colony	On colony	over 1 000 000
20 000	15 000	over 100 000	1 500	

INDIAN ANCESTRY

Although people in this group may exhibit all the social, cultural, and racial attributes of "Indianness", they are not defined as Indians in the legal sense. Members of this group are not considered registered Indians because their ancestors refused – or were not allowed – to make agreements with the Crown. Included in this category are those Indians who have undergone "enfranchisement"; that is, have lost their Indian status.

Enfranchisement can occur in several ways. For example, until 1960 an Indian had to give up legal status in order to vote in a federal election. An Indian may choose to give up Indian status by applying formally to Ottawa. In so doing, that person also surrenders status for all heirs.

One of the most common ways today of losing Indian status is through intermarriage. Under Section 12.(1)(b) of the *Indian Act*, any legally Indian female who marries a non-Indian male loses Indian status for herself and for her children. On the other hand, if an Indian male marries a non-Indian female, the female becomes legally Indian as do any offspring that may result.

FIGURE 1.2 *Indian land surrendered for treaties*

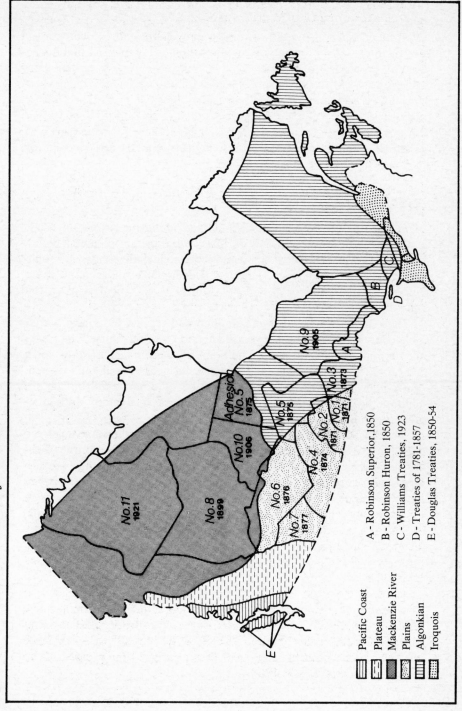

Pacific Coast
Plateau
Mackenzie River
Plains
Algonkian
Iroquois

A - Robinson Superior,1850
B - Robinson Huron, 1850
C - Williams Treaties, 1923
D - Treaties of 1781-1857
E - Douglas Treaties, 1850-54

In general, a move from Indian to non-Indian status is made on the basis of legal criteria that are set forth by the *Indian Act*. However, informal changes to the *Act* also affect movement between categories. For example, the Minister of Indian Affairs has recently announced that, at the request of band councils, the government will suspend certain sections of the *Indian Act* that discriminate against Indian women who marry non-Indians, as well as against their children. The Department of Indian Affairs has empowered the government to declare that any portion of the *Act* does not apply to any Indian individuals, groups, or bands. These powers under Section 4.(2) were recently invoked for members of certain bands in Quebec.

MÉTIS

Members of the Métis group are defined as having mixed ancestry. Initially, the title was confined to those with mixed French and Indian blood. However, it has now been broadened to include almost all people with partial Indian ancestry. These people, as well as those in the group entitled "Indian Ancestry", are not subject to the regulations of the *Indian Act*.

The Métis historically were defined and treated as a legal entity. The federal government, between 1870 and 1875, recognized the treaty and aboriginal rights of Métis. The Métis were given land or scrip worth $160 to $240, and medical and educational subsidies. If they wished, they could choose to "take treaty" and become registered Indians. In addition, crown lands were given to the provinces to set up Métis colonies.

In 1940, Indian Affairs changed its position and refused to acknowledge the existence of the Métis as a legal entity. At present, the Métis are re-emerging as an ethnic group in Canada, though they are not legally recognized by the federal government. A distinction between on-colony and off-colony Métis is necessary because, in Alberta, some Métis reside on specified land areas similar to Indian reservations. Because these Métis have a land base not available to other Métis, they have tended to develop more organized political structures.

INUIT

The category of "Inuit" has also undergone a number of redefinitions. Immediately after Confederation, the Inuit were placed under the control of the *Indian Act*. However, after a short time they were, and continue to be, placed under the direct jurisdiction of the federal government under the BNA *Act*.

When Canada began to develop the North, the government decided that a census was needed to establish the actual number of Inuit. As a result, a "disc" number was allotted to eack Inuk; for a time, only those with numbers were officially defined as Inuit. However, other definitions of Inuit have developed since and will continue to be used. For example, in the 1978 agreement between the Government of Canada and COPE, an Inuk was defined as a member of those people known as Inuit, Eskimo, or Inuvialuit who claim traditional use and occupancy of the land. In the case of the 1975 James Bay Agreement, an Inuk was defined as any individual who possesses a disc number, or has one-quarter Inuit blood, or is considered an Inuk by the local community, and such other persons as may be agreed upon.

RESULTS OF LEGAL DISTINCTIONS

Why have these legal distinctions been inflicted upon Canadian Natives? Those in power have surely been aware that such nominal distinctions have a "divide and conquer" effect. Natives became easier to control as they begin to fight among themselves. The distinctions between the non-treaty and the treaty Indians are particularly divisive: the two groups receive different privileges, different amounts of money from different sources, and different rights.

Red Power advocates are now attempting to point out the divisive effects of legal distinctions and to suggest ways of counteracting their influence. According to these advocates, legal status is irrelevant in the face of discrimination. Because the distinction between registered and non-registered Indians cannot be made visually, White Canadians cannot and do not distinguish between the two in daily interactions. All those who "look Indian" fall prey to the same stereotypes, and find themselves treated as though they were lazy, drunk, or happy-go-lucky. Moreover, Natives who fall under separate legal categories often lead similar life styles. Thus, the similarities among Natives frequently overshadow the legal differences.[4]

In a recent article, Dyck (1980) points out that the term "Native" is becoming increasingly popular with academics, lay persons, and politicians. This term, he argues, serves to cognitively combine peoples who, from a White Canadian perspective, are similar. Yet the various categories into which the Native population is divided are not irrelevant; indeed, under specific circumstances, these "internal" differences can be very important. As Dyck suggests, these differences can be exaggerated or ignored by the dominant group at will to suit its purpose. Distinctions can be emphasized to divide the Native population, or ignored through stereotypes and generalizations that avoid individual issues.

The History of Native-White Relations

In general, White Canadians have shown contradictory attitudes toward Native people. Whites have publicly proclaimed respect for Natives' rights while privately denying them such basic claims as the right to vote and the right to choose their reserves (Anderson and Wright, 1971; Washburn, 1965). Because an extended historical review of Native-White relations is beyond the scope of this book, the reader should consult the following sources for a thorough discussion: *Report on the Affairs of the Indians in Canada, 1844*; Jenness, 1937; Stanley, 1952; and Patterson, 1972.

This chapter will briefly examine the history of the relations between the two dominant Canadian groups and Native peoples. First the French policy will be considered, then the British. Conclusions have been based on documents and histories written during the time of contact; this gathering of information through historical documents is known as a content analysis. Analysis has been limited to formal and informal documents relevant to the times, including personal corrspondence between government officials.

FRENCH-NATIVE RELATIONS

French-Native relations must first be considered in the context of North America as a whole before we can turn specifically to Canada. A thorough review of the documents available on the attitudes of French settlers to the Indians reveals that no well-defined policy was established to govern French-Native relations. Generally, the French were attempting to exploit the land and to continue the "pseudo-colonization" of North America. However, initially, they did not intend to settle New France with any large stable population. Moreover, only a small number of French people wished to emigrate to New France; this fact, combined with France's mercantilistic philosophy[5] and the strong influence of Roman Catholicism, meant that no policy of cultural or physical genocide was invoked.

Initially the French were totally dependent on the Indians, but the relationship between the two soon changed to a symbiotic one. Intermarriage, or "wintering in", between French trappers and Indian women soon became common practice and was encouraged by French authorities who wanted to strengthen Indian relations so that the fur trade would continue. These marriages between French men and Indian women were not meant to be exploitive; the relationships were stable and the father was considered legally responsible for his wife and offspring.

In general, the French tried to expand their territories in North America by peaceful means. Usually they succeeded, because their agricultural style of life only minimally disrupted Native life.[6] After they had settled a territory, the French then asked the Indians to join in a treaty to acknowledge submission to the King of France. In this way, the French usually won territory without actually expropriating it. However, the process was not always so peaceful, and the French were certainly prepared to use force when they found it expedient to do so. When the Marquis de Tacy was placed in charge of Canada in 1663, his commissions included a provision for the use of arms to subjugate the natives if necessary. [7]

The two strongest ideological influences in seventeenth-century New France were Roman Catholicism and mercantilism, which was at its most popular as an economic theory. French policy, rather than treating Indians as distinct and inferior, tried to make them over into French citizens, at least in Canada.[8] This ideology of "Frenchification" is illustrated in various exchanges of letters between religious and state leaders of the day. For example, on April 6, 1666, Colbert wrote to Talon that:

> In order to strengthen the Colony in the manner you propose, by bringing the isolated settlements into parishes, it appears to me without waiting to depend on the new colonists who may be sent from France, nothing would contribute more to it than to endeavour to civilize the Algonkians, the Hurons, and other Indians who have embraced Christianity, and to induce them to come and settle in common with the French, to live with them and raise their children according to our manners and customs.

Talon replied, some seven months later, that he had tried to put Colbert's suggestions into practical operation under police regulations. Colbert then wrote, on April 9, 1667, as follows:

> Recommendation to mold the Indians, settled near us, after our manners and language.
> I confess that I agreed with you that very litle regard has been paid, up to the present time, in New France, to the police and civilization of the Algonkians and Hurons (who were a long time ago subjected to the King's domination) through our neglect to detach them from their savage customs and to obligate them to adopt ours, especially to become acquainted with our language. On the contrary, to carry on some traffic with them, our French have been necessitated to attract those people, especially such as have embraced Christianity, to the vicinity of our settlements, if possible to mingle there with them, in order that through course of time, having only but one law and one master, they might likewise constitute only one people and one race.

Another exchange of letters from the period demonstrates that this policy of assimilation was expressly favoured by the king. Duchesneau, in his letter to de Signelay, November 10, 1679, writes:

> I communicated to the Religious communities, both male and female, and even to private persons, the King's and your intentions regarding the French-ification of the Indians. They all promised me to use their best efforts to execute them, and I hope to let you have some news thereof next year. I shall begin by setting the example, and will take some young Indians to have them instructed.

In another letter to de Signelay, dated November 13, 1681, Duchesneau states:

> Amidst all the plans presented to me to attract the Indians among us and to accustom them to our manners, that from which most success may be anticipated, without fearing the inconveniences common to all the others, is to establish villages of those people in our midst.

Thomas, commenting on this letter, says:

> That the same policy was in vogue as late as 1704 is shown by the fact that at this time the Abnaki was taken under French protection and placed, as the records say, "in the centre of the colony." (1896: 544)

Through a policy, then, of assimilation rather than genocide, the French were able to maintain relatively amiable relations with the Native population for quite some time.

When war broke out with England in the eighteenth century, the demand for fur decreased and the French mercantilistic philosophy came to an end. War also brought a change in the French policy toward the Indians. Native land rights began to be systematically ignored (Harper, 1947: 131). Letters signed by Louis XV at this time give companies headed for New France full ownership of the land, coasts, ports, and havens of New France, and full right to dispose of these properties in any way they desired (B.F. French, 1851). Similar provisions can be found in the privileges, power, and requirements given to the Company of One Hundred Associates by Cardinal Richelieu nearly a century earlier.[9]

BRITISH-NATIVE RELATIONS

The Natives' experience with the English was considerably more negative than that with the French. This was partly due to the operation of different structural variables when the English made a serious bid to control New France. Mercantilism as an economic theory had been discarded and the importance of the fur trade was dwindling; colonization in the true sense was now important. In addition, the religious ideology of the British had a very different basis than that of the French. Manifest destiny and the Hamlite rationalization[10] pervaded the British secular way of life, exemplified in the Protestant ethic that hard work and no play would bring salvation.

A review of the documents relevant to the initial contact period between the English and the Indians in Canada reveals that Native concerns were completely overlooked and ignored. Little control was exerted over the British settlers as they expanded westward. As Thomas points out, the Indians were not even mentioned in discussions when land was given to companies.

> For example, the letters patent of James I to Sir Thomas Gage and others for 'two several colonies', dated April 10, 1606, although granting away two vast areas of territory greater than England, inhabited by thousands of Indians, a fact of which the King had knowledge both officially and unofficially, do not contain therein the slightest allusion to them. (1860: 550)

Although later charters recognized the existence of Natives, they did so in an extremely racist fashion. In the charters of Charles I, this statement, typical of several, authorizes the state to

> ...collect troops and wage wars on the barbarians, and to pursue them even beyond the limits of their province and if God shall grant it, to vanquish and captivate them; and the captive put to death....

Until 1755, the English followed a policy of expediency. At first they chose to ignore the Native population. When this was no longer feasible due to the need for westward expansion, the English chose to isolate Indians through the reserve system or to annihilate them, as they did the Beothuk Indians of Newfoundland. In 1755, Indian agents, today called superintendents, were appointed, formally establishing Canada's policy of treating Native people as wards of the state. Significantly, the Indian agents initially placed in control of the reserves were always military men.

By 1830, the federal governent was questioning the value of the Indian for Canada's future. Although it remained a concern for some, invasion from the south by the United States was no longer an immediate and direct threat. Because there were no other potential attackers, Indians were not likely to be needed for support in battle. Without their status as military allies, the Indians had no value for White Canada. Thus, in 1830, Indian Affairs was removed from military control and became a branch of the public service (Surtees, 1969). This change of jurisdiction allowed the British to adopt a more humanitarian attitude toward Natives.

The first *Indian Act* after Canadian Confederation was passed in 1876. It was first revised in 1880, and received minor alterations in 1884 and 1885. In 1951, the *Act* underwent a major revision which left it essentially in its present form. Interestingly enough, the 1880 version of the *Act* and the present one are remarkably similar, indicating that Indian Affairs has not undergone any major ideological shifts in the past hundred years of dealing with the Native population.

Conclusion

The policy governing Native-White relations was administered differently throughout Canada. In Ontario and Quebec, until 1860, the imperial government handled all the affairs and expenses of Native Canadians. At that time, a Crown Lands Department was established and a comissioner appointed to assume the role of chief superintendent of Indian Affairs. In other areas of Canada, the Indian Affairs office was administered directly by the various provincial or colonial governments.

Included in the BNA *Act* of 1867 was a special provision allowing for the administration of Indian Affairs to come under the control of the Government of Canada. Initially, Indian Affairs was the responsibility of the Department of the Secretary of State, but, in 1873, it was transferred to the Department of the Interior. In 1880, a separate Department of Indian Affairs was formed. In 1936, it was shifted to the jurisdiction of the Department of Mines and Resources, and, in 1950, it was again shifted to the Department of Citizenship and Immigration. From 1953 to 1966, Indians Affairs was handled by the Northern Affairs and National Resources Department. Since 1966, this has been called the Department of Indian Affairs and Northern Development. Hence, the administration of Indian Affairs has been shunted from one department to another, and never been allowed to develop consistent, humane policies.

Notes

1. In 1939 Duplessis was able to get northern Quebec Inuit redefined as Indians so that they came under federal, instead of provincial, control (Richardson, 1972).
2. *Indian Act*, R.A., c. 1-6, amended by c. 10 (2nd Supp.) 1974-75-76, c. 1/8, 1978, Hull, Minister of Supply and Services Canada, pp. 6-8.
3. One of the major concerns that DIAND has with regards to the changes in Section 12(1)(b) of the *Indian Act* is the financial cost. In a once-secret

document of DIAND entitled "Amendments to remove discriminatory sections of the *Indian Act*," the estimates run from $312 to $557 million. These figures are based on estimates of the number of women who would be reinstated as Indian and the percentage who would return to the reserves; the low estimate allows for a 30 percent reinstatement and a 30 percent return while the high estimate predicts a 100 percent reinstatement and a 70 percent return rate. In addition, approximately 57 000 children would be eligible for reinstatement.

The same document also estimates departmental costs for various other changes, such as altering the status of non-Indian men who marry Indian women and altering the status of the children of these mixed marriages. The document points out that Indian Affairs would not be the only department faced with escalating costs. National Health and Welfare, Canada Employment and Immigration, the Secretary of State, and the Department of Regional Economic Expansion would also be affected.

A federal-Cabinet discussion paper released in 1981 shows that settling land claims in the next 15 years could cost the government as much as $4.1 billion. About $1.8 billion of these claims concern land in British Columbia, where the fewest treaties were signed; most of the rest would be divided by Natives in the two Territories. The $4.1 billion includes reparation for hunting and fishing rights, payment for land, and the implementation of various programs and other benefits. In addition, another $500 million could be spent by the government in the next twenty years to settle specific claims. (*Indian News*, Vol. 22, No. 7, October, 1981)

4. See Davis, 1968, for a similar argument.
5. Mercantilism was the ecomonic theory that prevailed in Europe during the eighteenth century. Mercantilism held two basic tenets: the mother country was entitled to accumulate wealth in any form, and the mother country was entitled to exploit its colonies as a source for raw materials and a market for finished products, thereby maintaining a favourable balance of trade.
6. Because they used the seigneur system of agriculture, the French always remained near major waterways and did not intrude into the interior of New France.
7. For a more thorough discussion of this issue, see Cummings and Mickenburg, 1972.
8. Two additional factors contributed to the relatively peaceful relations between the French and the Indians: the military alliance of the Huron, the Algonkian, and the French; and the fact that the French settled in an area occupied by the Algonkian Indians who were migratory hunters (Jenness, 1967), had no real tribal organization, and were themselves recent arrivals in the area (Cummings, 1972).
9. See I. G. Shea, *Charlevoix's History of New France*, Vol 2, p. 39.
10. Manifest destiny, though it varied considerably, was the belief that Whites should control the world, or at least large parts of it. The Hamlite rationalization was the belief, taken from the Bible, that Ham was cursed by God and turned into a non-White person so that "he and his descendents should remain cursed and be subservient to Whites from then on." To the British, the Indians were clearly descendents of Ham.

2
The Indian Act

Introduction

The *Indian Act* is the foremost of the legislative Acts that affect Indians in Canada. Its importance cannot be exaggerated nor can its influence be minimized. It is the principal instrument by which the federal government and, indirectly, the provincial governments have exercised control over the lives of Indian people. Figure 2.1 on page 26, provides a brief chronological history of the development of the *Indian Act* as well as of the Department of Indian Affairs.

History of the Indian Act

The pre-Confederation period was characterized by the British view of Indians as a separate group to be dealt with in a specific manner. The colonial government saw a need for a policy to define and structure the relationship between Indians and non-Indians, a need which the federal government continues to uphold today. Whiteside argues that the *Indian Act* was intended to:

1. Undermine our traditional religion, leadership, and culture.
2. Sever our natural relationships with other Amerindians.
3. Ensure that the authority for all important decisions was removed from the influence of, and control of, our people .... As such, it should be known as "The Efficiency Act" which has over time inflicted mind-rape among some of our people.(1972:4,5)

The pre-Confederation period can be divided into two subperiods: military and missionary. Military influence over the Indians was predominant from 1746 to 1830 and missionary influence was foremost from 1830 to Confederation. Of course, neither military nor missionary influence can be so neatly categorized; the two overlap considerably (Whiteside, 1980).

In 1670, the British Parliament enacted the first legislation concerning Indians. This legislation was vague, but it established the paternalistic attitudes that have continued to this day, seeking to "protect" Indian people from "evil forces" and to promote the conversion of Indians to Christianity. At the end of the seventeenth century, the British colonial government in New York created the first Indian commissioner in North America and thus, indirectly, the first Department of Indian Affairs. Soon after, the British found it advisable to create and maintain alliances with such potentially important Indian tribes as the Iroquois; this new pragmatism became the basis of British policy until 1850.

The *Royal Proclamation* of 1763 publicly stated the following:

> It is just and reasonable, and essential to our interest, and the security of our colonies, that the several Nations or Tribes of Indians with whom we are connected, and who live under our Protection, should not be molested or disturbed in the Possession of such Parts of our Dominions and Territories as, not having been ceded to or purchased by Us, are reserved to them or any of them as their Hunting Grounds . . . .
>
> We do further declare it to be our Royal Will and pleasure, for the present as aforesaid, to reserve under our Sovereignty, Protection, and Dominion for the use of the said Indians, all the Lands and Territories not included within the Limits of our Said Three New Governments, or within the Limits of the Territories granted to the Hudson's Bay Company, as also all the Lands and Territories lying to the Westward of the Sources of the Rivers which fall into the Sea from the West and North West as aforesaid . . . .
>
> And we do hereby strictly forbid, on Pain of our displeasure, all our loving Subjects from making any Purchase or Settlements whatever, or taking possession of any of the Lands above reserved, without our especial leave and License for that Purpose first obtained.

Although this statement effectively specifies a procedure for the acquisition of Native hunting grounds by non-Natives, the major focus of legislation concerning Natives was limited until 1850 to single, special statutes regarding trade and alcohol. When the Indian Department was created in 1755, it was considered a branch of the military. Since the Indian Department was under military control, its legislation was aimed directly at the maintenance of Indians as allies. The Department was removed from the military in 1799, and returned to military control in 1816.

By 1830, the military importance of Natives in Canada was decreasing. Government bureaucrats had also begun to understand that Natives could no longer remain nomadic hunters and gatherers. The rapid influx of settlers and the upsurge in development meant that Natives would have to change their ways. Government commissions studied the problem and recommended that Natives take up agriculture. First, however, they would have to become "civilized".

Plans to civilize the Natives followed two separate, often conflicting, patterns. The first approach was to isolate Native communities but to enforce "British-agricultural-Christian" patterns of behaviour. The opposing approach was to place individual Natives among White settlers so that agricultural skills could be passed on naturally, by a process of enculturation. Experiments carried out by proponents of both policies experienced failure for a variety of reasons. The results were interpreted by officials at Indian Affairs as evidence that Natives were not capable of adapting successfully to the rapid social and technological change occurring at that time. To ensure that Indians would continue to have land upon which to reside and carry out agricultural endeavours, the *Crown Lands Protection Act* (1839) was passed. This assured Crown control and ownership of Indian lands.

In 1850, two *Acts* were passed that vested all Indian land and property into the hands of a Commissioner of Indian Lands[1]. In addition to protecting Indian lands, these *Acts* permitted no sale of Indian land without Crown consent and exempted Indians and their resident spouses from taxes in respect to Indian lands. More importantly, however, the *Acts* set forth the first legal definition of an Indian:

> First – All persons of Indian blood, reputed to belong to the particular Body or Tribe of Indians interested in such lands and their descendents.

> Secondly – All persons intermarried with any such Indians and residing amongst them, and the descendents of all such persons.

> Thirdly – All persons residing among such Indians, whose parents on either side were or are Indians of such Body or Tribe, or entitled to be considered as such; and

> Fourthly – All persons adopted in infancy by any such Indians, and residing in the village or upon the lands of such Tribe or Body of Indians and their descendents.

This definition was opposed on many fronts, and in 1851 was amended. The amendment forbade non-Indians to live among Indians and created the categories of status and non-status Indians.

In 1857, an *Act for the Gradual Civilization of the Indian Tribes* in the Canadas was passed. This *Act* explicitly stated the government's ideological position on the Indian role in Canadian society. The government felt that Indians must be assimilated in order to survive. To this end, the *Act* provided inducements for Indians to leave tribal societies and become enfranchised[2]; that is, to surrender Indian status. This *Act* remained more or less the same until Confederation, with the exception of a few highly specific changes. For example, the 1859 *Civilization and Enfranchisement Act* extended to the provinces of Canada the provisions regarding sale of alcohol to Indians, which had formerly applied only to Upper Canada.

The post-Confederation period, referred to by Whiteside (1980) as the "bureaucratic period", only ended recently, in the 1970s. During this period, bureaucrats wielded the ruling hand in Native affairs and exercised as much control over Native life as possible. The Department of Indian Affairs systematically ignored Native concerns and tried to convince Native leaders to behave like good children and not cause trouble.

The first stage in the post-Confederation era lasted until 1876, when the first comprehensive *Indian Act* was passed. During this time, the Secretary of State was given exclusive jurisdiction over Indians and Indian lands. The *Enfranchisement Act* of 1869 anticipated Canadian policy for the next hundred years, and was an early attempt to effect the assimilation of Indians into Canadian society. This attempt may have prompted the inclusion of Clause Six which, for the first time, stipulated that an Indian woman who married a non-Indian male would, along with her offspring, no longer be considered Indian.

By 1876, it became clear to the Canadian Parliament that acts relating to Natives were disjointed, contradictory, and generally peripheral in approach to the problem. The first comprehensive *Indian Act* was therefore designed, not to introduce new laws or amend existing ones, but to consolidate the many disparate laws that had already been placed on the statute books. Nonetheless, certain important changes were in fact made. For example, the use of location tickets was introduced to give individual Indians specific parcels of land on which to reside and carry out agricultural activities. Other amendments were legislated to regulate the surrender of reserve lands, the protection of reserves from encroachment and damage, the sale and management of Indian lands, the management and investment of Indian funds, and the election of chiefs and councils.

The new *Act* also effected some bureaucratic changes. First, it formalized the duties in the Canadian Cabinet of the Superintendent General of Indian Affairs. It also diminished the Governor-in-Council's authority respecting Natives, and gave much more discretionary power to the Superintendent-General.

As with all previous acts, Native input into the *Indian Act* was minimal. Some amendments were made to the 1876 *Indian Act* because of protests made by "advanced" articulate Indian groups. However, in general, Natives had little input into the decision-making process.

The decade after the first implementation of the *Indian Act* was one of rapid change for Natives on the prairies. The rapid depletion of the buffalo led to a loss of livelihood for prairie Natives and to a radical loss of cultural focus. White settlers encroached on Native territories in their drive to transform the prairies into farmland. Devastating epidemics and widespread famine completed the disruption of traditional Native lifestyles.

In 1880, the first separate Department of Indian Affairs was created under the Minister of the Interior, to address some of these issues. In addition, various amendments to the newly created *Act* were introduced at this time to cope with changes in the West. These amendments supported the policy of assimilation endorsed by the federal government. Enfranchisement was offered to the more "advanced" tribes and hand-outs were given to the "less-advanced" tribes. Members of marginal groups, such as the Métis, were encouraged to take land or money-scrip in exchange for a claim to Indian status.

The federal government also attempted during this time to address the issues of Native education and local government. These attempts culminated in the 1884 *Indian Advancement Act*, a statute that reflected the lack of agreement and general confusion surrounding these issues. For example, the federal government was still unclear as to how best to acculturate Natives through education. Should Natives attend White schools, or should they remain as isolated as possible? In the political sphere, should Natives be enfranchised or should they be allowed to retain their tribal system? The *Act* finally settled upon Native government by council, rather than chief, for each band. The Indian agent, a White man, acted as chairman of this council.

Two additional amendments were passed in 1884. The first seems to have emerged out of the unrest surrounding the Riel Rebellion in the West and banned the sale of fixed ammunition or ball cartridges to Natives. The second amendment was aimed more at assimilation; it barred the celebration of the Indian festival known as the Potlatch and the dance referred to as Tamanawas.[3] Around this time, also as a result of the Riel rebellion, Natives began to require permits to leave the reserve.

Even as it treated them like children, the government continued to encourage Natives to become self-sufficient and "civilized" throughout the late nineteenth and early twentieth centuries. On several occasions, this encouragement took the form of harsh acculturative measures by the Department of Indian Affairs. The refusal to pay annuities to certain bands and the systematic destruction of the tribal system were, according to official accounts, efforts to promote individualism and self-reliance.

The contradictory actions and attitudes of the federal government during this period reflected a transitional Native policy. This policy tried to protect the Natives and at the same time to provoke them to become more independent and less Native. In 1886 and 1887, amendments were introduced to the *Indian Act* to promote self-sufficiency; these measures included a general reduction of food, an extension of the *Act*'s enfranchisement provisions, and compulsory school attendance for Native children. Yet, even as it stressed Native independence, the federal government began to exert greater control over the lives of Native people. Increasingly, areas such as education, morality, local government, and land resources fell under government regulation. Significantly, the 1886-1887 amendments also attempt to "protect" Native concerns; they prescribe penalties for liquor abuse and prostitution, offer protection of lands from expropriation, and limit the exploitation of land for timber, mineral, and coal.

By 1906, amendments to the *Indian Act* had made it impossible to administer. Therefore, a new, consolidated *Indian Act* was introduced, consisting of 195 Sections.

Around this time, a new perspective on Native Canadians began to emerge. A tremendous influx of White settlers had entered the West, and the Native population began to be viewed as a barrier to Canada's general progress. In some cases, reserve boundaries interfered with urban growth; in other cases, the reserves prevented natural resource development. As a result of these issues, amendments to the *Indian Act* during the early twentieth century began to focus on the conditions under which land could be taken away from Natives. Provision had previously been made for the leasing of Indian lands to non-Indians; during World War I, such leasing was actively encouraged in an attempt to force Natives to use and increase the over-all productivity of their lands.

The regulations governing enfranchisement, always a concern of Indian Affairs, were once again amended in 1920. For the first time, the government could enfranchise Indians. The amendment read:

> The Superintendent General may appoint a Board to consist of two officers of the Department of Indian Affairs and a member of the Band to which the Indian or Indians under investigation belongs, to make enquiry and report to the fitness of any Indian or Indians to be enfranchised. The Indian member of the Board shall be nominated by the council of the Band; within thiry days after the date of notice having been given to the council, and in default of such nomination, the appointment shall be made by the Superintendent General. In the course of such enquiry it shall be the duty of the Board to take into consideration and report upon the attitude of any such Indian towards his enfranchisement, which attitude shall be a factor in determining the question of fitness. Such report shall contain a description

of the land occupied by each Indian, the amount thereof and the improvements thereon, the names, ages, and sex of every Indian whose interests it is anticipated will be affected, and such other information as the Superintendent General may direct such Board to obtain.

The *Indian Act* amendments of 1924 placed the Inuit under the jurisdiction of the Superintendent General of Indian Affairs. Up until this time, the Inuit had simply been considered Canadians; whenever relief was necessary, a minimal amount was provided. Originally, the 1924 Amendments were to include the Inuit under the definition of Indian. This was later changed so that the section simply read that the Superintendent General of Indian Affairs would be in charge of Eskimo (Inuit) Affairs.

Figure 2.1, following, highlights the structural and policy changes that have taken place in Indian Affairs since 1755.

FIGURE 2.1   *The development of the administration for Indian Affairs*

The following is a brief outline of the historical development of the administration of Indian Affairs. It is not meant to be a comprehensive listing. Rather, it is intended as a guide to correlate important legislative events with a particular departmental structure or organization.

1755	— Sir William Johnson was appointed Superintendent of Indian Affairs, Northern Department.
1763	— Jurisdiction over Indian Affairs in the old Province of Quebec was placed under the control of the Commander of the Forces.
1796	— Responsibility for Indian Affairs in Upper Canada was given to the Lieutenant-Governor.
1800	— Responsibility for Indian Affairs in Lower Canada was given to the Governor-General.
1816	— Jurisdiction over Indian Affairs in Upper and Lower Canada was transferred to the Commander of the Forces.
1828	— The position of Superintendent-General of Indian Affairs and Inspector General of the Indian Department was abolished and the office of the Chief Superintendent of Indian Affairs was created. Major-General H. C. Darling was appointed to this post.
1830	— The Indian Department was split into two offices. In Upper Canada, control was given to the Lieutenant-Governor. Colonel James Givins was appointed Chief Superintendent. In Lower Canada, control remained with the Military Secretary. Lieutenant-Colonel D.C. Napier, former resident agent at Montreal, was transferred to Quebec and made Secretary for Indian

Affairs. At this time, the reserve system was established in Upper Canada.

1841   — With the Union of 1841, the two offices of the Department were amalgamated and placed under the authority of the Governor-General.

1844   — Following the recommendation of the Commission of Inquiry into the Indian Department, 1842, a general reorganization of the Department was undertaken. The Civil Secretary was designated as Superintendent-General for Indian Affairs and the office of Chief Superintendent was abolished.

1860   — Responsibility for Indian Affairs was transferred from imperial control to the Province of Canada (23 Victoria Chapter 151). The Crown Lands Department assumed control of Indian matters and the Commissioner was designated as Chief Superintendent.

1867   — At Confederation, control of Indian matters was given to the federal government and responsibility was delegated to the Department of the Secretary of State for the Provinces. The Secretary of State became Superintendent-General of Indian Affairs.

1873   — The Department of the Interior was created (36 Victoria Chapter 4) and an Indian Lands Branch set up within it. A Board of Commissioners was established to administer Indian Affairs in Manitoba, British Columbia, and the Northwest Territories (P.C. 1873-111).

1875   — The Indian Boards were abolished and a system of superintendents and agents established. These were modelled on the Ontario administrative structure (P.C. 1875-1052/342D).

1876   — The *Indian Act* (39 Victoria Chapter 18) was passed which consolidated and revised all previous legislation dealing with Indians in all existing provinces and territories. A Board of Reserve Commissioners was set up to settle the Indian reserve question in British Columbia.

1880   — The Independent Department of Indian Affairs (43 Victoria Chapter 28) was set up. The Minister of the Interior, however, continued as Superintendent-General of Indian Affairs and presided over the new department.

1882   — The Central Indian Superintendency in Ontario was abolished and replaced by the various agencies already in existence.

1885   — Four new branches were created to revamp the departmental structure. These were a Statistics and School Branch, a Correspondence Branch, a Registry Branch and a Technical Branch. The Technical Branch prepared surveyors' drawings

and instructions. These joined the older Lands
Sales Branch and Accountant's Branch.

1886   — The Department was empowered to prepare and
register letters patent conveying Indian lands to
purchasers (49 Victoria Chapter 7). This created
the position of Registrar of Patents.

1889   — Two new branches were created. These were the Land
and Timber Branch and the Statistical, Supply, and
School Branch.

1894   — An independent School Branch was established.

1909   — A revamping of departmental structure took place.
Several distinct branches were set up to reflect the
expanded nature of the Department's activities.
These were the Secretary's Branch, Accountant's
Branch, Land and Timber Branch, Survey Branch,
Records Branch, and School Branch.

1912   — A Royal Commission on Indian Affairs for the
Province of British Columbia was appointed.

1916   — The Report of the Royal Commission on Indian
Affairs for the province of British Columbia was
completed.

1924   — An amendment to the *Indian Act* (14-15 George V
Chapter 47) brought the Inuit under the responsibility of the Superintendent-General of Indian Affairs.

1929   — An agreement was concluded respecting reserve lands
in Manitoba and Alberta, stipulating that they would
remain under federal control when these western provinces assumed control of their natural resources.

1936   — The Department of Indian Affairs was made a branch
of the Department of Mines and Resources. The branch
included the following components: Field
Administration (four inspectors, one Indian
Commissioner, and one hunderd and fifteen agents);
Medical Welfare and Training Service (responsible for
schools, employment, and agricultural projects);
Reserves and Trust Service (responsible for land matters
and timber disposal); Records Service (responsible for
current files and historical material).

1945   — Indian Health Services was transferred from the
Department of Mines and Resources to the Department
of National Health and Welfare. At this time, Eskimo
Health Services was also transferred from the responsi-
bility of the Northwest Territories Division of Lands,
Parks, and Forests Branch.

1947   — The Welfare and Training Division was split into a
Welfare Division (responsible for welfare, family
allowances, *Veteran's Land Act* administration, and
handicrafts) and an Education Division.

1949   — The Indian Affairs Branch was transferred to the
Department of Citizenship and Immigration. The

	administrative structure of the Branch remained virtually unchanged. A Construction and Engineering Service, however, was created.
1951	— A new *Indian Act* was passed after intensive study of the matter by a Special Joint Committee of the Senate and House of Commons, 1946-1948.
1959	— The Welfare Division was split into the Economic Development Division (responsible for resource management, industrial and agricultural projects, and placement services) and the Welfare Division (responsible for community development, family allowances, child welfare, and rehabilitation).
1960	— A new administrative region was created, the District of Mackenzie, with headquarters at Fort Smith.
1962	— The Indian Affairs Branch was reorganized. The Branch's functions were regrouped under three major activities: Education (responsible for all educational facilities); Operations (responsible for the activities of the Economic Development Division, economic planning, trusts and annuities, reserve lands and resources, welfare, field administration, and handicrafts); and Support Services (responsible for band councils, membership, estates, engineering, and construction).
1964	— A major reorganization of the Branch was undertaken in order to give more authority and responsibility to officers in the field. Three new directorates were formed: the Development Directorate (responsible for establishing and coordinating social, industrial, and resource development); the Education Directorate (responsible for establishing and carrying out educational policy); and the Administration Directorate (responsible for dealing with Indian lands and estates, membership, records management, field administration, and the provision of a secretariat and support services).
1965	— The Indian Affairs Branch was transferred to the Department of Northern Affairs and National Resources (P.C. 1965-2285).
1966	— The present Department of Indian Affairs and Northern Development (now also known as the Department of Indian and Northern Affairs) was established.

As Bartlett (1980) points out, by the Depression, the federal government appears to have reached a pinnacle in its regulation of and interference in the lives of the Native population. In 1927, the federal government once again consolidated the *Indian Act*. With the exception of amendments in 1938 which, among other things, repealed the *Indian*

Act's section on Inuit affairs, major changes were not made again until after World War II.

In 1936, a major restructuring of the Department of Indian Affairs was carried out. The Department moved from the Ministry of the Interior to the Department of Mines and Resources with the subsequent creation of four branches of Indian Affairs: Field Administration; Medical Welfare and Training; Reserves; and Trust and Records. This structure remained intact until 1945 when an Order-in-Council transferred the Indian Health Service to the Department of Nation Health and Welfare.

The amendments in 1938 instituted the first revolving-loan fund for Indians. This *Act* allowed the Superintendent General to make loans to Indian bands or individuals for the purchase of machinery and livestock or for the development of any project. In addition, the *Act* sought to ensure development of mineral, natural gas and petroleum deposits on reserves.

Because of world and domestic events, the federal government ignored Native Canadians from the late 1930s until the mid-1940s. After World War II, the Department of Indian Affairs emerged with a new direction in its policies and programs for Natives. Assimilation was discarded as a goal, and, as the Minister of Mines and Resources declared in 1946, the federal government decided to help Indians to retain and develop their Native characteristics while simultaneously taking on the full rights and responsibilities of Canadian citizens.

This new approach to Native issues was further reflected in the 1951 revised *Indian Act*. The new social conscience emerging out of a depression and two cruel wars led the Canadian government to rethink its programs and policies toward Natives. In 1946, a Special Joint Committee of the Senate and House of Commons was created to study the 1927 *Indian Act* and make suggestions for change. This committee reported the unqualified failure of the government's policy of assimilation. In addition, it found the *Act* itself replete with anachronisms and logical contradictions. The committee recommended that the *Act* be repealed and almost totally amended.

Although the revised 1951 *Act* was depressingly similar to the original *Act* of 1868, it did present some new ideas. Its two major innovations were the increased imposition of provincial laws and standards on Natives and the removal of excessive government control over local affairs on the reserves. The *Act* of 1951 emphasized: 1. Defining status more precisely. 2. Facilitating enfranchisement. 3. Allowing more responsibility to local bands. The end result, however, was a disappointment to most Natives in Canada. As Bartlett points out, even though the new 1951 *Act* was the culmination of a century of constant modification:

The astonishing feature of the amendments up to 1950 is how little, despite their frequency, they sought to accomplish. They were always preoccupied with details and never contradicted the basic rationale of the *Indian Act*, which demanded "civilization" and responsibility from the Indian population while denying them control over the forces affecting their lives. (1980:6)

A second Joint Committee of the Senate and the House of Commons continued studying the "Indian problem" and reported back in 1961. A further study of the educational, social, and economic conditions of Canadian Natives, now commonly called *The Hawthorn Report*, was made public in 1966. However, from 1951 until the present, no substantive amendments have been made to the *Indian Act*. Furthermore, few amendments of any type have been enacted during the past thirty years.

Our analysis of the *Indian Act* has revealed that, in the early development of Canada, few regulations were thought necessary to govern Native behaviour or Native-White inter-relations. If the government had invoked more stringent and encompassing legislation, it would surely have brought public opinion against it on a variety of fronts. However, as the population of Canada grew and the development of the land increased, pressures to regulate and control Native-White relations grew. The subsequent policy of assimilation and civilization was thought to be the best way to prepare Natives to enter the rapidly industrializing, larger Canadian society.

Since colonial times, the dominant group has changed in its ideology toward Natives. This change in ideology has been directly reflected by changes in the policy governing Native concerns. As pointed out by Leslie and Maguire,

Early concerns were the liquor traffic, unscrupulous traders, and land speculators. By Confederation, suspicion and fear had given way to benevolence and a desire to protect Indians until they chose to take their place in society. To that end, Indian legislation dealt mainly with protecting reserve lands from trespass and damage, and Indian people from the social evils of local towns.

By the turn of the century, society had grown impatient. It saw Indian people in possession of large fertile tracts of land, often not fully utilized, which were in many places a hindrance to settlement and commercial expansion. The protections in the *Act* were reduced and measures to acquire reserve land, with or without consent, were introduced.

By 1920 this impatience had become so great that compulsory enfranchisement was introduced in the *Indian Act*. Finally, after World War II, a time of concern with social problems, the *Indian Act* was changed to remove most of the more discriminatory and repressive provisions. However, there was no change in the underlying philosophy and assumptions about the relationship between Indian people and "White" society. (1978:192)

In the final analysis, we find that one feature of Canadian legislation concerning Natives has shown almost no variation since the late eighteenth century when the government first assumed responsibility for Native welfare. The Canadian government is still trying to "civilize" the Native, with all the underlying biases and assumptions that word implies.

In the past decade, a new cultural influence has begun to make itself felt in Native spheres. Whiteside (1980) refers to this decade as the "business period". He argues that, with the decline in power of the bureaucrat, the businessperson is now exerting a strong influence on Native activities. This influence is also being felt internally, as Natives themselves make demands on band councils to develop reserves. The impact of the business world upon Native life is too recent to fully comprehend. However, this new influence clearly brings with it attitudes which are peculiar to the marketplace and which are certainly at variance with the traditional value systems of Native cultures.

Conclusion

Theoretically, the rights of Canadian Indians are determined not only by the *Indian Act*, but also by the *British North America* (BNA) *Act* and by the Canadian Bill of Rights (CBR). As a Canadian statute, the *Indian Act* cannot amend the BNA *Act*. However, Section 91(24) of the BNA *Act* declares that Indians and lands reserved for Indians fall under the exclusive legislative authority of Parliament. Similarly, the CBR overrules any statute that denies an individual equality before the law by reason of race, national origin, colour, religion, or sex; however, "equality before law" has proven capable of very broad definition in the Canadian courts. In practice, then, the *Indian Act* continues to define the Indian rights.

The *Indian Act*, originally designed both to protect the Native population and to ensure assimilation, has not weathered the centuries well. Not only has it structured inequality, poverty, and under-achievement among Natives, but it has seriously encroached upon the personal freedom, morale, and well-being of Native people. Currently, Native leaders are trying to negotiate a new act that will protect land rights without restricting other areas of Native life. Native groups are therefore attempting to modernize the treaties and to seek reinterpretation in the courts for protection of lands and resources.

In summary, the *Indian Act* was administered in the interests of benign rule but its implementation created isolation, control, and enforced poverty. It has become the most vicious mechanism of social control that exists in Canada today. On the one hand, it has accorded Indians special status, legally and constitutionally; on the other, it has denied them equality in any realm of Canadian life (Berger, 1981).

The federal government argues that the *Indian Act* does not attempt to take Indians out of the scope of the ordinary law. Its major aim is to maintain Native culture and to provide Indians with additional rights and safeguards. However, these rights are not "vested"; even without amendments, much of the protection afforded Indians can be removed at any time under the *Act* by the Governor of Council (Cabinet) or by the Minister of Indian Affairs.

The *Indian Act* is particularly important today because within its structure lies the salvation of many Indian groups with land claims. At the same time, however, the Act denies other Natives a similar opportunity because of its definition of Indian status. It is the *Indian Act*, not the BNA *Act*, that defines who is Indian and who is not. The *Indian Act* allocates resources to those it defines as Indian and denies them to others of the same Indian ancestry. Between the legal Indians and the non-Indian rest the Métis, who receive special privileges under provincial legislation in western provinces only (Berger, 1981).

In 1981 and early 1982, Natives were preoccupied with making sure that their rights were enshrined in the proposed federal constitution. At the time of writing, the new constitution acknowledges the "existing" rights of aboriginal people in Canada. How these rights will be defined and reconciled with the *Indian Act* is yet to be determined.

Notes

1. On August 10, 1850, two acts were passed. One act was for the better protection of the lands and property of the Indians in Lower Canada. The other was for the protection of the Indians in Upper Canada from imposition, and the protection of the property occupied or enjoyed by them from trespass and injury.
2. For example, an enfranchised Indian could receive fee simple title to fifty acres of land and a specified sum of money.
3. Further controls of Indian customs and rituals were introduced in 1895, 1914, and 1933. The 1884 amendment was the first time the government seems to have acted in this fashion.

3

Indian Treaties in Historical Perspective[1]

Introduction

The premise on which the British occupation of what is now Canada is said to be based is that absolute title to the land was vested in the Crown – this paramount estate becoming a plenum dominium (full power to dispose of property at will) whenever the Indian title was surrendered or otherwise extinguished. The French, on the other hand, did not subscribe to the principle of an Indian or aboriginal title but rather, on acquiring the land, accepted a responsibility for the religious welfare of the indigenous peoples; Indian social affairs were attended to by the ecclesiastics.

An aboriginal title[2] can be interpreted not as a clear land title to a fixed occupational site but as the territorial range rights of an identifiable nomadic group over a wide but definable area for food-gathering, hunting, fishing and trapping. The idea that a nomadic existence equates with the principle of an aboriginal title is quite valid where it can be shown that this territorial imperative is maintained by force of arms, agreement or lack of serious competition, and this way of life can quite legitimately be referred to as "ancient" or "traditional".

At this point, however, cognizance should be taken of several divergences set in motion by the various occupying European powers fairly late in historical times which completely changed the ancient or traditional ways of most Indians and irrevocably modified those of the remainder. Prior to the various occupations, the traditional Indian ways in what is now Canada ranged from the conspicuous consumption of the Pacific coastal peoples, through the marginal subsistence levels of those in the north-central region to the ample subsistence provided the inhabitants of the eastern woodlands by the chase and the produce of their village plots.

The most dramatic change was, of course, the conversion of the Plains Indians to the horse culture. At least equal in impact was the emphasis placed by the early French and British entrepreneurs on the fur trade which, to provide the profits expected, wholly depended on a re-direction of Indian pursuits to the primary production (on a massive scale) of hides and furs for the world market. At this stage, at least for the French and the English, the wide-ranging nomadic Indian was a necessity.

In other quarters, however, the fur trade was not the be-all and end-all of the new land's potential. The dilemmas which are manifest to this day were early evidenced and the Indian people, already subject to dislocations and relocations beyond their control, were inevitably caught up in the resultant conflicts – to nurture the fur trade; to open the country to settlement and development; to support and protect the Indian people; to maintain effective trading facilities; and, above all, to uphold law, peace and good order.

These problems were resolved for the French Sovereign by the conquest of 1759. For the British, the existing dilemmas were not only becoming more apparent but paradoxes were gestating which would make the half-century between 1763 and 1814 most portentous for the future of the Indian people who found themselves under the suzerainty of the British Sovereign.

Historical Background

In 1713, by the *Treaty of Utrecht,* France ceded Acadian (excepting Cape Breton Island) to Great Britain, recognized the British Sovereign's suzerainty over the Iroquois people, relinquished all claims to Newfoundland, and recognized British rights to Rupert's Land. When the Charter for exploitation of Rupert's Land was granted by Charles II to the Hudson's Bay Company in 1670, it is doubtful that even the claimants were aware of the vast territory involved – all the land draining into Hudson Bay from Baffin Island on the northeast to the headwaters of the Saskatchewan in the southwest. For the next century and a quarter the western boundaries of Rupert's Land were to remain the firmest delineation of British America's western extent.

By the Peace of Paris, 1763, France ceded all her North American possessions to Great Britain, with the exception of St. Pierre and Miquelon Islands (which she retained) and Louisiana (which she ceded to Spain). In the spring of that year the crystallization of Indian misgivings gained expression through the activities of Chief Pontiac, although particular provisions in the *Royal Proclamation* concerning the protection of Indian-occupied lands were designed to allay such fears. The *Royal Proclamation* of 1763 did indeed define lands which were to remain, at the Sovereign's pleasure, with the Indians as their hunting grounds, but Rupert's Land and the old colony of Quebec were specifically exempted. In what was to become Canada, the hunting grounds in the east comprised a relatively narrow strip between the northern bounds of Quebec and Rupert's Land, along with all of what was to become Upper Canada; in the northwest, an amorphous area bounded by Rupert's Land, the Beaufort Sea, and the Russian and Spanish claims to the west and south.

In 1769, St. John's Island (renamed Prince Edward Island in 1798) became a separate government.

By the *Quebec Act*, 1774, in what has been described as a statutory repudiation of *Royal Proclamation* policy, Quebec's boundaries were extended to encompass all the land described in the preceding paragraph as the eastern Indian hunting grounds.

With the Revolutionary War of 1775 to 1783 the emphasis in the colonies of Nova Scotia and Quebec changed irrevocably to settlement, development, lumbering, fishing and trade; dissolution of the two hundred-year-old partnership between Indian and fur trader was well on the way. The most immediate effect was a 50 percent increase in population in the two colonies occasioned by the influx of United Empire Loyalists who were, primarily, interested in farming, homesteading and business. These were followed, particularly in Upper Canada after 1791, by a steady stream of settlers with like interests from the south. They brought with them the desire for peace, law, good order and the other concomitants of settled living.

The Treaty of Paris, 1783, established the boundary from the Atlantic to the Lake of the Woods. At one stroke Canada lost the entire southwestern half of the vast inland domain which French and British adventurers had discovered, explored and exploited with the help of the Indian people. Along with it went that portion of the Indian hunting grounds, established in 1763, bounded by the Great Lakes and the Ohio and Mississippi Rivers. A natural point of departure for the future boundary at the 49th parallel of latitude was also ensured. The inevitable dissension with the Indian people which followed, however, was reaped by the United States rather than Great Britain.

In 1784, as a result of the large-scale influx of United Empire Loyalists into the St. John River area the year before, New Brunswick was separated from Nova Scotia. Cape Breton Island also became a separate entity.

By the *Constitutional* (or *Canada*) *Act* of 1791, the Imperial Parliament divided Quebec into the provinces of Upper Canada and Lower Canada, abolished the concillar form of government which had existed in Quebec for two centuries, and established representative government in both provinces. Land was to be granted in freehold tenure in Upper Canada and could be so granted in Lower Canada, if desired.

In 1796, by the Jay Treaty, the fur-trading posts of Niagara, Detroit, Michilimackinac, and Grand Portage – which were still in British hands – were handed over to the United States in accordance with the boundary provisions agreed to in 1783. In order to facilitate what remained of the fur trade, an article in the Jay Treaty provided for the free passage of Indian trappers back and forth across the boundary with "their ordinary goods and peltries"; it is on this provision that the present Iroquois claim duty-free passage across the international boundary.

In 1803, by the Louisiana Purchase, the United States acquired that vast, vaguely-defined territory west of the Mississippi which had been ceded back to France by Spain in 1800. The consequent push westward, and the inevitable rivalries arising, would once again raise the contentious question of the boundary between British America and the United States.

On the Pacific coast, the leading protagonists changed over the course of time from Russia, Britain, and Spain to Russia, Britain, and the United States, but it was not from the sea that this contest was to be settled. Indeed, Captain Cook had made his landfall at Nootka Sound in 1778, but the traders who followed him lost their vessels and furs to the Spanish who were engaged in a last endeavour to enforce their claims to the northwest coast. In 1791, Captain George Vancouver arrived to acknowledge, officially, restoration of British rights after the Nootka Convention; concurrently, the Russians were pushing down from the north, following the seal and the sea otter.

The only firm and lasting links with the Pacific coast, however, would have to be by land and these were provided through: Alexander Mackenzie in 1793 by way of the Peace River canyon to Dean Channel; Simon Fraser in 1808 by the tumultous river which bears his name; David Thompson in 1811 down the Columbia to its mouth. These Canadian Scots were all members of the North-West Company and rivals, not only of the Spanish, Russians and Americans, but of the Hudson's Bay Company. The chain of discovery and exploration whose initial links were forged in the quest for furs along the Atlantic coast over the preceding two centuries was complete from ocean to ocean – all in the name of the fur trade. In each instance, the ubiquitous Scot was accompanied, guided, and sustained by Indian companions.

For the United States, Lewis and Clarke had, of course, paced the Canadians, reaching the Columbia in 1805. John Jacob Astor established the western headquarters of his fur company at the mouth of the Columbia in 1810.

In 1809, by the *Labrador Act*, Anticosti Island and the coast of Labrador from the St. Jean River to Hudson Strait were transferred from Lower Canada to Newfoundland. Not even the eastern provinces, however, were to be allowed to engage in such peaceful organizational exercises much longer. The improvement in relations which the Jay Treaty appeared to herald had not resolved the border ambiguities at the centre of the continent and the animosities of the American Revolution were by no means exhausted.

The outbreak of war in 1812 saw 500 000 British Americans (of whom less than 5 000 were regular troops) confronted by a population of 8 million in the United States. Great Britain was not only at war with the United States, but had her strength committed to the struggle with Napoleon. Through a combination of dogged determination on the part of the British Americans (aided by several hundred Indians under Chief Tecumseh) in throwing back invasion forces and ineffective planning on the part of the enemy, Canada managed to hold out until the defeat of Napoleon in 1814 allowed Britain to bring all her forces to bear in America. Having thus gained the initiative in no uncertain manner, it is hard to understand why the British did not seek more equitable boundary terms by the Treaty of Ghent in 1814, but both parties appeared content to settle the controversy through a mutual return of conquered territories. Thus were Canadian interests sacrificed to ensure American cordiality.

The United States considered the Jay Treaty of 1796 to be abrogated by the War of 1812-14, but the Convention of 1818 settled the outstanding boundary matters by confirming the border to the Lake of the Woods and extending it along the 49th parallel to the Rocky Mountains. The Treaty of Ghent reinstated the provisions of the Jay Treaty affecting Indian people but, as the conditions of the former were not considered to be self-executing, it became the individual responsibility of each of the governments concerned to give effect to the relevant provisions by appropriate legislation.

In terminating the international boundary at the Rocky Mountains, the Convention of 1818 left one major area subject to contention with the growing neighbour to the south – the so-called Oregon Territory, roughly half in and half out, jointly occupied by Britain and the United States. The first large-scale movement of American settlers into Oregon in 1842 naturally created a clamour for annexation to the United States. Fortunately, the contention was resolved through the Treaty of Washington in 1846 by which the boundary was continued to the sea along the 49th parallel and Vancouver Island confirmed as a British possession. With the agreement of 1825 between Britain and Russia on a description of the Alaska boundary, to all intents and purposes Canada's external boundaries now were fixed and her attention could be concentrated on consolidation.

Treaty Activity East to West

NEWFOUNDLAND

It is perhaps fitting that this section on negotiations and agreements with the Indians of Canada should begin, in reasonable detail, with those first encountered (in all likelihood) by the Viking adventurers at the end of the first millenium A.D., and by John Cabot midway through the second.

Newfoundland was claimed by Cabot in 1497 for his Sovereign, King Henry VII, and is spoken of as the first of England's overseas colonies. Eighty-six years later, in 1583, Sir Humphrey Gilbert reaffirmed England's suzerainty in the name of Queen Elizabeth and established at St. John's what is said to be England's first colonial government abroad. Until the Treaty of Utrecht acknowledged sole possession by Britain in 1713, however, Albion's hold on the island outpost was tenuous at best.

It was very likely that Basque fisherman were cropping cod off the Grand Banks at the time Cabot was making his claim. The Basques were soon joined by Bretons, Spaniards, Portuguese, and men from Devon and Normandy. The major difference between them (which probably gave an early, but fleeting, semblance of proprietorship) was the English practice of sun-curing their catch on the beaches. Having copious home supplies of salt, the others at first preferred to green-pack their catches aboard. As sun-curing produced a more widely-marketable product, it wasn't long before all were competing for beach space.

Government in general (and justice in particular) was understandably rough and ready under such circumstances; a semblance of order was maintained for specific intervals by a fishing fleet, "Admiral", selected from captains representing half a dozen nations. Punishments meted out, according to sea-going customs of the times, were harsh and summary. Even so, the first contact between Beothuk and English administrator was amicable and included the inevitable giving of presents.

The Beothuks immediately recognized the superiority of iron over stone, and net-twine over animal sinews and plant fibres. They found it harder to understand why such prodigious quantities of fish were required, or why the rough fishermen were less appreciative of their visits than the British administrators. What they couldn't obtain as presents they began to acquire by pilfering the stocks and stores of the beach camps. Summary justice having been what it was, it wasn't long before the fishermen were shooting the Beothuks on sight. Thereafter, the Indians avoided all Europeans (including the administrators) as best they could but continued taking whatever they found portable in hit-and-run raids on the curing beaches. In the fishermen's eyes the Indians were of no use. Exasperation ran high and, after an incident which resulted in loss of life to members of a French party, the French waged an all-out effort to hunt down and annihilate every remaining Beothuk on the island. (Although some early historical accounts hold that the French armed Micmac Indians from the mainland and set a bounty on the aboriginals, contemporary sources discount that theory for lack of supportive evidence. Whatever the case, most writings indicate that both French and British hunting parties were equally responsible for indiscriminate Beothuk slaughters.)

Throughout their tenure, the British administrators made sporadic attempts to contact the aboriginals. As a hunted remnant, however, the Beothuk ran for the woods at the first sign of a stranger. In addition, Beothuk numbers had fallen far below the critical levels for population survival and contact became increasingly a matter of mere chance.

Most of our direct knowledge of this tragic race comes from Shanawdithit, the last of the Beothuks, who was captured in 1823 along with her mother and sister; her father had drowned in attempting to evade the captors; the women were exhausted by starvation and couldn't flee. At that time, according to Shanawdithit, the total Beothuk population of Newfoundland was thirteen individuals. The three women were well-treated and were free to come and go as they pleased; however, the mother and sister died in Twillingate within the year. Shanawdithit lived in the households of several British administrators and, over the next six years, provided many drawings illustrating her people's culture. Having quickly gained a working knowledge of English, she filled in the existing gaps in European knowledge of the Beothuk language which was found to have little connection with any mainland tongue. Indeed, the ethnic connection seems just as tenuous. Shanawdithit died of tuberculosis in St. John's hospital on 6 June 1829 at the age of twenty-nine. After her death, no further contact with the Beothuk people was ever recorded.

For some reason British adherence to the principal of an "aboriginal title" did not apply insofar as the Beothuk people were concerned; in dealing with them treaty activity was never a consideration. There are Montagnais and Naskapi Indians, and Inuit people, resident along the coast of Labrador. Although no endeavour was made to extinguish their aboriginal title prior to Newfoundland's entry into Confederation in 1949, the Canadian government has provided funds to the Native peoples of Newfoundland to investigate claims related to land use and occupancy.

ACADIA

Although its borders were as vague as any of the time, there is little doubt that, by late in the seventeenth century, Acadia was a long-settled part of New France; certainly, what are now Cape Breton Island, mainland Nova Scotia, Prince Edward Island, and New Brunswick were then under the dominion of the French Sovereign. By the Treaty of Utrecht in 1713, France ceded Nova Scotia to Great Britain. What is now New Brunswick remained in dispute, while Cape Breton Island and Prince Edward Island were retained by France.

By the Peace of Paris in 1763, of course, all came into British hands along with the old colony of Quebec. In the *Proclamation* of 1763 the question of aboriginal title has been taken to equate with those lands "reserved for Indian use" and it has been claimed that because the Maritimes were not specifically exempted, as was Quebec, the aboriginal title has never been extinguished.

On the other hand, the rationale by which Quebec was exempted is that because the French occupation did not rest on the recognition of an aboriginal title, and because the land had been ceded to Britain by France under the Peace of 1763, all claims were extinguished. This argument is probably at least as valid concerning Acadia. As exampled heretofore in the case of Newfoundland, the matter of the aboriginal title serves to confuse as many issues as it clarifies. However, one might argue that if the Native residents of any particular part of Canada have, or had, an aboriginal title, then so had, or have, the Native residents of any other part.

PRINCE EDWARD ISLAND

The fur trade was never a significant feature of economic development in Prince Edward Island. To the beginning of the French era, the Micmacs had used it and Isle Royale (Cape Breton Island) merely as summer camping grounds. When it was granted (as Isle St. Jean) by the French Sovereign to the Compte de Saint-Pierre in 1719, it was practically devoid of exploitable animal life. In time the trees were cut down, the young men left the sea, and the rich soil was devoted to agriculture.

Immigration to Isle St. Jean began in 1728 with seventy-six Acadian families who wished to settle on French territory. The few Indians who resided there year round had little interest in mainland affairs. At the end of the French Régime in 1763, most of the Acadian settlers on Isle St. Jean returned to France, while some relocated in Nova Scotia or Quebec. Isle St. Jean was then placed under the government of Nova Scotia; the island was separated from Nova Scotia in 1769 and renamed Prince Edward Island in 1798.

Treaty activity, such as it was, was conducted to ensure Indian assistance or neutrality, as may be illustrated in the following quotation from Governor Cornwallis of Nova Scotia to the Lords of Trade in 1749: "The St. John's Indians I made peace with ... (were) a warlike people .... Treaties with Indians are nothing. Nothing but force will prevail." Prince Edward Island came into Confederation in 1873 and since that time the government of Canada has not conducted treaty activities with the Micmac Indians, either on its own or in concert with the provincial government.

NOVA SCOTIA

When French fisherman adopted the beach-drying process used by the English to cure cod, their greatest need was for extensive beaches safe from their rivals. Many turned to the beaches of Nova Scotia and Cape Breton Island. In so doing they were exposed to the Micmac Indians who were master trappers and curers of pelts. In view of the number of furs available, the French turned more and more to this profitable sideline; some, no doubt, decided to make the fur trade their major endeavour before the French monopolies came into being.

Even after the monopolies were in existence, fur-trading in Nova Scotia allowed more scope for the individual than in Quebec. From the start however, the colony had quite a varied economy; this was probably due to the haphazard and disconnected way in which settlement developed. In time, as the forests were depleted and the fur trade diminished, the varied nature of the economy became even more evident; eventually the principal emphasis came to be on fishing, ships, and trade routes. In none of these latter activities had the Indians of Nova Scotia any appreciable part.

Population expansion was a relatively early manifestation in Nova Scotia and few of the incoming people looked to the Indian residents as partners in the development of the peninsula. The contributing elements were returning Acadians, pre-Revolutionary New Englanders, the United Empire Loyalists, small groups of British, and other cohesive units such as the Lunenberg Germans. The Scots started to arrive in some numbers at the time of the Peace of Amiens (1802). During the course of some twenty years after the Battle of Waterloo (1815), roughly 20 000 Highlanders and Western Islanders arrived to populate northeast

Nova Scotia, Cape Breton, and Prince Edward Island. With the end of the Scottish movement, large-scale immigration to the area ceased.

As presently constituted, Nova Scotia's boundaries were fixed by the inclusion of Cape Breton Island in 1820. The province entered Confederation as a founding member in 1867.

Significantly, the principal treaty activity in Nova Scotia pre-dated the major period of immigration by several decades (the last important activity taking place in 1779). In the present instance the chronology of events establishes that this was more accident than design. The Maritime treaties stressed mutual peace and friendship, the objective being to ensure the assistance or neutrality of the Indian people. Provision was invariably made for the trade in Indian hides and furs; and mention was usually made that the Indian people were not to be disturbed in their normal pursuits of hunting and fishing. With the major influx of settlers, however, change was inevitable and the contribution the Indians were able to make was irrevocably curtailed.

NEW BRUNSWICK

In the summer of 1534, Jacques Cartier, the Breton master-navigator, followed the north shore of New Brunswick to his landfall on the Gaspé peninsula. The deep forests northwest of the Bay of Fundy appeared, however, to discourage the early fur traders; after an unsuccessful attempt to establish a trading centre on an island at the mouth of the St. Croix River, the Huguenot, Sieur de Monts, transferred his fur-trading headquarters back to the St. Lawrence in 1608.

The purposeful vagueness by which the boundaries of Acadia were defined in the Treaty of Utrecht (1713) left New Brunswick in a politically ambiguous position which lasted for nearly half a century. The situation was further complicated by the fact that neither the French nor the British were represented there in any appreciable numbers. In 1749 the matter became one of confrontation when the French erected Fort Beauséjour on the New Brunswick side of what was to become the provincial boundary and the British countered with Fort Lawrence on the Nova Scotia side. The impasse was resolved by the surrender of Fort Beauséjour to the British in 1755 and Nova Scotia's subsequent absorption of Acadia's remnants after the Peace of Paris in 1763.

During the hostilities, the indifference accorded New Brunswick's potential by the French and British overlords had not been shared by the British-American soldiers who had entered the area from the New England seaboard. Ostensibly, settlement from New England was to have been geared to the taking up of homesteads left by the expelled Acadians; however, it was not long before dissension arose all along the St. John River among established settlers, the half-pay soldiers, and ordinary immigrants from New England. Although these matters were eventually resolved (at least to the satisfaction of the administrators) the Indian residents were soon complaining to the authorities in Halifax that the settlers were killing their game and that game not killed was being driven away. The Indians were appeased by presents and persuasion, the governor having promised to restrain the settlers from hunting wild animals in the woods.

In the years immediately before and after the *Royal Proclamation* of 1763, settlement along the banks of the St. John was at times little more than a land-grab. The Indian residents were naturally hostile to the increased activity; the authorities viewed the situation with mixed feelings and uncertain loyalties. While there may be a question as to whether or not the "Indian hunting grounds" provisions of the *Royal Proclamation* applied to Nova Scotia (then including New Brunswick), the settlers and entrepreneurs certainly acted as if these had no bearing. Moreover, the rapid increase of settlement along the St. John from United Empire Loyalists after the American Revolution muffled what remained of the Indian hostility. Native protests were lost in the clamour of increasing development and virtually were stilled by the creation of the province in 1784.

For a time, some of the settlers endeavoured to combine the incompatible activities of timber-cutting, farming, fishing and the fur trade; however, the most obvious resource was timber and, as attention came to be focused on the fine stands of pine, it appeared the province was destined to become one vast lumber camp. After the War of 1812-14, lumbering activity along the St. John and in the valleys of the Miramichi and the Restigouche had completely supplanted the fur trade. With the passing of the latter, the value of the Indian as a substantial developmental factor in the province's economy was also reduced.

As was the case throughout the Maritimes (excepting Newfoundland), treaty activity concerning New Brunswick was mainly of the Peace and Friendship variety, designed to ensure the assistance or neutrality of the Indian people. The question of an aboriginal title does not seem to have been an issue. In any event, there is no documentary indication that any endeavour was made to deal with the matter either before New Brunswick entered Confederation (1867) or after.

QUEBEC

During his first voyage of exploration and discovery up the St. Lawrence in 1535-36, Jacques Cartier visited the Iroquoian villages of Stadacona (Quebec) and Hochelaga (Montreal). Under Sieur de Roberval, he participated in the first unsuccessful attempt to establish a colony in that area between the years 1541-43. Partly because of misunderstandings arising from Indian anxiety to obtain European tools and utensils of metal, Cartier had quarrelled with the Native people during the winter of 1541-42; with almost prescient dread of their hostility, he withdrew from the venture and returned to France. After an auspicious beginning, this experience was a portent of the bitter enmity which was to develop between the French and the Iroquois peoples.

At the time, Cartier believed that the Indian people had little to exchange for the goods they found to be so superior to theirs of stone, hide, bark, bone and wood. Sparked initially by the dictates of fashion concerning fur-felt, however, the demand for high-quality furs (particularly beaver) from the St. Lawrence area had so increased by the end of the century that the French decided only a state-supervised monopoly could effectively control the supply. As the Sovereign expected the monopolists to defend their investment (and themselves) by their own endeavours, it was concluded that colonists brought out by the monopolists would provide the most enduring protection.

Under Sieur de Monts, Samuel Champlain contributed his many talents to the establishment of the monopoly bases in Acadia; however, Champlain's potential was not put to full use until the centre of the fur trade was transferred, under his local direction, back to the St. Lawrence in 1608.

During the half-century between Cartier's departure and Champlain's arrival, the Iroquoian residents of Stadacona and Hochelaga (first encountered by Cartier) had been supplanted by nomadic Algonkian hunters from the north. The Huron branch of the Iroquoian peoples was established in the lands to the south and southeast of Georgian Bay. The Five Nations of the Iroquois were strategically located in what is now northern New York State, particularly in the valley of the Mohawk River. Although they were of the same ancestral stock, a cleavage had developed between the Hurons and the Five Nations and they were implacable enemies.

From the start, Champlain's relations with the Montagnais and Abenakis ranging the St. Lawrence and Ottawa valleys were good and it wasn't long before Indian cooperation in providing furs had subtly changed to a dependency on the Europeans for metal-wares, cloth, some foodstuffs, and, ultimately, firearms. Of course, the French depended at least as much on the Indians, not only for furs, but for vital wilderness expertise. The enterprising Hurons were quick to complete the chain, as middlemen, in getting furs from the interior to the Ottawa and St. Lawrence Rivers.

It was, perhaps, inevitable that Champlain would have to interest himself in the political affairs of his Indian partners, if only to show his good faith; but it was also unfortunate in that the common foe of all his allies happened to be the quick-witted and industrious Iroquois of the

Five Nations. The die was cast at sunrise on a day in July 1609 when he participated in one of the regular confrontations between the opposing groups which, up to that point, had been conducted on highly ritualized lines.

Champlain, along with several of his compatriots, had accompanied a war party of sixty Montagnais into Iroquois territory. Travelling along the shores of Lake Champlain at night, they met a group of Iroquois warriors and the Montagnais arranged a formal encounter for the following morning. The engagement is best described from Champlain's own writings:

> My Frenchmen were concealed in separate canoes belonging to the Montagnais. After equipping ourselves in light armour, each of us seized an arquebus and went ashore. Leaving their barricade, the enemy, numbering about two hundred strong and robust men, came toward us with gravity and assurance that greatly pleased me. Our Indians told me that those who carried the lofty plumes were the Chiefs and that I should do all I could to kill them. I promised to do my best.... When I saw them preparing to shoot their arrows at us, I raised my arquebus and aiming directly at one of the Chiefs, fired; two of them fell dead at this shot, and one of their companions received a wound of which he afterwards died. I had put four balls in my arquebus.... The Iroquois were greatly surprised at seeing two of their men killed so suddenly.... Whilst I was reloading, one of my companions fired a shot, which so astonished them anew that, seeing their leaders slain ... they ... fled into the forest; whither I pursued them and killed some others....

The following year saw another such encounter at the mouth of the Richelieu with much the same results, but in which the survivors were cut down instead of being allowed to retire as had been the custom.

These encounters not only upset the balance temporarily in favour of the Algonkian peoples but served to establish certain principles which were to hold from 1610 to the end of the century. The rules of Indian warfare were irrevocably changed. The combined role of the Indian as fur supplier and mercenary warrior was set. Fatefully, the Dutch had founded their colony on the Hudson River in the very year of Champlain's second successful skirmish with the Iroquois of the Mohawk and Hudson valleys. It took the Iroquois no time to learn the lesson of powder and shot and they immediately sought the Dutch as allies and suppliers of the lethal weapons. This alliance automatically transferred to the English as successors to the Dutch. As middlemen in the fur trade, the Iroquois were without peer; due to their inherent organizational talents, as mercenary warriors armed with the new weapons, they had little need of European raid captains; with vengeance an integral element of their philosophy, there was no need to spur them on. In consequence, an inordinate quantity of French furs found their way to the Dutch and English merchants of the Hudson Valley.

After they had experienced the rewards of the fur trade, the people of the Five Nations became dependent on the metal-wares and weapons of the Europeans as had the Native allies of the French. The contest between the French and the people of the Five Nations was actually for control, first of the fur trade and, secondly, of the St. Lawrence supply route. It was only a short portage from the head of the Mohawk River to Lake Ontario; from their heartland the waterways of Lake Champlain and the Richelieu River provided the Iroquois direct access to the St. Lawrence. From the first they thwarted the French plan of having the Hurons and Ottawas transport the furs provided by the Indians of the interior to the St. Lawrence. The Five Nations counter was simply to eliminate the competition and to divert the furs to the Hudson River merchants who, unencumbered by the niceties of state monopoly and the problems of organization or transportation, could provide a higher rate per skin in better quality trade goods.

It is unlikely that the Five Nations could have raised more than 4 000 fighting men even at the peak of their influence yet, at times, their activities practically brought those of the French to a standstill. Due to their ferocious battle style, Iroquois losses were unusually high but custom permitted the induction of prisoners (including Europeans) as replacements; even so, warrior numbers steadily diminished over the years.

In 1615 Champlain agreed to assist his Indian allies in a concerted plan to destroy the Iroquois heartland stronghold at Onondaga and, hopefully, to nullify the Five Nations threat for all time. The Andastes (from the Susquehannah River Valley) failed to link up with the Hurons, however; the latter failed to smash the stronghold; Champlain was wounded, and the Five Nations were left with a score to settle.

By the late 1640s, the Iroquois of the Five Nations had destroyed the Algonkians of the Ottawa Valley, scattered the remnants, and had launched their major campaign against the Hurons. The ruin and dispersal of the Huron Nation was completed in the spring of 1649, and a kindred people to the south and east, the Neutrals, immediately followed the same path to destruction. The Five Nations attacked and annihilated the Eries in 1655 and then turned on the Andastes. The latter group finally succumbed in 1676 and their remnants were absorbed into the Seneca Nation. The main representatives of the southern Algonkians, the Lenapes, were also subdued during this period. Of the subdued peoples, the Hurons, the Neutrals, the Eries, and the Andastes were of Iroquoian stock.

All this time the Iroquois continued to compete with the French. Their influence was felt from Albany to Lake Michigan and from Tadoussac to Hudson's Bay. For a half-century, the Five Nations of the Iroquois were actually at war with the French state and her Indian allies.

The Dutch and the English did little more than provide arms and encouragement; it should be borne in mind that the English did not take over from the Dutch in the Hudson Valley until 1674. Although victorious in the field, by the 1660s the Iroquois fighting force, including inducted enemy prisoners, was reduced by more than half.

In 1665, the experienced and professional regiment, the "Carignan-Salières" under the Marquis de Tracy, arrived in New France. In 1666, de Tracy led a mixed force of soldiers, habitants, and Indian allies into the Five Nations heartland. The Iroquois warriors, melting into the woods ahead of their enemies, generally refused direct confrontation; however, the invading force destroyed their crops and stores, burned out the villages and stockades, and laid the country to waste. The results were two-fold: the historic pallisaded Iroquois villages were not rebuilt; the French obtained a twenty-year peace. But while the peace curtailed large-scale armed activity on the part of the Iroquois, it did not hinder their fur-trading penchant or entirely inhibit their raiding proclivities.

At an earlier date the French authorities had considered trying to effect a reconciliation between the Hurons and the Five Nations; however, it was felt if this took place the Iroquois would merely lead the Hurons to trade with the Dutch. The ecclesiastics, on the other hand, felt that if they could convert the Iroquois of the Five Nations to Catholicism the warriors would not only be brought to godliness but could be weaned away from the Dutch and English traders. Having been unable to carry their religion effectively into the Five Nations heartland, they decided to settle as many converts as they could under their charge in New France; in this way those who were to become the Iroquois of Caughnawaga were established on the St. Lawrence in 1667. The Caughnawaga converts initially were won over to the French cause and participated extensively in raids against the British in New York and elsewhere in New England. They were represented in various forays against Albany, at Schenectady in 1690, and at Deerfield in 1704; they counted themselves out of the Haverhill raid in 1708, but took part in the extinction of the British garrison at Fort William Henry in 1757.

Naturally there was a strong disinclination on the part of the Caughnawaga people to participate in actions which might involve their relatives from the Mohawk valley, and this hesitancy became most pronounced in the 1750s. They also showed a preference to trade through Albany where fur prices were higher and the quality of trade goods better; in many instances they were joined in this endeavour by French trappers. Among the practices they brought with them to the Mission settlement was that of adopting prisoners, and their numbers were soon swelled with English, Dutch and German inductees from the Hudson Valley and elsewhere in New England. The Caughnawaga people, at different times, experienced all the apparent advantages (and obvious disadvantages) to which the Indian people of Canada were exposed during their interaction with Europeans. They were exhorted to be good Christians, and mercenary warriors; they were expected to participate in the fur trade, but were reviled if they traded where prices were best; they were adjured to temperence by the clerics, but coaxed to trade their furs for brandy. In the end, it was they who guided the British conquerors to Montreal in 1760.

With the destruction of the Hurons in 1649, the French entrepreneurs decided to dispense with middlemen and to seek the furs at source themselves. The voyageur and the coureur de bois thus came into their own and the wheel had turned inexorably in favour of the fur trade. To this end new transportation routes were explored, forts were established to ensure orderly delivery without Iroquois interference and new territory was explored as older sources of supply dried up.

The fate of the old colony on the St. Lawrence had been decided. The fur trade was hostile to settlement. Given a choice, the young men preferred the profit, freedom and excitement of the woods to the drudgery of the seigneury, so much so that, eventually, even the law couldn't keep them on the land. While the Catholic Church distrusted the freedom of the woods, there were Indian souls to be saved in the hinterland and brave clerics preferred the rigours of such duty to those of a St. Lawrence parish. Even when the fur monopolists paid service to their obligation and brought out colonists, the call of the wilds was practically the first sound the would-be settler heard. Lines were always overextended and dependence on the one cash-crop was always too great. All the while, the British colonies along the Altantic seaboard were growing in population and diversifying along economic lines. Granted, the British advantage was to last only a scant dozen years but there was time enough to bring the advantage to bear on New France. The curtain fell in 1760 with the fall of Montreal.

Although the Articles of Capitulation, 1760, promised amnesty to the Indian allies of the French Sovereign, all the Indian peoples realized they had lost with the cessation of hostilities. Up to this time the value of the Indian to the occupying powers was as a fur-collecting mercenary warrior. The consolidation of British America reduced the mercenary warrior's value to zero, no matter whose side he might have been on. The Indians were aware that the American colonists, as homesteading settlers, had invariably been cold-blooded about Indian allies – when their usefulness expired they were pushed aside. In this way, the Five Nations had become the Six Nations: the Tuscaroras, a southern people of Iroquioan stock, had been expelled from North Carolina in the years 1714-15 after reacting in the customary manner to wrongs inflicted on them by the settlers, and had joined the Mohawks, Oneidas, Onondagas, Cayugas, and Senecas in their northern redoubt.

Considering "wrongs inflicted", there is little talk herein of "Indian massacres" or "bloodthirsty cunning", or of the sufferings endured, for example, by Adam Dollard at the Long Sault (1660) and by the military garrison of Fort William Henry (1757); it is customary, of course, to cite the horrors experienced by the pioneering settlers of Lachine (1689) or of Deerfield, Massachusetts (1704). The principal victims in the story of North America, however, were, and are, the aboriginal peoples. For example, the contest between the Algonkian and Iroquian peoples for control of the St. Lawrence and the lower Great Lakes pre-dated the European occupation but did not degenerate to wholesale slaughter until the European antagonists had armed their so-called allies with weapons of long-range, mass destruction.

With its base in culture and religion, the aboriginal war was steeped in ceremony, ritual torture, and stoicism. We find it hard to appreciate that it was the captive warrior's right to be accorded as extended a death-rite as possible and this by the stoic endurance of torture. "You should not thus shorten my life for you would have no longer time to learn to die like men." Taking into account the warrior's right and the weapons used, there were relatively few deaths in preoccupation engagements.

The interaction of Indian and European corrupted both. The cultural and philosophic basis of Indian warfare was perverted, sometimes unconsciously, by European manipulators to mercenary terrorism, magnified beyond recognition through the use of firearms. Access to European goods and weapons became not just a desirable end for the Indian but a necessity maintained with anxiety and desperation; the most degrading acquisition was English rum or French brandy. The Indian may have won many battles after the occupation, but he lost every war.

After the Peace of Paris the French officers, administrators and many of the social elite returned to France. The British hoped to model the new Quebec on the colonies of the Atlantic coast, mainly by an infusion of English-speaking colonists. However, the influx was not what was expected or indeed wanted, and was limited to a few hard-headed Scots aching to enter the fur trade. The Caledonians had a natural empathy with the remaining 65 000 French inhabitants, an economic antipathy towards further settlement, and no respect for the objectives of the British administration. These entrepreneurs were just as determined to advance Quebec's fur-trading interests at the expense of the other colonies as were the French monopolists. They were equally determined to observe the "Indian hunting grounds" provisions of the *Royal Proclamation* only insofar as these fitted in with their aims for exploiting the fur resources of these lands. By design or good luck the Scots traders' objectives were achieved with the passage of the *Quebec Act* in 1774, whereby the colony's borders were restored to those enjoyed by New France – bounded on the north from the headwaters of the Mississippi to the Atlantic Ocean by way of the Hudson's Bay/Hudson Strait watershed, and including the vast triangle south of the Great Lakes between the Mississippi and Ohio Rivers. As was the case wherever settlement was curtailed, and the fur trade sustained, a modicum of benefit obtained to the Indian in his capacity as trapper and guide.

While it may appear that the American Revolution of 1775 and the *Treaty of Paris* (1783) made a mockery of the revised Quebec border pretensions, it is well to recall that it took the *Jay Treaty* of 1796 and several additional years of harassment to dislodge the Montreal traders from the area south of the Great Lakes to the confluence of the Ohio and the Mississippi (which was well inside the territory of the newly formed United States). Under the special provisions made for them in the *Jay Treaty,* the Indian trappers continued doing business back and forth. The Montreal-based traders consolidated in 1784 as the North-West Company.

The *Constitutional Act* of 1791 divided Quebec at the Ottawa River into Upper Canada (Ontario) and Lower Canada (Quebec); during the years before and after, the United Empire Loyalists, followed by a steady flow of settlers from the United States, populated the Eastern Townships of Lower Canada. By the *Labrador Act* of 1809, the coastline from River St. Jean (including Anticosti Island) to Hudson Strait was transferred to Newfoundland, and the area drained by the Hamilton River complex to Rupert's Land. The St. Lawrence coastline and Anticosti were returned to Lower Canada in 1825. The Province of Canada was formed by uniting Upper and Lower Canada in 1840 and this union continued until Confederation in 1867.

When considering the Indians of Quebec, a basic confusion arises involving the matter of treaty negotiation and the question of an Indian, or aboriginal, title to the land under consideration. While it can be said there was no negotiation regarding an unrecognized aboriginal title, it cannot be said that the type of arrangements which have come to be thought of as "treaty" arrangements were not entered into. Indeed, there is little difference between the type of arrangements that Champlain entered into with the Huron or Algonkian peoples and the Maritimes agreements heretofore described as "Treaties of Peace and Friendship". If anything, it might be argued that the type of agreements entered into by Champlain were even now more binding in that these were alliances whereby he agreed to assist his new allies regarding settlement of old scores. In succession, he promised such help in battle to the Montagnais, the Algonkians, and the Hurons. Considering that the commom enemy was the Iroquois of the Five Nations, the French cannot be said to have violated their basic treaty promises.

It should be acknowledged that it is easier, by hindsight, to align the interests of the French and their Indian allies than it is regarding the British. Whether it was official policy or not, the prime emphasis during the French regime was on the fur trade; in consequence, the abrasive pressures of a rapidly-increasing European population and ever-expanding areas of settlement did not exert their adverse effect on French-Indian relationships. In southern British America, relatively rapid trends in these areas tended to see the Indian peoples brushed aside or totally submerged by increasing numbers of settlers.

Champlain and his successors continued to form political alliances with various Indian groups whenever, or wherever, these were encountered and were successful in promoting the idea that only the French could provide protection from the Iroquois. Ostensibly the forts they erected were put up with the consent of the Indians who ranged the local regions, and who accepted the argument that these guaranteed the safety of the Indians using the French fur routes. Further evidences of French effectiveness were the promises of peace extracted from the Five Nations at Quebec in 1667 after de Tracy's destruction of the Iroquois heartland villages and again at Montreal in 1700 after Frontenac had levelled the rebuilt strongholds of the Oneidas and the Onondagas.

Other than the assurances provided in the *Articles of Capitulation 1760,* that the Indian allies of the French would not be penalized or disturbed on their lands, neither the British nor the Canadian governments subsequently entered into treaty negotiations with the Indian people of Quebec.

The question of an aboriginal title in Quebec is quite another matter. It has been said that French discovery and occupation meant absolute sovereignty over New France; the Indian had no recognizable title and, as a savage, no negotiable rights. The French felt an obligation to raise him to a state of grace and, if necessary, to set aside land under church direction where he and his family could receive religious instruction and be nurtured towards civilized life. In the *Royal Proclamation* of 1763, the British idea of an aboriginal title (concerning that rough trapezoid heretofore described as Old Quebec or Lower Canada) was dismissed as though extinguished by the prior French occupation.

The boundaries of Quebec remained unchanged from Confederation in 1867 until 1898 when that portion of the former Rupert's Land area south of the Eastmain River and the 52° latitude was added to the province. No reference was made to an Indian interest in the territory.

In 1912, the District of Ungava was transferred to Quebec, but this time the province assumed a statutory obligation to obtain a surrender of the rights of the Indian inhabitants therein. Although Quebec did not take any steps to fulfill this commitment for some sixty years, the province's announced plans in 1971 for massive hydro-electric development on the east coast of James Bay accentuated the need to resolve Indian claims in the region. The outcome was an agreement in 1975 involving the government of Canada, the government of Quebec, three Quebec crown corporations, namely Hydro-Quebec, the James Bay Development Corporation and the James Bay Energy Corporation, as well as the Grand Council of the Crees, and the Northern Quebec Inuit Association.

The James Bay and Northern Quebec Agreement redefined, in contemporary terms, the relationship between the two governments and Quebec Cree and Inuit. Although the Agreement has not been termed a "treaty" by either government, the effect has been the same. The Native peoples surrendered all their "claims, rights, titles, and interests, whatever they may be, in and to land in the Territory and in Quebec"; at the same time, however, the Cree and Inuit communities acquired a substantial degree of control over their own political, economic, and social evolution.

In 1978, the Naskapi Indians of Northeastern Quebec and the Port Burwell Inuit signed Complementary Agreements to the James Bay and Northern Quebec Agreement.

ONTARIO

In what was to become southern Ontario, the Native depopulation effected by the Iroquois of the Five Nations continued for many years; however, as the Iroquois threat diminished, Chippewa (O-jib-ewa) peoples from the north and west moved in to range the unoccupied lands. It was with these and subsequent groups that successive British and Canadian administrations negotiated for the surrender of the Indian title and to relocate the Six Nations at Brantford and the Mohawks at the Bay of Quinte. It is under these circumstances the matter of an aboriginal title presents its anomalies and automatically raises questions. With whom is the aboriginal title lodged? With those remnants whose direct antecedents were presumed to be in situ first, namely the Wyandots (Hurons)? With those who presumably gained the lands by conquest, namely the Five Nations? Or, as one is led to suspect, have successive administrations been presented with such increasingly complex Native conundrums (of which the evolving "aboriginal title" policy is one) that the exigent manner was to treat with those in situ?

Farther north, under the *Royal Charter* of 1670, the Hudson's Bay Company enjoyed its unfetterd dominion over the Canadian Shield, a substantial portion of which was to become northern Ontario. Apart from the period between 1682 and 1713 when the French had successfully contested for control, the Company was the law; fortunately for the Indian collectors ranging Rupert's Land, its jurisdiction was the fur trade. The collecting stations at Moose Factory and Fort Albany served as focuses for the Crees and other northern groups funnelling the wealth of premium furs over the cheap water route to England. The *Royal Proclamation* of 1763 specifically exempted Rupert's Land from its provisions.

After the American Revolution, by far the largest number of Loyalists (probably about 5 000) settled west of what is now Cornwall and along the north shore of Lake Ontario. White settlement was indeed a fact and the matter of aboriginal title was a major concern. Besides those who came to the Ontario region directly, a number of dissatisfied Loyalists from the Maritimes followed soon after the main movement. Then there were the "late Loyalists", who vastly outnumbered the refugees, seeking cheaper lands and a more orderly environment; some had been disquieted by the Revolution and others were impressed by the appearance that the British had little difficulty with the Indian people while the Ameicans seemed to be constantly at war with them. In the main, these were true settlers – pioneer homesteaders whose greatest ambition was to farm their own land. The resulting divergences between the English-speaking newcomers and the French-speaking residents were recognized in 1791 by the division of Quebec into Upper and Lower Canada.

By 1812 the settler population of Upper Canada had increased to 80 000 and the arrangements by which the newcomers were accommodated under the "Indian Lands" provisions of the 1763 *Proclamation* numbered roughly a dozen; two of these, the Haldimand Grant and the so-called Gunshot Treaty, are remarkable only as examples of mismanagement. The Gunshot Treaty was probably one of the most bungled transactions in the history of Indian treaties; negotiations probably started as early as 1783-84 and were concluded 139 years later in October and November of 1923.

Prior to the Revolutionary War, the tendency had been for the earliest settlers in Upper Canada to cluster at Cataraqui (Kingston), York (Toronto), and Niagara. As the Loyalists, and those who followed, filled in the gaps, the need to discharge the Indian title to the north shore of Lake Ontario became increasingly pressing. Consequently, Sir John Johnson, Superintendent-General of Indian Affairs (1782-1828), had an agreement drawn up to discharge the Indian title along the lakeshore from Toronto to Kingston. Although representative Indian leaders at the Bay of Quinte signed the agreement on September 23, 1787, the document was blank as far as describing the lands surrendered.

In one version of its history, the use of the word "Gunshot" is said to have meant that the back boundary of the tract to be ceded was to be the distance from the lakeshore that a gunshot could be heard on a still day.

At various times fragments of documents have been put forward which have appeared to support this version, or in which "as long as the sun shines" and such phrases are used. Invariably these fragments are felt by the holders to be portions of the missing treaty; however, the incomplete document of 1787 was clearly prepared to present more exact boundaries and the language used was much drier than the descriptive terms quoted, and more indicative of the officialese of the period. The terms quoted are generally illustrative of those used in preliminary treaty negotiations and the documentary fragments could be from the numerous exchanges which must have arisen between the principals. (For example, as a result of a direction dated 15 September 1783 from Governor General Haldimand, Sir John Johnson ordered Captain Crawford of the Indian Department to start making the necessary land purchases in the Bay of Quinte area from the Indian peoples concerned. There are indications that Captain Crawford exceeded his instructions and negotiated for many parcels; it is very like that one or more of these transactions gave rise to the Gunshot Treaty story.)

In any event, the matter was again brought to Sir John's attention early in 1791 resulting in the following intimation to the Deputy Surveyor-General: "I never received any deed from Crawford of the purchases he made . . . . The deed I had drawn up at the head of the Bay . . . was left in your hands to fill up the courses, since which I have never seen it." The indications are that the Surveyor never did complete the blank spaces and the agreement was considered invalid. In 1805, a relatively small parcel on the Etobicoke River, west of Toronto, was cleared of the Indian title and the shore west of that to Burlington Bay in 1806. The omnibus agreements of 1923 with the Chippewa and Mississauga peoples were considered to have rectified all the outstanding oversights attending the arrangements ostensibly entered into in 1787.

Concurrent with Governor General Haldimand's concern with the aboriginal title in the Bay of Quinte area during 1783-84 was his obligation to meet the Imperial commitment undertaken when Captain Joseph Brant (Thayendanega) had allied himself and his followers to the British cause in the American Revolution. The combined pressures attending these responsibilities, along with the influx not only of settlers but of other migrating Indian groups into the Upper Province, could well have given rise to the exigent nature of the measures taken during this period.

(Under the British regime, Joseph Brant became a protégé of Sir William Johnson, then Indian Superintendent of the Iroquois in Upper New York State. Sir William made the young Mohawk his assistant and, at the outbreak of the American Revolution, Joseph accompanied Sir William's nephew Guy Johnson to England. On his return, Joseph Brant received a commission and, under the commands of Generals Haldimand and Johnson, led the Mohawks, Senecas, Cayugas and Onondagas against the Americans during the American Revolution. Other factions of the Six Nations aligned themselves with the Americans or remained neutral.)

The first arrangements for the reception of Captain Brant (then on half-pay) and his followers were made by Governor General Haldimand early in 1784. The location was the Bay of Quinte area previously mentioned. (It should be borne in mind that this grant was in an area allegedly purchased by Crawford from the Mississaugas but for which a deed was never produced and also that the district, Tyendinaga, is outside the area covered in the 1923 settlements.) Captain Brant however, felt there were too many European settlers in that vicinity; on October 25, 1784, therefore, Haldimand reserved for the Mohawks and others of the Six Nations about one million acres of prime land in Southern Ontario – all the land for six miles on either side of the Grand River from its mouth on Lake Erie to its source. Unfortunately, Haldimand did not have the power to make the grant because the aboriginal title, ostensibly held by the Mississaugas in the north, had not been extinguished. Nevertheless, in 1784 Captain Brant and most of his followers removed to the banks of the Grand. Captain Deseronto, on the other hand, preferred the original agreement and, despite the arguments of Haldimand and Captain Brant, insisted on settling at Tyendinaga with 300 Mohawks of like mind.

With regard to the Grand River Tract, the aboriginal title deemed to be held by the Mississaugas extended only from the mouth of the Grand, on Lake Erie, for approximately two-thirds of its length; these southerly reaches were included in a title extinction negotiated with the Mississaugas on May 22, 1784. As the agreement however, was considered defective a corrected instrument was made on December 7, 1792.

Obviously, part of Haldimand's difficulty was in deciding with whom to negotiate as aboriginals in situ and, as has been observed, in some instances this decision was made precipitately. Under the circumstances outlined heretofore, it would not be remiss to suspect that nepotism, as well as exigency, was somewhere in play, and that if an immediate advantage was to be considered, it would hardly be in favour of the Chippewas or the Mississaugas.

Quite simply put, in the Grand River instance Governor-General Haldimand was giving away land he was not free to dispose of; this was very probably on the basis of inaccurate or incomplete advice. The instrument of Lieutenant-Governor John Graves Simcoe dated December 7, 1792, defined the boundaries of the title extinction more clearly, reconfirming that the original surrender did not include the headwaters of the Grand. The so-called Simcoe deed of January 14, 1793, moreover, did not state that the Haldimand Agreement was thereby superseded or abrogated, but did establish that the northernmost limit to which settlement along the Grand River could be reserved exclusively to Captain

Brant's people was that dictated by the title extinction in 1792.

Although Joseph Brant strongly protested the withholding of the northern reaches, it was evident he did not personally adhere to the principle that the lands of the Grand should be reserved for his people's exclusive use; on February 5, 1798, he sold approximately half of the entitlement including all the lands along the river from Fergus south to Paris. This practice was finally inhibited by the withholding of Crown consent to such alienation.

The reloction of the Iroquois groups in Upper Canada was the most dramatic feature of an odd sequel to the American Revolution, namely the influx of various Indian peoples. This was, of course, presaged by the movement of the Ojibeway who were subsequently dealt with as the aboriginals in treaty negotiations. While the late Loyalists were entering via the Lake Ontario entry points, Delawares were filtering in from the southwest, some of them becoming incorporated with the Six Nations people on the Grand River; representatives of the Ottawas and the Wyandots, a Huron remnant, were returning to their ancestral home in the upper province by way of Sault Ste. Marie, while the Ojibeway migration from the north and west continued.

No matter how badly the Indian peoples wanted to preserve their freedom and cultural heritage, their dependence on European manufacturers was almost total by this time; they naturally preferred to live and obtain their necessities in a friendly, or at least neutral, environment rather than in one of hostility, as was their lot to an increasing extent in the United States. If anything, the War of 1812 served to intensify Indian proclivities to view the British as allies and Canada as a refuge.

In 1821 the over-extended North-West Company gave up the struggle with advancing settlement and merged with its rival, the Hudson's Bay Company. Whatever else it had been, the North-West Company had been Canadian-based and Canadian-oriented; thereafter, the Canadian fur trade, along with those dependent on it for their livelihood, was directed from London and was no longer a major factor in the life of Upper Canada.

For some thirty-five years after the War of 1812, tens of thousands of British settlers moved into Upper Canada while the administration was concurrently endeavouring to accommodate hundreds of incoming Indians and to treat with those already established and their aboriginal titles. It was reasonably clear that the British administrators had hoped the Indian peoples would follow the pattern set by the British settlers and farm the lands allotted to them; however, the process was far from orderly. For example, some Indian people were glad to settle on Walpole Island, but the comprehensive reserve on Manitoulin Island planned by the British in 1836 never came to pass: the Indian people had their own ideas regarding where it would be best to locate. For many, the fur trade had provided the only material income they had ever known and farming was not considered by them to be an acceptable alternative.

Up to the year 1818, compensation for the lands was a once-for-all payment in goods or money at the time of negotiation. In 1818, annuities became a feature of most land surrender exercises and were initially paid in goods. Because the Indian recipients began to trade their presents for liquor, however, in 1829 Sir John Colborne, Lieutenant-Governor of Upper Canada, obtained permission from the Secretary of State to apply the annuities toward building Indian houses and farming implements and livestock. In 1840, the Upper and Lower Canadas were reunited to form the Province of Canada. The aboriginal title had been dealt with to the satisfaction of the administrators by some two dozen treaties and surrenders.

By the end of the 1840s, settlement on an agricultural basis was quite extensive throughout what had been the Upper Canada segment of the now united Province, up to and including the Bruce Peninsula. As we have seen, treaty activities up to that time in Upper Canada had been the most intensive of any conducted in Canada, although untidiness had attended the sequence of events along with overtones of exigency and undertones of irregularity and nepotism. The activities of 1850, however, were to be conducted *prior* to the extensive settlement contemplated for the more northerly reaches of the province; they were to reject the piecemeal in favour of the comprehensive, although exigency was as obvious a concomitant as ever.

The Robinson-Superior and Robinson-Huron Treaties of September 7 and 9, 1850, respectively, discharged the aboriginal title to twice as much land as had been affected in all other Upper Canada treaties put together. Discovered to be rich in minerals, the area was all the land north of Lakes Superior and Huron to the height of land separating Rupert's Land from Canada; the Indian peoples deemed to be ranging either tract were the Ojibeway. The Robinson Treaties (named after the Crown's representative, the Honourable William Benjamin Robinson) did not establish a formula for future treaty activities as is sometimes claimed, but they did establish a much tidier method. The principal features included provision for annuities, Indian reserves, and freedom for the Indians to hunt and fish on any unconceded Crown lands.[3]

The good agricultural land on Manitoulin Island did not go unnoticed. The government of the Province of Canada commissioned the Honourable William McDougall, then Superintendent-General of Indian Affairs, to effect a treaty with the resident Indians. McDougall obtained a surrender in 1862 from the Indians of the Island, excluding therefrom that portion of the Island east of Heywood Sound.

In 1867, the province of Ontario was created with the same boundaries as Upper Canada and entered Confederation as a founding member.

Rupert's Land was acquired from the Hudson's Bay Company by Canada in 1870 and the nucleus of Manitoba was formed at that time as the fifth province. Separating the settlers of Manitoba and those of Ontario was the North-West Angle (the Lake of the Woods district); this settlers' highway, known as the Dawson Route, was cleared of the aboriginal title in 1873 under Treaty No. 3. (As will be seen further on, the fledgling province of Manitoba and a contiguous area to the north and west had been covered by Treaties No. 1 and 2 in 1871.)

Although Treaty No. 3 was intended initially to be a matter of negotiation with the Ojibeway of the area, the outstanding features of the document were the specific provisions for the people of mixed blood in the actual wording: "by virtue of their Indian blood, claim a certain interest or title in the lands or territories . . . the said Half-breeds have elected to join in the treaty . . . it being further understood that the said Half-breeds shall be entitled to all benefits of the said treaty . . . " While the Adhesion of the Half-breeds may be an isolated incident in Treaty activity in Canada, it is a tacit admission of Mixed-Blood (Métis) interest or title in the land. Of course, one need only look at the *Manitoba Act* of 1870 wherein the Half-breed Grants were deemed "expedient towards the extinguishment of the Indian Title".

In 1889, most of the Treaty No. 3 area was included in Ontario's revised boundaries which advanced north to the Albany River. With Treaty No. 9, concluded in 1905 to allow for uninhibited railway construction, substantially all of Ontario had been cleared of aboriginal title. The province's present boundaries were fixed in 1912 and the additional territory was covered by an Adhesion to Treaty No. 9 in 1929-30.

Despite statements that Britain had been honouring the aboriginal title of North American Indians since 1670, the cornerstone for the type of negotiation we have come to think of in Canada as treaty activity was laid in Upper Canada in 1784. This may be ascribed to forces set in motion by the *Royal Proclamation* of 1763 and the American Revolution, with emphasis on clearing the land of its aboriginal title to facilitate full title transfer to others. It may be said that the land surrenders were just that, but on what authority? Obviously these imperfect exercises were designed for one purpose – to extinguish the Indian land title implied in the *Proclamation* of 1763. What might be considered oversights when comparisons are made with later activities were occasioned by lack of expertise and experience, not intent.

The provision of Indian reserves was not a feature of the early Upper Canada treaties and had to be fitted in at later dates. By 1850 the process had been so refined that reserves were provided and there was no confusion as to what extinguishment of the aboriginal title meant, including the limitation (as time went on) of Indian hunting and fishing to lands not taken up for settlement and development. The language of

Treaty No. 9 is even more precise and the limitations even more clearly defined; however, the rewards also reflect something of a growing social consciousness.

Ontario provides as cogent examples as may be found of the inequities which have resulted from treaty activities, no matter what the original circumstances and motives were; it also provides the longest continuous time scale, 1784 to 1923. There are some examples of groups considered to be well off and many who are considered to be poor. In some instances these circumstances can be related to the time when surrender of agreement was concluded (pre-Confederation, post-Confederation) or to the environs (southern Ontario, northern Ontario). In no instance was a treaty instigated by an Indian group and in very few cases did they influence the terms to any great extent. Ontario also provides a precedent wherein identified Indian groups received cash compensation specifically for their surrendered Indian title to hunting, fishing and trapping interests. This agreement is in two parts, one defined as a Treaty with the Chippewas dated October 31, 1923 and the other with the Mississaugas dated November 15, 1923. Also of significance therein is that this action concluded the arrangements, previously mentioned, initiated by Sir John Johnson on September 23, 1787.

THE PRAIRIE PROVINCES

Most of the post-Confederation "numbered" Treaties, particularly in Manitoba, Saskatchewan, and Alberta, predated the establishment of provincial boundaries and the result has been an overlapping of treaty/ provincial lines. A sequential look at the Western Treaties is mandatory in order to understand their role in Canada's expansion and development on the Prairies. In the 1870s in particular, Indian-treaty activity was conducted in quick succession throughout the Fertile Belt. As the regions north of the settled areas became desirable, the pace of treaty activity quickened again. The scenario began to develop, however, many years before Confederation.

In 1857, the Province of Canada's Chief Justice Draper testified before a Select Committee of the British House of Commons convened to consider the future of Rupert's Land. Admitting that his Province was not then ready to take on the responsibility for all the lands in question, the Chief Justice suggested instead that Canada could eventually take over the Hudson's Bay Company's land holdings bit by bit and that a railway link with the St. Lawrence could be built; the Committee accordingly recommended that the Red and Saskatchewan River districts be ceded to Canada. Although the recommendation was not immediately acted on, the exercise was evidence of a growing national consciousness.

In the drive toward geographical unity, the more reluctant and tardy elements were to receive the usual assistance in making up their minds from concurrent events in the United States. During the American Civil War (1861-65), the victorious North built up a particularly powerful, effective, and well-armed force. The completion of the Union Pacific Railway in 1864 saw American settlement westward accelerated beyond belief. The 1860s also saw the citizen settlers of newly-created Minnesota eyeing the fate of the Red and Saskatchewan River districts with interest.

In 1867, Canadian Confederation began with the founding provinces of Nova Scotia, New Brunswick, and Canada (from which were created Ontario and Quebec). Three years later, the new Dominion acquired Rupert's Land and the North-Western Territory, and admitted the postage-stamp size province of Manitoba into the Union. In 1871, British Columbia entered on condition that an east-to-west railway would be started in two years and completed within ten.

The year 1871 was also the beginning of the most intense and comprehensive treaty activity yet undertaken in Canada – Treaties No. 1 and 2 in the Red River district, 1871; Treaty No. 3, the Lake of the Woods link, 1873; Treaty No. 4, southern Saskatchewan, 1874; Treaty No. 6, most of the North Saskatchewan River district, 1876; Treaty No. 7, the remainder of the South Saskatchewan River system (Alberta), 1877. The spate not only encompassed the immediate prospective areas of Western settlement, but also included the most likely lands for railroad rights-of-way with options. In addition, Treaty No. 5 in 1875 prepared the way for steam navigation via Lake Winnipeg and the Saskatchewan River.

From part of the Northwest Territories (Rupert's Land and the North-Western Territory) were created the provisional Districts of Assiniboia, Saskatchewan, Athabaska, and Alberta in 1882. These, along with the enlarged District of Athabaska (1895), were the areas absorbed by the newly-constituted provinces of Saskatchewan and Alberta in 1905. Earlier, Treaty No. 8 (1899) to the northwest of Treaty No. 6 had extinguished the Indian title to the area between Edmonton and the access route to the Yukon gold-fields; subsequently, Treaty No. 10 (1906) took in the remaining unsurrendered portion of Saskatchewan. Finally, Adhesions to Treaty No. 5 in 1908-10 preceded Manitoba's boundary extensions of 1912.

.   .   .

For much of its history, the story of Manitoba is the story of the Hudson's Bay Company. By design, the Company's effect on the Indian people of the area was curiously indirect although nevertheless profound. From the beginning it was the Company's intent to have its agents attend to business at York Factory grading and processing furs brought direct to the point of embarkation by Indian collectors. Economically, the combination of low transportation costs from Hudson's Bay ports and relatively cheap, good-quality trade goods was hard to beat; competition from the French and then from the hard-driving Nor' Westers, however, forced the Company into active inland promotion and exploration. Despite the disruptions caused by the rivalries of the various traders, the Indians suffered more from the ravages of alcohol and European diseases than they did at the hands of the Company's agents who, on the whole, enjoyed a good working relationship with the Indian people throughout Rupert's Land.

The most serious rupture occurred over the Red River Colony whereby the Company went into the land settlement business in 1812 under a major shareholder, Thomas Douglas, Earl of Selkirk. The chief opponents of this enterprise were ostensibly the gentlemen of the North-West Company and the Indian bystanders were occasionally treated to the spectacle of Scottish trappers murdering Scottish settlers (or vice versa). Settlement was, of course, even worse from the Indian point of view but this colony was to develop along lines which would have pained its highminded founder.

In 1817, the Earl of Selkirk, on behalf of King George III, entered into negotiations with chiefs and warriors of the Saulteaux and Cree Nations for the extinction of title to lands adjacent to the Red and Assiniboine Rivers. As was recorded much later by Manitoba's lieutenant-governor, the Honourable Alexander Morris, the Indian signators to the Selkirk Treaty were "made to comprehend, the depth of the land they were surrendering, by being told, that it was the greatest distance, at which a horse on the level prairie could be seen, or daylight seen under his belly between his legs." The consideration for the surrender was the annual payment of one hundred pounds of tobacco to each Nation.

Initially Selkirk intended the Red River Colony to be a model of Scottish husbandry and propriety. With the union of the North-West Company and the Hudson's Bay Company in 1821, however, the fierce rivalries of their agents were resolved and the colony became the logical place in which to establish the Indian wives of the Company's employees. The union had also set in motion the release of old employees, both French and British, and many of these also set up Mixed-Blood households in the settlement. The numerous offspring gave the Colony its greatest single spurt of growth and served to stabilize two new population elements – the English-speaking "Scotch" or "Hudson's Bay" Indians, and the French-speaking Métis. Although the stiff-necked original Highland settlers stuck to Gaelic and to farming, the attention of the colony's majority was once again concentrated on the fur trade, even to the extent of surreptitious dealings with the Company's American rivals "south of the line".

In time all the people of mixed blood came to be thought of as "Métis", at least by the European settlers. Many Mixed Bloods, through ties of blood and empathy, came to cast their lot with the Indian peoples. There was also considerable inter-marriage not only between the two major Mixed-Blood language groups but with their Indian affiliates. The resultant re-combination of Native genes would make their Métis descendents as least as "Indian", on the basis of "blood content", as many of the registered Indians in the East. Additionally, we are told that being Indian is as much a state of mind as a matter of blood content; from their close association and affinity over the generations with their Indian affiliates, the Métis have every right to consider themselves representatives of the present Indian way of life rather than as a people set apart. The Métis are as much children of the fur trade as are the redirected Indian peoples whose ancestors' existence since the 1600s depended on the European drive for Canadian furs.

In 1870, the Hudson's Bay Company sold its proprietary rights over Rupert's Land to the government of Canada; in that year, the nucleus of Manitoba, comprising a good part of the Red River Colony, was formed as the fifth province. To many of the colonists, and particularly to the established Indians and Métis, it appeared that the Company had sold them as well. All were well aware that it was the intention of businessmen and other Eastern (Toronto) interests to open up the West – and their inter-dependent fur-trading enclave – to full-scale development.

The resultant discontent was manifested in Louis Riel's provisional government, a stop-gap designed to safeguard Native and Métis rights in Red River by dictating the terms on which the Colony would become part of Canada. The rights of the Métis were fulfilled somewhat in the *Manitoba Act*; 1 400 000 acres of the new province were set aside for the Métis and their children and all existing titles and occupancies were to be respected. Altogether the new province covered some 11 000 square miles.

As noted previously, the North-Western Territory and Rupert's Land were admitted into the Dominion on July 15, 1870. An enabling Order-in-Council of June 23, 1870 gave the Canadian Parliament full legislative power over the new territory. The transfer was made upon the following terms: that Canada should pay Hudson's Bay Company £300 000 sterling; that the Company should retain the posts they actually occupied in the North-Western Territory, and might within twelve months of the surrender, select a block of land adjoining each Post outside of Canada and British Columbia; that, for fifty years after the settlement, the Company might claim 5 percent of the land set apart for settlement in the Fertile Belt (bounded on the south by the United States, on the west by the Rocky Mountains, on the north by the North Saskatchewan River, and on the east by Lake Winnipeg, the Lake of the Woods and the waters connecting them). In addition, all land titles conferred by the

Company up to March 8, 1869 were confirmed. A significant provision regarding the Native inhabitants, however, was Article Fourteen:

> Any claims of Indians to compensation for lands required for purposes of settlement shall be disposed of by the Canadian government in communication with the Imperial government; and the company shall be relieved of all responsibility in respect of them.

Needless to say, Treaties Nos. 1 and 2 of August 1871, took in practically every square inch of Selkirk's sixty-year old colony including large areas *outside* the embryonic province. (Manitoba's boundaries did not catch up until the extensions of 1882.) With relatively minor variations, the treaty activities of September 1875 likewise anticipated Manitoba's final boundaries by some thirty-seven years. Treaties No. 1 and 2 made absolutely no provision for the Indian and Métis peoples to continue their pursuits of hunting, fishing, and trapping, while Treaty No. 5 allowed restrictive hunting and fishing to the Indian people. The aboriginal title, however, had been neatly tied up province-wide. The indications are, of course, that the Indians were expected to adopt farming as their livelihood, at least in the Assiniboine and Red River areas; this has been put forward as a reason for the lack of hunting, fishing, and trapping provisions in Treaties Nos. 1 and 2.

For the most part, Treaties Nos. 1 to 11 all featured similar provisions. With a few subtle differences, all the Western treaties provided for: reserve lands; monetary payments, and occasionally medals and flags, at the treaty signing; suits of clothing every three years to chiefs and headmen; yearly ammunition and twine payments (Treaties Nos. 1, 2 and 9 excepted); and some allowance for schooling. Treaty No. 6 was exceptional as it was the only one in which provisions were made for medical treatment, and for "assistance in the case of pestilence or famine." The medical provision decreed that "a medicine chest shall be kept at the house of each Indian agent for the use and benefit of the Indians at the direction of the agent"; this has been made a claim for comprehensive medicare, in the modern sense, on behalf of the Indian people concerned.

To obtain a proper appreciation of Indian treaties, one should read them in historical context. If the treaties provisions are read as symbolic promises of more comprehensive services to be adapted to changing circumstances, they take on a very different meaning than if they are read as plain statements meaning precisely and exactly what they say. Many of the commissioners' promises (in and out of treaty) were "once-for-all commitments" and any or all "recurring expenditures" were related to real requirements at the time.

On the formation of Manitoba, considerable numbers of nomadic

Métis withdrew westward from settlement, depending for their liveli-hood on the dwindling buffalo herds. The detachment of the Mixed-Blood people from the Indian people was achieved from 1874 onward by treaty activity, the separation being emphasized by the provision of reserves exclusively for Indians under treaty. Some Mixed-Blood people were included in the treaty activities of particular bands but the majority went the way of the Métis. Those who took treaty thus adopted "Indian" status. Those who chose not to take treaty were eligible for half-breed scrip.

With the esablishment of reserves "for the sole and exclusive use of Indians" as an accompanying feature of treaty activities, the necessity to define "Indian" became imperative. The latter step, however, and the establishment of treaty paylists and band lists (1951), have served to introduce and perpetuate a peculiarly mechanistic way of determining Indian status. "Treaty Indian" has become a label of differentiation currently used (especially in the West) by the Indian people themselves and by many of the news media. Misuse of the expression has served to create barriers between peoples sharing a common cultural heritage and similar ways of life.

On December 31, 1873, Indian Commissioner J. A. N. Provencher summarized the advantages of dealing with the Indians by the treaty system and how this would help the Indian people make the necessary adjustment to a new style of living:

> There are two modes wherein the Government may treat the Indian nations who inhabit this territory. Treaties may be made with them simply with a view to the extinction of their rights, by agreeing to pay them a sum, and afterwards abandon them to themselves. On the other side, they may be instructed, civilized and led to a mode of life more in conformity with the new position of this country, and accordingly made good, industrious and useful citizens.

> Under the first system the Indians will remain in their condition of igno-rance and inferiority, and as soon as the facilities for hunting and fishing disappear, they will become mendicants, or be obliged to seek refuge in localities inaccessible to immigration or cultivation.

> Under the second system, on the contrary, they will learn sufficient for themselves, and to enable them to pass from a state of tutelage, and to do without assistance from the Government.

No story of the Western treaty-making process would be complete without mention of the North-West Mounted Police. Established in 1873 to maintain order on the Prairies, these mounted riflemen were a formi-dable presence at treaty negotiations; they not only added pomp to the ceremonies but they had come to be trusted and recognized as representatives of the Queen's good faith. The force also played a significant role in encouraging roving bands of Indian buffalo hunters to settle on reserves. This was particularly important when the last appearance of the buffalo on the Canadian Prairies in 1879 left destitute hundreds of starving Indians around Fort Walsh.

Construction of the railway was scheduled to start in 1873 (in accordance with the British Columbia agreement) but was disrupted in that year on political grounds which also cost the life of Sir John A. Macdonald's government. The railway matter, however, was to be kept alive by more than just the protestations of British Columbia until Sir John's return; obviously, the disparate segments of the new country had to be linked as soon as possible for survival and rapid settlement was necessary to sustain its development. That an east-west railway would provide the most immediate and practical resolution was evident to the most sceptical.

The expedience with which treaty activities were conducted between 1871 and 1877 merely reflects the haste with which the Dominion was stitched together and should not be taken to imply that government's motive was to steal Indian land or to obtain it by trick or fraud. Since 1763, successive administrations had been burdened with the liability of the "Indian title" inferred from the *Royal Proclamation*; what title the government in right of the Sovereign was obliged to purchase had not been clearly defined in that legislation. The method of dealing with the question evolved from imprecise beginnings in the late 1700s to the ritualized, rather mechanistic, method used so extensively and expediently in the 1870s.

Upon study, one is left with the impression that the treaty commissioners operated within quite narrow areas of discretion regarding what actually could be given; that they felt the tactics used were justified as long as the Indian people were adequately "looked after" with integrity, according to the conscience of the times. Needless to say, from today's viewpoint the Indian signators had relatively little choice, and even less expert counsel. In such circumstances, that there should be divergences concerning what the people thought they were getting as opposed to that which was actually written into treaty is understandable; that these divergences would become even more significant as the standards of literacy and militancy rose was inevitable.

Treaty No. 4, concluded in 1874, covered the arable southern portion of what was to become Saskatchewan[4] and was the first in which trapping, despite its early significance, was officially recognized as a feature of Indian life. In conjunction with Treaty No. 7 (concluded in 1877), the jagged treaty line from Georgian Bay to the Rockies containing the most likely areas of expanding settlement was completed – roughly two degrees of latitude north of the international boundary.

In 1875, steam navigation via Lake Winnipeg and the Saskatchewan River was the best mode of transportation from Manitoba to the regions of the Fertile Belt; construction of the railway had not yet progressed past Winnipeg. Thus, in September of 1875, Alexander Morris, Lieutenant-Governor of Manitoba (and the Northwest Territories, ex-officio) met with representatives of the Saulteaux and Swampy Cree tribes to negotiate Treaty No. 5; he succeeded in obtaining the surrender of their rights and title to 100 000 square miles to the north of Treaties 2, 3, and 4. The western extremity of the treaty was at Cumberland House on the Saskatchewan River.

Prior to the negotiations of Treaty No. 6, Lieutenant-Governor Morris was well aware that the Indian people of the Saskatchewan River districts were becoming apprehensive for reasons other than the pending negotiations. American whisky-jacks and other unscrupulous traders had been active throughout the Canadian West; recent epidemics of measles, scarlet fever, and smallpox had taken a terrible toll; and the threat of starvation was ever present due to the accelerating reduction of the buffalo herds on which they depended. While the need to change their way of living was appreciated, the Indians fully realized that no one could change from hunter to farmer without proper preparation and training. The presence of the railway survey parties working through their area had also caused anxiety. The signing of Treaty No. 6 accounted for all the land drained by the North Saskatchewan River in the central areas of what were to become Saskatchewan and Alberta.

During his term of office, Governor Morris officiated over Treaties No. 3, 4, 5, and 6; there is no doubt that he adapted the method developed in the earlier exercises, particularly in the Robinson Treaties, to his needs. Although the governor repeatedly told the Cree chiefs throughout the negotiations for Treaty No. 6 that Her Majesty could not provide greater benefits than had been extended in the previous treaties, it was at the Cree's insistence that the medicine chest, pestilence and famine provisions were written in. As Morris explained, it was the Queen's way to provide relief in the case of national famine and medical care in the case of national pestilence; writing appropriate provisions into the treaty would not affect these policies and would serve to allay the specific and valid fears of a particularly stricken group; equally, in view of the Indian's recent experiences and consequent dread of sickness, a box of medicine to be kept and administered by the Indian agent could not be considered an unreasonable concession. Obviously the governor also had to admit that hunters could not become farmers overnight and, as the people had lived with famine at their tent-flaps, he felt he could not deny the need for assistance during the transition – thus his provision for their insurance ($1 000 each year at seed time for the first three years). None of these provisions had been included in previous treaties and, with the exception of Treaty No. 8 where spring provisions for several years were included, they were not repeated.

From his own writings, ambivalence may be noted in Governor Morris's promises to preserve the traditional Indian way of life as countered by his emphasis on the adoption of stock-raising and general farming as the acceptable means of livelihood. On the one hand we find him telling the people, "Understand me, I do not want to interfere with your hunting and fishing. I want you to pursue it through the country as you have heretofore done", and on the other, "I said you would get seed; you need not concern yourself so much about what your grandchildren are going to eat; your children will be taught, and they will be as well able to take care of themselves as the Whites around them." It is evident that the governor felt that while the children would be fully able to fend for themselves on an equal basis in the larger society, assurance had to be given many of the hunters he addressed that the life they knew would not be swept away arbitrarily to be replaced by a dreaded, unknown future:

> You know my words are true; you see for yourselves and know that your numbers are lessening every year . . . . We want you to have homes of your own where your children can be taught to raise for themselves the food from mother earth. You may not all be ready for that, but some, I have no doubt, are, and in a short time others will follow.

While he may have misjudged the time factor, Alexander Morris genuinely liked and admired the Indian people and spent a large part of his life

> devising means whereby the Indian population of the Fertile Belt can be rescued from the hard fate which otherwise awaits them, owing to the speedy destruction of the buffalo, hitherto the principal food supply of the Plains Indians, and that they may be induced to become, by the adoption of agricultural and pastoral pursuits, a self-supporting community.

Governor Morris was also a practical man, conducting his treaty activities in full realization that extinguishment of the Indian title would "enable the government to throw open for settlement any portion of the land which might be susceptible of improvement and profitable occupation." Concerning the value of the railway, his views expressed regarding Treaty No. 3 are explicit: "And so was closed a treaty whereby a territory was enabled to be opened up, of great importance to Canada embracing as it does the Pacific Railway route to the Northwest Territories – a wide extent of fertile lands, and, as is believed, great mineral resources." In 1880, looking back with understandable pride to his own contributions, he wrote, "Since 1870, no less than seven treaties have been concluded, with the Indian tribes, so that there now remains no Indian nations . . . inside the Fertile Belt, who have not been dealt with."

It is evident that Governor Morris considered that the Indian peoples' need and desire to hunt, fish, and trap for food would diminish as their skill (and consequent yield) in the agricultural-pastoral field improved. That his views and those of today's Indian people are at variance is equally evident. While the governor speaks of "permission to the Indians to hunt over ceded territory and to fish in the waters thereof, excepting such portions of the territory as pass from the Crown into the occupation of individuals or otherwise," many Indian people today view hunting, fishing, and trapping as inalienable prerogatives which were confirned, not limited, by treaty. Unfortunately, the actual wording of the treaties contradicts both viewpoints, giving rise to charges either that "ancient treaty rights" are being flouted by goverment or illegally curtailed. The very wording of any treaty plainly indicates that curtailment is inevitable. As time goes on, more and more land will be taken up for "settlement, mining, lumbering, trading or other purposes"; just as inevitably, game retreats with advancing development. By the same token, no matter how inevitable the curtailment of opportunity, no treaty provision was ever made that hunting, fishing or trapping would cease by a given date (apart from that implied in the Chippewa-Mississauga agreements of 1923). In every treaty since Confederation, government has reserved the right wherever hunting, fishing or trapping is mentioned to make "regulations".

The signing of Treaty No. 7 at the Blackfoot Crossing of the Bow River in September 1877 under Governor Morris's successor, the Hon. David Laird, "completed the series of treaties, extending from Lake Superior to the slopes of the Rocky Mountains." This cleared not only the lands of the Fertile Belt but also the northerly route first proposed for the Canadian Pacific Railway and the more southerly route finally decided upon. By the time Western construction had started (1880), what the Indian people may have thought of the matter was hypothetical; the Indian title to the last link in the Prairie chain (southern Alberta) had been extinguished in 1877. The rapid prior resolution of the Indian interest undoubtedly contributed to the speed of construction. The railway company not only received an initial construction subsidy of $25 million and all trackage previously built, but also obtained a 25-million-acre grant of prime settlement land; this land was to be chosen, by the company, in blocks twenty-four miles deep on either side of the line (alternating with equal government blocks) from Winnipeg to Jasper House. Within *ten years*, the West had passed from the influence of a company whose primary concern was the fur trade to that of a company whose major interests centred on settlement and development.

The pace of treaty activity slowed considerably when the coverage was complete in the Fertile Belt. Except for an Adhesion (covering an additional 11 066 square miles) in 1889 to Treaty No.6 by certain Wood Cree tribes in the vicinity of Montreal Lake and Lac La Ronge, the further extinction of the Indian title to new areas considered for development was not deemed necessary until 1899. The immediate need then was to clear the route from Edmonton to the Pelly River in the Yukon. The route was used mainly by miners, but more and more people each year were travelling along it and through the Peace River and Lesser Slave Lake districts. The Indian people here appeared less concerned than those further south and were not particularly interested in reserves or agricultural pursuits.

The "domino" effect in treaty activities, however, was as evident as ever. Anyone who looks carefully at the treaty question invariably asks, "Why didn't more people hold out?" The major hurdle, of course, was to get the first group to sign; once this had been accomplished, the cash and other immediate benefits lured others to do likewise. The anxiety of the masses worked on the representatives, resulting in an inability to manoeuvre effectively and an eagerness to sign. Under such circumstances, there was no need for sharp practice or large-scale misrepresentation.

The territory (324 900 square miles) cleared under Treaty No. 8 was greater than that of any previous treaty; as well as the northern half of Alberta, it took in the southeast portion of the Mackanzie District in the Northwest Territories, the northwest corner of Saskatchewan, and the northeast quarter of British Columbia. Particular difficulties have attended the application of Treaty No. 8 in the Northwest Territories and these will be examined in the appropriate section on the Territories. As the lands in the northeast quarter of British Columbia are contiguous with those of the Peace River area and share the same features, the western boundary of Treaty No. 8 was established at the Rocky Mountains; the Dominion assumed all costs and no objection was lodged by the provincial government.

In 1905, the province of Saskatchewan was created with its present boundaries. The remainder of the province came under the treaty with the signing of Treaty No. 10 in 1906. From 1901 to 1911 Saskatchewan's population increase, mainly from the influx of settlers, was the most spectacular in Canada – nearly 400 percent. During that period, well over a million people settled in the Prairies and British Columbia. The Indian population in all three Prairie provinces was roughly 22 500 people in 1900.

Alberta was the first, and only, of Canada's constitutent parts to be created a province *after* the Indian title has been substantially extinguished. Except for a small corner on its eastern border at the fifty-fifth parallel (included in Treaty No. 10 of 1906), the future province was completely cleared of the aboriginal title with the signing of Treaty No. 8 in 1899-1900. As with Saskatchewan, provincial status was achieved in 1905. Population growth was hardly less spectacular – over 400 percent in the decade from 1901 to 1911.

Of course, the treaty benefits accorded their western and southern neighbours encouraged the Indians to follow suit at Norway House, Cross Lake, and Fisher River in 1908; at Oxford House, God's Lake, and Island Lake in 1909; and at Deer Lake, Fort York, and Fort Churchill in 1910. In all, an area of 133 400 square miles was covered in Adhesions to Treaty No. 5 and included in Manitoba's boundary extensions of 1912.

BRITISH COLUMBIA

In many aspects British Columbia differs considerably from the rest of Canada; this difference has greatly affected the conditions for human habitation both in prehistoric and historic times. Essentially this is a matter of geography and climate, governed in part by the great mountain ranges which separate most of the province from the rest of Canada.

It has been estimated that prior to its discovery by Europeans the vast area we know as Canada supported less than 250 000 people; of these, approximately 100 000, or 40 percent, were concentrated between the mountains and the Pacific Ocean. Because humans had ranged Canada for uncounted generations, the conclusion is inescapable that they found the ocean beaches and salmon rivers of the future province most favourable to their survival. The waters teemed with food; the forest provided housing, fuel, clothing, and utensils. As the sea supplied a sustained yield, this was the only part of prehistoric Canada in which the inhabitants developed a thoroughly dependable economy of surplus; consequently, social organization was advanced, artistic expression sophisticated, technology was at a relatively high level, and trading activities were extensively engaged in.

Initially, European exploratory activities in the area tended to focus on the products of the sea and were peculiarly confined to the last quarter of the 1700s. The original Spanish and English competitors appeared off the coast in the 1770s, with the Russians and Americans entering the fray in the 1780s. As noted previously, the Scots-Canadian representatives of the North-West Company arrived late on the scene, overland, around 1800.

Not until its amalgamation with the North-West Company did the Hudson's Bay Company extend its trading influence into the area. In 1849, under the same unlikely rationale found wanting in New France two centuries earlier, the Company was charged with settlement and colonization of Vancouver Island while still retaining full trading rights on the Island and on the mainland opposite. In 1851 the Company's Chief Factor at Fort Victoria, James Douglas, became governor without relinquishing his former position.

The fur trade and settlement were, of course, no more compatible in the 1850s than they were in the 1650s. Colonization languished. The few settlers who ventured into the enclave did serve, however, to warn the Indian residents of things to come. To allay Native fears, Governor Douglas in his first few years of office negotiated a series of aboriginal title surrenders (which included provisions for village reserves) in the northeastern and southeastern parts of the island; these, and the almost accidental inclusion of the northeast quarter of the province in Treaty No. 8 in 1889, represent the only formal treaty activities in which the Indian people of British Columbia have participated.

As a result of the disruption caused by the rapid influx of miners, the mainland (controlled by the Hudson's Bay Company as New Caledonia) was erected to the status of a Crown Colony in 1858 and renamed British Columbia. The new colony was brought under Governor Douglas' sway on the condition that he sever his connection with the Company.

In 1861, Governor Douglas directed that village reserves be clearly defined throughout British Columbia, stipulating that the bounds were "to be pointed out" by knowledgeable Indian persons. Thus, for the first time, we find fixed aboriginal occupational sites of long standing not created but confirmed as reserves. However, with the intention of protecting the reserves from pre-emption, the governor declared them to be held by the Crown in trust for the Indian people.

First we were presented with treaties without reserves; now, we encounter reserves without treaties. The anomalies thus created are as prodigious as any previously met. What are the aboriginal range rights of fixed communities? What happens to the principle of the aboriginal title? The *Royal Proclamation* of 1763 can hardly be held to apply to an area whose existence was a matter for conjecture at the time; geographer John Rocque's map of 1761 North America showed all the land north and west of what are now Lakes Winnipegosis and Manitoba as "intirely unknown" (sic). On moral grounds alone, however, one could argue if the principle of the aboriginal title holds in any part of Canada it holds in every part.

Governor Douglas retired from office in 1864; two years later British Columbia achieved its present boundaries through union of the two Crown Colonies with the Stickeen Territory. Although its discovery and exploration had come last, British Columbia was the first of the larger provinces to be marked out (as a Colony, nonetheless); its northern boundary, the 60th parallel, eventually became that of all the Western provinces.

As has been related, British Columbia entered Confederation in 1871 on the understanding that construction of the Canadian Pacific Railway would be started within two years and completed by ten. At that time, the policy of allotting and holding lands on behalf of the Indian people put into practice by Governor Douglas was clearly defined; by 1912, most of the reserves had been properly identified and were conveyed to the Dominion. Arising from the railway agreement, two extensive tracts of land identified as the "Railway Belt" and the "Peace River Block" became the subjects of negotiation between the Dominion and the Province: the Railway Belt was a patchwork of blocks extending from the Alberta border between Jasper and Field to North Vancouver; the Peace River Block covered 3 500 000 acres entirely within the British Columbia portion of Treaty No. 8. The Dominion interest in these lands was returned to the province in 1930 on the stipulation that reserves therein "shall continue to be vested in Canada in trust for the Indians."

YUKON

Some of the most ancient sites of early humanity in Canada are to be found in the extreme north of the Yukon Territory and in its southerly reaches. From Asia, the most likely initial migration route would have been through Alaska's Seward Peninsula, eventually intersecting with the north bank of the lower Yukon River. The probable northerly route into the present Territory would have been via the Procupine River; the southerly, would have been through the upper reaches of the Yukon.

Historically, the Yukon's destiny was more directly linked to the settlement of the Alaska boundary, primarily with Russia, than to the "Indian territory" proviso, extending somewhere to the west of Rupert's Land, mentioned in the *Royal Proclamation* of 1763.

To the Russians, Alaska was "Russian America" although, particularly in the early stage, the Russian claims to sovereignty in North America were often just as nebulous and pretentious, as those shared by the other occupying powers. In the early 1700s, the North Pacific was essentially a huge area for geographic speculation. Lands were projected which did not exist, and whether Asia and America were connected at their northern extremities was the subject of acrimonious debate. This latter question obsessed Peter the Great and to resolve it he chose Vitus Bering, a Dane in the Russian naval service. Peter died before Bering's expedition to the Siberian coast got underway; however, Peter's widow, Catherine I, continued the plan. Unknown to Peter, Catherine, or Bering, was the fact that the question had been resolved nearly a century earlier (about 1640) by a group of Cossacks who had coasted Arctic Siberia to its eastern limits in a boat held together with willow withes; their report lay buried in the files at Yakutsk.

Bering's first expedition in 1730 was considered inconclusive; he was again commissioned to conduct a voyage of exploration, this time to discover America. Along with Captain-Lieutenant Cherikov in an accompanying ship, Bering mapped the northwest shoulder of the North American continent in the summer and fall of 1741. Cherikov had also explored the Aleutians, encountering the fur seal and the sea otter. Unfortunately, Russia had meanwhile acquired a new empress, Elisabeth, and Russian America was turned over to the promyshlenniki (independent Russian fur traders) who were interested only in reaping the rich harvests of the coastal waters.

In 1762, Catherine the Great succeeded to the throne of Russia and her dreams of empire included America. Strangely enough, the other colonizing powers had not realized that Russia had been reaping enormous profits for over twenty years from the sale to China of fur seal and sea otter pelts taken off the Aleutians and Alaska; the orientals had assumed that the source was the coast of Siberia. At a diplomatic function, Catherine declaimed that not only would she extend Russia's fur-gathering along America's western coast, but she would assert her suzerainty over that area by the establishment of permanent Russian settlements therein. The immediate reaction was a flurry of activity by the British and Spanish in the late 1700s.

Russia of course did not lack men to support Catherine in America, and by 1784 shore posts (hardly settlements) were established at Attu, Agattu, and Unalaska in the Aleutian Islands and on Kodiak Island off the mouth of Cook Inlet; eighteen months later, a shore settlement was established on the mainland fronting Cook Inlet. By 1807, New Archangel on Baranov Island in Sitka Sound was a thriving community and the ostensible capital of Russian America. The first resident Chief Manager, Alexander Baranov, had formed an enduring mercantile alliance with American shipping interests and fur-poachers; along with Aleuts in American ships, joint forays regularly invaded the coast of Spanish California. By the 1820s, forty forts were functioning in Russian America, including Fort Ross, built and manned by Russians on the coast of California.

As a result of internal crises compounded by difficulties abroad, and under mounting pressure from the navy, Russia suddenly declared that Russian America extended south to latitude 51° (the Queen Charlotte Strait), that no foreigner was to trespass and, further, that no foreign ship was to approach within a hundred miles of shore. This, of course, was too much for the United States who, in concert with a very concerned Great Britain, applied immediate pressure. The upshot was a treaty (1824) whereby the United States rolled back the border 54° 40' and Russia agreed to establish no more posts or forts outside the newly prescribed bounds. In 1825, Britain agreed to the southern limitation but also insisted on entry rights along the narrow coastal strip and establishment of the border which still exists between Alaska and the Yukon Territory. The Alaska purchase by the United States in 1867 did not substantially alter any of these provisions; certainly, not as far as the Yukon was concerned.

As administrators and colonizers, the Russians showed very little respect for the lives of their officers, colonists, and fur traders. This attitude was passed on, and the treatment accorded aboriginal peoples by Russian officers, colonists, and fur traders was sometimes barbaric and occasionally little less than bestial. Apparently, the experiences of the Aleut, Tlingit, and Kutchin peoples at the hands of the Russians contributed to the general distrust by the Northern peoples for Europeans and Native disinterest in treaty activities. American military control, imposed during the first ten years after the Alaska purchase, did nothing to improve the situation.

The Yukon was at first included in the North-Western Territory, but isolation between the Great Divide and United States territory led to its creation as a separate Territory in 1898. Other than a small area covered by Treaty No. 8 in 1899 in the southeast corner of the Territory east of the Great Divide, there has been no treaty activity in the Yukon. Mining and other developmental activities have helped to deplete or drive away the traditional resources on which the Indian people depend.

NORTHWEST TERRITORIES

Before the explorations of the Hudson's Bay Company's Samuel Hearne (1769-72), the depth of country between the northwest confines of Rupert's Land and the Pacific coast was unknown to the British: as Hearne stated, "The continent of America is much wider than many people imagine." Owing to Hearne's efforts, and those of his Cree guide Matonabbee, the lands from the Slave River, Great Slave Lake, and the Coppermine River north to the Arctic were accurately reported. Later, Alexander Mackenzie, an agent of the North-West Company, who was yet hopeful of finding a river route to Cook Inlet on the coast of Russian America, set out from Fort Chipewyan in 1789; instead, he found the river which now bears his name and followed it to the Arctic Ocean.

By the early 1800s, a number of posts had been established along the Mackenzie River; the areas fur resources were being thoroughly exploited and contact had been made with a Russian fur-trading post in what was to become the Yukon Territory. Although the Hudson's Bay Company's agents were officially confined to Rupert's Land, the North-West Company's traders were free to collect furs in roughly three-quarters of the area north of the 60th parallel. While Mackenzie's loyalties were with the North-West Company, he felt that the constant frittering away of the two Companies' energies in internecine strife was disastrous considering the ever-increasing competition from Russian and American traders. His hopes were realized with the merger of the Hudson's Bay and North-West Companies in 1821, followed by a working agreement between the revitalized Company and the Russian Americans which was to last until the Alaska purchase in June 1867.

The Alaska purchase in itself was one of those strange, but quite frequent, incidents in history which originate with a fallacy, grow through guile and deception, and terminate in bitterness and misunderstanding. The Czar was told that under the rule of "Manifest Destiny" the United States would eventually take Russian America by force. He believed that, by offering to sell, he would accommodate American interests and perpetuate American goodwill; he did not want to sell. The United States Congress was told that the rush in Canada to confederate was bound to include Russian America and that the United States must acquire the territory by purchase; they did not want to buy. Finally, through persuasion, each of the major parties was convinced that it was doing the other a favour and the deal was made for $7 200 000. The chief Russian negotiator was eventually accused of fraud and bribery and spent the rest of his life in exile. The Czar was accused, albeit in secrecy, of peddling holy Russian soil and Russian subjects. The charges in the United States included everything from malfeasance to corruption. Alaska was dubbed "Seward's ice-box" and sentenced to ten years' military occupation under a noted Indian fighter who felt his assignment was a logical continuation of his career. In Canada, the event was hardly noticed; Confederation (July 1867) was the more immediate concern.

From 1867 to 1870, the recently consolidated Hudson's Bay Company held undisputed sway over most of Canada. In effect, through the efforts of the Canadian Indian people, the fur trade reigned supreme. At one stroke, all this changed, however, with the transfer of Rupert's Land to Canada in 1870. At the time, the founding provinces, with the exception of the Maritimes, were mere shadows of what they were to become; British Columbia was a British Crown Colony; all the rest became the Northwest Territories, under Dominion administration.

As was the case earlier in the East, an immediate result of the opening of the West was the commencement of intense treaty activity throughout the Fertile Belt; this took place in order to clear the lands of the Indian title in advance of anticipated settlement and to clear any prospective route for the proposed east-to-west railway. Neither of these developmental considerations had immediate bearing in the lands north of the 60th parallel and the only activity of consequence in the Northwest Territories was inclusion in 1900 under Treaty No. 8 of the area to the south of the Great Slave Lake, mainly because of mining exploratory activity in the lands between it and Lake Athabasca.

In 1880, British rights to the Arctic Islands passed to Canada and were lodged with the Northwest Territories; in 1898 the Yukon Territory was separated. In 1912, with the final demarcation of the provinces, the Northwest Territories attained its present boundaries. In 1925, Canada's northern boundary was extended to the North Pole in accordance with the "sector principle".

The partnership with the Canadian Indian peoples fostered by the Hudson's Bay Company in the late 1600s was maintained well into the twentieth century in the Northwest Territories. Long after the Company's scope had been curtailed elsewhere and pelts had become scarcer, the Territories, well outside the areas coveted for settlement, still provided subsistence for the fur-gatherer and profits for the Company. Then, a sudden change took place with its usual immediate effect: oil was discovered at Fort Norman in 1920 and Treaty No. 11 was signed everywhere within the Mackenzie District in 1921. According to the fiat first laid down in 1763 and interpreted in the early 1780s, as soon as the land was found to have gained significant value, or was wanted for development purposes, it had to be cleared of its aboriginal title with all possible dispatch.

Treaty No. 11 possessed one significant difference; noting the baneful effect on the people south of the Great Slave Lake in Treaty No. 8, the Treaty No. 11 people were not going to be relegated to reserves. Although provision was made in both treaties for reserves on the basis of one square mile per family of five (or, in treaty No. 8 only, 160 acres per person for those who chose to live apart), until 1974 not a single reserve site was chosen anywhere in the Mackenzie District, nor in the small corner of the Yukon covered by treaty No. 11.[5] As had been the case in 1787, the treaties were signed, dated, and proclaimed, but critical elements were left hanging. This raises pertinent questions concerning: the prospective life of treaty negotiations; the time required to observe or fulfill a condition; and, whether the penalty or voidance principles common to most other types of material settlement agreements apply.

As is provided in the treaties, federal conservation regulations are applicable throughout the Territories and the Yukon including for protection of migratory birds, muskoxen, polar bear and female caribou. However, developmental and sporting activities have, as in the Yukon, reduced the traditional game resources on which the Indian people depend.

Conclusion

From the time the first European set foot on what was to become Canada, until the present limits were fixed by the inclusion of Newfoundland in 1949, European sovereignty over the land was essentially a matter of effective occupation. On the East coast, the Vikings barely established a toehold and disappeared almost without a trace; the bitter contest between the French and, first the English, then the British after the Union of the Crowns, was finally resolved by force of arms in 1759-60 following three centuries of contention. On the West coast, despite the claim said to have been established by Drake at the 38th parallel in the sixteenth century, Spain held the coast well north of the 40th parallel until pushed out of contention. The Russian claim to all the coast from the 55th parallel north was never seriously contested by Britain, yet Russian America passed rapidly to the United States by purchase in 1867.

With the extension of international rivalries on the North American continent, traditional inter-tribal conflicts were often intensified. Group migrations became more frequent and were subject to manipulation by the competing European factions, both in colonial wars and through the fur trade. The fur trader needed the Indian collector and from this need grew esteem and understanding. However, as fur resources were depleted and large-scale settlement became a factor, the Indian could not escape the unappreciative attention of the incoming developers and home-steaders.

Indian treaty activity in Canada began with the Maritime "Peace and Friendship" agreements during colonial struggles, in which the principals agreed to aid each other in conflict or remain neutral. There was no mention of land title and, invariably, the Indian people were assured they would not be disturbed in their traditional pursuits of hunting, fishing, and trapping. Between 1725 and 1779, there were as many as eight agreements of this type.

The most significant date in Canadian Indian treaty matters is October 7, 1763, when, by *Royal Proclamation*, the British Sovereign directed that all endeavours to clear the Indian title must be by Crown purchase. In effect, the *Proclamation* applied to lands then west of the settled areas, Old Quebec and the Maritimes having been passed over as if they had been adequately dealt with. The anticipated influx of settlers was accelerated by the American Revolution (1775-83) and then by the War of 1812; hence, the half-century between 1775 and 1825 witnessed a comprehensive land surrender scheme to extinguish Indian title to most of what is now southern Ontario. Compensation to the Indian groups deemed to be in situ was sometimes in cash, sometimes in goods. The land so "cleared" or "ceded" was considered freed of all encumbrance with plenty of room for Indians and non-Indians alike.

Thereafter, the exigent elements of Canada's growth westward and northward dictated the pace and direction of treaty activity. The discovery of minerals north of Lakes Superior and Huron precipitated the negotiation of the Robinson Treaties in 1850 with the Ojibeway.

Plans to settle the region of the Fertile Belt in the Prairies exerted similar pressures as the Indian peoples and the Crown in right of Canada signed Treaties Nos. 1 through 7 between 1871 and 1877. Subsequent treaty activity continued ad hoc: the discovery of gold at the Klondike River (1897) led to Treaty No. 8 in 1899, thus clearing the access route from Edmonton to the Pelly River; plans for construction of roads and railways precipitated the signing of Treaty No. 9 in 1905; Treaty No. 10 in 1906 immediately followed the attainment of provincial status for Saskatchewan and Alberta; the discovery of oil at Norman Wells in 1920 preceded Treaty No. 11 by one year.

The commissioners saw the treaties in one way; the Indians in quite another. A reading of the reports of the Commissioners and of Lieutenant-Governor Morris' book[6] shows that the two groups came together with radically different expectations. The Indians sought to be protected from land-grabbing settlers and from the evils they sensed. Buffalo herds were diminishing and the railway was projected; the Indians sought wide ranges which they could call their own and over which they could live much as they had in the past. The Commissioners saw Indian reserves as places where Indians could learn to be settlers and farmers. Some Indian spokesmen appeared to accept the idea of farming, but it is unlikely they fully understood all that was entailed.

The 1923 Chippewa and Mississauga Agreements in Ontario involved compensation for surrender of Indian hunting, fishing, and trapping rights. These agreements notwithstanding, there has been no "treaty activity" in Canada since.

In the 1970s, loss of "traditional livelihood" through hydro-electric power development (James Bay) and oil-producing schemes (Northern pipelines) has precipitated a strong dialogue between Native groups and government. This time, by combining a higher degree of research with consultation and negotiations on both sides, compensatory agreements have been or are being worked out in many non-treaty areas of Canada. In those areas already covered by treaties, the federal government has stated that it will honour its "lawful obligations"; to this effect it has provided research funding for Indian bands and organizations to investigate claims or grievances relating to the fulfilment or interpretation of Indian treaties.

Notes

1. This chapter was written by George Brown and Ron Maguire, Ottawa, 1979. Reprinted with the kind permission of the Research Branch, Department of Indian and Northern Affairs.
2. "Aboriginal title" has not been defined in Canadian, British, nor International law. The Judicial Committee of the Privy Council in *St. Catherine's Milling*

and Lumber Company v. The Queen (1888) 14 App. Cas. 54, 58 described the tenure of the Indians as a "personal and usufructuary right, dependent upon the good will of the Sovereign"; as a "mere burden" upon the Crown's "proprietary estate in the land."

3. The post-Confederation Treaties, Nos. 3 to 11 inclusive, also allowed Indian hunting, fishing, and trapping on unoccupied Crown lands, but further restricted them to "such regulations as may from time to time be made" by Her Majesty's Canadian Government. Federal Fish and Game Acts, to name a few, are examples of "such regulations".

4. A cartographical error at the time caused Maple Creek to be named as the western extremity of Treaty No. 4. Later maps show the intended stream to be Seven Persons Coulee, with Maple Creek in its present location (some 70 miles to the eastward). This oversight was never corrected in the Treaty No. 4 text, upon which depended the subsequent boundary descriptions of Treaties Nos. 6 and 7.

5. A reserve of 52 square miles was set aside for the Hay River Band of treaty No. 8 by Order-in-Council P.C. 387 of 26 February 1974.

6. The Hon. Alexander Morris, P.C., *The Treaties of Canada with the Indians of Manitoba and the North-West Territories*, Toronto, Belfords, Clarke & Co., 1880; reprinted by Coles Publishing Company, Toronto, 1971.

4

Indian Claims in Canada[1]

Introduction

The Native peoples of Canada have come under European influence in various ways, in differing degrees, and at different historical periods. Little impact was made on the Arctic until this century and most of that has occurred since World War II. On the other hand, the Indians of the Atlantic coast and along the shores of the St. Lawrence encountered Europeans early in the sixteenth century. As a result of this contact, the Beothuk of Newfoundland were destroyed. Other Indians in the more southerly parts of the country have since largely moved towards a Euro-Canadian way of life. In northern areas, more continuity has been preserved with traditional patterns of living. Nowhere has Native life been entirely unaffected by the advent of the European settlers and their domination of territory that was once the exclusive domain of Native peoples.

European-Native interaction has taken many forms. The fur trade significantly altered the way of life of a large segment of the Indian population, economically as well as socially. While the fur trade introduced European goods and commercial values, it also brought with it White Western moral and religious persuasions. At the same time, social interaction brought into being the people of mixed ancestry often referred to as Métis.

The later occupation of land for settlement was further instrumental in modifying the economic and socio-cultural bases of Native societies. Resource exploitation in almost every part of the country additionally disturbed the lives of Native peoples both directly and indirectly through its environmental effects. Such activity continues today, with similarly disruptive results.

From an early period, the government of the colonizing society made itself specifically responsible for the relationship between the immigrants and the Natives. At law, the Native interest in land and other natural resources could not be acquired directly by the newcomers, but rather through the agency of their government. In addition, the government assumed much of the direction of Native societies, particularly those whose traditional way of life was most disrupted. The historical relationship of the government to Native groups accounts for their insistence on continuing special status as the original people of Canada. The Crown became the target of Native grievances and claims respecting land, resources, and the management of Native affairs. These claims are based on aboriginal rights or on agreements made with government which were based on the Indians' position as unconquered indigenous occupants of the land.

To implement the policy of dealing with Native peoples differently from other citizens, it became necessary to determine the membership of the Native societies. Racial mixing and changing patterns of living have in many cases blurred the distinction between the original and immigrant peoples. The solution that has evolved is that people of Indian ancestry in Canada fall into two major classes in their position vis-à-vis government. There are those recognized by the Canadian government as so-called status Indians, and a second group that includes those who are termed non-status Indians, as well as Métis. Status Indians are registered by the Department of Indian Affairs and Northern Development and possess certain rights and are subject to some limitations set forth in the *Indian Act*. That *Act* and its administrative interpretation determine what Indian status means, in practice, for the 250 000 persons who hold it.

Non-status Indians are people of Indian extraction who for varying reasons were not registered as Indians by the Department. Estimates of their numbers vary depending on the criteria applied; there are at least half a million. The category includes women who have lost or whose ancestors have lost, Indian status through marriage. In addition, it encompasses those who voluntarily renounced their Indian status through what is called enfranchisement. One particularly large group without Indian status is the Métis, who form a distinct society with a group identity of its own.

Unless everyone with any Indian ancestry were to be accorded Indian status, a dividing line had to be adopted to encompass the group. Pre-Confederation Indian legislation set down loose definitions based on heredity and social factors, and these criteria were carried over into the

Dominion's own early Indian legislation. In western Canada, inclusion in the treaties came to be the mark of status; hence status Indians there are frequently referred to as "treaty Indians". The list of registered Indians has been built up by ad hoc methods which often seem to have been quite arbitrary. It is for the persons and bands on this list only that the federal Department of Indian Affairs and Northern Development has accepted responsibility under the *Indian Act.*

Non-status Indians and Métis are recognized as holding a status no different from that of other Canadians. While the government of Canada has assumed special responsibilities for education, health, welfare, and economic development for status Indians, the non-status and Métis people rely on the same agencies as other Canadians for these services; this usually means the provincial governments. The *British North America Act* assigned to the Dominion Government responsibility for "Indians, and Lands reserved for the Indians" but gave no clearer specification of those terms. Non-status Indians and Métis argue that the government does not have the constitutional authority to limit these responsibilities by restricting the meaning of "Indian" only to those defined in the *Indian Act.* This question of status and membership in the status group is therefore an important element in the consideration of Native claims and grievances.

The Inuit or Eskimos are a third group. Partly because of their location in the far hinterland of northern Canada, they were for long left with an ambiguous status outside these systems of administration. Some social services were provided by missionaries and traders, and through different levels and departments of government. The northerly extension of Quebec in 1912 was taken by the federal government to mean that the province became liable for its Inuit inhabitants. Meanwhile, serious deterioration of the Inuit economy was increasing the costs of providing relief. The question of jurisdiction was resolved in 1939 when the Supreme Court of Canada declared the Inuit to be Indians for the purposes of the *British North America Act.* While they are therefore a federal responsibility, the *Indian Act* excludes them from its operation and they are dealt with separately by the government.

These, then, are the major groupings of Native people, from a legal standpoint. Their claims are significantly influenced by these distinctions. There are three general categories of claims: aboriginial rights, treaty and scrip settlement grievances, and band claims. The notion of aboriginal rights underlies all other Native claims in Canada. Native people claim that their rights to land derive from their original occupancy, and point out that aboriginal title has been recognized by the dominant society through various judicial decrees and actions of government. It is important to note that no treaties under which Native people ceded their lands were ever made for about half the territory of Canada. On this basis, both status and non-status Indians, as well as the Inuit, are now developing or negotiating claims.

Treaty Indians have a number of claims that relate to the agreement for the cession of their lands through treaty. Some of these rest on an insistence that specific treaty terms have not been fulfilled, and that the broader spirit of the treaties has not been assumed by the government. A frequent claim is that verbal promises made at the time of the negotiations were not included in the written texts. In some areas, Indian people also emphasize in their treaty claims that these transactions constituted inadequate settlements, even if all their terms were fulfilled. These claims involve assertions about the way in which treaties were negotiated, the disparities between the two contracting parties, and the alleged unfairness of the terms.

Most status Indians belong to bands, which possess rights to reserve lands held in common. There are approximately 550 Indian bands in Canada holding rights to 2 200 reserves. Most bands, whether in treaty or non-treaty areas, likely have specific claims to broach. The most numerous and widespread are those stemming from reserve land losses. Reserve lands were sometimes lost through squatting or re-surveys, though most typically as a result of formal surrenders and expropriations. Claims may be based on the specific nature and legality of these occurrences or on the general propriety of such forms of alienation. Management of band funds and reserve resources and the administration of band affairs, particularly with regard to economic development, are central features of many potential band claims.

As will be evident, land is an extremely important element of Native claims in general. Native peoples are becoming more articulate about their unique relationship to the land both past and present, and about the meaning it has for them. At the same time, they are aware that the material standard of living that has been achieved generally in Canada derives ultimately from the land and its resources. As a consequence, they seek not only a role in determining the way in which the land and other resources are used, but also a just portion of the benefits derived from their exploitation. This theme is basic in the aboriginal rights claims, but it also appears in treaty claims, where the original land agreements may be in question, and in band claims concerning lost reserve land or other natural resources.

For the Native people, trusteeship, a fundamental element in Native claims, involves both protection and assistance. When the federal government assumed political control over Native people, undertook responsibilities for reserve land and band finances, and imposed special limitations on Indians as a feature of Indian status, it adopted a protective role over Indians and their affairs analogous to that of a guardian or trustee towards a ward or beneficiary. From this relationship flow grievances and claims which pertain to the government's management of Indian resources.

The Nature of Claims

ABORIGINAL RIGHTS

The concept of Native or aboriginal rights to land stems from a basic fact of Canadian history: that Indian and Inuit peoples were the original, sovereign inhabitants of this country prior to the arrival of the European colonial powers. The Indian understanding of the legal content of aboriginal title has been described in a statement tabled before the House of Commons' Standing Committee on Indian Affairs and Northern Development by the National Indian Brotherhood. It said,

> Indian title as defined by English law connotes rights as complete as that of a full owner of property with one major limitation. The tribe could not transfer its title; it could only agree to surrender or limit its right to use the land. English law describes Indian title as a right to use and exploit all the economic potential of the land and the waters adjacent thereto, including game, produce, minerals and all other natural resources, and water, riparian, foreshore, and off-shore rights.

While its content has never been clarified in Canadian law, aboriginal title has been referred to by the judiciary as "a personal and usufructuary right", or right of use and occupancy, "dependent upon the good will of the Sovereign".

The British colonists felt wholly justified in their encroachment on Indian lands because of their belief that their civilization, especially as it was manifested in powerful Christian states supported by sedentary agriculture and a developing technology, was inherently superior to Native cultures based on hunting, fishing, gathering, and sporadic horticulture. In their view, this superiority and its accompanying ideology unquestionably carried with it a right and a duty to prevail. But while denying Native sovereignty or full land-ownership, the British Crown came to acknowledge the existence of a certain Native right to the land. While such recognition was not always honoured, it gained increasing legal force in colonial times: in the policy of treating with the Indians to acquire lands for settlement, in colonial statutes, in instructions transmitted to colonial governors, and eventually with full Imperial authority in the *Royal Proclamation* of 1763.

A most significant document in the controversy which has surrounded the notion of aboriginal title, this *Proclamation* delineated lands that were to be reserved to the Indians at that time. These consisted of land outside the Hudson's Bay Company's territory and the new colonies of Quebec East and West Florida, and west of the "Sources of the Rivers which fall into the Sea from the West and North West as aforesaid". Partly designed to cope with serious abuses which had sparked forceful Indian reaction, it included a general prohibition against purchasing "any Lands whatever, which, not having been ceded to or purchased by Us [The Crown] as aforesaid, are reserved to the said Indians, or any of them".

In order that Indian territory could be legally acquired in those areas in which settlement was to be encouraged, that is in Nova Scotia and old Quebec, the *Proclamation* outlined a policy under which such lands could be purchased at a public meeting of the Indians "to be held for that Purpose by the Governor or Commander in Chief of our colony respectively within which they shall lie...". Such a procedure underlay the pre-Confederation treaties made in Upper Canada, now southern Ontario.

Since Confederation, recognition of aboriginal title has been expressed in the major treaties, in which various Indian tribes agreed to "cede, release, surrender, and yield up" their interest in the land; and in a substantial number of government agreements, Orders in Council, policies, and legislation pertaining to land in general and to Native peoples.

One important example of these was the transfer in 1870 of Rupert's Land and the North-Western Territory from the Crown to the Dominion of Canada. A schedule to the Orders in Council effecting this convey-ance provided that Indian claims to compensation for lands required for settlement would be "considered and settled in conformity with the equitable principles that have uniformly governed the British Crown in its dealings with the aborigines". In 1875, the Canadian government exercised its right over provincial legislation by disallowing the *British Columbia Crown Lands Act,* because it failed to recognize Indian rights in the land. The 1912 *Boundaries Extension Act,* by which much of what is now northern Quebec was annexed to that province, provided that Quebec would recognize the Indians' territorial rights "to the same extent, and will obtain surrenders of such rights in the same manner, as the Government of Canada has heretofore recognized such rights and has obtained surrender thereof...". As a final example, the 1921 Order in Council authorizing the negotiation of Treaty No. 11 in the Northwest Territories stated that it was "advisable to follow the usual policy and obtain from the Indians cession of their aboriginal title...".

This traditional acceptance of the concept of aboriginal title has not, however, been consistently honoured or practised. The title has not been extinguished by treaty in large areas of Canada, including Quebec, most of British Columbia, the Yukon, the Inuit areas in the Northwest Territories, and the Maritime provinces. In addition, extinguishment has been challenged in the Indian areas of the Northwest Territories. Native claims respecting their title have been formally advanced for well over one hundred years in British Columbia, and subsequently in all the non-treaty areas. Although such claims differ in some respects from region to region, they basically take one of two forms. The first consists of a demand for formal legal recognition of a subsisting title and the rights that flow from it. The second is a demand for adequate, fair compensation for the loss or extinguishment of this title.

In the unsettled areas of northern Canada where the traditional pursuits of hunting, fishing, and trapping persist, the Indian and Inuit proposals for claims settlement are more heavily oriented towards achieving the affirmation of aboriginal rights, in the belief that cultural integrity and development can best be maintained through active participation in the control of the development and use of Northern lands. The President of the Indian Brotherhood of the Northwest Territories recently explained that his people

> ...see a land settlement as the means by which to define the Native community of interest in the North, and not to obscure it. This is why we stress ... that formalization of our rights is our essential goal, rather than the extinguishment of those rights ....
>
> ... Now we seek, through a land settlement, a resource base under our own control, which ensures our autonomy and our participation as equals in those decisions which affect our lives.

In contrast, the southern, more populated areas of Canada where the land has become densely settled, aboriginal title claims place more emphasis on compensation for the extinguishment of the title, and the restitution of rights such as hunting and fishing, and exemption from taxation. In all of these areas, the Native peoples view a possible settlement as a means by which they may develop and achieve control of their lives and communities.

INDIAN TREATIES AND SCRIP SETTLEMENTS

While the land rights of Native peoples in Canada have by no means been treated uniformly, there did develop in British North America a consistent body of precedent and tradition which was utilized on new frontiers where fairly rapid settlement or resource exploitation was being promoted. This involved the making of treaties under which Native peoples surrendered most of their territorial rights and gained various forms of compensation. Although numerous land surrender treaties had already been made in the Thirteen Colonies, it was not until after the American Revolution that the system was first systematically used in Canada.

Algonkian-speaking peoples formed the Indian population of southern Ontario when the European claim to territorial sovereignty passed from the French to the British in 1763. However, European settlement did not occur there to any degree until twenty years later. In these post-Revolutionary years, the separation of the Thirteen Colonies from British North America created an urgent need for land on which to settle disbanded soldiers and other Loyalists. The unsettled areas of British North America provided a ready solution to the problem.

About 10 000 United Empire Loyalists moved into the area of the St. Lawrence-lower Great Lakes. In presiding over this settlement, the Imperial Government did not simply grant land to these newcomers without regard for the Indian inhabitants. As has been seen, the *Royal Proclamation* of 1763 declared that Indian land rights could only be alienated at a public meeting or assembly of the Indians called for the purpose, and then only to the Crown. Although often honoured only in the breach, the *Proclamation* principles were respected in what became southern Ontario through a complicated series of formal treaties and surrenders.

To the government, these treaties were little more than territorial cessions in return for once-for-all grants, usually in goods, although there is contemporary evidence that some of the Indians involved considered that the government was assuming broader trusteeship responsibilities as part of the bargain. Annuities, or annual payments for the land rights ceded, appeared in a treaty in 1818, after which they became usual. At this stage, the provision of land for Indian reserves only occasionally formed part of the surrender terms. Similarly, the right to continue hunting and fishing over ceded territories was very rarely mentioned in the written terms of surrender. Not until 1850, when cessions of land rights were taken by William Robinson along the northern shores of Lakes Huron and Superior, were treaties made that granted to the Indians all four items: once-for-all expenditures, annuities, reserves, and guarantees concerning hunting and fishing. It was for this reason that Alexander Morris, most widely known of the government's negotiators, wrote of the Robinson Treaties as constituting the "forerunners of the future treaties" to be made by the recently created Dominion.

The provisions of many of the southern Ontario treaties and surrenders are quite discordant with more recent agreements conveying far greater benefits to Native peoples elsewhere. Most cessions made in Ontario after 1830 were concluded in trust. The government assumed responsibility for disposing of the ceded lands on the Indians' behalf, with the proceeds of sales usually going to the particular Indians involved. As with those made earlier, which were ofttimes outright surrenders with the government as purchaser, there are strong arguments that inadequate compensation was given. Surrenders concluded prior to 1818 provided for a lump-sum payment along with a nominal yearly rent: in one 1816 surrender of Thurlow Township, for instance, the yearly rent was fixed at one peppercorn. In an 1836 surrender, it was considered sufficient to promise the Chippewa claimants vague agricultural and educational aid in exchange for their surrender of one and one-half million acres south of Owen Sound. The Robinson Huron and Superior Treaties, as well, supplied only minimal payments to the Indians, although they contained provisions for a limited augmentation of annuities in the future. One oversight in the Huron Treaty presumably left aboriginal rights intact at Temagami.

Treaties Nos. 1 to 7 were made during the 1870s in the territory between the watershed west of Lake Superior and the Rocky Mountains in what was then Canada's newly acquired North-West. These treaties utilized many features of the earlier transactions, but were far more comprehensive in their provisions and more consistent and uniform with one another. Their characteristics and relative similarities were not due to a broad policy worked out in advance by the federal government. Indeed, immediately before the first of these treaties was made, the government had little information about the Indians of its new territory, let alone a policy. It proceeded to deal with the Native occupants in an ad hoc fashion as necessity dictated. Almost inevitably the patterns of earlier Canadian experience were adapted to a new time and place. The seven treaties which emerged were partly shaped by the Indians themselves and were indirectly influenced by United States' practice.

The government's purpose in negotiating treaties in the North-West was to free land for settlement and development. A corollary of this was the urgent desire to satisfy the Indians sufficiently so that they would remain peaceful. The nature and extent of Indian rights to the territory were not discussed at the negotiations nor were they defined in the treaties themselves. It is evident from the texts, nevertheless, that the government intended that whatever title the Indians might possess should be extinguished, since the opening clauses of all seven agreements deal with land cession. This emphasis was not reflected in the preliminary treaty negotiations. There the stress was on what the Indians would receive rather than on what they were giving up. The commissioners gave them assurances that the Queen understood their problems and was anxious to help them.

The loss of control over land use and the diminishing game supply threatened the traditional Native way of life. While the Indians attempted to retain as much control as possible over their own territory and future, a secondary desire was the attempt to gain sufficient compensation and support to ensure their survival amidst rapidly changing conditions. As a result of hard bargaining, Indians did manage to have some additional provisions included in the treaties beyond those the government had originally intended. These included agricultural aid and certain liberties to hunt and fish.

Indians today make several points in relation to these treaties. The major one is that the treaty texts do not reflect the thrust of the verbal promises made during the negotiations and accepted by a people accustomed to an oral tradition. They state that their ancestors understood the treaties to be specifically designed to protect them and help them adapt to the new realities by developing an alternative agricultural base to complement their traditional livelihood of hunting and fishing.

Indian associations strongly deny that the treaties obligate the government only to fulfil their terms as they appear in the bare texts. They uniformly insist that the written versions must be taken together with the words spoken by the government's agents during the negotiations. In a submission to the Commissioner on Indian Claims, the Federation of Saskatchewan Indians states that:

> In his various addresses to Chiefs and Headmen at treaty meetings, Commissioner Morris had a single message for the Indians: The Queen was not approaching the Indians to barter for their lands, but to help them, to alleviate their distress and assist them in obtaining security for the future. "We are not here as traders, I do not come as to buy or sell horses or goods, I come to you, children of the Queen, to try to help you. The Queen knows that you are poor; the Queen knows that it is hard to find food for yourselves and children; she knows that the winters are cold, and you[r] children are often hungry; she has always cared for her Red children as much as for her White. Out of her generous heart and liberal hand she wants to do something for you . . . ."
>
> These verbal assurances and statements of Crown intent, and the many others like them, given by Morris in his address to Chiefs and Headmen, cannot be separated from treaty documents because they were accepted as truth by the assembled Indians.

The nature and extent of the implementation of the treaty provisions are another source of grievance in this area. The government's open policy of detribalization, which held as its goal the assimilation of Indian people into the dominant society, motivated a number of specific policies which were destructive of Indian efforts to develop within the context of their own cultures. The field of education is one of the most conspicuous examples of this process, as it was easy to appreciate the effects of isolating children in residential schools where they were taught that their parents' language and culture were inferior, and had instilled in them a set of alien customs and values.

In the Indian view, during the late nineteenth and early twentieth centuries, the government failed to provide the expected agricultural assistance, and unduly restricted Indian agricultural development. It encouraged the surrender of some of the best agricultural land from the reserves when its efforts failed to turn the Indians into farmers.

All of the Prairie Native organizations, along with the Grand Council of Treaty No. 3 in northern Ontario, view as desirable the rewording of the treaties in terms that will embody their original spirit and intent. As in aboriginal title areas, the results of such settlements could, they say, provide the basis for revolutionizing the future development of Indian peoples and reserves on Native terms. The treaty-Indians' organizations have outlined some specific objectives and proposals for an approach to development. A primary characteristic of these is their rejection of the concept of assimilation or detribalization, and stemming from this the conviction that the Indian people must initiate and control the development effort themselves.

Only at the turn of the century, when mineral exploitation provided the impetus, were treaties made to the north of the areas surrendered during the 1870s. Treaty No. 8 was concluded in the Athabaska District, Treaty No. 9 in northern Ontario and Treaty No. 10 in northern Saskatchewan. In addition, adhesions to Treaty No. 5 were taken in northern Manitoba to extend the limit of ceded territory to the northern boundary of the province. Finally, in 1921, following the discovery of oil at Norman Wells, Treaty No. 11 was made in the Northwest Territories.

A major question has arisen respecting Treaties Nos. 8 and 11 as to whether the agreements involved the cession of Native land rights, since both the oral testimony from surviving Native people who were present and the reports of those discussions which took place at the treaty-making raise substantial questions about this. The address of the Treaty No. 8 commissioner at Lesser Slave Lake in 1899 dealt only with what the Indians would receive; there is no reference in the extant text to ceding territory, and, as with Treaty No. 11, there is little evidence that the Native people were aware that land cession was involved. Nevertheless, the commissioners made it clear that the country would be opened up for settlement and development. The Indians understood that they were not to interfere with those coming into the country for lawful purposes; in return, they sought protection for themselves in their hunting, trapping, and fishing way of life.

The treaty terms were modelled closely on those of the Prairie and Parkland treaties. The provisions for reserves of land and for agricultural aid which were suited to southern conditions were applied in the North where much of the territory was not suitable for agriculture. The Indians at Fort Chipewyan reportedly refused to be treated like Prairie Indians and to be placed on reserves, since it was essential to them to retain freedom to move around. Why then did the Indians sign the treaties? Testimony from those present at the negotiations indicates that they were given ample assurances that they would not be adversely affected by accepting treaty. They would neither be confined to reserves nor lose their hunting, trapping, and fishing rights.

In addition to those Native people whom the federal government was prepared to recognize as Indians having an aboriginal right in the soil, there was also in the western interior of Canada a large population of Métis. for the most part, they considered themselves a group separate from both Indians and Europeans. Despite this, they regarded themselves as Natives of the country and entitled, like the Indians, to some special consideration. When it appeared that they were being ignored, they forced themselves on the attention of the government in 1869-70 by denying entrance into the Red River Settlement to the Canadian appointee sent to govern the territory.

Métis had never before been dealt with as a group. Nevertheless, in 1870 the Dominion parliament passed the *Manitoba Act* which, among other things, made provision for a distribution of land to the children of Métis heads of families in Manitoba. The *Act* accorded statutory recognition to the Métis' aboriginal title. Subsequently the heads of families themselves were included in the grant, and they were each to be given a 160-acre parcel of land, to be chosen in any section open to colonization. Alternatively, they were entitled to negotiable certificate (scrip) enabling them to acquire such an area, an arrangement which played into the hands of speculators.

The Métis people of the North-West outside Manitoba were not included in these grants. While the treaties were being made with the Indians of the North-West in the 1870s, almost nothing was done to settle the Métis' claim. The *Dominion Lands Act* of 1879 enabled land grants to be made to Métis in the Northwest Territories, but this statutory provision was not acted upon until early in 1885 when an Indian and Métis rebellion was anticipated. The Street Commission then appointed to screen Métis applicants for scrip was intended to be an instrument of pacification, as the *Manitoba Act* had been fifteen years earlier. Eventually, the Métis' claim was met through an issue of scrip throughout the region where Indian title had previously been extinguished by treaty.

The different methods adopted for dealing with Indians and Métis, which had been first applied in Manitoba, were in this way extended further into the Western interior. In 1899, they were extended into the North; two commissions were appointed to deal with the Indians and the Métis respectively within the Treaty No. 8 area. The same principle was followed for Treaties Nos. 10 and 11, except that the Indian-treaty negotiators then acted simultaneously as scrip commissioners for the Métis.

The Métis' claims rest upon the same general foundation as those of persons deemed to have Indian status, that is, upon an aboriginal right to territory. Métis were admitted into Indian treaties in western Canada only as an exception to a general rule. Such admission applied only to those most closely identified with the Indians, although some element of choice was permitted. The *Indian Act* of 1876 specifically excluded them, barring exceptional circumstances, while later amendments provided for their withdrawal.

The *Manitoba Act* had pointed the way to the policy to be adopted for extinguishment of Métis rights, and this differed significantly from that employed for Indians. It was not negotiated, but was unilateral, proceeding by legislation and Orders in Council. Furthermore, while the Métis were treated as persons having aboriginal title, and therefore different from other Canadians, it has never been government policy to create and maintain them as a category of persons with special status like the Indians. The Dominion assumed no unique, continuing responsibility towards the Métis and non-status Indians as part of its constitutional jurisdiction over Indians.

Métis claims are likely to fall into three categories. There will be claims that the distribution of land and scrip, especially under the *Manitoba Act,* was unjustly and inefficiently administered. As well, there may be a general claim that this form of compensation was inadequate to extinguish the aboriginal title enjoyed by the Métis community, particularly since few of them gained very much from scrip. This argument would be similar to that made by some treaty groups that the treaties constituted an imposed settlement and that they were unfair by reason of insufficient compensation. This type of claim may be reinforced by the fact that people of mixed blood have generally received no compensation beyond the western interior of Canada but are making claims jointly with status Indians in several regions of Canada such as British Columbia and the Yukon Territory. This situation helps to support the third type of claim, that Métis are Indians under the terms of the *British North America Act,* if not under those of the *Indian Act,* and are entitled to special consideration from the federal government.

BAND CLAIMS

The third major class of claims encompasses the multifarious, scattered claims of individual Indian bands. Several categories of these can be identified at present, and include claims relating to the loss of land and other natural resources from established reserves, and issues pertaining to the government's stewardship of bands' financial assets over the years. Underlying all these claims is the difficult question of trusteeship.

The full story of the government's management of reserve resources and band funds across Canada is only gradually being pieced together from the files of the department, missionaries, and others, and from the oral testimony of Indian people themselves. The resources include not only land itself but also minerals, timber, grazing lands, and water. Band funds in most cases derive from land and other resource sales. Where land was surrendered and sold off from reserves, the capital went into band funds, to be administered by the federal government.

Land losses from established Indian reserves account for by far the majority of band claims so far brought forward. Groups of them are probably sufficiently similar to be classified on a regional and historical basis. Grievances arising in New France have certain elements in common, as do Indian claims in the Maritimes, in Ontario, in the southern Prairies, and in British Columbia. The problem of pressure for reserve land acquisition by speculators and settlers is central to all.

The French, who were the first European power to control the northern half of North America, were the first to establish any sort of Canadian Indian policy. Their approach was pieced together as geographical distance from the mother country, overwhelming Native military strength, a fur trade economy, and negligible settlement dictated. They sought, if unsuccessfully, the Indians' assimilation into French-Canadian society and saw the converted Natives as equal in civil and legal status to France's European subjects.

There are conflicting interpretations as to whether Indian territorial rights were affirmed or extinguished under the French régime; treaties were never concluded for territory either in New France or in Acadia. As to White colonists, land was given to Indians through imperial grace. However, the Crown, instead of granting such tracts directly to the Native people, handed them in trust to the most efficient civilizing and Christianizing agencies then known, the religious orders. Six Indian reserves were formed in this manner.

With the British takeover in 1760, France's Indian allies were secured in the use of their lands. In 1851, 230 000 acres were set aside as Indian reserves and a further 330 000 acres were similarly appropriated by the *Quebec Lands and Forests Act* of 1922. Additional reserves were created through the transfer of land from the provincial to the federal government by letters patent issued by Quebec, through direct purchase by the Dominion from a private party, or thorugh private leases.

The Native peoples of Quebec have, over the years, sought increased compensation for land lost from these reserves; settlement of disputes between bands and tribes over reserve ownership; restitution for damages done through logging, fishing, and canal construction; and compensation for questionable band-fund management. The existence of these grievances suggests a basic difference in view between the Indians and the federal government, which has historically tended to judge the issues solely on their legal merits as seen by the Department of Justice.

In the nineteenth century, for instance, the complaints of the Hurons of Lorette and the Montagnais of Pointe-Bleue against White squatters went unnoticed. Charges that the municipality near the Iroquois Oka reserve had unjustly taken over land to allow for the construction of three roads were only briefly considered, as was the Caughnawaga claim for land sold as a clergy reserve. The St. Regis Iroquois' protests against the Quebec government's unilateral renewal of leases to, and sale of, islands in the St. Lawrence, along with their claim to compensation for the flooding of additional islands by the Cornwall Canal, were to no avail. Dozens of claims to islands, first voiced in the eighteenth and nineteenth centuries, remain unsettled, and many of the current disputes over expropriation, whether by settlers, clergy or the Crown, go back to these earlier years. At the root of much of this lack of responsiveness is the government's and the courts' persistent denial of the Indians' contention that they owned the land initially granted to the religious orders, on the grounds that title thereto had been given directly to those orders, and not to the Indians themselves.

The arrival of the British in New France, so far as the Indian people were concerned, did not favourably alter the Natives' condition. The same could be said for the Maritimes. As British settlement and power increased, large tracts were set apart for Indian use and occupation. Although these lands were called Indian reserves, they were not guaranteed to the Indians through treaties, and were subsequently reduced as the land was required for settlement. Further pressures on these reserves in the Maritimes in the early nineteenth century, coupled with problems in dealing with flagrant non-Native squatting, motivated the colonial governments to appoint commissioners to deal with and supervise reserves. These officers apparently had and certainly exercised the right to sell reserve lands without Indian consent. With Confederation, the existing reserves were transferred to the jurisdiction of the federal government, though for a long time the underlying title lay with the respective provinces.

Claims have been presented to the federal government for past reserve-land losses. Within this category, several main types of claims are emerging. A large number contest the legality or status of surrenders of reserve lands. These include submissions on surrenders processed without proper Indian consent, uncompleted sales of surrendered land, sale of lands prior to their being surrendered, lack of letters patent for completed sales, and forged Indian signatures or identifying marks on surrenders. In Nova Scotia, a general claim has also been presented contesting the legality of all land surrenders between 1867 and 1960. This is based on the argument that the Micmac Indians of that province constituted one band; that under the *Indian Acts* of the period, surrenders could only be obtained at a meeting of a majority of all band members of the requisite sex and age. Another group of Maritime band claims against the federal government arises from the contention that a number of reserves transferred to the federal government after Confederation were subsequently listed or surveyed by the Department of Indian Affairs as containing smaller areas than the original acreages listed, or were simply never surveyed and registered as reserves at all.

There are also Maritime Indian claims against the federal government relating to the latter's trusteeship role. The Union of Nova Scotia Indians has put forth a number of claims concerning mismanagement by the government of its obligation to ensure adequate and proper compensation for reserve lands surrendered or expropriated for highway rights-of-way, utility easements, and other public purposes.

The sources of Indian claims in southern Ontario are similar to those in Quebec and the Maritimes. Probably the bulk of them have not yet been disclosed: at any rate, no formal comprehensive claims statement has emerged. In common with Quebec, though, past cases of recorded claims for such losses abound. Some have been rejected by the Departments of Indian Affairs and Justice, or by the courts; many, however, lie dormant. It would not be unreasonable to expect these, and new contentions based on them, to be advanced in greater numbers in the near future.

Indian people have claimed that cessions concluded under unjust circumstances and legally questionable government expropriations of reserved lands were common. Government initiatives, along with pressure from White speculators and settlers, were, as usual, dominant factors. The Six Nations' Grand River surrender in 1841, the Mohawks' cession of Tyendinaga Township in 1843, the Moore Township surrender made by the Chippewa later that year, and the 1847 cession by the St. Regis Iroquois of Glengarry County, are prime examples of contentions that surrenders were attained under pressure. All these were ceded in trust, although there is evidence that the trust provisions were not always upheld. Similar grievances pertain to the government's acquisition of unceded islands. Equally familiar was the variety of expropriation which allowed the sale of individual lots from Indian reserves for clergy and state purposes. Disputes over the status of territory, too, were prevalent. These were generally related to squatter infiltration and occasionally extended into inter-tribal conflicts for reserved lands and, accordingly, for annuities.

The social and economic factors underlying the loss of Indian reserve lands in central and eastern Canada soon found expression on the Prairies. In the years following the making of the treaties and the setting aside of the reserves, the southern prairies were gradually settled. Towns and cities sometimes grew on the very edges of reserves or even around them, and railways ran through them or along their boundaries. As in

Ontario, so on the Prairies, reserves located on good farming land were coveted by settlers. For all these reasons, political pressure frequently developed for the surrender of all or a portion of a reserve. In many cases the Indian Department responded by obtaining a surrender of the reserve land in question; proceeds from the sales of such land were credited to the particular band's fund, and administered under the terms of the *Indian Act*.

In recent years, the bands and Native associations of the Prairies have clearly articulated several claims arising from previous government policies in relation to land surrenders. At present, they are examining both the justification for these surrenders in general, and the legality and propriety of specific cessions, such as those involving Enoch's Band, near Edmonton. Three surrenders took place. The entire Passpasschase Reserve was ceded shortly after most of the band members left treaty and took Métis scrip. The remaining members moved elsewhere, and subsequently the band and its assets were amalgamated with Enoch's Band, residing on the Stony Plain Reserve. In 1902 and 1908, political forces largely supported, if not generated, by the Minister responsible for Indian Affairs himself, compelled the surrender of portions of this reserve. In taking the surrenders, government officials used approaches which appear to have been morally and legally dubious. Such questions surround many other surrenders in the Prairie region and northern Ontario.

At the heart of many Indian grievances in the northern Prairie Provinces is the issue of unfulfilled treaty entitlements to land. Complex in themselves, such claims have been further complicated at the outset by the need for provincial assent to any proposed transfer of lands to Indian Reserve status. Under the 1930 *Natural Resources Transfer Agreements,* the three Prairie Provinces obliged themselvesd to transfer to the federal government, out of the unoccupied Crown lands, sufficient area to meet unfulfilled treaty obligations. Native people have felt that there has been provincial reluctance to comply with this and disputes have arisen over the exact nature of the commitments. The Island Lake bands in Manitoba, for instance, have raised the matter of what population base should be utilized in the granting of unfulfilled treaty entitlements. A substantial proportion of the bands' allotments under Treaty No. 5 were made in 1924, but the land assigned was approximately 3 000 acres short, if based on the populations at that date and on the treaty terms. The bands maintain that their total entitlement should be computed using a recent population total, with the 1924 allotment simply subtracted from the new allocation.

In addition, this case points to the inequality amongst the various treaties' land provisions throughout the West. In common with other treaties in Manitoba, Treaty No. 5 provides for 160 acres per family of five, compared with the 640-acre figure used for treaties elsewhere. Since the land in this region of Canada is non-arable, an additional inequity is present relative to more southerly, fertile regions. The bands contend that a fair solution, satisfying the twin criteria of population datum and uniform treaty terms, would be an allocation of almost 300 000 acres.

In British Columbia, the history of Indian reserves is substantially different from that elsewhere. During the 1850s, when Vancouver Island was still provisionally governed by the Hudson's Bay Company, certain minor surrenders were concluded by the Company's Chief Factor, James Douglas, for several parcels of land there. But these, along with the territory in the northeastern corner of the mainland included in Treaty No. 8, are the only areas covered by treaty. The dual governorship of the two colonies – Vancouver Island and British Columbia – under Douglas in 1858 was soon accompanied by the establishment of comparatively liberal reserves both within and outside the treaty areas. But then, expanding White settlement motivated Douglas' successors to reverse his policy of allowing the tribes as much land as the Indians themselves judges necessary, and accordingly to reduce the reserves wherever possible. Only with great reluctance did the colonial government allot new reserves in areas opening to settlement.

By 1871, when the colony entered Confederation, Indian complaints concerning the failure to allot adequate reserves and reserve land reductions were already numereous. Yet, the Terms of Union that year did nothing to allay these grievances. Fundamentally, the Terms provided for the transfer of responsibility for reserves to the Dominion, and for the conveyance of land from the province to the Dominion for new reserves. As no amounts were agreed upon, a dispute immediately arose between the two over the appropriate acreage to be alloted per family. The province declared ten acres sufficient; the federal government proposed eighty. An agreement establishing an Indian Reserve Commission was concluded in 1875 to review the matter, but there continued to be provincial resistance against attempts to liberalize reserve allotments.

This is one source of Indian claims in British Columbia. A recent report by the Union of British Columbia Indian Chiefs, entitled *The Lands We Lost,* details others. This includes the by-now familiar pattern of encroachment by non-Indian people, together with questions about various government surveys and Commissions, federal Orders in Council, and reserve land surrenders. A prime cause of such losses, and the major grievance expressed in this regard, was the work of the federal-provincial McKenna-McBride Commission, set up in 1912 to resolve the outstanding differences between the two governments respecting Indian land in British Columbia. The Commissioners were appointed to determine the land needs of the Indians and to recommend appropriate alterations to the boundaries of Indian reserves. All reductions were to require the consent of the bands involved, but in practice this stipulation was not followed. The recommendations were subsequently ratified by both governments under legislation which authorized these reductions irrespective of the provisions of the *Indian Act* controlling the surrender of reserve lands. Eventually, some thirty-five cut-offs, aggregating 36 000 acres, were made, while lands of far less value, although of larger area, were added to reserves.

Dealing with Native Claims

COURTS AND CLAIMS COMMISSIONS

Only occasionally have the courts in Canada been asked to adjudicate issues concerning the rights of Indian people. Although there are exceptions, in general the judicial system has not responded positively or adequately to Native claims issues. Respecting aboriginal rights, the judiciary decreed that any European colonial power, simply by landing on and laying claim to lands previously undiscovered by White European society, became automatically the sovereign of this "newly discovered" land. Occupation was taken to confirm that right. Rather than obligations which came with the assumption of sovereignty, Native rights were conceived as matters of prerogative grace by both government and courts.

Indian people have faced clear social and cultural obstacles in becoming litigants in a legal system largely foreign to their experience. And even if some might have considered taking action through this forum, they had until very recently little or no capacity to pay the necessary legal fees. As a result, most of the early but significant decisions in the area of fundamental Indian rights have been handed down in cases where the Indian people affected were not directly represented. Many of these cases involved disputes between the federal and provincial governments over questions of land and resources. Indian rights became material to the cases only because the federal government sought to rely upon them to reinforce its own position by citing its exclusive constitutional responsibility for Native people and lands.

What was, until very recently, the only significant case on the question of aboriginal title in Canada was decided by the Judicial Committee of the Privy Council in 1888. This, the *St. Catherine's Milling* case, involved litigation between the federal government and the province of Ontario over the question of whether the former could issue a timber licence covering lands eventually declared to lie within Ontario. The Indians themselves were not represented. The federal government, for its part, argued that it had properly acquired the title to the land from the Indian people; the Judicial Committee of the Privy Council denied that Native people, at any time, had "ownership" of their land in the sense that Europeans understood the term, and stated ". . . that the tenure of the Indians, was a personal and usufructuary right, dependent upon the good will of the Sovereign". The Law Lords went on to say that the effect of signing treaties with Indian people was to extinguish this "personal and usufructuary right", and to transfer all beneficial interest in the land covered by the treaty immediately to the province. Nearly a century was to pass before the nature of aboriginal title would receive further consideration by Canada's highest court of appeal.

The courts have also rendered judgments on the nature and effect of the treaties. At least three possible interpretations of the Indian treaties have been put forward. Some have been regarded as transactions between separate and independent nations. Such has been the traditional claim of many Six Nations Indians. Secondly, they have been characterized as special protective agreements in which Indian peoples surrendered their rights to land in return for irrevocable rights conferred upon them by the government. Thirdly, they might be interpreted as according the Indians no rights "beyond a promise and agreement" analogous to any commercial contract made at the time with the government. A judgment written by the Judicial Committee in 1897 opted for this last interpretation in a dispute amongst the Attorneys-General of Canada, Ontario, and Quebec. Indian people have thus found themselves constrained by adverse precedent before they had begun to make their own arguments in court.

In addition to the rights at stake in this case, the courts have also dealt with the promise of continued hunting and fishing rights. Their decisions have affirmed the federal government's right to break express promises made by treaty. However, on occasion the judiciary has questioned the morality of such legislative action. Many of the most fundamental treaty promises regarding social and economic development have not yet reached the courts. It would require a radical departure from established precedent for the courts to accord such obligations the character understood by the Indians.

Cases touching the many reserve-land-loss grievances have on occasion come before the courts. Little can be learned about the direction which the courts might take in future land-loss claims from a reading of these judgments, as they disclose no clear pattern of judicial thought. Decisions on claims concerning the mishandling of Indian monies have been equally rare and uninstructive. The fundamental question of the relationship between the federal government and Indian people in the areas on management of land and monies remains legally undefined. Indian people regard this relationship as one of trust and the federal government has often referred to it in these terms. This fiduciary obligation places a very heavy burden on the federal government to act in good faith and always to consider the best interests of Indian people to be of paramount concern.

As an avenue for Canadian Indian claims, the legal system could only have been seen in Native eyes as an incomprehensible gamble. Only in recent years have the courts responded more favourably to these claims, not in the sense of fully and satisfactorily resolving them, but rather in providing a basis from which Indian people might negotiate with the government.

The first Canadian attempt to hear and settle Indian claims outside the courts came with the establishment by parallel legislation, in 1890-91, of a three-man Board of Arbitrators. Appointed to inquire into disputes between the Dominion and the provinces of Ontario and Quebec, the Board, with one federal and two provincial members, considered respective federal-provincial responsibilities in the area of Indian affairs. Claims were presented by the Department of Indian Affairs on behalf of the Natives. The Department generally stated that the satisfaction of Native grievances was the obligation of the old Province of Canada before 1867, and of Ontario and Quebec thereafter. The provinces countered that such obligations rested solely with the Crown in right of the Dominion.

In all, some twenty cases were placed before the Board, which was heavily dependent on the opinions of the governments' legal and administrative officers. This system proved unsatisfactory, since the claims became embedded in federal-provincial conflicts. The Board itself had no final adjudicatory power, and by the early 1900s had waned into insignificance. With few exceptions, the Indians derived no benefit from its activities.

Realization on the part of both Native and non-Native people in the United States that the ordinary courts were unsuitable forums for the presentation and resolution of Native grievances and claims brought forward a response that was increasingly to preoccupy Canadian governmental and Native thought. Efforts which began in the 1930s in the United States to establish a special adjudicatory body with powers to hear and determine Indian claims culminated in 1946 with the creation of an Indian Claims Commission. In Canada, the Joint Committees of the Senate and House of Commons on the *Indian Act* and on Indian Affairs, which sat in 1946-48 and 1959-61 respectively, recommended establishing a similar, though more limited, body. As a result, enabling legislation received first reading in the Commons in December 1963, and the draft bill was sent to Indian organizations, band councils, and other interested groups for comment; a slightly amended version of the proposal was introduced in June 1965.

The terms of the bill provided for a five-person Indian Claims Commission, one member of which was to be a status Indian, with a chairman who was a judge or lawyer of at least ten years' standing. The jurisdiction of the commission would have been limited to acts or omissions of the Crown in right of Canada or of the United Kingdom, but not in right of a province. Because of this and stipulations about evidence, there was substantial doubt as to whether it would have been able to decide on the merits of the aboriginal title issue in British Columbia, a claim which comprised one of the main rationales for the creation of the body.

The suggested Canadian commission would have lacked jurisdiction to hear classes of cases which, in the United States, formed the bulk of those heard. These included claims for the government's failure to act "fairly or honourably" where land was involved, as well as others requiring that treaties be re-opened on grounds such as unconscionable consideration. The Canadian legislation would have permitted the commission to consider only failure to fulfil treaty provisions, not the general question of re-opening treaties. The bill also ignored the Native organizations which were emerging as a force at that time. Instead, the proposed commission was to be authorized to hear claims on behalf of bands, as defined by the *Indian Act;* regional Native organizations, however, might not have been recognized as claimants. Further, the commission would have been given authority only to make money awards, not to restore land.

Because of these and other inadequacies, this proposal for an adjudicatory commission met with Indian opposition. On second reading, it was referred to a Joint Committee of both Houses of Parliament, but was allowed to die following the dissolution of Parliament later in 1965. Nothing further was done towards establishing a commission, although the government's intention to do so appeared to be unchanged. In September 1968, the Minister of Indian Affairs stated that he proposed to introduce a bill "in the weeks to come" to establish an Indian Claims Commission, and he reaffirmed this intention the following December. On this occasion, though, he remarked that the bill had been referred for amendment to the Cabinet Committee on Health, Welfare, and Social Affairs. This appears to have been the government's last public discussion of the projected commission before the announcement of a new Indian policy in June 1969. This demise was attributed to consultations with Indian representatives and the review of Indian policy which had preceded the drafting of the new *White Paper.*

THE WHITE PAPER AND THE INDIAN CLAIMS COMMISSIONER

The first of a series of contemporary responses to Indian claims started with the 1969 *White Paper on Indian Policy.* That event marked the beginning of a new era of unprecedented claims activity. The government proposed an approach which is said would lead to equality of opportunity. This was described as ". . . an equality which preserves and enriches Indian identity and distinction; an equality which stresses Indian participation in its creation and which manifests itself in all aspects of Indian life". To this end, the *British North America Act* would be amended to terminate the legal distinction between Indians and other Canadians, the *Indian Act* would be repealed, and Indians would gradually take control of their lands. The operations of the Indian Affairs Branch would be discontinued and services which had previously been provided on a special basis would be taken over by the federal or provincial agencies which serve other Canadians. Economic development funds would be provided as an interim measure. In short, Indians would come to be treated like all other Canadians: special status would cease.

In laying out these proposals, the government continued to recognize the existence of Indian claims, and proposed the establishment of an Indian Claims Commission, but solely as an advisory body. It was made clear that the government was not prepared to accept aboriginal rights claims: "These", the *Paper* said, "are so general and undefined that it is not realistic to think of them as specific claims capable of remedy except through a policy and program that will end injustice to Indians as members of the Canadian community. This is the policy that the government is proposing for discussion." Treaty claims, while acknowledged, were also placed in a dubious light:

> The terms and effects of the treaties between Indian people and the Government are widely misunderstood. A plain reading of the words used in the treaties reveals the limited and minimal promises which were included in them. . . . The significance of the treaties in meeting the economic, educational, health, and welfare needs of the Indian people has always been limited and will continue to decline. . . . [O]nce Indian lands are securely within Indian control, the anomaly of treaties between groups within society and the government of that society will require that these treaties be reviewed to see how they can be equitably ended.

The government apparently felt that while the central aboriginal and treaty claims had little virtue, and were directly at odds with the proposed policy, there were instances where claims might be accepted. Lawful obligations would be recognized.

Rather than proceeding with the kind of commission discussed in the 1960s, it was decided that further study and research were required by both the Indians and the federal government. Accordingly, the present form of commission was established under the *Public Inquiries Act* to consult with the Indian people and to inquire into claims arising out of treaties, formal agreements, and legislation. The Commissioner would then indicate to the government what classes of claims were judged worthy of special treatment, and recommend means for their resolution.

Given the nature of Indian views on their rights and claims as we now understand them, it is not surprising that their reaction to the *White Paper* was strongly negative. The National Indian Brotherhood immediately issued a statement declaring that,

> . . . the policy proposals put forward by the Minister of Indian Affairs are not acceptable to the Indian people of Canada . . . We view this as a policy designed to divest us of our aboriginal, residual and statutory rights. If we accept this policy, and in the process lose our rights and our lands, we become willing partners in cultural genocide. This we cannot do.

In the following months, Native groups across the country forcefully and repeatedly echoed this response. When the Commissioner, Dr. Lloyd Barber, was appointed in December 1969, the National Indian Brotherhood rejected his office as an outgrowth of the unacceptable *White Paper,* viewing it as an attempt to force the policy on Native people. Indians saw the *White Paper* as the new articulation of a long-resisted policy of assimilation. The proposal was denounced as a powerful, threatening extension of traditional Indian policy in Canada.

In rallying to oppose this apparent challenge to their rights, the Native peoples have in turn produced extensive statements of their own positions. While difficulties were encountered in arranging for research funding, sufficient government monies were made available to finance some of this work. The resulting statements, together with concerted legal and political action on the part of Indians, have led to significant changes in the government's approach.

An early response occurred in August 1971, when in reply to submissions from the Commissioner and Indian leaders, the Prime Minister agreed that the former would not be exceeding his terms of reference if he were to "hear such arguments as the Indians may wish to bring forward on these matters in order that the government may consider whether there is any course that should be adopted or any procedure suggested that was not considered previously". The Commissioner took this to mean that he was free to look at all types of grievances and claims, including aboriginal rights issues.

In August 1973, the government made a substantial change in its position on aboriginal rights by announcing that it was prepared to negotiate settlements in many areas where these had not been dealt with. Then, in April 1975, on the basis of proposals developed through consultations between Indian leaders and the Commissioner, the government accepted an approach to the resolution of Indian claims based upon negotiations.

ABORIGINAL RIGHTS

In the non-treaty areas of Canada, criticisms of the *White Paper* centred around the proposed transfer of responsibility for Indian Affairs from federal to provincial authority and the *Paper's* refusal to recognize or deal with aboriginal rights claims. The Union of New Brunswick Indians, for example, announced its complete rejection of the policy, and the Indians of Quebec stated through their Association that they would have nothing to no with its implementation until a treaty had been concluded with them. Then, in September 1971, Indian representatives from across Canada completed their succinct position paper on "the territorial aspects of Indian claims based on aboriginal title". This statement was later supported by a Parliamentary Standing Committee during the life of a minority government, but never brought to a vote in the Commons.

In July 1972, a substantial answer to the government's denial of aboriginal rights claims was presented in the *Claim Based on Native Title* by the Union of British Columbia Indian Chiefs. The Union asked the Prime Minister and the government of Canada

> ... to realize what a shock it was to the Indians, especially of British Columbia, to be told in 1969 that grievances relating to claims based on Native (aboriginal) title to land "are so general and undefined that it is not realistic to think of them as specific claims capable of remedy" except through the new policy then proposed – a policy which, if unaltered, totally rejects that historic claim. For the Indians of British Columbia, sometimes as individuals, sometimes as organized groups, have for generations maintained a claim for compensation, adjustment, or restitution based on denial, without their consent and without compensation, of their ancient rights to use and enjoy the land that was theirs.

The submission declared that the Native people must be compensated for the loss of their rights to the land throughout the whole of British Columbia, including the loss of surface, subsurface, riparian, and foreshore rights. This claim was based squarely on the doctrine of aboriginal title, and contains lengthy arguments supporting the validity of the concept. In doing so it distinguished between a claim to present title, as was being asserted in the courts by some British Columbia Indians, and its own contention that the Indians had oboriginal title prior to the coming of non-Indian settlers, but are now largely denied the rights of occupancy and use which that title carries with it. Except for hunting and fishing rights, the claim is primarily for compensation, not restitution.

The Union did not consider the courts an acceptable means of achieving settlement, and declared that only the federal government and parliament, whether through an overall legislative settlement or an adjudicatory commission, could effectively deal with the issues. Either method would have been acceptable, though on balance at that time the Union favoured the second. Since then an approach through direct negotiation has gained acceptance.

The adjudicatory commission's function would have been to determine the amount of compensation due various claims. The claim to aboriginal title would have been recognized in legislation constituting the commission, which would avoid the time-consuming process whereby each group of Indians must establish the fact and extent of its title. The objective would be to determine the possibility of restitution, especially in questions of hunting and fishing and riparian or foreshore rights, and, in most cases, the amount of compensation for loss of rights.

The value of the land was to be assessed at the time the Indians lost the use of it: the date of the treaty in the British Columbia treaty areas, and the date of establishment of reserves elsewhere. This amount would be converted to a present dollar equivalent and compensation paid at 5 percent simple annual interest. The resulting fund would be administered by a province-wide development corporation owned and managed by Indian people. This proposal, its authors believed, would not only settle the grievances of the past, would lay a foundation for the social and economic development of the Indian communities of the province.

Well before this statement of the British Columbia land claim was presented, the Nishga Indians of the northwestern part of the province had begun their search through the courts for a judicial declaration that their aboriginal title had never been surrendered by treaty or otherwise extinguished. The case, *Calder v. Attorney-General of British Columbia,* was first heard in British Columbia Supreme Court in 1969. Dismissed by that court, it was appealed to the British Columbia Court of Appeal where it was again dismissed. Finally, it was taken to the Supreme Court of Canada where, in January 1973, seven judges divided four to three against the Nishga claim. Six of the bench supported the notion of an aboriginal title "dependent upon the good will of the Sovereign", but there was no agreement on the fundamental questions of how such rights might be extinguished or evaluated.

Three of the judges held that aboriginal rights are without value unless the government obliges itself to pay by enacting compensation legislation. They also held that such rights can be extinguished implicitly through land legislation necessarily denying their continued existence. Three other judges declared that aboriginal rights cannot be extinguished without compensation or without specific direct legislation removing the right to compensation. Occupation, they said, was a proof of the continued existence of aboriginal rights, and the Nishga appear to have been in possession of the Nass Valley from time immemorial; they have never made any surrender agreement with the Crown.

The Nishga lost their case on the collateral and technical point that the issue could only properly come before the court with provincial authorization. The substantive issue as to whether the Nishga have aboriginal rights remains unresolved by the courts, as it does for all other Native peoples in Canada pursuing aboriginal rights claims. The judgment has left unanswered many questions as to the nature of aboriginal title, its worth, the manner by which it can be extinguished, and the degree of proof necessary to establish a valid claim to aboriginal title.

The decision not to pursue the issue further through the courts seems to have been chiefly a result of a change in attitude by the government. The prime minister, speaking to a delegation from the Union of British Columbia Indian Chiefs immediately after the Supreme Court decision, told them that the judgment had led him to modify his views. He appeared to be impressed with the minority judgment and remarked, "Perhaps you have more legal rights than we thought you had when we did the *White Paper*".

At the same time, both the Native people and the Canadian government were aware of the negotiated agreement made between the United States' government and the Native peoples of Alaska, which had become law in December 1971. The indigenous Indians, Inuit, and Aleut had laid claim to almost all the land area of the state, an area which they had continued to use and occupy. Native action, prompted by oil and gas leases, resulted in a land freeze in 1966 pending settlement of their claims. Several bills were subsequently presented to congress under different sponsorships: the legislation which emerged as the *Alaska Native Claims Settlement Act* of 1971 marked a radical departure from any previous Native land settlement policy in the United States, or elsewhere.

The *Act* provides for the transfer to Native peoples of both land and money and for the setting up of Native corporations to administer both. Alaskan Natives are entitled under the *Act* to a total of 40 million acres divided amongst 220 villages and 12 regional corporations. This amounts to about 15 percent of the state's area. The villages acquire the surface estate to 22 million acres, while the regional corporations receive the subsurface estate to that land, together with full title to 16 million acres. The remaining 2 million acres are for sundry purposes including protection of existing cemeteries and historical sites. There is also provision for allotments from this amount, not to exceed 160 acres per capita, to individual Natives living outside the villages. In addition, a land-use planning commission, of which at least one member must be a Native person, was established. The commission's functions are advisory, not regulatory.

The monetary settlement, to be administered by the regional and village corporations, is comprised of approximately half a billion dollars from the United States Treasury over an eleven-year period, and an additional half-billion from mineral revenues from lands conveyed to the state. The latter would otherwise have become state revenue. In this way, the state is sharing in the settlement of Native claims.

Native people in Canada have always been keenly aware of the treatment of their brethren in the United States, and this settlement received wide publicity. The professed rationale behind the settlement was that it should not only satisfy legal and moral claims but should provide a foundation for the social and economic advancement of the Native people. It has undoubtedly affected thinking in Canada on the nature of any future settlement in aboriginal rights areas in this country.

Shortly after the Calder decision and the prime minister's statement to the British Columbia Chiefs, the Yukon Native Brotherhood presented its paper, *Together Today for Our Children Tomorrow,* to the prime minister and the minister responsible for Indian Affairs. The paper, undertaken with financial support from the Indian Claims Commissioner, contains the Brotherhood's proposal for negotiation and settlement of the claims of the Native people of the Yukon Territory. It describes the difficulties experienced by Yukon Indians in the face of recent changes there, and outlines the Brotherhood's intention of obtaining a settlement that would help Native people to influence and adjust to the rapid development of the North. This would be accomplished by ensuring them an economic base under their own control from which they might work to develop their own lives and cultures on an equal footing with the non-Native population.

Such a settlement would involve the setting aside of land for the Indian people, to be held in trust in perpetuity by the Crown and controlled by Native municipalities created for that purpose. Sufficient lands should be set aside to provide for municipalities where the Indian people could have permanent homes; for historic sites and cemeteries; for hunting, fishing, and trapping camps; and for economic development. Until the selection of these lands is completed, a land freeze should be imposed on all unalienated crown lands in the Yukon. In addition to land, the Brotherhood proposed that the Indian people should receive a part of all government royalties from gas, oil, mineral, and forest production, and from commercial hunting in the Yukon. Further, they proposed a lump-sum cash settlement as compensation for all past grievances and individual claims.

Native participation would be guaranteed in all matters pertaining to land and water control and development and wildlife management by their representation on the relevant boards or agencies. The right to hunt and fish for food, and to trap on unoccupied lands would be guaranteed. For a period of twenty-five years, free health services would be provided and income earned on Indian lands would be free of taxation. A general corporation would be formed to manage Indian funds and provide training and resources, but control would gradually devolve upon the municipalities themselves.

The Yukon Native Brotherhood asked that a negotiating committee be established, a request which was supported by the Indian Claims Commissioner. This was agreed to by the prime minister. Although the task was clearly not going to be an easy one, the government's decision to commence negotiations was a significant step forward in settling aboriginal claims throughout Canada.

In August 1973, this response to the Yukon Native Brotherhood was broadened into a statement by the Minister of Indian and Northern Affairs of general policy on the claims of the Indian and Inuit people. At the outset, the statement reaffirmed the government's recognition of its continuing responsibility for Indian and Inuit people under the *British North America Act,* and referred to the *Royal Proclamation* of 1763 as "a basic declaration of the Indian people's interests in land in this country". It then recognized the loss of traditional use and occupancy of lands in British Columbia, northern Quebec, the Yukon, and the Northwest Territories, in areas where "Indian title was never extinguished by treaty or superseded by law". For these areas, the government offered to negotiate and enshrine in legislation a settlement involving compensation or benefit in return for the Native interest. In making this offer, it expressed an awareness that "the claims are not only for money and land, but involve the loss of a way of life". The statement also pointed out that while the federal government has the authority to deal with claims in the two northern territories, elsewhere provincial land is involved. It urged that the provinces concerned be prepared to participate in the negotiations and in the settlements.

While the statement went a considerable distance in recognizing Indian claims in non-treaty areas, there are two problematical aspects. First the policy did not cover southern Quebec and the Atlantic provinces, where the land claims were said to be of a different character from those in the regions where original land rights were recognized. More study of the situation in these areas by both the Native people and the government was suggested. In addition, there are several "non-treaty" groups in other parts of Canada, such as the Iroquois, the Sioux, and various bands within the treaty areas. Second, there has been a great deal of concern amongst Native people that the policy was heavily oriented towards the removal of rights and the provision of compensation; they would like to retain and entrench as many of their rights as possible, particularly as they pertain to land. The Inuit, for example, insist that their hunting rights be formally recognized by federal legislation and be on the basis that they have a prior right to hunt game for food or livelihood on their land.

Furthermore, while the policy provided the opportunity for dealing with claims in at least some non-treaty areas, it offered very little in relation to treaty claims and individual band claims concerning such things as reserve lands and band funds. The statement reiterated the government's pledge to honour lawful obligations, but his does not really provide anything more than all Canadians expect of the government on a regular basis. Nevertheless, it did refer to the Queen's statement to Indians in Calgary in July 1973, that "You may be assured that my government of Canada recognizes the importance of full compliance with the spirit and terms of your treaties".

THE MACKENZIE VALLEY AND JAMES BAY

Two areas in northern Canada, the Northwest Territories and the James Bay region of Quebec, have been especially significant in the litigation and negotiation of aboriginal title claims since the Calder decision and the opening of the Yukon negotiations. In both areas, aboriginal title has been asserted in attempts to cope with intrusive large-scale economic development and to retain the maximum of Native control over their traditionally held regions. In the Northwest Territories, the Native peoples are faced with a huge development project, the Mackenzie Valley pipeline, which threatens to disrupt their life. They have consistently, but unsuccessfuly, requested that the federal government impose a land freeze pending the resolution of their claims to the land, and have challenged the assertion that the treaties made in the area have extinguished their aboriginal title. They contend that the agreements they made were solely treaties of peace and friendship.

On April 2, 1973, the chiefs of some sixteen Indian bands filed a caveat in the Land Titles Office in Yellowknife claiming aboriginal rights to almost half the land in the Northwest Territories. The effect of the caveat would have been to make any future land grants in the area subject to the claim of the Indians if it were subsequently found that they had a valid legal interest in the land. The caveat was referred to the Supreme Court of the Northwest Territories for a decision as to whether it should be accepted, and during the ensuing hearing evidence was heard from Indians involved in the treaty-making.

The following September, an interim judgment was handed down by the court, which upheld the caveat in saying, ". . . that there is enough doubt as to whether the full aboriginal title has been extinguished, certainly in the minds of the Indians, to justify the caveators [sic] attempt to protect the Indian position until a final adjudication can be obtained". This judgment was appealed by the federal government and was set down for hearing by the Appellate Division of the Supreme Court of the Northwest Territories in June 1975. Meanwhile, attempts to achieve negotiations led in January 1974 to a joint announcement by the president of the Northwest Territories' Indian Brotherhood and the minister of Indian and Northern Affairs that a committee would be established "to engage in preliminary discussions to develop the groundwork for a comprehensive settlement of Indian claims in the Northwest Territories".

The position of the Northwest Territories' Indian Brotherhood, like that of the Inuit Tapirisat of Canada, is that a settlement of Native claims must precede the pipeline or any other major development projects. Although this had not yet been fully or openly accepted by the federal government, there is clearly an acceptance that a settlement must be reached as soon as possible and that negotiation is the preferred approach.

Like the Mackenzie Valley, the James Bay area is part of the Hudson's Bay Company's territories transferred to Canada in 1870. When the boundaries of Quebec were extended in 1912 to include much of this particular part of the territory, the federal government required that Quebec agree to recognize and obtain surrenders of the rights of its Native inhabitants. This stipulation was not fulfilled. In a report published in 1971, the Dorion commission appointed by the Quebec government found that the province did indeed have such an obligation and recommended that immediate steps be taken to honour it. Subsequently, the Indians of Quebec Association began working with the Quebec government to set up a framework for the negotiation of a settlement of their land rights. In May 1971, while these preliminary steps were being taken, the provincial government announced its intention to develop the hydroelectric power resources of the James Bay territory. Three months later, before any meetings had taken place between the Indian and provincial negotiators, the Quebec legislature established the James Bay Development Corporation, and made it responsible, with the powers of a municipal government, for developments within the affected region.

Environmental impact studies subsequently carried out found that the project would have a severe effect on the ecology of the region and specifically on the traditional livelihood of the Native populace. This threat and the provincial government's refusal in negotiations to delay or modify the project led the Native people to initiate legal proceedings to protect their rights. Thus, on November 7, 1972, the Grand Council of the Cree (of Quebec) and the Northern Quebec Inuit Association served notice on the governments of Quebec and Canada and the James Bay Development Corporation that they intended to seek an interlocutory injunction to suspend the project until their aboriginal title had been acknowledged and dealt with.

After a year of hearings and deliberations, the Quebec Superior Court, in November 1973, granted the injunction asked for and ordered a halt to the project. The Court found that the Cree and Inuit retained their aboriginal title, in stating that,

...at the very least the Cree Indians and Eskimo have been exercising personal and usufructuary rights over the territory and the lands adjacent thereto. They have been in possession and occupation of these lands and exercising fishing, hunting, and trapping rights therein since time immemorial. It has been shown that the government of Canada entered into treaties with Indians whenever it desired to obtain lands for the purposes of settlement or otherwise. In view of the obligation assumed by the province of Quebec in the Legislation of 1912, it appears that the Province of Quebec cannot develop or otherwise open up these lands for settlement without acting in the same manner that is, without the prior agreement of the Indians and Eskimo.

One week later the Quebec Court of Appeal suspended the injunction.

After an unsuccessful attempt by the Indians and Inuit to have the Supreme Court of Canada consider the case, the Quebec Court of Appeal, on November 21, 1974, unanimously overturned the lower court's judgment. One justice said, for the Court, "I am of the opinion that the Indian right to the territory in question has doubtful existence and that the recourses arising out of it, if they exist, do not entitle them to obtain an injunction to stop work on the project" (*Unofficial translation*).

Meanwhile, negotiations had led to the signing one week earlier of an Agreement in Principle by the James Bay Cree, the Inuit of Quebec, the province of Quebec and the government of Canada. The agreement contained the proposed terms under which the Native people would surrender their interest in 400 000 square miles of land comprising the areas transferred to Quebec by the 1898 and 1912 *Boundaries Extension Acts*. It provided for a continuation of negotiations to establish the final terms of settlement by November 1, 1975, and for the continuation of the hydro-electric project, as modified by the agreement, without threat of further legal action. Nevertheless, a path was left open for litigation to be pursued if a final agreement was not reached by that date.

Under this agreement, the Native peoples would receive 5 250 square miles of land in some form of ownership (Category I lands). Of this land, 1 274 square miles would be administered under the *Indian Act* on behalf of the Cree. Another 60 000 square miles would be set aside as exclusive hunting, trapping, and fishing areas for the Native peoples (Category II lands). These could be expropriated by Quebec for the purpose of development, providing that they were replaced, or, with the consent of the Native people, compensation were paid. In addition, Native people would have exclusive hunting and trapping rights over certain animals over the whole of the territory ceded, and would participate on an equal basis with the provincial government in administering and controlling hunting, trapping, and fishing.

While nearly 600 acres per capita of surface and subsurface rights passed into corporate Native control under the Alaskan settlement, the James Bay Cree would gain surface rights averaging some 200 acres per capita, and 2 600 acres per capita of Category II lands. This difference in emphasis illustrates the local Grand Council's interest in an agreement that would encourage the Native people in their traditional way of life.

The monetary compensation would consist of $75 million in cash to be paid over a ten-year period, of which the federal government would contribute half. This federal contribution is based on that government's responsibilities for the extinguishment of Native title in the area ceded to Quebec by the 1898 *Boundaries Extension Act*. That legislation did not specify a provincial responsibility as did the 1912 *Act*. In addition, the Native people would receive a further $75 million from the royalties from the hydro project, and, for twenty years, 25 percent of royalties on any non-hydro development begun in the region within fifty years of the settlement. The province would own mineral and subsurface rights, but on Category I lands would be obliged to negotiate consent and compensation or royalties for any exploitation of those assets.

A provincial government scheme ensuring an annual minimum income to those who wish to pursue hunting, trapping, and fishing is contemplated by the agreement, as well as some special economic development programs. Federal and provincial programs and funding, and the obligations of the two governments, would continue to apply on the same respective bases as to other Native peoples in Canada and the province, "subject to the criteria established from time to time for the application of such programs". At the federal level, these apparently refer to such matters as education, housing, and health.

Native concerns regarding their environment are reflected in two further terms of the Agreement in Principle. One is the provision for extensive modifications and remedial measures to the hydro project to minimuze its impact on Native communities and culture. The second such term provides for assessment studies of environmental and social impacts of any future developments in the territory, with Native involvement in the decision-making based on such statements.

It has yet to be seen what effect this Agreement in Principle will have on the outcome of other negotiations currently under way in aboriginal title areas. In response to Inuit concerns, the Minister of Indian and Northern Affairs has affirmed that he does not regard the Agreement as a model or benchmark for the settlement of land claims by Native groups elsewhere in Canada. Nevertheless, there are indications in a recent government working paper presented to the Yukon Indians that the approach taken in the James Bay Agreement is of interest to the government in relation to other areas.

TREATY AREAS

The *White Paper*'s implication that treaty rights are neither perpetually entrenched nor socially desirable aroused a quick, firm response from Indians in the southern treaty areas. In June 1970, the Indian Chiefs of Alberta presented a counter-proposal to the prime minister. Entitled *Citizens Plus,* but soon known as the *Red Paper* on Indian policy, the Paper castigated the government for its efforts to impose a policy which it said "offers despair instead of hope". Recognition of Indian status is essential for justice and for the preservation of Indian culture, the *Paper* asserted; moreover, the treaties are "historic, moral, and legal obligations" which constitute the basis for Native rights in Alberta. The Chiefs expressed the general view of treaty Indians that the spirit of the treaties, so long ignored, must now be fulfilled.

In October 1971, the Manitoba Indian Brotherhood presented a proposal to the government entitled *Wahbung: Our Tomorrows.* Like the *Red Paper,* it stressed the belief that, "The Indian people enjoy 'special status' conferred by recognition of our historic title that cannot be impaired, altered, or compromised by federal-provincial collusion or consent. We regard this relationship as sacred and inviolate." The following year, the Grand Council of Treaty No. 3, in presenting the minister with its brief on economic and social development, stressed in addition that:

> Our treaty must speak to our people in the present if it is to have any meaning at all to us . . . The value of the lands ceded by the Indians to Her Majesty has increased many times. We Indians recognize this and accept the terms of our treaty. It is in this spirit of recognizing that our treaty was not frozen in time but was signed to affect the future of the descendents of the two signing parties that now ask you to examine with us how the two economic clauses must speak to our people today.

Later, the Federation of Saskatchewan Indians presented a report to the Commissioner on Indian Claims which emphasized the specific content and interrelation of treaty rights. It said that:

> . . . the Saskatchewan treaties, when placed in their proper historical context and interpreted in relation to the severe problems facing Plains tribes, emerge as comprehensive plans for the economic and social survival of the Saskatchewan Bands. To regard the treaties as "mixed bags" of disparate and unrelated "rights" and "benefits" – though these rights and benefits have undeniable reality – is too simplistic an analysis and fails to acknowledge their full scope and intent.

The reaction on the part of treaty Indians to the government's *White Paper* has served as notice of the types of treaty claims that will eventually be brought forward. These Indians have been quite reluctant to advance their claims piecemeal. Indications are that their general claims may be ready for presentation within a year or two. In the meantime, there is some interest in preliminary discussions on pressing treaty issues such as education, and hunting and fishing rights. Eventually, other matters such as economic development, taxation, health services, and the central grievance concerning the erosion of tribal government and community fabric, will come to the fore.

While the government has received and studied the various papers submitted by treaty-Indian associations, these papers have not been seen as official claims, and there has been no significant response except for the continuing assurance that the government will honour all lawful obligations, and the indication in the August 1973 policy statement that the spirit and terms of the treaties will be upheld. Outside the Northwest Territories, provincial involvement remains a problem, since agreements on a number of issues might require provincial co-operation.

Consideration of treaty claims will need to be closely tied to efforts at revising the *Indian Act*. Treaty Indians in Alberta and Saskatchewan, at least, see the revision to the *Act* as a vehicle for consolidating recognition of their treaty rights. It would seem that any fundamental changes in the *Act* must await resolution of basic issues in both treaty and non-treaty areas.

BAND CLAIMS

Since 1970, when the federal government began funding Indian research into claims, there have been a sizable number of claims presented by Indian bands. Nearly all have had to do with losses of land from Indian reserves. They have come primarily from the Maritime Provinces and the Prairies, with a lesser number from Quebec, Ontario, and British Columbia. Some of these claims have been submitted to the Department of Indian Affairs and Northern Development; others have been directed through the Claims Commissioner.

The presence of these claims has put substantial pressure on the government to react. Judging from the urgency behind some of the issues and the fact that there are potentially hundreds, if not thousands, of similar claims, this situation will probably become more acute. While a few of these claims are being resolved on an ad hoc basis, there are basic problems that must be dealt with before the bulk of them can be resolved. This is necessary to avoid the possibility of seriously prejudicing the interests of the larger Indian community. While there is urgency in dealing with some individual band claims, there is also recognition that every effort must be made to resolve the key questions in a way which involves full Indian representation from the area affected. In contemplating this approach, it must be appreciated that most of the issues are comlex, and that it will take time before the majority of bands have carried out sufficient research and deliberations to enable them to bring their issues forward. At present, there does not appear to be any government policy in relation to these claims, other than the honouring of lawful obligations. Until there is agreement between the government and Indians on the fundamental questions, it will be difficult to deal with individual band claims effectively.

A NEW APPROACH TO RESOLUTION

In April 1975, at a meeting between the National Indian Brotherhood and a committee of federal cabinet ministers, a proposal for claims processes that had been developed through consultation between Prairie Indians and the Indian Claims Commissioner was put forward and accepted in principle by the ministers.

The primary procedure for dealing with claims would allow basic issues to be brought up through provincial and territorial Indian associations and presented directly to cabinet ministers. The issues would be discussed in this forum to determine whether there was a basis for agreement. Through this process, general principles and parameters for settlement mechanisms might be established. Such agreements would allow detailed treatment of the issues to be delegated. In some cases, this might require negotiations at a secondary level. In others, administrative machinery might be appropriate, while in further instances, it might be desirable to refer matters to the courts or specially created arbitration tribunals. In this way, the settlement processes would be tailored to the issues and based on fundamental agreements in principle. To facilitate such negotiations, a new impartial commission is proposed.

The agreement contemplates a totally original and innovative institution for dealing with claims issues. Its implementation should create a new negotiation-centred era of activity towards claims resolution.

Notes

1. This chapter is reproduced by permission of the Minister of Supply and Services Canada.

5

Native Treaties and Claims

Origin of Treaties

When the Hudson's Bay Company (HBC) surrendered Rupert's Land in 1869, Canada inherited the responsibility for negotiating with the resident Native tribes. Prior to the transfer, the *Royal Proclamation* had established the "equitable principles" governing the purchase and surrender of Native lands. The Imperial Order in Council that transferred this responsibility is stipulated in Article 14:

> Any claim of Indians to compensation for lands required for purposes of settlement shall be disposed of by the Canadian Government in communications with the Imperial Government; and the Company shall be relieved of all responsibility in respect of them.

The administrators subsequently appointed to negotiate federal treaties with the Indians were inexperienced and unfamiliar with Native customs. Lacking firsthand knowledge, these administrators fell back on the legacy of the HBC's treatment of Natives as well as on some sketchy reports of the negotiations behind the Robinson Treaties of 1850 and 1862 and the Manitoulin Island Treaty.

Preliminary negotiations between the Indians in Manitoba and the representatives of the government began in 1870. By 1871, Treaties Nos. 1 and 2 were signed, and in 1873 the lands between Manitoba and

Lake Superior were ceded in Treaty No. 3. Northern Manitoba and the remainder of the southern Prairies were surrendered by the Natives between 1874 and 1877 in Treaties Nos. 4, 5, 6, and 7.

The land taken by the Canadian government under Treaties Nos. 1 through 7 provided sufficient land for the mass settlement of immigrants entering Canada. However by 1899, the pressures of settlement and mineral development again caused the government to negotiate for new lands from the Natives. Although these later treaties, Nos. 8 through 11, differed in many respects from the earlier ones, they were clearly modelled upon Treaties Nos. 1 through 7.

The federal government decided to negotiate with the Natives largely because its own agents forsaw violence against White settlers if treaties were not established. However, this was not based on particular threats or claims on the part of the Natives, who simply wished to carry out direct negotiations with the government to recompense them for their lands prior to White settlement. After the first treaty was signed, neither the government nor the Natives attempted to find alternative means to deal with "Indian claims". Government officials based future treaties on prior ones and Indians insisted on similar treatment to that received by those who had signed prior treaties.

Despite specific differences, the contents of all the treaties are remarkably similar. Treaties Nos. 1 and 2 created reserve lands granting 160 acres per family of five. They also offered annuities of three dollars per person, a gratuity of three dollars per person, and a school on each reserve. (Other promises were also made orally during the negotiations; some of these were later given formal recognition by an Order in Council.[1]) Treaty No. 3 contained the same provisions as Treaties Nos. 1 and 2, except that its reserve allotment was increased to 640 acres per family of five.[2]

The federal government desired treaties that were brief, simple, and uniform in content. Nonetheless, although constrained by these government limitations, negotiators were often forced to make minor additions to a treaty; sometimes these took the form of verbal promises, presumably to avoid deviations from the standard written form. For example, the government negotiators for Treaty No. 6 were forced to add several benefits such as medicine chest and provisions for relief in times of famine.

In general, however, the government negotiators had by far the best of the bargaining. Indeed, most treaties were written by the government and simply presented to the Indians for signing. The terms, for example, of Treaty No. 9 were determined by the Ontario and Canadian governments well in advance of discussions with Indians. Moreover, there is evidence that, in many cases, hard-won oral promises have never been recognized or acted upon by the government.

In their negotiations with the Natives, treaty commissioners always avoided discussing the nature or extent of aboriginal land rights. Although the commissioners obscured the issue, however, the Indians clearly surrendered land claims by signing the treaties. In many cases, the commissioners argued that the Indians had no land rights at all; if the Native negotiators objected to this argument, the commissioners would enlist support from missionaries or traders whom the Natives trusted. No Indian treaty was ever brought before Parliament. Instead, the treaties were presented to Cabinet and ratified by Order in Council. This suggests that they were accepted by the government of Canada both as a recognition of Native land claims and as a means of their negotiation and resolution.

Under Section 31 of the *Manitoba Act,* 1870, approximately 1.4 milion acres were set aside for "the benefits of the families of the half-breed residents". The land was to be divided "among the children of the half-breed heads of families" residing in the province at the time of its transfer to Canada. Initially, the amount of land set aside was thought to provide each child with 290 acres. However, due to miscalculations, the government also had to issue money scrip in lieu of land. In 1874, the "half-breed heads of families" themselves were given grants of 160 acres or $160 in scrip, although after 1876 they became eligible only for the scrip. By 1885, the government had alotted 1 448 160 acres and $509 760 to Métis in Manitoba. In all, the government handled more than 24 000 Métis claims (14 000 in the Northwest Territories, Saskatchewan, and Alberta, and 10 000 in Manitoba). These claims involved over 2.5 million acres of land and in excess of $3.6 million.

British Columbia was a special case in its handling of treaties. Between 1849 and 1854, James Douglas, the governor of the colony, negotiated a series of treaties with the Indians on Vancouver Island. After 1854, this policy was discontinued: although the colonial office in England supported the treaties, it would not provide Douglas with monies to continue them. The White British Columbian settlers refused responsibility for negotiations with the Indians and would not release public funds to settle land claims.

As Berger (1981:222-23) points out, British Columbia's House of Assembly had initially recognized aboriginal land titles. However, when told by London that it would have to provide the funds to settle those titles, the House of Assembly withdrew recognition of Indian land claims. This meant that, technically, the Indians were not entitled to any compensation.

No further treaties were ever made in British Columbia, although Treaty No. 8 does cover the northeastern part of the province. With the entry of British Columbia into Confederation in 1871, the administration of Indians and Indian lands in the province fell under the jurisdiction of the federal government. However, the federal government's interpretation of this jurisdiction has remained controversial up to the present.

When British Columbia entered Confederation, the actual terms concerning the treatment of Natives were unclear. The terms of union clearly stated that all public lands were to be the property of the provincial government; this meant that the federal government owned no land outright in the province to give to the Natives. Some provision was made, however, for Native lands. The province agreed to relinquish the federal government "tracts of land of such extent as it had hitherto been the practice of the British Columbian government to appropriate for that purpose" (Berger, 1981:224).

Unfortunately, the practice of the British Columbian government was to supply considerably less land than did the federal government. When alloting land, the province had simply set aside a number of acres per family. Although White settlers had received 320 acres of land per homestead, Natives had been granted considerably less. In 1873, the federal government asked the province to determine the size of the reserves by relinquishing 80 acres per Indian family. The province set aside only 20 acres per family, a much lower acreage than that set aside for other Natives by the Canadian government. Understandably, Indians in BC objected strongly and insisted on their aboriginal land rights.

The British Columbian policy effectively undermined federal negotiations with the Natives. A federal-provincial commission was established to investigate the allocation of Native lands. By 1910, despite Native objections, a number of reserves had been established in the province.

The British Columbian Natives continued to oppose the establishment of reserves and to argue title to their own lands. The federal government dissolved its commission in 1910 after the provincial government refused to sanction any more reserves. In the early 1900s, Indians sent delegations to Victoria and to England in an attempt to argue their claims for aboriginal rights. The federal government partly supported these claims and tried, unsuccessfully, for a hearing before the Supreme Court of Canada. The province refused to comply.

In 1913, a Royal Commission was established partly to adjust the acreage of the reserves in British Columbia. In 1916, the Commission produced a report detailing lands to be added to and removed from existing reserves. The added land was to be twice the size of the land taken away; however, the land to be taken away was, at that time, worth twice as much money.

As the federal government tried to implement this report, it met increased opposition from the provincial government and from the Natives. The province finally confirmed an amended verson of the report in 1923. But the Natives never accepted it. The Allied Indian Tribes of

British Columbia (AITBC) emerged to become a powerful political force uniting Native opposition to the decision. In 1923, the AITBC presented a list of far-reaching demands to the federal government and agreed to relinquish their aboriginal-title claim only if the demands were met. These demands were remarkably similar to those met by previous treaties in other provinces, namely 160 acres per capita, hunting rights, and the establishment of reserves.

The AITBC demanded that either a treaty be negotiated or their aboriginal-title claim be submitted to the Judicial Committee on the Privy Council. In essence, they argued that, contrary to the beliefs of the federal and provincial governments, there had been no final settlement of their claims.[3] As a result of the Indians' petition, a special joint committee of the House and Senate was convened to hear evidence and make a decision. This committee decided that the Indians had not established any claims to land based on aboriginal title. However, it did recommend that an annual sum of $100 000 be spent for the good of Indians in British Columbia.

In order to prevent an appeal of this decision, the federal government passed an amendment to the *Indian Act* that prohibited the collection of funds from Natives for the advancement of a land claim. This amendment remained law until the middle of this century. As a result, Natives became powerless to press their claims and were successfully ignored by the federal government throughout the Depression and World War II. Of necessity, local issues replaced larger concerns during this time: the Native Brotherhood of British Columbia was established in 1931 and, in 1942, became prominent in its fight against income tax for Native fishermen. But Native land claims did not emerge again as an issue until the 1960s, when they played an important role in the creation of the Indian Land Commission.

After World War II, the federal government returned its attention to domestic affairs, including Native issues. During this time, new and reorganized organizations were establishing linkages with non-Native groups in support of Native claims. These groups focused on the general welfare of Natives as well as on settlement infringements upon their treaty rights. Because many rights were outlined only vaguely in the treaties, precise definitions and claim boundaries were often left to the discretion of the courts. Federal-provincial disputes also posed innumerable problems for solving Native claims; the exact boundary for control of natural resources is unclear even today.

By 1945, the federal government realized that Native claims were serious and would not disappear. A joint committee of the Senate and House was created to look into Native issues. The United States had already established an Indian Claims Commission which the Canadian committee felt was worth emulating. Following the American lead, the committee recommended that Canada establish a Lands Commission. However, the Minister of Citizenship and Immigration, who at the time held jurisdiction for Indian affairs, argued that Native claims in Canada were much more amendable to the court system than those in the United States.

In 1959, a second joint committee was established to look into a larger and more varied number of Native claims. Again the committee recommended that a Lands Commission be established. The first draft of a paper to create an Indians Claims Commission was written in late 1961. However, an Indian Land Claims Commission was not actually appointed until 1969.

The reasons for the delay are complex. First, elections resulted in a number of changes of federal government. Second, the federal government was waiting to find out the results of various court actions concerning Native claims. Third, the federal government decided to involve Natives directly in the formation and administration of the claims commission; this process created a number of delays. And fourth, the change in the federal government's philosophy toward Natives that took place in the late 1960s further complicated matters.

In the end, a Claims Commissioner was appointed to receive and study the grievances of Indians and, when advisable, to recommend measures to resolve those grievances. However, the Commission was only *advisory* and did not have explicit powers of adjudication.

Native Claims Policy: 1867-1980

Because of their recent media exposure, Native claims appear to be a relatively new phenomenon. However, despite appearances, Native claims against various parties have been going on for well over a century. There are many reasons why these cases were not settled a long time ago. Until 1951, certain sections of the *Indian Act* forbade a non-Native advocate to take up a case on behalf of Natives. Also until 1951, a claim against the Crown required government approval before it could go to court. In general, the federal government has always made it difficult for Natives to press claims; at one point, neither band funds nor personal contributions by Natives could be used for this purpose. This policy was partly the result of the federal government's belief that it alone could assess and guard the interest of its Native "wards". The realization that Natives can act independently in a manner contrary to government policy has occurred only recently.

The word "claim" suggests that a complaint is based upon a legal or political right. Before the Office of Native Claims was created, the Department of Indian Affairs had no special section for dealing with Native rights. Until 1974, the Department simply used one of two filing systems: "petitions and complaints" or "claims and disputes". If a case was filed under "petitions and complaints", no legal action would be taken. The decision as to which file a case would be placed in was largely made according to how formally it was presented to the Department. As Daniel points out, "When a grievance or complaint was put in the form of a clear statement of rights and violations of those rights, it was likely to be considered a claim" (1980:196). At any rate, no consistent policy existed for determining which cases were grievances and which were claims.

In order to transfer a case from the "complaints" file to the "claims" file, the assistance of a claims advocate has generally been required. Historically, the missionaries played this role; because they could read English documents and understand British law, the missionaries established a long tradition of acting as mediators between Natives and government, particularly in the signing of treaties. Much later, Native leaders and organizations took on the role of advocate for Native claims. Recently, however, Natives have found that legal training is needed to most effectively pursue a claim. In addition, they now recognize a need for individuals with special skills in anthropology, political analysis, history, and linguistics.

Until 1974, the federal government did not develop any special structure or mechanism by which to process and adjudicate comprehensive claims. Cases were simply handled through the normal administrative channels. Often, a special investigator, litigator, or commission was appointed to gather evidence before the case was decided. These special bodies were advisory only and lacked decision-making authority. Special advisory appointments generally reflected a desire by the federal government to avoid formal adversary proceedings when deciding Native claims. This avoidance could also be seen in the government's reluctance to use the court system as the mechanism for claim settlement (DIAND, 1981).

In place of court actions, the federal government has favoured a negotiating stance, followed by an out-of-court settlement procedure (Colvin, 1981). In the few cases that went to the courts, such as the Nishga case, the specific points of law were not addressed. The absence of formal procedures and court restrictions allowed specific individuals an inordinate degree of control over the outcome of particular claims. As Daniel points out:

... our research found many instances in which the federal government's disposition towards a claim had the appearance of having been altered to a significant degree by a change in personnel associated with the case . . . (The) policy with respect to the comprehensive claim of the Chippewas and Mississaugas seems to have been more liberal after the appointment of R.V. Sinclair, a man known to have been an advocate of several Indian claims, and an occasional critic of Indian Affairs policy. (1980:216, 246)

Not only did the government's settlement procedures fail to produce satisfactory claim settlements. They also added to the already considerable grievances of Native Canadians.

Reeling from the negative reaction to its newly introduced *White Paper*,[4] the federal government began finally to consider establishing a claims commission. This change in ideology was masked by a full program of procedures for claim settlement. First, guidelines for a funding program controlled by the Privy Council were set forth (1970-73). Then, an Indian Claims Commissioner was appointed (1972-73) and the Rights and Treaty Research Program was established (1972-76).

The early programs were very general and exploratory in nature. Later, programs and funds were provided to Natives to establish more specific claims. In addition, loans became available for claims research and development. As of 1979, the federal government had contributed nearly $16 million outright and $23 million in loans for the research and development of Native claims.

Figure 5.1 identifies areas in Canada that are included in the comprehensive claims of Native peoples. As the map shows, ownership of a sizable portion of Canada is claimed both by status and by non-status Natives. Some of these claims, such as that affecting the James Bay region, have already been decisively settled, while others, such as that affecting the Western Artic Inuit, have only reached the "agreement-in-principle" stage. However, much of the area under claim by Natives has not been negotiated to a satisfactory conclusion.

In 1974, the Office of Native Claims (ONC) was created under the Department of Indian Affairs to co-ordinate all federal negotiations concerning Native claims. The ONC also conducts basic research and formulates policies for claim development and negotiations. Since 1974, the federal government has also established various commissions to explore Native rights. The most publicized of these has been the Berger Commission, although others, such as the Hartt and Lyshk Commissions, have also gathered substantial amounts of evidence concerning Native claims.

Despite its mandate, however, the ONC has not so far resolved many specific claims. Few Natives are willing to directly negotiate with the ONC because of their firmly entrenched distrust of DIAND. Natives argue

FIGURE 5.1   *Comprehensive claims: areas claimed by Native associations*

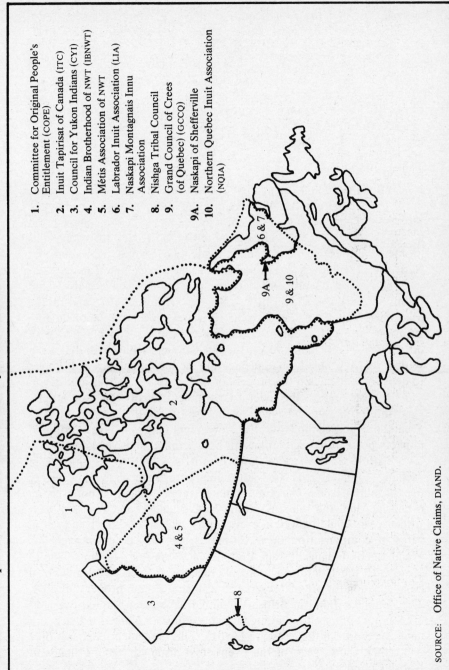

1. Committee for Original People's Entitlement (COPE)
2. Inuit Tapirisat of Canada (ITC)
3. Council for Yukon Indians (CYI)
4. Indian Brotherhood of NWT (IBNWT)
5. Métis Association of NWT
6. Labrador Inuit Association (LIA)
7. Naskapi Montagnais Innu Association
8. Nishga Tribal Council
9. Grand Council of Crees (of Quebec) (GCCQ)
9A. Naskapi of Shefferville
10. Northern Quebec Inuit Association (NQIA)

SOURCE: Office of Native Claims, DIAND.

that one body cannot act as both the representative of the federal government and the representative of Native claims. Furthermore, because the ONC determines the rules that govern negotiations, Natives feel that the negotiation process is tailored to the advantage of the federal government. Figure 5.2, showing the number of claims submitted to the ONC as well as the disposition of the cases, suggests that the Natives' view of the ONC may well be legitimate.

In 1975, the National Indian Brotherhood (NIB) agreed with the federal government to form joint committee to investigate Native issues and to discuss principles and parameters for settling Native claims. However, in 1978, the committee was disbanded when the NIB withdrew from it.

Under the 1930 *Natural Resouces Transfer Agreements,* Native claims, particularly in the West, require the relinquishing of land by the provinces. The federal government may recognize land claims, but the province still has to provide the actual land. To try to resolve this problem, various tripartite councils, made up of federal, provincial, and Native representatives, have been established throughout Canada.

The federal government has recently begun to take Native land claims seriously, as shown by the Nisgha decision of 1973 and by the Mackenzie Valley Pipeline decision. However, the interpretation, administration, and enforcement of claims continue to be plagued with difficulties. For instance, even though the James Bay issue has been settled, recent problems in implementing the settlement have led Natives to question once again the process of taking treaty. Natives argue that, as with past treaties, the federal government is adhering to a strictly legal interpretation and ignoring the "spirit" of the agreement. The events surrounding the James Bay Agreement may well have a profound impact upon future negotiations for other comprehensive claims.

As of 1982, the federal government is willing to pay money in exchange for land rights but is not willing to negotiate Native sovereignty over disputed lands. Current estimates suggest that this policy is an expensive one: the bill for settling Native land claims over the next fifteen years could be well in excess of $4 billion. Indeed, given present rates of compensation these estimates are very conservative. The Wagmatcook Indians of Cape Breton Island, the first Maritime band to settle with the federal government, recently received $1.2 million in compensation for original reserve lands taken without proper authority. The Penticton Band in British Columbia have been granted over $14 million in compensation, along with the return of some 12 000 acres of land severed from their reserve in 1916. This agreement concerns only one, albeit the largest, of the twenty-two disputed "cut-off" lands of British Columbia.

FIGURE 5.2 *Specific claims submitted for settlement to the Office of Native Claims*

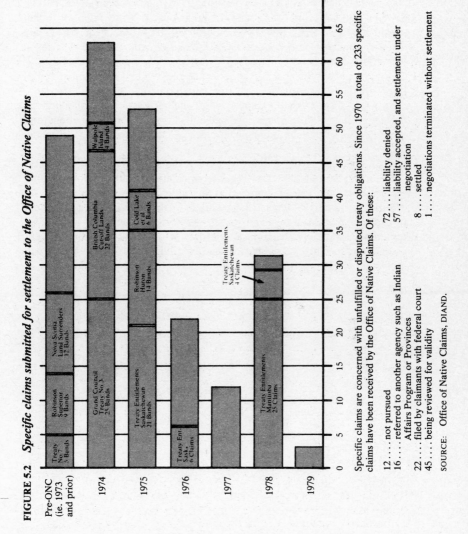

Specific claims are concerned with unfulfilled or disputed treaty obligations. Since 1970 a total of 233 specific claims have been received by the Office of Native Claims. Of these:

12 . . . . not pursued
16 . . . . referred to another agency such as Indian Affairs Program or Provinces
22 . . . . filed by claimants with federal court
45 . . . . being reviewed for validity

72 . . . . liability denied
57 . . . . liability accepted, and settlement under negotiation
8 . . . . settled
1 . . . . negotiations terminated without settlement

SOURCE: Office of Native Claims, DIAND.

Notes

1. In 1981, the Ontario Supreme Court decided that Native peoples who have treaty rights can legally hunt and fish out of season on Crown land in Eastern Ontario. The decision, involving the 1818 treaty with the Mississauga Indians, was partially based upon oral records of the day. The decision states that the minutes of a council meeting between the deputy superintendent of Indian Affairs and the Indians in 1818 recorded the oral portion of the 1818 treaty and are as much a part of the treaty as the written articles of the provisional agreement.
2. The increased allotment of 640 acres in Treaty No. 3 became standard for all future treaties except for Treaty No. 5, which reverted to the 160-acre allotment. Other changes that became standard included assurances of continued hunting, fishing, and trapping rights, an annual budget for ammunitions, and the provision of agricultural supplies, such as cattle, seed, and farm implements.
3. In their submission, the Indians noted that the secretary to the Governor-General had assured them that, if they were dissatisfied with the Commission's report, they could appeal their case to the Imperial Privy Council.
4. The *White Paper* (1969) was a document put forth by the federal government to end the special status of Indians. In essence, the government wanted to terminate the reserve structure and integrate Indians as Canadian citizens without any special legal rights, privileges, or obligations. The document was shelved after extremely negative reaction and has not been acted upon.

PART II

The second section of this book provides the reader with a profile of Native peoples in Canada today. We will begin by presenting an in-depth statistical profile of Natives to illustrate their overall position within Canadian society. When possible, we will also try to report major developments or trends over time for specific indicators.

The statistical information presented in the following chapters has been collected from a number of different sources; as a result, the "totals" from various tables may not always be the same. Despite minor discrepancies, however, statistical information is essential to interpret and determine the success of federal policies and programs concerning Native people. For example, statistics tell us that federal expenditures for Natives were increased by only 14 percent per capita between 1970 and 1978, as compared to increases of over 100 percent per capita in other federal social programs.

Urbanization is one of the major social issues now facing Native Canadians. As the Native population has continued to increase in size, more and more individuals have migrated to the cities. The consequences have been dramatic and revealing. As seen in Chapter 7, Natives have generally not adapted well to urban life and have encountered a host of social problems.

A profile of contemporary Native Canadians would be incomplete without a look at the organization that has been created to act as their trustee. Chapter 8 examines the structure, mandate, and budget of the Department of Indian Affairs and Northern Development.

Although Native people have played a minimal role in the development of Canadian society over the past century, they have recently begun to take a more active part in Canadian politics. Chapter 9 explores various voluntary Native associations that have developed with a political thrust. As evidenced by the recent constitutional debates, many Native organizations have become active lobbying groups that are strong enough to force the government to concede to some of their demands.

The position of Native people in Canadian society is certainly changing over time. However, as we will see, these changes do not reflect any progress toward a fixed goal. Changes in federal policy appear random and directionless, offering little evidence that any goals have been developed or pursued. And the demands of the Native peoples frequently also lack focus and direction, or fail to consider financial costs and problems of implementation.

6

Demographic and Social Characteristics

Introduction

Before we can examine the demographic conditions of Canadian Natives, we must point out that the demographic data on the Native population continues to be plagued with two sources of potential bias. First, most of the information is taken from the Department of Indian Affairs and Northern Development (DIAND). And second, the definition of a Native Canadian remains problematic.

Three national agencies collect most of the statistics on the Native population: the Vital Statistic Section of the Health and Welfare Division of Statistics Canada; DIAND; and the Decennial Censuses of Canada. These three differ widely in their terms of reference and in their methods of enumeration; as a result, statistics emanating from any one agency are not strictly comparable with statistics from the others. At present, no attempt has been made to reconcile the statistics produced by these major sources.

Needless to say, the lack of standardized data severely limits the accuracy of short-term trend analyses and makes future projections difficult. Moreover, because the definition of an Indian has changed over time, statistics reported by all three agencies show wide discrepancies; in some cases, revised definitions of Indian status have meant that statistics related to an initial cohort are no longer appropriate at a later time.

Our socio-demographic profile of Natives in Canada will begin with a discussion of population growth, including births, deaths, and migration. It is a mark of the confusion brought about by unclear and inconsistent definitions that the meaning of migration has been expanded to include those who have been redefined either as Indian or non-Indian.

Population Growth

The figures in Table 6.1 show a three-fold increase in the absolute size of the registered Indian population over the past century. During the same period, however, the Indian population has come to constitute a smaller and smaller proportion of the total population, decreasing from 2.5 percent in 1881 to 1.2 percent in 1980. Since the late 1950s, the natural increase rate for registered Indians has hovered around 3 percent. In 1968, it was over 3.4 percent, but by 1970, the rate had dropped to 2.8 percent. Since 1970, the rate has slowly decreased, but it is still double the national Canadian average of 1.4 percent.

Between 1960 and 1975, the Indian population grew rapidly. As a result, the age distribution of Natives is very different to that of the general Canadian population. Figure 6.1 shows the rate of population increase for registered Indians in graph form.

The Department of Indian Affairs projects that, given medium fertility, the registered Indian population will increase to nearly 350 000 by 1986. By that time, the growth rate will have dropped to the national average of 1.4 percent.

Three factors affect the growth rate of the Native population: the birth rate, the death rate, and the rate at which people gain and lose Indian status, otherwise called the "in-out" migration rate. Figure 6.2 graphically illustrates the natural increase (births minus deaths) of Indians and Inuits from 1962 to 1974 as compared to the national average for those years. The Indians declining natural-increase rate is due generally to a lowering of their birth rate. In 1921, the crude birth rate for Indians was nearly 51 per 1 000 population. By 1962, it had dropped to 46 per 1 000, and, by 1976, to 28.5 per 1 000, which is still nearly double the national average of 15.7. The death rate for Indians has also dropped somewhat over the past twenty years from 10.5 to 8.3, and now is very similar to that of the overall Canadian population.

The birth rate is significantly influenced by the average age of marriage. Although, overall, the proportion of married Indians is lower than the national average, the proportion of married Indians in the highest-fertility age-group of twenty to twenty-four exceeds that of non-Indians. Moreover, the fertility of Indians between twenty and twenty-four appears to be twice the Canadian average.

TABLE 6.1   *Population of Native people in*
                Canada, 1881-1980

Year	Registered Indian population
1881	108 547
1901	127 941
1929	108 012
1934	112 510
1939	118 378
1944	125 686
1949	136 407
1954	151 558
1959	179 126
1960	185 169
1961	191 709
1966	224 164
1971	257 619
1974	276 436
1980	320 000

SOURCES:
Information Canada, *Perspective Canada I,*
(Ottawa: Queen's Printer, 1974), 240; *Perspective
Canada II,* (Ottawa: Queen's Printer, 1977), 282.

There are, however, considerable regional variations in Native birth
rates. Native women living in Eastern Canada have similar fertility rates
to those of White women, while Native women in the Prairies have
much higher rates. One band in Northern Saskatchewan is alone responsible for over 7 percent of all Native Canadian births.

In 1971, nearly 60 percent of all status-Indian births were illlegiti-
mate. This may be partly due to unwillingness on the part of Native
women to lose Indian status through marriage to non-Indian men.

In 1970, a Native's expected average life span was sixty years while
for Whites it was sixty-nine. The average age at death is markedly lower
for Natives than the national average: as Table 6.2 shows, for Natives
the average age at death is forty-three and for non-Natives, sixty-seven.

The in-out migration pattern refers to the number of Indians added
to or deleted from the federal roll of registered Indians. Table 6.3 shows
the number of Indians who were enfranchised between 1955 and 1975.
Unfortunately, the number of individuals who gained Indian status other
than through birth cannot be determined. The number of non-Indian

FIGURE 6.1   *Registered Indian population, 1924-76, and projections[1] for 1980 and 1985*

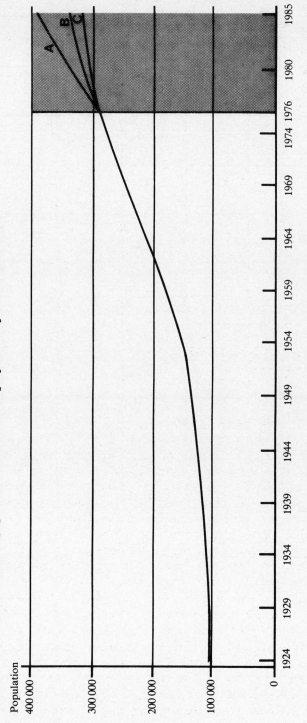

[1]The projections involve three different assumptions of fertility among registered Indians: (a) high fertility, (b) medium fertility, and (c) low fertility.

SOURCE: Program Statistics Division, DIAND, 1976; Information Canada, *Perspectives Canada III*, (Ottawa: Queen's Printer, 1980), 177.

FIGURE 6.2   *Natural increase of the registered Indian, Inuit, and Canadian populations*

Rate per 1 000 population

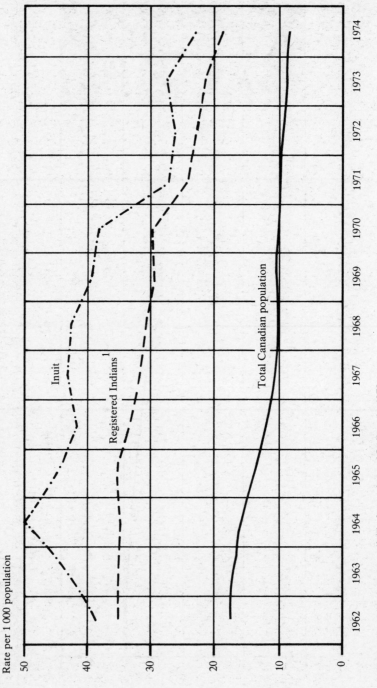

[1]No national figure was available for registered Indians in 1972.

SOURCE: Information Canada, *Perspective Canada II,* (Ottawa: Queen's Printer, 1977), 282.

females marrying Indian men was estimated at 300 in 1969 and over 500 in 1977. However, figures are unavailable concerning whether these women had children prior to their marriages and how many children they had after marriage.

Based on information in Table 6.3, the annual enfranchisement rate per 1 000 Indians has varied between 6.3 and 1.1. Despite this apparently low rate, however, over 13 000 Indians lost their status between 1955 and 1975. Moreover, the offspring of these 13 000, now old enough to have their own children, also surrendered their Indian status.

TABLE 6.2 *Specific measures of mortality among registered Canadian Indians and among Canadians as a whole*[1]

	A	B	C	D	E
	Crude death rate	Infant mortality rate	Average age at death	Male life expectancy	Female life expectancy
1960					
Indians	10.9	79.0	—	59.7	63.5
All Canadians	8.0	27.3		68.5	74.3
1965					
Indians	8.7	52.6	36.0	60.5	65.6
All Canadians	7.5	23.6	64.0	68.8	75.2
1970					
Indians	7.5	43.2[2]	42.0	60.2	66.2
All Canadians	7.5	18.8	66.0	69.3	76.4
1976					
Indians	7.5	32.1	43.0	—	—
All Canadians	7.4	16.0	67.0		

[1]Due to the difficulty in obtaining data, the data in any given cell above may be for a different year than for that shown. The difference is never more than two years and usually only one, and in any such cases of discrepancy the data is more recent than the date shown.

[2]This figure is an average of the rates for 1969 and 1971, since the 1970 data are unreliable due to incomplete reporting that year.

A Death per 1000 population.
B Deaths of children in first year of life per 1000 live births.
C Sum of the age at death of all persons dying in a given year ÷ the number of people dying that year.
D & E Age to which a person can be expected to live, calculated at time of birth.

SOURCES: Medical Services Branch, *Health Data Book* (Ottawa: Department of National Health and Welfare, 1978); Ponting and Gibbins, 1980.

As Table 6.3 shows, over 80 percent of enfranchised Indians lost their status through marriage to a non-Indian. Indeed, a close analysis of the data suggests that voluntary applications for enfranchisement have virtually ceased. The most recent statistics on enfranchisement show that nearly all Indians who surrender their status do so involuntarily as a result of the "marriage rule" enforced by the *Indian Act*.

TABLE 6.3 *Enfranchisements[1] of registered Indians, 1955-75*

	Enfranchisements upon application		Enfranchisements following marriage to a non-Indian		Total enfranchisements
	Adults	Children[2]	Women	Children[2]	
1955-56 to 1959-60	912	724	2 078	484	4 198
1960-61 to 1964-65	401	239	2 198	694	3 532
1965-66 to 1969-70	207	107	2 440	655	3 409
1970-71 to 1974-75	54	20	1 823	117	2 014

[1]On enfranchisement, an Indian permanently gives up all rights under the *Indian Act*. Enfranchisement in this sense has nothing to do with the possession of voting rights which were guaranteed to all Indians in 1960.

[2]Prior to 1972-73 minor, unmarried children were automatically enfranchised with their parent(s). Since 1972-73, minor, unmarried children have been enfranchised only when it is requested by the parent(s) and when the application is approved by the Department of Indian Affairs and Northern Development.

SOURCE: Information Canada, *Perspective Canada II*, (Ottawa: Queen's Printer, 1977), 285.

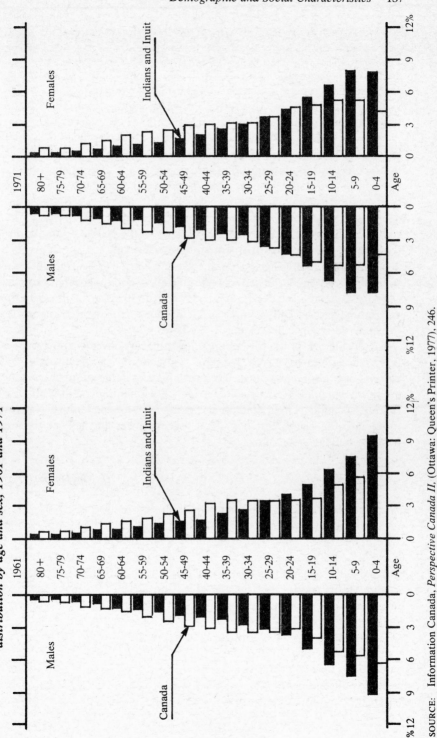

FIGURE 6.3 Indian and Inuit population as compared to the total Canadian population: distribution by age and sex, 1961 and 1971

SOURCE: Information Canada, *Perspective Canada II*, (Ottawa: Queen's Printer, 1977), 246.

Distribution by Age and Sex

Figure 6.3 and Table 6.4 show the distribution of Native Canadians by age and sex relative to that of the total Canadian population. The figures reveal a very young population: almost half the Native population are younger than fifteen and two-thirds are younger than twenty-five. Of the total Canadian population, only about one-third are younger than fifteen.

Clearly, the proportion of young people in the overall Native population is growing. Nonetheless, at 37 percent, the proportion of Natives between fifteen and forty-four is quite similar to the 41 percent found in the non-Native population. It is in the forty-five to sixty-five category that serious discrepancies arise: fewer than 10 percent of Natives, but nearly 20 percent of non-Natives, belong to this group. Similarly, in the sixty-five and older category, only 5 percent of the Native population is represented, as opposed to 8 percent of non-Natives.

The above figures carry a number of implications. Clearly, there is a stable Native population-growth rate, meaning continued high growth, as well as a decreasing death rate. Unless birth rates also decrease, more and more Natives will belong to the prime employment category of fifteen to forty, and the demand for jobs will increase.

As Table 6.4 shows, the dependency ratios are already over twice as high for Natives as for the general population; this means that the working-age population must already support a large number of non-productive people. (See Table 6.4, page 139.) Unemployment is already rampant among Native Canadians. And, as more and more Natives move into the prime employment category, fewer and fewer jobs are likely to become available.

Geographical Distribution

Almost every Indian is affiliated with one or more "bands". A band is a group of Indians who share a common interest in land and money and whose historical connection is defined by the federal government. The word "band" is also a political label; it is often arbitrarily imposed on Native groups, regardless of cultural differences, for the government's administrative purposes. Because the Minister of Indian Affairs can create and destroy band designations, the number of bands often varies from year to year.

When the federal government first divided various Indian tribes into bands, it showed very little concern about the impact of these divisions on Indian culture. For example, some tribes were matrilineal, tracing descent through the mother's side, while others were patrilineal. Yet, when the band system was established, tribes were arbitrarily thrown

TABLE 6.4   *Age distribution of the registered Indian population*

| | Age Group | | | | | Dependency Ratio[1] | | | |
| | 0-14 years | 15-64 years | 65 years and over | No age given | Population | Young | | Aged | |
						Indian	Non-Indian[2]	Indian	Non-Indian[2]
	percent								
1924	32.2	51.2	5.9	10.7	104 894	62.9	56.5	11.5	7.9
1934	34.7	55.4	6.2	3.7	112 510	62.7	50.3	11.1	8.8
1944	37.5	55.9	6.6	—	125 686	67.0	42.4	11.8	10.2
1954	41.7	53.2	5.1	—	151 558	78.5	49.0	9.6	12.5
1964	46.7	49.1	4.2	—	211 389	95.0	58.1	8.6	13.1
1974	43.2	52.4	4.2	0.2	276 436	82.4	47.5	8.1	13.0
1976	42.4	53.2	4.4	—	282 762	79.3	45.3	8.2	12.6

[1]The dependency ratios reflect the relationship between the groups least likely to be involved in the work force (i.e. the young and the elderly), and the working-age population.

[2]Data was not available for the corresponding year; the years represented are: 1921, 1931, 1941, 1951, 1961, 1971.

SOURCE: Information Canada, *Perspective Canada II,* (Ottawa: Queen's Printer, 1977), 287.

together and all treated as patrilineal. This produced serious social disorganization, and a wide-ranging disruption of tribal culture.

Under the *1951 Indian Act,* Section 2(1), "band" means simply a body of Indians. At present, over 200 000 Indians live on reserves and belong to 573 different bands; the largest of these is the Six Nations band, near Brantford, Ontario, with a population of 8 200. Each band is administered by one of eighty-seven agencies across Canada; the Caughnawaga agency handles only 1 band, and the New Westminster agency handles 32.

Canada has some 2 241 reserves, though this number, like the number of bands, varies over time according to the policy of the federal government. Reserves can vary in size. Although there is no minimum area, 160 acres per person is the maximum; some reserves in British Columbia cover only a few acres, while the largest is 500 square miles. In Eastern Canada, each band is generally limited to one reserve. In the West, one band may hold several reserves; British Columbia has over 1 600 reserves, but less than 200 bands (Allan, 1943).

Band designations are not the only means of differentiating Indian peoples. Two further criteria are language and cultural lifestyle. Indians have been divided into ten traditional linguistic groups: Algonkian, Iroquois, Sioux, Athabasca, Kootenay, Saliash, Wakash, Tsimish, Haida, and Tlingt. Six major cultural areas have also been established: Algonkian, Iroquois, Plains, Plateaus, Pacific Coast, and MacKenzie River. There is, of course, a considerable overlap between the two categories.

Over time, White Canada has systematically obliterated many Native cultural and linguistic distinctions. The forced migration of some groups from one area to another has caused cultural and linguistic mixing. For example, the Ojibeway were originally from southeast Quebec and eastern Ontario. By 1750, they had moved into an area of the Great Lakes, and by 1805, they were established in Saskatchewan. Other groups, such as the Assiniboine and Chipewyan, have been split through migration, with some group members moving north, and others, south.

Table 6.5 identifies the number of Indians living in specific provinces as well as the percentage they form of the total population. The figures demonstrate that 22.3 percent, nearly one-quarter of the Indian population, lives in Ontario. British Columbia is next, with 18.4 percent of Canada's Indians, and then Saskatchewan, with 15.2 percent; in all, over 60 percent of Canadian Indians reside in the four Western provinces. However, the Indians' lack of social and political impact can be better understood by looking at the percentage of Indians relative to the total provincial population. Here we find that Indians only make up a sizable proportion of the total in the Northwest Territories and the Yukon. Throughout the rest of Canada, Indians make up less than 5 percent of the total population.

TABLE 6.5   Distribution of the Indian population and Indian lands, 1977

Province	Indian Population				Indian Lands		
	Number	Percent of Canadian Indian population	Percent of total provincial population	Percent off-reserve[1]	Number of bands	Number of reserves and/or settlements	Approximate area (1979) of reserves (hectares)
Maritimes	11 093	3.7	0.5	26.2	29	64	31 800
Quebec	30 175	10.2	0.5	18.1	39	39	85 450
Ontario	66 057	22.3	0.8	31.6	115	171	736 210
Manitoba	43 349	14.6	4.4	25.2	57	103	235 120
Saskatchewan	44 986	15.2	4.4	29.8	68	124	645 010
Alberta	35 162	11.9	2.7	21.9	41	96	725 010
British Columbia	54 318	18.4	2.4	36.1	194	1 629	372 300
NWT	7 541	2.5	17.4	3.6	16	29	–
Yukon	3 217	1.1	12.7	17.6	14	26	–
Canada	295 898	99.9	1.3	27.6	573	2 281	2 830 940

[1]Here and in the text "off-reserve" is used to mean "off reserve, off crown land".

SOURCES: Ponting and Gibbins, 1980; DIAND, 1980.

Table 6.5 also gives the percentage of the Indian population considered "off-reserve" in 1977. The term "off reserve" refers to registered Indians who do not claim reserves as their places of residence. The determination of the exact population of off-reserve Indians varies over time. The variation among the provinces for this statistic, however, is quite narrow: Ontario is highest with 32 percent of its Indians off-reserve, while Quebec is lowest, with 18 percent.

On average, more than a quarter of the Indian population of Canada was considered off-reserve in 1977. While this figure reflects a dramatic increase in the number of off-reserve Indians over the past twenty years, it still shows that reserves remain home to nearly three-quarters of the Indian population. Clearly, the reserve still provides security and roots for most Indian people. The reserve is where the majority of Indians have grown up among family and friends. Even for those who leave, it continues to provide a haven from the pressures of White society. These factors, combined with the prejudicial attitudes of White culture, create a strong internal pull and external push toward remaining on the reserve.

Even if an increasing number of Indians leave the reserve, the absolute population of those who remain will still show a sizable increase. This could pose a number of problems for White Canada. Reserves are potential hot-beds for political and social discontent. In addition, if Indians on reserves become economically developed, they could pose a competitive threat to some Canadian corporate structures. Already, in British Columbia and Alberta, Indians have angered local businessmen by building housing developments on reserve lands close to major cities.

The nature of the reserve system is a major source of the recent growth in Indian identity. Because the reserve is a closed spatial area, it fosters an ease of communication among Natives and renders communication with outsiders difficult. When communication takes place only within a group, contrast conceptions of other groups emerge: one's own group is seen as "good", while the other group is seen as "bad". If outside communication is discouraged, internal communications become susceptible to group censorship; that is, members cannot criticize their own group or praise the other group without inviting negative sanctions. For example, an Indian who suggests that the federal government's position might contain some legitimate points becomes open to accusations of complicity or gullibility. As a result, information that might change the group's stereotypic, negative evaluation of government behaviour cannot be processed. Through this dynamic, the reserve can easily become a centre for radical, militant activities. This is clearly a major reason for the federal government's desire to abolish them.

The recent trend in the residential patterns of Canadian Indians indicates that an increasing number of them are moving to urban areas. Of these, over half are relocating in large metropolitan areas of more than 100 000 people. There are two explanations for the migration to large cities. First, unskilled employment is easier to obtain in large cities than in small towns. Second, Native ghettos are developing in various cities such as Winnipeg, Toronto, and Edmonton; once a sizable population of an ethnic group resides in a given poverty area, other members of that group find it easier to move there.

Siggner (1980) has looked at the migration patterns of registered Indians by comparing census data from 1966 and 1971. He found that only 20 percent of the Indian population moved one or more times during this period as compared to 25 percent of the national population. Over half (52 percent) of the Indian migrants were headed toward an urban area. Siggner also found that nearly one-fourth of all Indian migrants had moved more than three times during this five-year period.

The migrant population is a very young group, between twenty and twenty-five. However, this population is not comprised solely of single adults, as might be expected. Indeed, evidence suggests that many Indian migrants are parents moving with small children.

The average population size of Indian bands in Canada has increased to well over 500 people; in 1950, the average was 200. Most Indians currently live in bands of less than 1 000; the modal category, containing 39 percent, is 300 to 1 000 (see Table 6.6). Another 31 percent have a population of 101 to 300. Only sixteen bands are very large, with over 2 000 members; these are located in Ontario, Manitoba, and Alberta.

Approximately 2 240 separate parcels of reserve land make up a

FIGURE 6.4 *Reserve lands: number of acres of reserve lands per capita (Indians on reserves)*

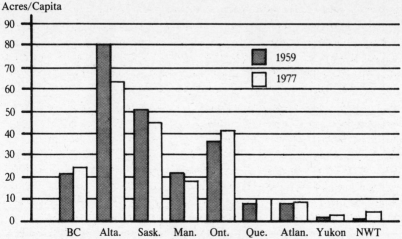

SOURCES: *Annual Report,* Indian Affairs Branch, Dept. of Citizenship and Immigration, 1959; *Registered Indian Population by Sex and Residence, 1977,* Program Statistics, DIAND; *Number and Acreage of Indian Reserves by Band, December 31, 1971,* Program Statistics, DIAND.

TABLE 6.6   Numerical and percentage distribution of Indian bands by size and geographic location, for regions, 1977

Region	Total bands		Distribution of bands by population size										Distribution of bands by geographic location							
			0-100		101-300		301-1000		1000-2000		2000+		Remote		Rural		Semi-Urban		Urban	
	#	%	#	%	#	%	#	%	#	%	#	%	#	%	#	%	#	%	#	%
Maritimes	29	100	5	17	10	35	12	41	2	7	–	–	–	–	13	45	10	34	6	21
Quebec	39	100	5	13	6	15	17	44	10	26	1	3	14	36	5	13	15	38	5	13
Ontario	115	100	20	17	40	35	40	35	10	9	5	4	34	30	52	45	21	18	8	7
Manitoba	57	100	3	5	6	11	32	56	12	21	4	7	25	44	26	46	5	9	1	2
Saskatchewan	68	100	2	3	11	16	41	60	12	18	2	3	10	15	43	63	13	19	2	3
Alberta	41	100	4	10	9	22	18	44	6	15	4	10	7	17	19	46	12	29	3	7
BC	194	100	54	28	81	42	53	27	6	3	–	–	53	27	77	40	41	21	23	12
NWT	16	100	–	–	6	38	9	56	1	6	–	–	8	–	7	–	1	–	–	–
Yukon	14	100	2	14	10	71	2	14	–	–	–	–	13	–	–	–	–	–	1	–
Canada	573	100	95	17	179	31	224	39	59	10	16	3	164	29	242	42	118	21	49	9

SOURCES: Statistics Division, *Registered Indian Population by Sex and Residence, 1977*, (Ottawa: Program Reference Centre, IIAP, 1979); Ponting and Gibbins, 1980, 35.

little less than 3 million hectares of land (more than 6 million acres). The total area of reserve lands per capita has decreased over the past twenty years (see Figure 6.4). In 1959, there were 32 acres per capita, but by 1991, there are likely to be only 27 acres per capita.

About 65 percent of the Indian population on reserves are located in rural or remote locations; this can be compared to a national average of 25 percent. (See Table 6.6.) Rural bands refer to those over sixty miles from the nearest urban centre, while remote bands are all those lacking roads for transportation to an urban centre. However, Indians have not remained as socially isolated from modern non-Indian society as this statistic would suggest. Nationally, fewer than 30 percent live in remote locations. This figure varies by region, with a low of 5 percent in the Maritimes and Alberta, with 55 percent in Manitoba, and with a high of over 80 percent in the Yukon.

Language Use and Retention

Price (1981) has investigated the potential for the survival of Native languages in Canada. He found that long-term future viability has been secured for at least nine Native languages by a minimum of 1 000 speakers. An additional twenty-six languages are spoken by an estimated 100 to 1 000 Natives.

While Natives still maintain a relatively high degree of adherence to their mother tongue, this is slowly diminishing. In 1941, fewer than 10 percent of Natives claimed English as their mother tongue.[1] The figure reached 15 percent in 1951 and over 25 percent in 1961; another 2 percent claimed French. By 1971, 53.9 percent still claimed a Native language as their mother tongue. Of the 30 percent who claimed English, fewer than 5 percent were bilingual. Of those who claimed Native dialects as their mother tongues, more than 40 percent were "somewhat" bilingual.

In reviewing various surveys from the 1970s, Price (1981) found that the percentage of Native-language speakers varied from a low of 62 percent in Toronto and Vancouver, to 73 percent in Winnipeg, and up to 100 percent on many reserves. He also found Saskatchewan to be most conservative in the retention of Native languages. However, Stanbury and Siegel (1975) found that only 18 percent of Vancouver Indians used their Native languages in their homes.

The overall diminishing of Native-language use is somewhat mediated by special schools and language instruction programs. As a result, Natives are increasingly bilingual. Like other ethnic minorities, they have learned that, to integrate into the larger society, they must learn to speak English. Thus, to a certain extent, the decreasing number of

TABLE 6.7 *Persons with Indian-Inuit mother tongues as a percentage of all Indian-Inuit ethnic group members*

	1951	1961	1971
Under 15 years	85.0	69.3	54.5
15-24 years	87.1	75.1	53.2
25-44 years	89.0	81.1	58.6
45-64 years	91.1	87.4	66.2
65+	94.4	91.0	73.2
All ages	87.4	75.7	57.1

SOURCE: Information Canada, *Perspective Canada I,* (Ottawa: Queen's Printer, 1974), 250.

Native-language speakers reflects an increasing move away from the reserves and an increasing contact with non-Natives. Of course, the educational process has also increased the number of English-language speakers, though the high Native drop-out rate at elementary levels has minimalized its impact on language retention and use. However, as Natives increasingly recognize the value of English-language education, their languages and dialects may disappear even more rapidly.

Table 6.7 expresses the number of individuals with Indian-Inuit mother tongues as a percentage of all Indians and Inuit. The figures clearly show that the younger population is rapidly losing its Native mother tongues.

Religion

According to present statistics, 56 percent of Indians in Canada are Catholics. This, of course, reflects the early Jesuit and Oblate missionary work among the Natives. The second largest Indian religious group is Anglican, with 25 percent. Another 12 percent of Indians belong to the United Church, and the remaining 7 percent are evenly distributed between the other Christian churches in Canada.

The above information is based on official government statistics. However, no information has been gathered as to the extent to which Natives have internalized Christian beliefs and the extent to which they still adhere to pre-Christian religious beliefs. Apparently, a significant proportion of Natives have retained their indigenous religious ideologies.

Nonetheless, Christianity has had a definite impact on Native culture during the past few centuries. Its ideology of acceptance and obedience has contributed significantly to widespread conservatism and fatalism among Native peoples.

Marital Status

Figures on the marital status of Natives do not support the stereotype of the broken Native family. According to Table 6.8, only 6.7 percent of registered Indians are widowed or divorced as compared to 7 percent of the overall White population.

There are however, a number of explanations for this statistic. Because Native people are frequently poor, they often avoid the court costs and alimony payments that accompany formal divorces by simply separating from or deserting their families. Moreover, many women,

TABLE 6.8 *Marital status of Indians and of the total population, 1961*

		Indians	
Single	Married	Widowed and divorced	Total
19 702	1 987	17	
9 219	8 053	58	
6 354	19 837	353	
2 214	15 589	720	
1 086	11 612	1 203	
613	7 398	1 757	
456	5 331	3 737	
39 644	69 807	7 845	117 296
33.3%	60%	6.7%	100%

		All Canada	
Single	Married	Widowed and divorced	Total
1 361 734	70 395	430	
649 440	531 833	2 373	
451 417	2 101 900	18 790	
251 747	2 087 405	50 733	
191 438	1 585 916	101 150	
140 054	980 370	169 046	
145 376	757 485	488 293	
3 191 206	8 115 304	830 815	12 137 325
26%	67%	7%	100%

SOURCE: Statistics Canada, *Marital Status by Ethnic Groups,* Bulletin 1.3-7, 106, 1961. Reproduced by permission of Information Canada.

even though they live with a man and bear children, never officially get married. Instead, they live common-law or marry according to tribal ritual, which has not been recognized by the federal government since 1957. Native women may choose not to marry for various reasons. Unmarried women with children receive a fairly substantial income through the baby-bonus scheme: an unmarried Native women with three children receives about three times as much money in social welfare as a married-but-separated woman with three children. Unmarried Indian women are also eligible for several educational and vocational-training programs not available to maried women. And, finally, unmarried women do not risk losing their Indian status.

The low official divorce rate of Natives, then, should not be used as an indicator of family stability. However, some anthropologists have argued convincingly that White North American standards of family stability should be used only for White North Americans and not for members of other cultures. The definition of stability is so open to various culturally-based interpretations that no attempt to apply it to another culture can be free of ethnocentric bias.

Other statistics also suggest that Native family patterns depart radically from White norms. About 60 percent of the Native population are officially married as compared to 67 percent of the overall Canadian population. However, young Natives between fifteen and nineteen are much more likely to marry than are other Canadian teenagers (Anderson, 1978). Both of these statistics have implications for the illegitimacy rate. In 1965, 32 percent of all Indian children were illegitimate, markedly in excess of the national average.

Socio-economic Status

The social and economic status of Canadian Natives is largely determined by three indicators: income, occupation, and education. We will begin by discussing income, and then focus upon occupational and educational attainment.

INCOME

In 1966, Hawthorn et. al. established that the per capita income per year for Natives was about $300, and for Euro-Canadians, about $1 400. The yearly earnings per Native worker were $1 361, and for a Euro-Canadian worker, $4 000.

In 1978, the per capita annual income in various bands ranged from well over $10 000 to as low as $550. With few exceptions, the percentage

TABLE 6.9 *Income of reserve Indian families, 1967*

	$1 000 or less (%)	$1 000 – 3 000 (%)	$3 000 or more (%)
PEI	64.4	31.2	4.2
Nova Scotia	65.5	26.4	8.1
New Brunswick	49.4	42.4	8.2
Quebec	47.5	32.2	20.3
Ontario	24.3	53.7	22.0
Manitoba	60.8	34.3	4.4
Saskatchewan	57.3	35.8	6.9
Alberta	33.2	50.3	16.5
BC	29.3	44.6	26.1
Canada	40.5	43.0	16.5

SOURCE: Departmental Statistics Division, DIAND, 1971.

of people receiving welfare increases as the per capita income decreases. However, the Indian superintendent, who represents the federal government on the reserve, largely determines the amount of welfare actually provided to Indians; if the superintendent takes a liberal view, more welfare will be granted.

Income can be divided into two categories: "wage" and "non-wage and transfer". On the average, the non-wage category accounts for about 45 percent of the total income of a Native community, as compared to a national average of about 10 to 15 percent.

When income level is looked at by province, a clearer picture emerges. Table 6.9 shows that only in three provinces did more than 20 percent of the total Native population earn over $3 000 in 1967. Moreover, nearly half the Natives earned less than $1 000.

In 1970, 62 percent of employed Natives earned less than $2 000. Only 27 percent earned more than $6 000, as compared to the national figure of 51 percent. Even when employed, the average wages and income for Natives continue to be well below the national average (Ponting and Gibbins, 1980).

As stated earlier, per capita income varies for Natives across Canada. Recent increases in gas and oil prices and direct per capita payments currently result in a very high per capita income for some Prairie bands; in 1978-79, mineral revenues from oil and gas amounted to well over $100 million, over 80 percent of which was distributed among five reserves in Alberta. Regional disparity becomes an even more important consideration when the per-capita-income figures are collapsed into family-income statistics.

OCCUPATION

Table 6.10 shows the degree to which Native representation in various occupational categories has been over or under its representation in the general population.[2] To make the data more meaningful through the comparison, similar "over-under" statistics have been included for British-Canadians.

Natives have been substantially over-represented in the "primary and unskilled" category of workers. This situation does not appear to be improving: from 1931 to 1961, the over-representation in this area hardly decreased at all. In addition, Natives are consistently under-represented in white-collar occupations, a situation that actually worsened between 1931 and 1961. Preliminary analysis of 1976 data suggests that these over-under figures remained stable from 1961 to 1976.

Statistics for the British "charter" group, included for comparison, show an opposite trend. British under-representation between 1931 and 1961 increased only for low-prestige jobs. Moreover, British over-representation in the professional and financial category increased from 1.6 percent in 1931 to 2 percent in 1961. The table seems to substantiate the old adage that "the rich get richer and the poor get poorer."

Darroch (1980) has extensively examined the over-under occupational representations of various ethnic groups. Using an index to measure the discrepancy between an ethnic group's occupational distribution and that of the entire labour force, Darroch determined the ethnic job distribution for 1971, and compared his findings with previous data. Darroch found that, for most ethnic categories, occupational differentiation had been substantially reduced. However, for Native people, comparison of the 1951 index (23.9) with the 1971 index (29.0) shows a considerable increase.

About 20 percent of Natives in the labour force are classified as farmers or farm workers. An additional 36 percent are evenly split between production work and traditional activities, such as hunting and trapping. Some 15 percent are loggers and another 24 percent work at non-specific low-status jobs. Only 3 percent of Native workers occupy managerial or professional positions: this can be compared to the managerial and professional representation of the French (8 percent), the British (12 percent), and the Jews (40 percent).

The data for 1971 show that many Natives are leaving labouring jobs and becoming more involved in the commercial and social-service sectors. However, this shift is much less pronounced than that found in the wider Canadian population. Thus, while Natives are gaining in absolute terms, in relative terms they are falling further and further behind.

So far, we have confined our discussion to those Natives actually in the labour force. The over-all labour-force participation rate for Natives

TABLE 6.10   *Over-under representation of the male labour force*

Occupational Category	British	Indian and Inuit
1931		
Professional and financial	+1.6	-4.5
Clerical	+1.5	-3.7
Personal service	-0.3	-3.1
Primary and unskilled	-4.6	+45.3
Agriculture	-3.0	-4.9
All others	+4.8	-29.1
1951		
Professional and financial	+1.6	-5.2
Clerical	+1.6	-5.2
Personal service	-0.3	-0.6
Primary and unskilled	-2.2	+47.0
Agriculture	-3.2	-7.8
All others	+2.5	-28.2
1961		
Professional and financial	+2.0	-7.5
Clerical	+1.3	-5.9
Personal service	-0.9	+1.3
Primary and unskilled	-2.3	+34.7
Agriculture	-1.5	+6.9
All others	+1.4	-29.5

SOURCES: *Census of Canada,* 1931, monograph 4, Table 67, and Vol. 7, Table 40; *Census of Canada,* 1951, Vol. 4, Table 12; *Census of Canada,* 1961, Vol. 3.1-15, Table 21. Reproduced by permission of Information Canada.

is close to the national average: 56 percent as compared to 61 percent, respectively. However, depending on the statistical source, while between 10 and 12 percent of the total population are unemployed, between 40 and 60 percent of Natives are out of work. Moreover, the most recent data show that about 35 percent of working Natives are employed for less than a half a year (DIAND, 1980) although this is considerably better than the 51 percent reported in the early 1960s, it is still over three times the national rate.

Certain regions of Canada are considered high-unemployment areas and offer few opportunities to either Natives or non-Natives. As Figure

6.5 shows, Natives are heavily concentrated in areas of high unemployment. Even when economic expansion in the West or North provides increased opportunities, the high-level training required generally restricts Native participation.

In addition to regular federal employment programs, the Department of Indian Affairs provides a number of services to help Natives find jobs and relocate if necessary. Since 1974, DIAND has assisted in the relocation of nearly 700 families at a cost of nearly $700 000. DIAND has generally encouraged Natives to move off reserves in high-unemployment areas and to enter areas with higher job-potential. An off-reserve housing program has been established to provide equity and loan assistance to Natives who purchase houses in non-Native communities. In 1978-79, approximately 200 families used this service at a federal cost of slightly over $1 million. In some provinces, DIAND works along with Outreach programs designed specifically for Natives. Outreach programs have been in operation since 1972; between 1975 and 1979, they had an annual expenditure of nearly $700 000.

These federal programs are attempting to raise Natives to an average Canadian standard of living. Unfortunately, the programs offer too little to be more than bandaid measures; they also operate only for short periods of time as pilot projects. In addition, the programs are generally designed only to meet the needs of middle-class Natives. Finally, the independent structure of the programs reflects a lack of wide-ranging, integrated federal policy.

DIAND summarizes the bleak employment outlook for Indians as follows:

> The increase in the working-age population of 50 000 to 60 000 over the next 10 to 15 years will far exceed recent rates of on-reserve job creation and will occur in an off-reserve employment market already saturated by the earlier national "baby boom".

> The low levels of labour-force participation reflect a continuing reliance on traditional pursuits as well as dependence on social support.

> In the absence of successful job creation, social support for increasing numbers of unemployed Indians may double over the next 10 to 15 years.

> Despite improvements in education and shifts toward more active involvement in professional pursuits, Indian earnings are still below national levels.

> Both expanded on-reserve economic development and improved access to off-reserve labour and commodity markets cannot be achieved in time to provide sufficient job opportunities on reserves for the rapid increase in the working-age population over the next 10 years, without an immediate and massive focus on Indian economic development. (*Survey*, 1980)

FIGURE 6.5   *Local labour market: percentage of the Indian population of living in high unemployment areas*

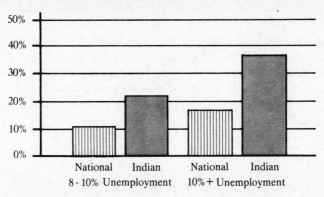

SOURCES: CEIC; Statistics Canada; Statistics Division, DIAND.

The average duration of employment per year for Natives is 4.8 months. Looking at more specific figures, Hawthorn et al. show that about 25 percent of employable males worked for less than two months in 1966. About 65 percent of employable males worked for less than six months, and 10 percent were employed for six to nine months. Although specific data are not available, sources from DIAND suggest that most Indian females have, at one time or another, been in the labour force; however, fewer than 5 percent of these have worked for more than six months in a year. Only 28 percent of the total employable Native population were employed for longer than nine months. In another study, Buckley, Kew, and Hawley (1963) found that of 2 200 northern Saskatchewan Indians and Métis in the labour force, fewer than 200 had year-round jobs. More recent data show that these trends have scarcely varied since.

About 20 percent of the employable Native population does not participate at all in the labour force. However, as Table 6.11 shows, of those who do participate, over 12 percent will remain permanently unemployed. These figures should be approached warily. The criteria that determine the active labour force are largely based upon White middle-class values and include only those Natives who have worked or looked for work during the past week. Moreover, because primary and unskilled jobs are extremely susceptible to seasonal factors, the time of year has a disproportionate impact on the Native employment rate. However, even taking these factors into account, Native unemployment is still three times higher than the national average.

Table 6.12 shows a breakdown of employment rates for Natives by residence. The data reveal that the participation rate in the labour force for Natives off the reserve is not much higher than for those on the reserve: 35.7 percent and 27.9 percent respectively. However, the higher participation rate of off-reserve Natives is not balanced by a corresponding increment in the actual employment rate; indeed, the employment increase is less than half the participation increase. Clearly, then, only about half of those who leave the reserve can expect to find employment.

TABLE 6.11   Indian[1] and Canadian labour force and employment rates, 1961

	Rate of employment		Participation rate		Labour force[2]	
	Indian	Canadian	Indian	Canadian	Indian	Canadian
Newfoundland	95.8	91.4	22.2	42.7	72	113 771
PEI	96.0	97.4	19.3	51.3	25	34 339
Nova Scotia	83.6	95.7	24.2	49.7	415	238 750
New Brunswick	89.7	94.1	25.2	48.5	362	179 702
Quebec	79.7	95.5	30.5	52.4	3 259	1 178 710
Ontario	90.3	96.6	34.4	56.8	9 264	2 404 812
Manitoba	84.5	97.2	25.8	55.3	3 868	343 938
Saskatchewan	90.6	98.0	29.1	53.5	4 462	326 736
Alberta	91.5	97.2	32.6	56.9	4 746	491 487
BC	84.7	94.7	28.4	51.9	5 847	581 395
Yukon	74.6	94.9	34.0	66.9	418	6 257
NWT	95.0	97.8	30.9	54.2	911	7 463
Canada	87.7	96.1	30.3	54.0	33 649	5 907 360

[1]On- and off-reserve Indians.

[2]Number of people 15 years and older employed or seeking employment during the week before enumeration.

SOURCE: *Brief to Special Senate Committee on Poverty 1970*, DIAND, 14: 170-171. Reproduced by permission of Information Canada.

TABLE 6.12   Indian labour force and employment by residence, 1961

	On-reserve			Off-reserve		
	Labour force	Employment rate	Participation rate	Labour force	Employment rate	Participation rate
Newfoundland	—	—	—	72	95.8	22.3
PEI	22	95.4	17.2	3	100.0	—
Nova Scotia	296	81.1	20.9	119	89.9	40.2
New Brunswick	307	88.5	23.9	55	96.4	35.5
Quebec	3 152	80.3	31.3	107	63.6	17.2
Ontario	5 009	88.9	28.8	4 255	91.9	44.4
Manitoba	2 464	80.7	23.4	1 404	91.2	31.6
Saskatchewan	2 712	89.1	21.3	1 750	92.9	34.3
Alberta	2 673	90.1	31.0	2 073	92.3	34.8
BC	4 464	86.9	27.8	1 383	77.7	30.6
Yukon	27	77.7	38.6	391	74.7	33.7
NWT	—	—	—	911	95.1	30.9
Canada	21 126	86.3	27.9	12 523	88.4	35.7

SOURCE: *Brief to Special Senate Committee on Poverty, 1970*, DIAND 14:172-73. Reproduced by permission of Information Canada.

Because Natives usually work at seasonal or part-time jobs, they have little job security. And, even in seasonal jobs, Natives are often discriminated against. La Rusic (1968) found that highly skilled Indian men employed by mining-exploration companies as line-cutters and stakers never received the same high pay or good working conditions that Whites received. Thus, the low income of Natives does not only reflect the seasonal nature of their jobs.

EDUCATION

Canadian culture places a great deal of emphasis on the value of education. Education is generally seen as essential to success; young people who do not show academic potential are usually regarded as early failures. Certainly, education has a great impact on lifestyle and life chances. Yet, for a variety of reasons, not all Canadians are able to use the educational system as effectively as possible. Native Canadians, in particular, are excluded by several factors from the benefits of White education.

The federal government does appear to have fulfilled its responsibility to Natives in the area of finance for education (Frideres, 1972). Federal expenditure for Native education was $13.5 million in 1956 and $52 million in 1967; by 1980, it reached well over $270 million, or 39 percent of the total Indian-Inuit Affairs budget. However, less than 1 percent of this money has gone directly to Native communities for Native control. Most has been spent on the creation of various federal administrative and bureaucratic positions or on capital grants to provincial and local governments to purchase "seats" in non-Native schools. Natives themselves have had little control over the money allotted for their education and have had little input into the educational process. In each province, the curriculum used in Native schools is regulated by the provincial government and is the same as that designed for White, middle-class students in all the other public schools (Waubageshig, 1970). This process is now undergoing scrutiny.

History of Native Education   For many years after Britain took control of Canada, Native education was controlled by the military, acting for the Crown. Then legislation was passed in 1830 and provincial or local governments assumed the responsibility.

> Several legislatures had made provisions for the attendance of Indians at schools serving non-Indian children, including the payment to local authorities in both Upper and Lower Canada for the incorporation of Indian reserves into established school districts or school sections and some provision had been made in the statutes for the financing of Indian education. (Special Senate Hearing on Poverty, 1970:14, 59)

In general, White settlers were indifferent to Native education: a public fund was not established for this purpose until 1848. In some cases, White settlers encouraged the school enrolment of Native children to pressure the province to establish more schools. However, as the density of the White population increased, Native education was increasingly ignored. Later, the federal government was reluctant to operate schools for Indians, and passed the responsibility to other, mainly religious, agencies.

With passage of the *British North America Act,* Canada's Parliament was given the power to administer Native affairs, including education. In 1876, the *Indian Act* was passed, providing the legal basis for federal administration of Native education. In addition, most treaties signed after 1871 contained a commitment:

> To maintain schools for instruction on the reserve and whenever the Indians of the reserve shall desire it or to make such provision as may from time to time be deemed advisable for the education of Indian children.

Federal and provincial government policy on Native education can be considered in two phases. The first, from 1867 to 1945, has been labelled the "paternalistic ideology" while the second, from 1945 to the present, has been called the "democratic ideology" (Hawthorn et al., 1967). The second phase simply refers to the "open door policy" that enabled Natives to attend school off the reserve.

The paternalistic policy, by which Natives were considered backward children, was adopted and perpetuated by various religious orders in Canada. After Confederation, the first schools for Natives were quasi-educational institutions set up by religious groups. Under Sections 113 to 122 of the *Indian Act,* the federal government could legally arrange for provincial governments and religious organizations to provide Native education. Four churches – Roman Catholic, Anglican, United, and Presbyterian – began to "educate" Natives in their denominational or residential schools.[3] Of these, the Catholics and Anglicans have had the greatest impact on Natives in Canada, and continue to do so.

Education has traditionally been viewed by the churches as the best way to acculturate Native people. The religious missionaries who, up until recently, controlled Native education, were far more concerned with the instilling of White language, values, and religious ideology than with teaching useful knowledge and skills. Because they felt that Natives would always live in isolation, the missionaries made no attempt to prepare them for successful careers in Canadian society. Instead, they concentrated on eradicating all traces of Native languages, traditions, and beliefs.

Paying little attention to the multitude of linguistic and other cultural differences among the tribes, and the varied traditions of child-rearing in preparation for adulthood in the tribal communities, the government entered the school business with a vigour that caused consternation among the Indians. The package deal that accompanied literacy included continuing efforts to 'civilize the natives' .... Children were removed – sometimes forcibly – long distances from their homes, the use of Indian languages by children was forbidden under threat of corporal punishment, students were boarded out to White families during vacation times, the Native religions were suppressed. (Fuch, 1970:55)

Because religious ideologies are fundamentally conservative, they discouraged protest and revolt on the part of the Natives. For example, Roman Catholicism holds that poverty is not a social evil, but is God's will. Instead of struggling against God's will, Catholics are encouraged to humbly accept their fates to ensure a place in heaven. Thus Roman Catholicism discourages social change, particularly that which involves force: in heaven, "the first shall be last and the last shall be first".

Churches that operated schools were given land, per capita grants, and other material rewards for their efforts.[4] Often, these grants resulted in the material exploitation of the Natives as churches pursued property and profits (McCullum & McCullum, 1975). Even today, the churches' continuing opposition to integrated joint schools, Native teachers, Native language use, and so on suggests a greater concern for their vested financial interests than for the quality of Native education. As Hawthorn et al. point out:

We note that the greater the educational resources possessed by a church or the greater its investment in Indian education, the greater its anxiety to maintain the status quo. On the contrary, the faiths having the least material interests in Indian education are much more open to innovation. (1967:61)

Well over half of Canada's Natives today are Roman Catholic. A special joint Senate-House of Commons Committee (1946-48) interpreted Sections 113 to 122 of the *Indian Act* to stipulate that, when the majority of Native band members belong to a given religion, members of that religion must be in charge of education in that school. This suggests that religious groups will continue to control many Native schools, despite their proven antipathy to Native independence.

Until 1945, Native schooling was "education in isolation":

During this period, schools and hostels for Indian children were established, but scant attention was paid to developing a curriculum geared to either their language difficulties or their sociological needs. A few Indian bands established schools for their children on the reserves, but the majority of them had neither the financial nor leadership resources to establish and operate their own schools. Provincial governments were too preoccupied with their own priorities to become involved in Indian education. Missionaries provided a modicum of services, but their "noble savage" philosophy effectively insulated the Indians from the mainstream of society. (Special Senate Hearing on Poverty, 1970:14, 59)

Residential schools were almost all built in the country, far from White settlements. Contact between Native children and their parents was minimized. The schools were highly regimented and insisted on strict conformity. There were few adults, and most of these were non-Native: as a result, normal adult-child relations could not develop. Few of the teachers were well qualified; they neither stimulated the children nor acted as positive role models. The average annual staff turnover was never less than 21 percent and often more, particularly in later years.

In 1945, the "open door policy" was introduced that allowed students to travel off the reserve to receive an education. This was a radical departure from the earlier policy of isolation, and residential schools began to decline in enrolment. Particularly since the early 1960s, the number of Native children attending residential schools has been drastically reduced. The unpopularity of these schools should come as a surprise to no-one.[5]

Types of Indian School   Today, Natives can attend either federal schools or integrated joint schools. There are four types of federal school: day schools; denominational (also called residential or religious) schools; boarding and hospital schools; and band schools.

Day schools form the largest group under federal control. They are located on the reserve and provide education only for those who live there, including the non-Native children of teachers and so on.

Denominational schools are those operated by a religious group. Since the late 1930s, DIAND has also operated residential schools; at first DIAND acted through the churches and, more recently, directly. When day schools were established in 1950 for elementary education, residential schools began to provide secondary education only. Since the late 1960s, these schools have been systematically shut down; as of 1979, there were fewer than twenty, mostly in Saskatchewan.

Hospital schools provide classes for Natives in government hospitals from the pre-school level through to adult education. Boarding schools are for Native orphans or children from broken homes, and may or may not be on the reserve.[6] All boarding schools are presently under government-financed church control, mainly Roman Catholic. While technically integrated, they have a majority of Native students.

Band schools are a recent phenomenon. Each band school is operated directly by a band or bands, but is financed by the federal
government. At present, only 8 percent of federal schools for Natives
are band-operated.

Integrated joint schools are not controlled by the federal government. Essentially, these are provincial schools that allow Natives to
attend. The structure and curricula of these schools are no different
than in those controlled by the federal government. The difference lies
with the administration and financing. Although education is a provincial responsibility, the federal government pays each local school board
a per diem fee for each Native child enrolled there.[7]

In 1963-64, approximately 55 000 Indians were enrolled in elementary and secondary schools. Of these, 59 percent were in federal day
schools, 13 percent were in residential schools, and 1 percent were in
hospital schools. The remaining 27 percent were attending integrated
joint schools. Data from the Indian Inuit Affairs Program (IIAP) shows
the number of joint school agreements that were operating in 1976. (see
Table 6.13.) Over 600 agreements were made reserving over 41 000
spaces for Native children. Preliminary estimates for 1980 suggest that
the number of agreements has increased to nearly 700, comprising over
50 000 spaces. Table 6.14 breaks down this enrolment distribution into
elementary and secondary categories. It also adds categories for special
schools and Natives who are absent from the reserve.

TABLE 6.13   *Integrated joint school agreements,*
31 March 1976

Region	Number of Agreements	Spaces reserved
Maritimes	13	1 248
Quebec	29	3 404
Ontario	123	7 273
Manitoba	76	5 772
Saskatchewan	130	7 685
Alberta	81	5 626
British Columbia	155	10 021
Yukon	16	481
Canada	623	41 510

SOURCE: Elementary and Secondary School Division,
Education Branch; prepared by Program
Statistics Division, IIAP, December, 1976.

TABLE 6.14 *Indian enrolment by school and grade*

Year and Type of School	Grade				Special	Absent from reserve[1]	Total
	Pre-1	1-6	7-8	9-13			
1961-62	3 560	32 746	5 698	3 381	739	1 616	47 740
Federal	3 403	24 256	3 361	596	739	–	32 355
Non-federal	157	8 490	2 337	2 785	–	1 616	15 385
1962-63	3 759	34 035	5 772	3 830	590	1 924	49 910
Federal	3 407	24 262	3 004	737	590	–	32 000
Non-federal	352	9 773	2 768	3 093	–	1 924	17 910
1963-64	3 897	35 453	6 161	4 065	770	4 575	54 921
Federal	3 575	24 791	3 089	750	506	–	32 711
Non-federal	322	10 662	3 072	3 315	264	4 575	22 210
1964-65	4 027	36 229	6 758	4 761	804	4 686	57 265
Federal	3 422	24 067	3 292	768	509	–	32 058
Non-federal	605	12 162	3 466	3 993	295	4 686	25 207
1965-66	3 660	38 929	7 107	5 220	1 013	5 466	61 395
Federal	3 093	24 566	3 203	716	462	–	32 040
Non-federal	567	14 363	3 904	4 504	551	5 466	29 355
1970-71 Federal and Non-federal	6 836	29 321[2]	25 568[3]	5 149[4]	1 575	–	68 449
1975-76 Federal and Non-federal	8 582	27 990[2]	27 557[3]	6 332[4]	1 356	–	71 817

[1]Pupils (and parents) living off the reserves in communities with educational facilities usually attend non-federal schools, but school records are not maintained by Indian Affairs.
[2]Grade category is 1-6. [3]Grade category is 7-8.
[2]Grade category is 1-4. [3]Grade category is 5-9. [4]Grade category is 10-13.

SOURCE: *Summary of Indian Enrolment by Grade, Canada, 1961-76*, Program Reference Centre IIAP.

Table 6.14 shows the distribution on Native enrolment from 1961 to 1976. Clearly, Native children are increasingly attending non-federal schools. In 1961, over two-thirds of Native elementary and high-school students went to federal schools. In 1966, this had dwindled to 52 percent. And by 1971, nearly two-thirds of Native elementary and high-school students were enrolled in non-federal schools. This trend has continued to the present, and shows no sign of abating.

Since the late 1960s, the Department of Indian Affairs, under pressure from various sources, has begun to emphasize the development of Native-controlled schools in Native communities. This is particularly true in the Western provinces. Indian Affairs has found that, when Natives control the education of their children, the secondary participation of the community rises and the retention rate for students increases. At present, it is too early to assess the impact of band-operated schools. However, although band schools did not exist in 1966, by 1979 they had gained 8 percent of the Native student population.

School Attendance: Primary and Secondary   Most Native children attend federal schools until grade six, then switch to non-federal schools for their secondary educations. Fewer than 10 percent continue in the federal school system, due to a lack of federal secondary schools. The remainder are forced to attend non-federal schools whether or not they choose to.

The switch from one school-system to another has a serious disruptive influence on the educational and social development of Native children. The change of social milieu has the greatest negative impact. Initially, Native children enter federal schools as a distinct cultural group with a minimal knowledge of English or French. However, because they all share a similar social status no one is at a disadvantage. When these students transfer, they are broken up and sent to different provincial schools where they become outsiders among White students who have spoken English or French from birth.

Native students at provincial schools face considerable discrimination. On the reserve, these students have already met indirect, institutionalized racism; however, as Lyon et al. (1970) have shown, Native students in integrated schools are exposed daily to direct discrimination by teachers and other students. In the long term, racism results in a serious and permanent distortion of the Native children's self-concepts. The more short-term effects of dicrimination include lower marks and a tendency to drop out at an early age.

Elliott (1970) draws attention to age differences as a disruptive factor for Native students in provincial schools. As Hawthorn et al. (1967:132) show, only 12 percent of Native students are in the same age-grade as their White counterparts.[8] On average, Native students are about

TABLE 6.15 *Student enrolment[1] as a percentage of the corresponding Indian population*

| | Age groups | | | | |
	4-5 years	6-9 years	10-13 years	14-18 years	Total 4-18 years
	percent in school				
1969-70	42.9	90.0	91.2	57.7	74.1
1970-71	40.1	94.5	98.6	68.5	80.0
1971-72	41.1	92.3	99.1	69.3	80.1
1972-73	39.6	88.1	100.0	73.4	80.0
1973-74	48.6	90.2	101.9	67.5	80.8
1974-75	60.3	98.6	97.1	64.7	82.6

[1]Includes non-Indian children, such as the children of teachers living on reserves, who are enrolled in federal and band-administered schools. Figures may therefore be somewhat inflated and exceed 100.0 percent in some categories.

SOURCE: Information Canada, *Perspective Canada II*, (Ottawa: Queen's Printer, 1977), 290.

two-and-a-half years older than their White classmates. At the federal schools, all the students are Native; therefore, in any one grade-level, they are all over-age to the same degree. However, in an integrated school, the Native students face feelings of inferiority as they are placed in classrooms with White students who are considerably younger than they are.

Elliott also claims that the competitive environment in provincial schools poses problems for Native children. The competition for achievement is greater in integrated schools than in federal schools. Native children, not used to the intense competition that exists among White, middle-class students, may become psychologically uncomfortable and begin to lose academic ground. Native children do not get adequate counselling prior to or following placement in integrated schools. Not surprisingly, these social disruptions eventually result in a high drop-out rate among Native students.

Table 6.15 looks at the student enrolment of Indians from 1969 to 1975 as a percentage of the corresponding general Indian population. For each age group, there has been a clear increase in the number of Indians attending school. Virtually all Indians attend school between the ages of six and thirteen, resulting in a participation rate comparable to that of the general Canadian population. The rate for four-to-five years olds is low, but still comparable to the national average. However, for the age category of fourteen to eighteen, the participation of Indians is markedly lower than the national average. Fewer than two-thirds of the Indian population in this age group are attending school.

Overall, the educational enrolment figures since 1971 show that most Native children are now enrolled in school, if not actually attending full-time. By 1979, nearly 75 000 Native students were enrolled, representing approximately 83 percent of all Native children between the ages of four and eighteen.

Successful school completion to grades twelve or thirteen still much lower among Native students than among Canadians as a whole. In 1966, fewer than 10 percent of Indian students remained in school throughout the twelve or thirteen years. Although dramatic increases have since occurred, Figure 6.6 shows that the rate for Indians remains less than one-quarter of the national rate.

The enrolment and drop-out rates show that, in 1969-70, 57.7 percent of the registered Indian population between fourteen and eighteen were enrolled in school. This figure increased to 73.4 percent in 1972-73, then decreased to 64.7 percent in 1975-76, according to the latest available

FIGURE 6.6　*Retention: percentage of Indian students remaining to grade 12 from grade 2, ten years earlier*

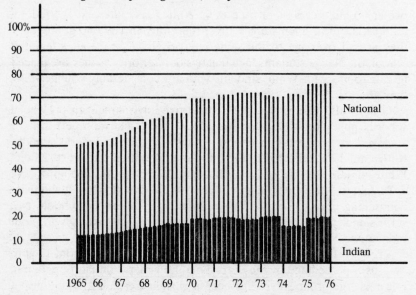

SOURCES:　*Education in Canada,* Cat. no 81-229, Statistics Canada; Re-calculation of Table E-1, E-11 in *Socio-Economic Forecasts for Registered Indians in Canada 1976-77 to 1989-90,* D.E. Stewart, P.R.E., DIAND, 1977.

TABLE 6.16 *Enrolment of registered Indians by type of school (in percent)*

	Kindergarten	Grades 1-8	Grades 9-13	University	Vocational	Other[1]	Total Students
1959-60	–	93.2	5.6	0.1	0.1	1.0	40 637
1964-65	7.2	78.6	8.8	0.2	1.9	3.3	53 464
1966-67	6.1	77.0	8.8	0.2	2.3	5.6	60 840
1968-69	8.5	71.4	10.2	0.3	2.6	7.0	67 658
1970-71	8.6	64.5	11.2	0.5	2.9	12.3	79 395
1972-73	9.3	61.8	11.8	1.1	4.1	11.9	84 223
1974-75	10.8	60.0	11.6	2.4	4.3	10.9	86 144

[1]Includes full-time students enrolled in special courses, nursing training, upgrading, other miscellaneous courses, and teacher training.

SOURCE: Information Canada, *Perspective Canada II*, (Ottawa: Queen's Printer, 1977), 289.

TABLE 6.17   *Enrolment of registered Indians in kindergarten,*
high school, and university, 1949-77

	Kindergarten enrolment	University enrolment	High school enrolment as a percentage of total school enrolment[1]
1949-50	—	9[2]	3 0
1953-54	—	—	4 6
1957-58	2 562	27	5 9
1961-62	3 560	50	8 1
1965-66	3 583	131	10 2
1969-70	6 807	321	13 3
1973-74	8 666	1 055	16 5
1974-75	9 273	2 047	16 2
1975-76	8 582	2 071	17 1
1976-77	8 668	—	17 3

[1]Students in grades 9-13 as a percentage of all students enrolled in grades 9-13.
[2]Figure is for 1948-49.

SOURCES: Departmental Statistics Division, DINA; Information
Canada, *Perspectives Canada III,* (Ottawa: Queen's
Printer, 1980), 178.

statistics. Apparently, the enrolment of fourteen- to eighteen-year-old Natives has reached a peak and is now declining. The rate of mid-year school drop-outs for this age group supports this conclusion: between 1974-75 and 1976-77, the drop-out rate increased from 3.1 to 9.6 percent.

Table 6.16 shows the enrolment of registered Indians in various types of school. The data show that, in 1960, very few Indians went beyond the elementary level. However, by 1974-75, over one-quarter of Indians were enrolled beyond that level. Table 6.17 shows that the high-school enrolment of registered Indians is increasing substantially and, in 1977, made up nearly 20 percent of the total Native school enrolment.

Quality of Native Education   The quality of Native education is determined by a variety of factors. These include operation and maintenance costs, pupil-teacher ratios, the proportion of Native teachers, educational expenditures, and overall per-student education costs.

Except in Manitoba, the pupil-teacher ratio for federal schools is lower than that for provincial schools. While this suggests that the quality of Native education is inferior, two factors qualify this somewhat. First, because federal schools have few students and high instruction costs, there is a tendency to combine several grades into a single class. Second, an increasingly large number of Native students are no longer attending federal schools.

Operation and maintenance costs for Natives in federal and provincial schools have escalated rapidly, rising from approximately $65 million in 1970 to $164 million in 1980. These increases appear to be keeping pace with increasing Native student enrolments and with the general increase in all educational costs.

Between 1970 and 1980, total educational expenditures for Natives decreased relative to the total DIAND from nearly 50 percent to 39 percent. In current-dollar terms, expenditures per student have doubled since 1970, matching the national average. In constant-dollar terms, this represents a modest 3 percent decline. In 1979, for each Native student, $2 600 was spent in federal schools and $2 250 in provincial schools; the national average is $1 900.

The proportion of Native teachers in federal schools tripled between 1966 and 1979, to approximately 27 percent. However, although 90 percent of the teachers in Native schools have formal teaching credentials, only about 13 percent are university graduates.

Educational Attainment   In terms of financial aid, DIAND appears to be providing adequate educational opportunities to Native students. Yet most Natives attain only a low level of educational achievement. Tables 6.18 and 6.19 present data on the educational attainments of Native Canadians.

Table 6.18 shows that, in 1961, nearly a quarter of the registered Indian population over fifteen had no formal education. An additional quarter had less than five years of formal education. Younger people appeared to be better educated; only 10 percent of Indians between fifteen and thirty-four had no formal education compared to almost 50

TABLE 6.18   *Educational achievement of Indians 15 and older, 1961 (in percent)*

Age	None	Elementary 1-4	Elementary 5+	Secondary	University
15-34	10.4	18.5	50.6	20.1	0.4
34-55	26.3	27.4	38.2	7.8	0.3
55+	48.2	29.0	19.7	3.0	0.2
Total 15+	21.0	22.7	42.0	13.8	0.3

SOURCE: Statistics Canada 1961 *Census of Canada.* Reproduced by permission of Information Canada.

TABLE 6.19   *Educational attainment of Native people and all Canadians by selected age groupings, 1971 (in percent)[1]*

| | Age group | | | |
| | 15-19 years | | 20 years and over | |
	Indians and Inuit[2]	All Canada	Indians and Inuit[2]	All Canada
Grades 1-8	58.7	12.8	79.6	36.8
Grades 9-13	39.0	75.3	15.0	36.0
Some university	0.5	4.9	1.7	11.9
Other post-secondary	1.8	7.0	3.7	15.3
Total	100.0	100.0	100.0	100.0

[1]Includes only those individuals who were not full-time students of any educational program or institution.
[2]Includes only those Indians and Inuit who reported Indian or Inuit languages as their mother tongue in the 1971 Census of Canada.
SOURCE: Information Canada, *Perspective Canada II,* (Ottawa: Queen's Printer, 1977), 290.

percent of those fifty-five and older. However, all Indians over fifteen lagged far behind their White counterparts. In general, nearly 90 percent of Indians had not finished high school.

Table 6.19 presents more recent data on Natives over fifteen-years-old, and allows for a comparison with the national population. In 1971, the number of Natives between the ages of fifteen and nineteen who had reached secondary school was almost five times lower than the national average. Among those twenty and over, the proportion is less extreme but still marked; this is largely due to substantially lower educational achievement in the White population. At the higher educational levels, the number of Natives with "some university" or "other post-secondary" education is less than half the national figure.

Table 6.20 looks specifically at the educational attainments of the Native population between fifteen and sixty-four, comparing them to the national average. The overall pattern remains the same, but the focus on the working-age population gives us some indication as to the success of Natives in the labour force. Between 1971 and 1976, the educational achievement of Natives apparently increased, particularly at the "some high school" level which, by 1976, was nearly equal to the national average. However, Native representation in the "some post-secondary" level has decreased since 1966, relative to the national figures (DIAND, *Survey,* 1980).

TABLE 6.20 *Educational attainment of selected working-age populations, 1971 and 1976 (in percent)*[1]

	1971		1976	
	Indians and Inuit[2]	Canada	Non-status Indians and Métis	Canada
Grade 8 or less	79.6	36.8	49.8	24.6
Some high school	15.0	36.0	47.7	49.5
Some post secondary	5.4	27.2	2.5	25.9
Total	100.0	100.0	100.0	100.0

[1]Comparisons between the data for 1971 and 1976 should be made with caution. The figures represent different Native population groups and have been collected by different statistical agencies.
[2]Includes Indians and Inuit who reported a Native language as their mother tongue in the 1971 *Census of Canada.*

SOURCES: 1971 *Census of Canada,* unpublished data; *Survey of Métis and Non-Status Indians,* Native Council of Canada and Native Employment Division, Canada Employment and Immigration Commission, Ottawa, 1977.

Post Secondary School Attendance Beyond the elementary-school level, and particularly beyond the secondary level, the pattern of Native student enrolment diverges sharply from the Canadian norm. As Table 6.19 shows, fewer than 1 percent of Natives attend university, as compared to nearly 7 percent of the general population. Of all Native students involved in any form of post-secondary education, 60 percent are enrolled in vocational training; this refers to programs in such areas as carpentry, sheet metal work, motor mechanics, and farming. Another 30 percent of Native post-secondary students are enrolled in "upgrading" courses; although these can range from courses on canning preserves to courses in advanced mathematics, they most often signify the former type. It seems clear that nearly all Natives who enrol in post-secondary training are being prepared for jobs at the semi-skilled level or lower (DIAND, *1978-79 Annual Report*).

Table 6.21 offers a more specific breakdown of Native participation in post-secondary courses. The figures show a curvilinear pattern. Until the mid-1970s, Native enrolment steadily increased in professional and vocational courses. Since then, however, Native enrolments have dramatically decreased in all areas but teacher training. This decrease is

TABLE 6.21　Indian enrolment in professional and vocational courses

	1967-68	1968-69	1969-70	1970-71	1978-79
Adult education					
Basic literacy	2 224	3 415	4 388	5 471	1 700
Other adult programs	6 833	9 652	11 964	14 638	3 000
Total	9 057	13 067	16 352	20 109	4 700
Vocational training					
Pre-vocational	598	1 443	3 888	4 285	1 500
Vocational skills	1 029	1 393	2 114	1 778	1 000
Technology	274	364	414	529	—
University	180	235	321	459	—
Teacher training	27	38	49	48	600
Nursing	18	20	24	24	30
Other	180	340	2 007[1]	2 248[1]	1 200
Total	2 306	3 833	8 817	9 371	4 330
Employment relocation					
Short term	8 135	8 676	6 292	6 236	—
Regular	3 206	3 460	5 697	5 966	—
In-service training	144	330	218	218	—
On-the-job training	95	257	269	530	—
Family relocations	287	509	502	416	—
Apprenticeship	—	—	73	125	—

[1]All courses were shorter than four months.
SOURCES:　DIAND, *Annual Report, 1969-70; 1970-71.* 1978-79 data is from survey.
　　　　　Reproduced by permission of Information Canada.

partly the result of some program cut-backs. It also reflects increased Native enrolment in provincial community colleges as well as an increased use of programs funded through the Canada Employment and Immigration Commission (CEIC). This conclusion would seem to be supported by the increased expenditures of CEIC and DIAND, as illustated in Figure 6.7.

Figures 6.8 and 6.9 show a dramatic increase since the early 1960s in the number of Natives attending university. A number of universities have tailored special programs to meet the interests and needs of Native students, while others have provided remedial services to assist Natives who are entering university. However, even though the increase in Native

FIGURE 6.7 *Technical training expenditures*

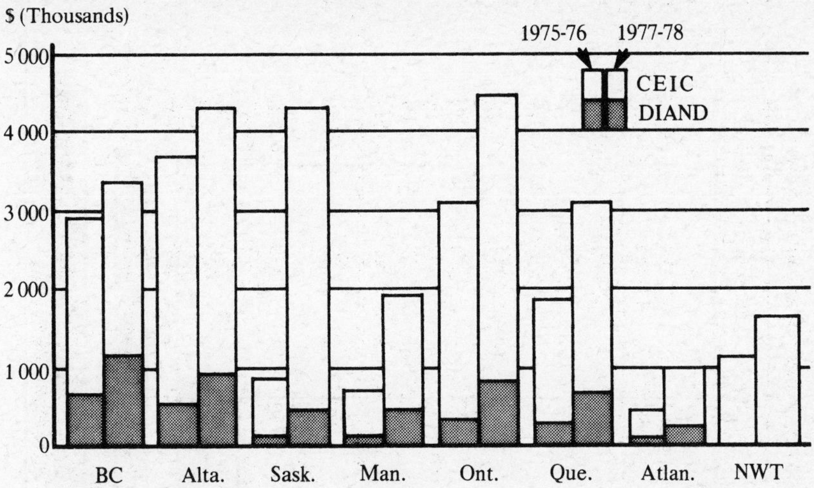

SOURCE: *Indian Survey, 1980,* DIAND, 86.

employment has been rapid, the Native participation rate is still less than one-half the national level. For example, in 1975, 12 percent of the Canadian population between the ages of eighteen and twenty-four were enrolled in universities, and only 5 percent of the Native population.

Even more dismal than the enrolment figures are the statistics that reflect the rate of graduation from universities. According to Table 6.22, 156 Native students were enrolled in universities in 1967-68. Of these, 17 percent withdrew voluntarily during the year and 15 percent failed one or more courses, generally resulting in automatic exclusion under the terms of their special-entry program. The rest passed all their courses, but, at the end of the program, only 6 percent remained to graduate. In 1970, 432 students were enrolled in universities and only 12 percent graduated. Clearly, a Native student's chances of finishing university are still quite small. Language and cultural differences, as well as the effects of discrimination, have not been adequately addressed and continue to place Native students at a serious disadvantage in the university system.

More recent information from Indian Affairs shows that, although Native enrolment in university increased substantially in the mid-1970s, it is once again decreasing. Table 6.23 shows an increase from slightly over 1 000 in 1974 to about double that figure in 1975 and 1976. This rapid increase largely resulted from increased enrolment in three areas: Saskatchewan, British Columbia, and the Yukon.

FIGURE 6.8   *University enrolment of Indians between 1957 and 1979*

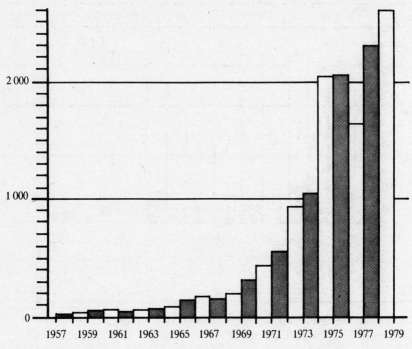

SOURCE: Employment and Related Services Division, DIAND, 1978.

FIGURE 6.9   *University enrolment: percentage of Indian population 18-24 years*

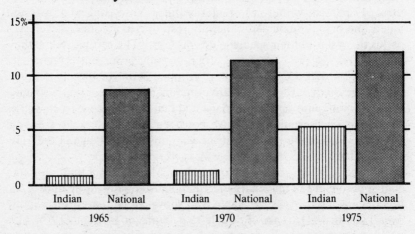

SOURCES: *Education in Canada,* Cat. no. 81-229, Statistics Canada; *Post-Secondary Courses for Indian Students,* 1965, 1975, DIAND; *Registered Indian Population by Age, Sex and Residence for Canada,* 1965, 1970, 1975, DIAND.

TABLE 6.22   *Performance of Indian university students*

	1964-65	1965-66	1966-67	1967-68
Enrolment	88	131	150	156
Graduates	5	8	13	10
Completed course	57	76	79	97
Failed course	5	7	15	23
Withdrew	21	40	43	26

SOURCE: *Brief to Special Senate Committee on Poverty, 1970,* DIAND, 14:65.
Reproduced by permission of Information Canada.

The reasons for the high drop-out rate among Native students are complex but straightforward. According to Castellano,

> ... the distorted reflection of himself which is presented to the Indian child is not even the chief source of the sense of incongruity which most Indian children experience in the White school system. Far more significant and handicapping is the fact that the verbal symbols and the theoretical constructions which the Indian child is asked to manipulate bear little or no relation to the social environment with which he is most familiar. (1970:53)

The Canadian educational system has been developed and refined by and for a White, urban, middle-class culture. This system becomes alien and meaningless in the context of life on a reserve (Fisher, 1969). The subject matter is largely irrelevant to the Native child's everyday life. Classes are taught by teachers who are almost always White and who seldom become involved with the local Native community. The competitive hierarchical structure of the school is foreign to Native values. And the curriculum is set firmly within a White, middle-class system of values, bearing little relation to local Native concerns. Not suprisingly, Native students are alienated from their educational system at a very young age.

Native students also have to contend with the poor image of themselves projected by the mass media, including films and books used in the schools. A recent study of social-studies texts for grades one through eight revealed that Natives were generally portrayed, if at all, as evildoers, non-entities, or savages (VanderBurgh, 1968). These portraits have a serious impact on the personal development of Native children. As Kardiner and Ovesey (1951) have pointed out, people who are continually ascribed negative traits will eventually begin to incorporate them into their identities. Someone who is continually called inferior will eventually believe it to be true.

Hawthorn et al. (1967), Elliott (1970), and others have argued that lack of parental support is an additional factor in the drop-out rate.

TABLE 6.23   *Indian university students*

Region	Year			
	1974	*1975*	*1976*	*1977*
Maritimes	108	108	66	213
Quebec	161	323	283	171
Ontario	157	231	319	122
Manitoba	309	343	410	190
Saskatchewan	43	470	446	447
Alberta	171	287	287	298
BC and Yukon	106	285	260	191
Canada	1 055	2 047	2 071	1 632

SOURCE: Statistics Section, Program Services Branch, IIAP, December 1978.

However, there are many structural reasons for this. Not surprisingly, because Native parents have no control over curriculum, choice of textbooks, or staff, they have come to regard the educational system as an "outside", racist institution, to be tolerated but not supported. In some provinces, Indians still cannot be school-board members.[9]

Active adult community support for education will only develop when Natives who live on the reserve are allowed to hold teaching and administrative positions. To blame parental neglect for the high drop-out rates is naive: when all the structural variables are considered, the reaction of Native parents to the educational system is not apathetic, but actively, and understandably, hostile.

Living Conditions and Quality of Life

Living conditions refer to specific objective factors that affect a Native's ability to maintain a quality of life commensurate with that of other modern Canadians. This includes such considerations as the availability and quality of housing and the provision of community services such as health care and welfare. As pointed out previously, the life expectancy of Natives is still ten years lower than the national average. Other indicators, such as the rates of suicide, violent death, and alcohol abuse, demonstrate a general increase in social problems and a lowering of the quality of life among reserve Indians.

HOUSING

The federal government has no legal or treaty obligation to provide housing units or repair existing ones for Natives. However, it does have a historical commitment to provide housing for Indians which, so far, it has chosen to continue.

Table 6.24 provides information with regard to general housing conditions on reserves. The actual number of houses on reserves has increased by 64 percent since the late 1950s. However, in 1977, over 1 000 Indian families lived in houses that were recorded as "needing replacement". Moreover, despite the increase in houses, crowding has become a way of life on the reserve. In 1977, nearly 65 percent of reserve houses contained two families, and an additional 4 percent of the reserve families were living in overcrowded conditions.

In 1977, DIAND estimated that 11 000 new housing units were needed on reserves. Because Native houses have a life span of fifteen years compared to a national average of thirty-five years, DIAND would therefore have had to double its current production rate to 4 400 units per

TABLE 6.24 *Housing Conditions on Indian reserves, 1958-75 (in percent)*

	1958	1963	1967	1971	1975
Portion of house per family[1]	87.8	86.3	87.7	89.2	91.5
Families requiring new housing[2]	31.6	20.3	24.3	25.4	—
Houses in good repair	40.4	50.7	49.7	47.4	51.4
Occupied houses requiring major repairs	80.0	7.3	11.1	15.9	28.2
Houses with:					
1-2 rooms	—	34.1	27.0	18.4	11.9
5 or more rooms	—	24.7	31.9	43.4	57.2
Electricity	—	44.8	57.3	79.0	81.2
Running water	—	13.8	19.2	30.2	34.1
Indoor toilet	—	8.5	12.1	23.1	32.7
Indoor bath	—	7.2	10.0	19.3	26.8
Telephone	—	10.2	16.4	25.2	33.1

[1]This represents the number of houses available on reserves divided by the number of families residing on the reserve. A figure of 100.0 would indicate there is one house per family. Figures less than that indicate that there are more families than houses.
[2]Figures are based on standards established by DIAND.
SOURCE: *Indian Housing Survey,* Program Statistics Division, DINA, 1958-75.

TABLE 6.25　Condition of housing on reserves[1]

	Good	Fair	Poor		Total	
		percent		percent	percent	number
All houses						
1958	40.4	30.2	29.4		100.0	22 809
1963	50.7	28.7	20.6		100.0	25 123
1969	49.6	26.5	23.9		100.0	28 417
1973[2]	45.9	30.6	23.5		100.0	27 071
Frame and other houses						
1958	—	—	—		—	—
1963	59.4	27.7	12.9		100.0	19 053
1969	55.0	26.8	18.2		100.0	24 111
1973[2]	47.9	31.5	20.6		100.0	24 929
Log houses						
1958	—	—	—		—	—
1963	23.3	31.6	45.1		100.0	6 070
1968	19.6	24.8	55.6		100.0	4 306
1973[2]	22.4	21.0	56.6		100.0	2 142

[1]The evaluation of the condition of Indian housing is based on a set of standards established by DIAND.
[2]No data were reported for the Brantford (Ontario) District, the Saddle Lake/Athabaska (Alberta) District, and for 23 bands in the Manitoba Region.
SOURCE:　Information Canada, *Perspective Canada II*, (Ottawa: Queen's Printer, 1977), 288.

year for the next five years. In addition, the number of houses requiring major repairs nearly doubled between 1971 and 1975. By rating housing conditions as good, fair, or poor, Table 6.25 provides an overview of housing conditions on reserves. Generally, slightly less than half the houses are in good condition.

Natives on reserves can obtain housing through a subsidy-housing program. In 1977, a new housing policy was established in an attempt to increase the number of housing units. However, the construction rate of new houses has not kept up with the demand.

TABLE 6.26   *Accessibility to Indian reserves and settlements, 1970*

		Means of access			
	Road	Road and rail	Water only		Total
	percent				settlements
Maritimes	48.4	40.6	11.0	100.0	64
Quebec	28.2	38.5	33.3	100.0	39
Ontario	32.0	28.5	39.5	100.0	172
Manitoba	20.6	32.4	47.0	100.0	102
Saskatchewan	49.2	26.7	24.1	100.0	120
Alberta	37.0	36.0	27.0	100.0	89
British Columbia	34.2	11.2	54.6	100.0	1 300
Canada[1]	34.7	17.7	47.6	100.0	1 886

[1]Includes the Yukon and the Northwest Territories.

SOURCE: Information Canada, *Perspective Canada II,* (Ottawa: Queen's Printer, 1977), 287.

Off-reserve Natives can obtain a small housing subsidy if they qualify for a regular mortgage; that is, if they are "assimilated", with a steady job and an income above the poverty line. Because of the rising cost of housing and spiralling interest rates, the fund has scarcely been used. Since 1967, only 2 339 houses have been subsidized under this program at a cost of nearly $20 million.

INFRASTRUCTURE SERVICES

The number and extent of government services available to Natives has a considerable impact on their quality of life. A major factor in the provision of services is accessibility by road or rail; without good transportation access, services are difficult and costly to provide. Yet, as Table 6.26 shows, only about a third of the reserves even have road access. Nearly half of all reserves and settlements are accessible only by water. And only 18 percent are accessible by both rail and road.

Figure 6.10 outlines the actual number of communities with electricity, sewage disposal, and running water. The data show that, on the average, 90 percent of reserve houses have electricity, 45 percent have sewage disposal, and 50 percent have running water. The percentage of reserves with adequate fire protection equipment has increased since 1970, but is still only about 35 percent. In Manitoba, less than 10 percent of reserves have sufficient equipment, but in the Yukon and the Atlantic provinces nearly 70 percent have adequate fire protection.

FIGURE 6.10   *Housing on Indian reserves with specified facilities*

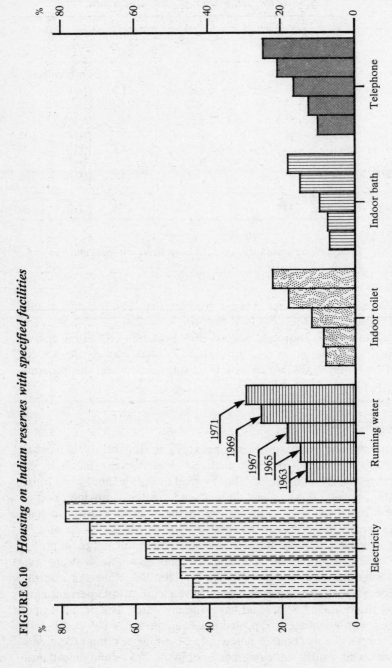

SOURCE: Information Canada, *Perspective Canada I*, (Ottawa: Queen's Printer, 1974), 249.

TABLE 6.27 *Government-financed assistance to Indians residing on reserves and crown lands, 1973-74*

	Reason for assistance				Average monthly number of persons[4] receiving assistance		Annual assistance per person	Total assistance
	Health[1]	Social[2]	Economic[3]	Total	Total	As percentage of 1974 reserve and crown lands' population		
	percent of persons receiving assistance							dollars
Maritimes	11.2	27.5	61.3	100.0	6 453	83.4	513	3 311 179
Quebec	10.7	19.7	69.6	100.0	6 348	27.3	461	2 927 077
Ontario	29.5	–	70.5	100.0	7 611	18.7	475	3 615 077
Manitoba	21.1	20.9	58.0	100.0	14 763	47.6	464	6 844 827
Saskatchewan	11.7	29.7	58.6	100.0	16 743	56.7	541	9 065 093
Alberta	17.2	28.1	54.7	100.0	15 400	57.9	488	7 515 127
British Columbia	17.1	41.7	41.2	100.0	11 102	32.3	727	8 072 260
Yukon	16.3	26.1	57.6	100.0	1 018	44.6	502	511 100
Canada[5]	16.8	24.3	58.9	100.0	79 438	40.7	519	41 861 740

[1]A family head or single person is unable to work or has inadequate earnings because of physical or mental disability, including advanced age.

[2]A family head or single person is unable to work or has inadequate income because he or she is giving care to an incapacitated spouse or parent, or is giving care and supervision to the dependent children in the family. Health and social reasons are combined in Ontario.

[3]A family head or single person does not come within either of the first two categories but is unable to work or has inadequate earnings because of a lack of employment opportunities.

[4]Includes family members dependent on the head of the family.

[5]Excludes Northwest Territories.

SOURCE: Information Canada, *Perspective Canada II*, (Ottawa: Queen's Printer, 1977), 291.

SOCIAL ASSISTANCE

The amount of social assistance provided to Natives indicates much about the quality of life on the reserve. As Tables 6.27 and 6.28 show, nearly 60 percent of federal assistance from 1972 to 1974 took the form of investments in economic programs while an additional 24 percent was directed at social problems. In all, over 40 percent of the 1974 reserve/crown-land population received assistance of some kind. About $519 dollars were spent per capita per year, comprising an annual expense of nearly $42 million.

These figures show considerable regional variation. In Ontario, 19 percent of Indians on reserves receive assistance, as compared to over 80 percent in the Maritimes. British Columbia and Manitoba use minority categories for the provision of assistance. Table 6.29 provides a more detailed breakdown of all federal expenditures for Indian-assistance programs, comparing the figures for 1970-71 with those from 1978-79.

TABLE 6.28   *Social assistance to Indians residing on reserves, 1972-73*

Administrative region	Reasons for assistance				Total amount of assistance
	Health[1]	Social[2]	Economic[3]	All	
	assistance per person in dollars				
Maritimes	581	549	486	511	2 869 565
Quebec	451	380	362	377	2 697 047
Ontario	428	—	428	428	3 319 658
Manitoba	498	445	265	347	5 251 259
Saskatchewan	481	450	432	442	8 464 499
Alberta	464	477	328	391	6 321 123
British Columbia	670	700	569	635	7 809 935
Yukon	423	487	464	470	604 290
Canada	498	514	395	442	37 337 376

[1]The family head or the single person is unable to work or has inadequate earnings because of physical or mental disability, including advanced age.
[2]The family head or the single person is unable to work or has inadequate income because he or she is giving care to an incapacitated spouse or parent or is giving care and supervision to the dependent children in the family. Health and Social reasons are combined in Ontario.
[3]The family head or the single person does not come within either of the first two categories and he or she is unable to work or has inadequate earnings because of a lack of employment or other earning opportunities.
SOURCE: Information Canada, *Perspective Canada I,* (Ottawa: Queen's Printer, 1974), 252.

Clearly, no major changes in priorities have occurred. Medical and social services still remain the focal point of federal programs and comprise over 80 percent of program expenditures.

In 1974, over half the total Indian reserve population received social assistance or welfare payments as compared to 6 percent of the national population. In addition, over 70 percent of the Indians who received welfare payments were employable. Moreover, quality of housing, health, and other social services provided on the reserves is lower than those provided elsewhere in Canada. These facts taken together suggest that social assistance is offered as an alternative to employment. As the rate of social assistance grows, it becomes increasingly evident that poor social conditions and economic opportunities will continue to keep Natives in a state of economic dependency.

FATALITY RATES

Poor health and high mortality rates on reserves are directly related to poor access to medical facilities, lack of sewage disposal, unchecked exposure to disease, and a general lack of health-care services. The mortality rate for Indians in 1963 was extremely high, 25 per 100.

TABLE 6.29 *Social support expenditures: all federal programs for Indians (including medical services)*

	1970-71		1978-79	
	$ *Thousands*	*%*	*$* *Thousands*	*%*
Social assistance	34 627	41.1	104 049	43.0
Child care	11 680	13.9	24 788	10.2
Alcoholism	167	0.2	5 539	2.3
Other social services (adult care, day care welfare aids	1 095	1.3	9 880	4.1
Medical services	36 599	43.4	94 002	38.8
Sports and recreation	99	0.1	2 211	0.9
Legal services and Native justice	—	—	1 689	0.7
Total	84 627	100.0	242 158	100.0

SOURCES: Financial Management Reports, DIAND; Financial Services, Health and Welfare Canada; Fitness and Amateur Sport Branch, Health and Welfare Canada; Solicitor General, Canada; Department of Justice.

Although this had decreased to 12 per 1 000 by 1977, it remains much higher than the national rate of 7 per 1 000. Infant mortality (up to four weeks) and post-neonatal mortality (four weeks to one year) have also been very high. In 1963, the post-neonatal mortality rate was 60 per 1 000, compared to 9 per 1 000 for the national population. By 1977, this rate had decreased substantially; however, at 15 per 1 000, it still remained twice as high as the national rate.

Accidents, violence, and poisoning account for over one-third of all Indian deaths, as compared to 9 percent of other Canadian deaths. Suicide has also become a significant cause of deaths, particularly for Natives between fifteen and thirty-four. The suicide rate for Natives generally is three times the national average; for those between fifteen and thirty-four, suicides account for well over one-fourth of accidental deaths. *The Indian News* claims that suicide among Natives is significantly under-reported; reporters found that, in Alberta, suicide accounted for one in every ten Native deaths.

Although the extent of Native alcoholism has been insufficiently researched, some officials estimate that 50 to 60 percent of Native illnesses and deaths are alcohol-related. *The Indian News* claims that, in its investigation of Native deaths, it found that more than 30 percent of deaths were directly due to the misuse of alcohol. Alcoholism has become a serious problem and has been recognized by DIAND as such. Table 6.29 shows a substantial increase since 1970 in funding to address alcoholism.

Deviance

As Schmeiser (1974) points out, any observer of the Canadian penal system cannot help but be aware of the immense social problem concerning Native offenders. The percentage of Natives in jail is far greater than the national average, and recidivism rates are also much higher.

Table 6.30 compares Native and non-Native inmates in federal penitentiaries. The two populations do not differ substantially except that far more Natives committed violent offences. The tables also show that, although Natives represent only 1.2 percent of the Canadian population, they comprise 9 percent of the inmate population in federal prisons.

As Table 6.31 shows, the percentage of Natives in provincial jails is astronomical, far greater even than in federal penitentiaries. Moreover, in most provinces, the rate of Native admissions is increasing. Much of this problem concerns Native women: in provincial jails, they constitute a much greater proportion of the female population than Native men do of the male population.

TABLE 6.30 *Selected characteristics of Native and non-Native inmates in federal penitentiaries, 1979*

Selected Characteristics	Inmates	
	Native[1]	Non-Native
Number[1]	802	8 442
Percent	8.7	91.3
Age group	%	%
Under 20	3.0	3.0
20-34	69.0	69.0
35 and Over	28.0	28.0
Total	100.0	100.0
Offence type	%	%
Violent[2]	48.0	27.0
Non-violent	52.0	73.0
Total	100.0	100.0
No. of previous commitments	%	%
0	62.0	65.0
1	19.0	21.0
2	12.0	9.0
3+	7.0	5.0
Total	100.0	100.0
Length of sentence	%	%
Under 2 yrs	7.0	4.0
2-3 yrs.	24.0	18.0
3+ yrs	69.0	78.0
Total	100.0	100.0

[1]Includes registered non-status Indians, Métis, and Inuit, except in the number of Native inmates which excludes Inuit.
[2]Violent offences include murder, rape, assault, etc.; non-violent offences are not against persons.
SOURCE: Information Systems and Statistics Division, Minister of the Solicitor General, July, 1979; prepared by DIAND, 1979.

Natives are most often incarcerated for three reasons: violation of the liquor act, traffic violation, and non-payment of fines. Non-payment of fines alone accounts for well over half of the Natives admitted to jails. While research into recidivism rates is sketchy, information from

TABLE 6.31 *Percent Native admissions to provincial correctional institutions by province, 1966-71*

	BC	Alberta	Saskatch-ewan	Manitoba	Ontario	Maritimes	Yukon & NWT
1966	–	31	–	39	–	–	–
1968	21	34	–	45	–	–	–
1970	15	26	54	45	–	–	–
1971	14	23	58	51	8	4	60

SOURCE: Schmeiser, 1974; *Statistics Handbook*, Minister of the Solicitor General, 1974.

TABLE 6.32   **Sentences and institutional histories of Native and non-Native inmates in federal penitentiaries on 31 December 1976 (in percent)**

	Natives	Non-Natives
Length of sentence		
Less than 2 years	11.5	5.3
2-5 years	55.1	44.3
5-10 years	18.8	25.5
10 to 20 years or more	6.7	14.6
Life	7.2	8.8
Other	0.7	1.6
Total	100.0	100.0
Number of previous incarcerations in a federal penitentiary		
None	56.1	58.0
1-2	33.3	29.1
3-5	9.4	11.1
More than 5	1.2	1.8
Total	100.0	100.0

SOURCES: Operational Information Services, Canadian Penitentiary Service; Information Canada, *Perspectives Canada III,* (Ottawa: Queen's Printer, 1977), 188.

Alberta and Saskatchewan shows that Natives currently incarcerated have more prior records than do non-Natives. This does not mean that Natives are discriminated against when sentenced: Hagan (1974) shows that sentences are generally made on the basis of the legal-technical merits of each case. Table 6.32 illustrates the distribution of sentences given to Native and non-Native inmates in federal penitentiaries. The data suggest that, although Natives tend not to be involved in "serious" crimes, such as murder and armed robbery, they are nevertheless sentenced to terms of life imprisonment almost as often as are non-Natives (Schmeiser, 1974).

Because alcohol use is highly related to Native crimes, many provinces are implementing legislation that permits the detention of intoxicated persons for a limited period of time without laying a charge (Verdun-Jones and Muirhead, 1979-80). This legislation may soon be reflected by a decrease in the rate of Native admissions to jails.

The Métis Commission (1977) found that most criminal offenses committed by Natives occurred in the city; this suggests that many Natives have not adjusted successfully to urban life. The Commission also found that Native inmates came from poorer backgrounds than White inmates, and were less likely to receive parole, temporary passes, or entrance into halfway houses. In general, Native inmates follow a "revolving-door" pattern: they enter prison, serve their time, leave, and soon return (Bienvenue and Latif, 1974).

Conclusion

As we have seen, Native people in Canada reside in scattered communities, and are divided by geographical boundaries, cultural differences, and legal distinctions. However, Native Canadians do share one common feature: across Canada, they lead marginal lives, characterized by poverty and dependence. Indeed, many people argue that Natives are members of a culture of poverty. Not only are they alienated from middle-class Canadian society through White racism, but also through the destructive mechanisms by which one class profits at the expense of another.

The position of Natives in today's society is not the result of any single factor, but of a complex of historical and contemporary events. The alienation of Native Canadians began with historical subjugation and subsequent economic displacement. This was followed by a failure to recognize and guarantee certain inalienable Native rights.

The subjugation and control of Native Canadians has been continued through a process of individual and institutional racism. The federal government has neglected to consult with Natives concerning their welfare, has failed to develop and finance effective programs to assist Natives, and, at times, has actively prevented Natives from becoming organized in pursuit of their rights. The political organization of Natives has also been hindered by the factionalism that has developed within different segments of Native society. All these factors, and others, have led to the marginality of Natives in Canada.

Both Natives and government decry the poverty and associated ills that currently face Native people. Since 1960, considerable efforts have been made to raise the social and economic status of Natives. DIAND has substantially increased its expenditures and attempted to develop a new philosophical perspective through which to solve the "Indian Problem". But, as the data presented in this chapter have illustrated, the efforts of DIAND have not been successful. Although Natives have achieved some absolute gains in income, education, and occupational level, they are falling further and further behind other ethnic groups in Canada.

Notes

1. Statistics Canada defines "mother tongue" as the language a person first learns in childhood and still understands.

2. The data show how many percentage points each group is over or under its representation in the general labour force. This is, if ethnicity were not a factor in occupational placement, the proportion of each ethnic group in every occupational category would be the same proportion of that group to the total population. For example, if Natives made up 1.2 percent of the total population, they would make up a similar percentage in each occupational category, Ideally, the over-under representation should hover around zero.

3. Schools founded and operated by a particular religious group.

4. Religious schools receive a fixed amount proportional to the number of pupils for the administration, maintenance, and repair of their buildings.

5. See Caldwell, 1967, and the *Canadian Superintendent*, 1965.

6. All of these schools were founded by the federal government, but are operated by religious orders.

7. In certain provinces, such as Nova Scotia, the Department of Indian Affairs has a master agreement with the province concerning payment for Native students in provincial schools.

8. According to national norms, students aged six should be in grade one, those aged seven in grade two, and so on.

9. This policy of exclusion is now under review. Natives now use school committees to communicate their desires and objections. These committees are set up by the band council and authorized to act on behalf of the Native community, but under regulations drawn up by Indian Affairs.

7

Native
Urbanization

Introduction

The effects of urbanization on Native Canadians have not been adequately studied, despite the concern expressed by the federal government. Partly this is due to a lack of data to support the claims of Native leaders and municipal governments as to the issue's importance. Because urban Natives are highly transient and tend to blend into the general urban poor, statistics are particularly difficult to obtain; politicans, as well as academics, tend to concentrate their efforts elsewhere. However, the issue of urbanization has recently been pushed to the attention of municipal, provincial and federal governments by indirectly related issues such as social services, unemployment, and urban crime.

In the mid-1960s, approximately 16 percent of the Indian population was considered as living off the reserve. As Table 7.1 shows, by 1976, 27 percent of Indians lived off the reserve. In 1980, this estimate reached nearly 30 percent.

Nearly 80 percent of off-reserve Indians are living in large metropolitan centres. Table 7.2 shows the rate of growth in the Native population for selected cities between 1951 and 1971. Clearly, a rapid growth has taken place in the number of Natives moving to the city. However, Table 7.2 does not reflect the number of Natives who have entered the city as other than full-time residents or whose lifestyles have frustrated the attempts of an enumeration agency to count them. Only a few cities in Canada have tried to gather up-to-date and dependable data, with often surprising results: on the basis of its own figures, Regina has predicted that, by 1985, over one-fourth of its population will be Native. Tables 7.2 and 7.3 illustrate the contrast between the official figures and the estimated actual Native populations in selected urban centres. The discrepancies can be considerable: in 1971, Calgary officially claimed slightly more than 2 000 Natives, yet a number of agencies placed the estimated figure at between 5 000 and 10 000.

Table 7.2 shows a steady increase in the urban Native population since 1966. Presently there is some debate as to whether the urbanization process has peaked or will continue to increase. So far, the evidence suggests that Native urbanization will continue to rise in the near future.

The number of off-reserve Indians varies widely from province to province. In 1978, of the more than 100 000 off-reserve Indians in Canada, nearly one-quarter lived in British Columbia. Each Prairie province had between 8 000 and 12 000 off-reserve Indians, and other provinces had about 5 000 each. In British Columbia, nearly 40 percent of Indians live off their reserves. In Ontario and Saskatchewan, about one-third are off-reserve. Manitoba, Alberta, and the Atlantic Provinces are all slightly under the national average with 27 percent of Indians off-reserve. In Quebec, this figure is only about 15 percent.

Migration is a reciprocal process, measuring the movement of Natives both into and out of the city. In some cases, Natives who move off the reserve settle permanently in the city; others only sojourn to the city, remaining for a while, then moving back to their reserves.

Before examining the process of migration in detail, a brief characterization is useful of the Natives who presently live in Canadian cities.

Urban Indian Profile

Table 7.1 shows that, in 1976, nearly one-third of the Indian population between the ages of twenty-five and forty-four lived off the reserve. This proportion of off-reserve Indians increased substantially from the early 1960s until the early 1970s. However, when age groups are compared, no substantial difference emerges in migration patterns. This suggests that members of all age groups migrate in almost equal numbers to urban centres, although somewhat fewer Natives over sixty-five migrate. The high proportion of children up to fourteen-years-old shows that many Natives bring their children with them as they enter the city.

Vincent (1970) found that in Winnipeg over half the Natives were younger than thirty; other studies have since supported this finding, with slightly different figures (Indian Association of Alberta, 1971; Denton, 1972). Vincent also found that 60 percent of urban Natives were married, though not necessarily living with their spouses.

TABLE 7.1 *Percentage distribution of the registered Indian population residing off-reserve by age group, 1966, 1972-76[1]*

				Age Group				
Year	0-14	15-19	20-24	25-29	30-44	45-64	65+	Total
	%	%	%	%	%	%	%	%
1966	12.8	12.8	19.1	22.8	22.8	18.4	12.7	15.9
1971	21.5	18.2	25.8	32.3	29.8	23.8	16.4	23.4
1972	22.6	19.5	25.6	32.7	30.5	24.3	17.3	24.3
1973	23.9	20.6	25.4	32.8	31.1	24.9	17.7	25.1
1974	25.1	23.5	27.0	33.9	32.9	26.8	20.9	26.8
1975	25.8	24.4	27.9	33.5	32.7	26.6	22.2	27.2
1976	26.0	24.8	27.0	32.8	32.9	26.6	22.2	27.4

[1]The 1966, 1971-73 off-reserve population has been adjusted for a change in the residence definition which occured in 1974, in order to make the trends historically comparable.

SOURCES: *Registered Indian Population by Age, Sex, and Residence, for Canada, 1966 to 1977.* Program Reference Centre. IIAP; *Unpublished worksheets,* Research Support Section, Research Branch, IIAP, 1979.

TABLE 7.2 *Indians and Inuit in urban centres[1]*

	1951	1961	1971[2]
Calgary	62	335	2 265
Edmonton	616	995	4 260
Hamilton	493	841	1 470
London	133	340	1 015
Montreal	296	507	3 215
Prince Albert	211	225	1 045
Prince Rupert	—	880	1 780
Regina	160	539	2 860
Saskatoon	48	207	1 070
Toronto	805	1 196	2 990
Vancouver	239	530	3 000
Winnipeg	210	1 082	4 940

[1]The cities chosen were those which in 1971 had the largest number of Indian residents. The numbers are probably understated since many arrivals in a city are itinerant and are, therefore, very difficult to count in a census.
[2]Does not include Inuit.

SOURCE: Information Canada, *Perspective Canada I,* (Ottawa: Queen's Printer, 1974), 244.

TABLE 7.3   *Estimated off-reserve concentrations of Natives*

Province	Centre	Indians	Indians and other Natives	
British Columbia	Vancouver	6 500	15-20 000	
	Chilliwack	—	865	
	Kamloops	—	515	
	Nanaimo	—	665	
	Port Alberni	—	830	
	Prince George	—	1 155	
	Prince Rupert	—	2 325	
Alberta	Calgary	—	5-10 000	
	Edmonton	—	10-15 000	
Saskatchewan	Regina	5 300	15 150	
	Saskatoon	1 800-2 000	—	
		—	5-10 000	
	Prince Albert	1 600-1 750	—	
	North Battleford	700-800	—	
Manitoba	Winnipeg	6 000-16 000	—	
		—	15-20 000	
Ontario	Sault Ste. Marie	—	1 505	
	Toronto	—	15-20 000	
Quebec	Montreal	—	700-800	permanent
		—	7 500	transient
		—	10-15 000	
Atlantic	Sydney Mines	—	1 210	

SOURCE: DIAND, 1980, 106.

TABLE 7.4   *Labour force participation and unemployment among Vancouver Indians off-reserves (in percent)*

	Participation			Unemployment		
	Stanbury	UNN	Ward	Stanbury	UNN	Ward
	1971	1976	1978	1971	1976	1978
Male	40.0	49	55	55.9	58	46
Female	65.5	82	83	48.3	52	33
Total	56.4	66	71	50.5	54	37

SOURCES: Stanbury and Fields, 1975; *United Native Nations Manpower Survey,* 1976; Bob Ward Associates, 1978; DIAND, *Indian Survey,* 1980, 190.

According to the male-female ratio, there are about 10 percent more Native females in urban centres than males. This figure does not include females who have been forced off the reserves through marriage to non-Indian men.

Levels of education for off-reserve Indians are significantly lower than the national average (Stanbury and Fields, 1975; Federation of Saskatchewan Indians, 1978). However, when compared to the educational levels of on-reserve Indians, the difference is not significant.

The low educational levels are reflected in low-status jobs and high unemployment rates. Tables 7.4 and 7.5 show the results of three independent surveys. These surveys demonstrate that the unemployment rate for off-reserve Natives is six times higher than for non-Natives. In a 1980 Calgary study, fewer than 20 percent of those contacting Native Outreach (a Native employment office) had held a job for more than six weeks during the past year (Frideres and Ryan, 1980).

All three surveys attributed unemployment among off-reserve Natives to a lack of training and a need to attend to family responsibilities. However, Stanbury and Fields (1975) also found that discrimination in employment contributed significantly. Because of the low labour-force participation rate, high unemployment, and low educational attainment, the income levels of urban Natives are very low. Stanbury (1975), studying Natives in British Columbia, found that over half (54 percent) of urban Indians made less than $2 000 per year as compared to only 24 percent of the provincial urban population. At the higher end of the income scale, only 13 percent of off-reserve Natives, compared to 33 percent of the provincial population, earned more than $8 000 per year.

TABLE 7.5 *Percent of British Columbian off-reserve Indians employed in each occupational category compared to the national average*

	BC Indians off-reserve		National
	1961	1971	1971
Managerial/professional/technical	6	10	24
Service/recreation	17	19	12
Primary	41	31	8
Production/craftsman	16	22	24
Labour/unskilled	12	9	4
Clerical/sales	8	7	22
Other	0	2	6

SOURCE: DIAND, *Indian Survey,* 1980, 141.

Decision to Migrate

Most studies of Native migration have focused upon the individual. The effects of the reserve community upon migration have seldom been investigated. The work of Gerber (1977, 1980) is an exception to this, and merits an extended discussion in any analysis of Native urbanization.

The structures of particular reserves have an important influence on Native migration patterns. Gerber found that Prairie reserves are very communally oriented, while Eastern reserves tend to be much more individualistic. For example, Eastern Indians are more likely to hold "location tickets" to land,[1] which they can will or sell to other Indians. This has considerable implications with regard to migration.

The specific structural factors of reserves that Gerber found important in affecting Native urbanization were: proximity of the reserve to an urban centre; the size of the band; road access; the degree of community development; Native-language use; and male-female ratio. Gerber found that bands exhibiting low migration were large, were located on the Prairies, were not close to urban centres, had a high degree of community development, and retained some use of Native languages. On the other hand, as Table 7.6 shows, high-migration bands were small, close to urban areas, had a low degree of community development, were not in the Prairies, and were largely English-speaking. In addition, the sex ratio of high-migration bands was, on average, 141 men to 100 women.

Gerber found that the development of personal resources and group resources were particularly important in determining migration patterns. Table 7.7 shows the typology she developed to indicate potential migration patterns.

Bands in Cell 1 are "inert", in that they are not adapting to the larger dominant culture or attempting to develop internally. Those in Cell 2 are "pluralistic". They are high in community development yet low in personal resources; while considerable economic social development has taken place, individuals have not participated in the education system or labour force to any great degree. In contrast, the bands in Cell 3 are "integrative". They have prepared individuals, through education and job experience, to enter the dominant culture, but have not created opportunities within the community; as a result, individuals must move to the outside world. Finally, the "municipal" Natives of Cell 4 are highly developed in both community and personal resources. "Municipal" Natives have a high rate of migration, but opportunities exist on the reserve for those who choose to remain.

In short, as one moves counterclockwise from Cell 1 in Table 7.7, the likelihood of urbanization increases. Apparently, the band itself provides the basic structural context that determines the rates of and reasons for urban migration. Those bands with high community development provide opportunities for their members of remain on the reserve. Those communities with high personal-resource development encourage their members to migrate to the city, when, in additon, community development is low, individuals are forced off the reserve but can compete successfully in the urban context. However, as Gerber argues, an increase in off-reserve residence also results when community development stimulates out-migration to compensate for a lack of personal-resource development.

Clearly, the structural conditions that govern reserve life determine, more or less, the decisions of individual Natives to migrate off the reserve. Denton (1972) also points out that, in addition to social factors, cultural factors come into play. According to Denton, reserves are governed by strong "village norms and social control mechanics which encourage work, independence, and earning one's own money" (1972:55). Thus, from an early age, young children are socialized into work roles and, as they grow older, make increasing contributions to family maintenance (Honigman, 1967). Often, conflicts result between children and parents: children are taught to be self-reliant and independent, but at the same time must bend to the will of their families.

These structural, social, and cultural conditions, then, are instrumental in "pushing" the young Indian off the reserve and into the urban context. Moreover, a decision to return to the reserve is also influenced by these factors: community development must be such as to easily absorb the returnee.

A number of academics have divided Native city-dwellers into transients, migrants, commuters, and residents. The *transient* moves

TABLE 7.6 *The characteristics of high-migration bands*

Band size	Less than 400 members
Employment	Tradition of working off-reserve; poor on-reserve opportunities
Urban Proximity	Semi-rural, urban, poor road access to urban centres for daily commuting
Education	Higher than average attainment; high proportion at integrated schools
Language	English or French spoken on reserve
Band Government	Poorly formulated

SOURCE: L.M. Gerber, *Trends in Out-Migration from Indian Communities Across Canada,* Department of the Secretary of State, 1977.

continually from one place to another without establishing full residence in any urban area (Nagler, 1971). The *migrant* simply transfers a
social network from a rural base to an urban one, moving to the city but
only interacting with other Natives. The *commuter* lives close enough to
an urban centre to spend large amounts of discontinuous time there, yet
retains residence on the reserve. The *resident* has been born in the city
and has spent a great deal of time in an urban context.

Many researchers have assumed that the longer an individual Native
resides in an urban area, the more likely integration into the dominant
society becomes. This assumption is true only for a certain segment of
the urban Native population. Some Natives, in order to become socially
and politically integrated into White society, terminate most social and
family ties with their band. But most Natives are unable to integrate into
the larger society, whether or not they desire to.

Although social factors undoubtedly play a part, most Natives tell
investigators that they have come to the city to participate in the labour
force. This provides a legitimate explanation to non-Natives and allows
Natives to apply for welfare aid more easily. However, Natives are very
much aware of the poor opportunities for steady employment in the
city. What, then, are the reasons for urban migration?

First of all, as pointed our previously, an increase in population has
created overcrowding on the reserve, specifically in the areas of housing
and employment. Most reserves are rural-based and can only provide
jobs for a limited population. As Deprez and Sigurdson (1969) point out,
because the economic base of most reserves is incapable of supporting
the existing Native population, out-migration is essential.

Each Native must assess the chances of obtaining work and housing
on the reserve. Because both are scarce, a great deal of competition
exists among reserve residents. As in most social organizations, access
to housing and employment is partly controlled by a relatively affluent
social elite. The housing needs of young, single males and females are
not considered high priority: young singles are seen as capable of entering
the world outside the reserve and generally lack the social network on
the reserve needed to entail a "quid pro quo". In particular, unmarried
females, with or without children, receive low priority in housing alloca-

TABLE 7.7   *Gerber's typology for migration patterns*

		Level of community development	
		Low	High
Level of personal	Low	1	2
resources	High	3	4

SOURCE: Gerber, 1979

tions. This partly accounts for the high ratio of males to females on certain reserves, as well as for the high proportion of children under fifteen who have moved off the reserve.

Migration away from the reserve is much more the result of push factors than of pull factors. The urban setting is attractive only to those who are qualified to actively participate in it; few Natives are able to do so. Most Natives "decide" to leave the reserve only when they are forced to by an absence of housing and employment opportunities.

Entering the City

In the early stages of urban migration, the first Native institutions to emerge in a city are bars with large Native clienteles. From these first interactions, cliques then emerge and create a social network for Natives to enter and leave at will. Through these cliques, the second stage of urbanization evolves; Native social and cultural centres develop, along with more extended social networks. Price (1979) calls these centres "second-stage" institutions. The centres inhibit integration into the city, yet increase the odds for urban survival. In addition, they promote and facilitate a chain migration of Natives to the cities.

The third stage of urbanization, institutional completeness, has not yet been reached. Institutional completeness is the creation and maintenance of a set of institutions, such as schools, churches, and employment agencies, that meet most social, cultural, and economic needs of the ethnic group. Native institutional completness has failed to develop in the urban centres for a number of reasons. The leaders of Native bands generally remain on the reserve, even though regional, provincial, and national government offices are located in urban areas. Native political organizations continue to focus on rural issues, such as band claims and treaty rights. Due to internal rivalries between Native factions, urban Native leaders have failed to gain political momentum. Moreover, because urban Native organizations, such as Friendship Centres, are continually preoccupied with crisis situations, they have not been able to address the general social and economic needs of Natives.

Clearly, few Natives enjoy the stable social networks in cities that would permit institutional completeness, develop. Native urbanization will not be complete until agencies are developed and staffed by Natives to provide employment and services to the Native community. At this time, Natives have become heavily involved in social and cultural centres, provincial political associations, and local Native political organizations. However, each urban area is developing somewhat differently, and according to varying schedules.

Progressive urbanization is producing more and more urban Natives. What happens after the Native enters the city? What kinds of experience take place? Of course, this largely depends on the lifestyle of the individual. For the purposes of discussion, urban Natives can be divided into transients and residents.

Transients are those individuals who are unable or unwilling to integrate into White society. Because they retain a rural orientation and possess few skills, transients are not able to participate in the social or economic fabric of Canadian society. As a result, they become more and more dependent on the same social-service organizations that, ironically, encouraged them to migrate in the first place.

Table 7.8 lists some of the value differences that exist between Natives and Whites. Of course, both value systems are in a state of flux and neither is as straightforward as it appears. For example, the introduction of social welfare, combined with the Natives' lack of control over their destiny, has led to a "dependency ethos" that did not exist before contact with White culture.

There is great deal of discontinuity between life on the reserve and life in the city. As they reach the city, Natives enter a world that is generally alien, frightening, frustrating, and hostile. Many Natives express total confusion as to "how Whites work".

Of course, the reaction of Natives to White society varies: some find it extremely bizarre and hostile, while other quickly adapt to the White ethos. The extent to which Natives can reconcile the "two solitudes" of reserve life and city life depends on early socialization experiences and past interactions with White society. Insofar as the structure of Canadian society plays a large role in socialization experiences, it has a profound effect on the ability of Natives to integrate into urban life.

TABLE 7.8   *Cultural differences between Whites and Natives*

White	Native
Man dominates, exploits, and controls nature	Man lives in harmony with nature
Future-oriented	Past- and present-oriented
Doing- and activity-oriented	Being-in and becoming oriented
Individualistic	Collaborative (tribal)
Capitalistic (commercial)	Communal
Nationalistic	Commual
Human nature evil but perfectible	Acceptance of human nature

Social Organizations
and Native Urbanization[1]

In Europe, state-funded social services have been used to extend the rights of citizenship and to encourage members of the lower classes to participate politically (Bendix, 1964). Mass education has been developed to raise literacy levels and to provide the formal qualifications necessary for employment in urbanized settings. In addition, social welfare organizations have been expanded to ensure an educated population and to provide support for an urbanized labour force. These social services pulled people from peripheral areas into the mainstream modern economy and, by so doing, played a part in the urbanization of European society.

In Canada, the federal government has tried to repeat this process through the urbanization of Native people. However, this policy is highly suspect. The federal government is trying to encourage Natives to abandon their reserves and treaty rights, mobilizing them as Canadian citizens but not as "citizens plus" (*White Paper*, 1969; Weaver, 1980); "citizens plus" refers to the view that, since Indians were the first inhabitants of Canada, they should be afforded special status and rights. By curtailing services on the reserves, most noticeably in the extent and quality of available housing, the federal government has tried to push Natives into the city, especially during winter. In addition, by transferring the provision of services from the federal to the provincial system, the federal government has attempted to reduce its treaty obligations.

Unlike in Europe, the federal government does not have jurisdiction over those social services, particularly education and social welfare, that have been used to expand citizens' rights and to urbanize members of the lower classes. In Canada, these services generally are provided by provincial agencies. While the provincial educational system has made some effort to increase the Native levels of literacy and formal certification, the welfare system has not been expanded to incorporate Natives into urban society. Although the number of Natives on welfare has increased in cities, they generally receive only short-term services that relieve temporary problems of urban subsistence (Stymeist, 1975).

The lack of educational qualifications continues to prevent full urban integration for most Natives. As stated earlier, Natives who claim a desire for employment as the primary reason for moving to the city generally do so because of the requirements of the welfare system rather than because they perceive actual employment opportunities for themselves. For some, such as single mothers with children, provincial welfare services allow a higher standard of life in the city than on a reserve or Métis colony. For most, however, government social services are not sufficient to encourage Natives to remain in cities. As a result, an increasing number of urban Natives can be classed as transient.

More and more young Natives are moving back and forth between urban and rural residences, generally on a seasonal basis. Faced with an inability to secure employment, or even to understand and use various government and private agencies, they commute into the city for short periods of time and leave, their frustrations intact (Frideres and Ryan, 1980). Even though these Natives may spend large amounts of discontinuous time in the urban context, they retain their social ties in the rural area.

A second group of Natives has succeeded in establishing residence, if not employment, in the cities. This group is predominantly female with young dependents (Gerber, 1977). In lieu of employment, these Natives rely on the support of relatives and friends in addition to government services. For example, of an Edmonton sample, 76 percent of urban Natives had relatives in the city when they first entered and 65 percent had friends (City of Edmonton, 1976).

A third, much smaller group of Natives appears to have successfully settled into urban society. Members of this group most closely approximate the White, middle-class, urban family: they live in single-family units as married adults with children; they have full-time employment; and they live in acceptable housing. Successful entry into urban society appears to be contingent upon attaining a level of education, health, and welfare possessed by the vast majority of non-Native citizens of Canada.

The Transition

Natives move into the urban context in a series of stages.[1] Although these stages are serial, they are not necessarily "step-wise sequential"; that is, all of the steps are not essential in order to achieve the final stage. Also, progression through the stages is usually not completed in one continuous sequence[2]. As this diagram indicates, Natives are exposed to a funnelling effect: although most Natives are exposed to service organizations, few become independent of the service organization and even fewer are successfully placed in the city. (See Figure 7.1.)

Natives move from Stage 1 to Stage 2 largely as a result of the recruitment procedures of service organizations. The type of service organization and its policy plays an important role in determining the rate of rural-to-urban transition. Service organizations influence the degree to which Natives can successfully adapt to the urban centre.

The issue of whether government or voluntary agencies should deal with Native problems has long been debated in Alberta. Although the Alberta government recognizes a partnership between the two sectors,

FIGURE 7.1   *Stages of advancement of Native people in final adaptation to urban milieu.*

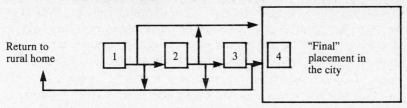

1. Entering the city.
2. Becoming a client of a service organization.
3. "Graduating" from the service organization.
4. "Final" placement in the city.

it has tried to maintain the primacy of government both in policy formation and in program maintenance. Private agencies do not have the complex network of contacts and services that government programs can provide. Nonetheless, a policy of subsidiarity, by which governments refuse to replicate the services offered by private citizens, has taken precedence. As a result, the government has become essentially a financier, relying upon the private sector to provide primary services to those in need.

Native Organization Contact

Although some Natives on reserves or Métis colonies find the sponsorship necessary to receive an advanced education, most Natives are poorly prepared for urban life. Educational standards on the reserves and colonies have been considerably below those in other Canadian schools. The quality of social services, particularly for housing and health, has been well below national norms. Not surprisingly, the lifestyle of the rural Native has adapted to inferior levels of education, work experience, housing, and health.

Even disregarding social and cultural factors, the vast majority of Natives entering cities do not have the qualifications necessary to get work, obtain social services, or even to succeed in school. Most Natives cannot even qualify for unemployment insurance. Their poverty, combined with their unconventional lifestyles, exposes them to much higher than average levels of detention and arrest by the police. In the end, most Natives are unqualified failures at city life.

Because of their unique position, urban Natives are much more likely than Whites to come into direct contact with service organizations that regulate and monitor social behaviour. Natives have consistently posed problems to these organizations in their attempts to establish public order and provide various services. Organizations that attempt to deal with Native urban problems can be broken down into four categories: public-service; acculturating-service; accommodating-service; and member organizations. Table 7.9 outlines the attributes of each type.

PUBLIC-SERVICE ORGANIZATIONS

Public-service organizations generally are designed to provide a single, functionally-specific service, such as justice, education, or welfare, to the general public. They work within the prevailing Canadian system of values and beliefs and are typically staffed by middle-class executives, clerical workers, and members of service-oriented occupations.

From one perspective, public-service organizations are designed to provide certain minimum levels of service to the general public. As a citizen, each individual has the right to a basic education, a basic standard of living, and equal treatment before the law. In return, the individual guarantees school attendance from age six to fifteen, the personal maintenance of public health and welfare standards, and submission to the police and the courts in all matters pertaining to public order.

From another perspective, public-service organizations, especially education and justice systems, are important mechanisms for encouraging the participation of individuals in society. For example, educational achievement draws individuals out of their immediate locales and moves them into a socio-economic framework through entry into the labour force. Similarly, the basic requirements of public health and order permit and encourage social behaviour.

In Alberta, according to available studies, public-services have failed to integrate Natives into urban society. Natives who have come into contact with these organizations have tended to become virtually permanent clients, as evidenced by recurrent patterns of detention and arrest, high rates of hospitalization and premature death, and the inability of most Natives to leave the welfare rolls. In the educational system, where permanent subsistence is not permitted, Natives tend to drop out before achieving the minimum standards of attainment for success in the labour force.

Public-service organizations do not assist most Natives to live in the city as competent citizens. Indeed, as currently constituted, these organizations more often present a barrier that denies Natives entry into the mainstream of urban Canadian life.

TABLE 7.9 *Attributes of types of service organizations*

Organizational type	Selected attributes of organizations					
	Organizational effectiveness	*Value representative*	*Membership recruitment*	*Extent of services*	*Ethnic comp. of staff*	*Ability to place clients*
Public Service	High	Middle-class	Mass[1]	Singular	Middle-class; White	High
Acculturative Service	High	Middle-class	Very[2] selective	Multiple; integrated	Middle-class; White	High
Accommodative Service	Low	Native	Mass	Singular	Mixed-Native; middle-class; White	Low
Member	Moderate	Native	Mass; Native	Singular	Native	Low

[1]Recruitment is selective, yet the services offered are considered the right of all citizens.
[2]Recruitment is usually based on a sponsorship basis.

ACCULTURATING-SERVICE ORGANIZATIONS

Like the public service, acculturating-service organizations draw their staff from the middle-class and act to promote or maintain the assimilation of Natives into White culture. A few Natives on Indian reserves or Métis colonies that display a potential for academic achievement are maintained through secondary school and then referred to a post-secondary institution, usually a college or a university. Once sponsored, these Natives have a high incidence of success in the system. However, Natives have found it difficult to obtain services from these organizations because they have difficulty understanding and coping with non-Native rules and procedures.

In Alberta, acculturating-service organizations include post-secondary institutions, such as colleges and universities, provincial apprenticeship branches, the Central Mortgage and Housing Corporation, and the Alberta Opportunity Fund (a source of credit for small businesses). These agencies share many characteristics with regard to Natives. They usually obtain many, if not most, of their clients through a system of referrals. Whenever possible, they exercise discretion when accepting prospective clients, taking only those who have a good chance of succeeding in their program. Once accepted, their clients typically do succeed: formal and informal counselling services, along with other sources of support, minimize the drop-out rates.

Acculturating-service agencies are also similar in that their clientele includes very few Natives. Most Natives simply do not have the minimal qualifications necessary to be referred to or accepted into such programs.

ACCOMMODATING-SERVICE ORGANIZATIONS

Accommodating-service organizations attempt to compensate for the lack of preparation revealed by certain visible-minority groups in their contacts with White society. These agencies are often funded by public-service organizations to deal with problematic clients. For example, the Special Constables Program of the RCMP, the Courtworkers' Program, and the Race Relations Units of municipal police forces all attempt to handle the problems that have arisen among Natives, the public, and the courts. These agencies try to protect the rights of Natives and, at the same time, render the legal system more efficient. Other acculturating-service organizations support the work of accommodating-service organizations; examples include the Native Counselling and Native Studies Programs on the campuses of various universities.

The ability of an accommodating-service organization to actually alter the fate of its clients is extremely limited. These agencies support the work of public- and acculturating-service organizations and generally operate within a White, middle-class value system. They have managed to attract Native clients by hiring a greater proportion of Native staff members and by modifying some operating procedures to reflect their clients' cultural background. However, because funding often depends on enrolment figures, this "accommodation" of Native interests is not entirely altruistic.

Because funding is almost always limited to support for a particular project for a limited time, programs offered by these organizations usually lack scope and continuity. Accommodating agencies are generally expected simply to direct their clients to existing services provided elsewhere. Indeed accommodating-service organizations often are limited to simply registering, screening, and referring their clients to other organizations. Moreover, they are unable to offer any real assistance to Natives in their dealings with those other organizations.

MEMBER ORGANIZATIONS

Unlike the other three types of service organization, member organizations tend to work against the assimilation of Natives into the mainstream of Canadian society. Member organizations represent the interests of Natives as members of a distinct ethnic group. They provide some employment for Natives, promote the revitalization of Native culture, and attempt to provide the broad range of social support necessary to allow people to lead a Native lifestyle. Some organizations, like the Native Indian Brotherhood, are working to develop and document a case for entrenched Native economic and political rights. Others, like the Indian Friendship Centres, are attempting to promote a Native lifestyle in the cities. These organizations also function to encourage the emergence of a Native elite that has not been co-opted into the staff of public-service organizations.

Although member organizations successfully provide services to urban Natives in the city, their effectiveness is attenuated by a virtual absence of employment for Natives as Natives. Member organizations have tried to promote the institutional completeness needed for in-group cohesiveness and solidarity. However, this institutional completeness cannot be achieved without the creation of jobs for their members. To remedy this problem, Natives, like Hutterites, could establish and run their own businesses; at present, there is only one urban Native enterprise – Can Native Housing. And, like Roman Catholics, Natives could control the beliefs, values and skills taught in government-supported schools.

At present, an inability to establish jobs for their membership stymies the success of Native organizations. Like those who rely on public-service organizations, Natives who belong to member organizations continue to be excluded and stigmatized by White, urban society. However, unlike the clients of public-service organizations, Natives in member organizations are less likely to regard themselves and their fellows as failures.

THE EMERGENCE OF ACCOMMODATING
SERVICE ORGANIZATIONS

As more and more Natives moved to the city in the late 1960s, public- and acculturating-service organizations came under increasing pressure. In coping with the influx of Natives, public-service organizations experienced a disproportionate decrease in effectiveness and a disproportionate increase in costs. Although the schools experienced some problems in assimilating Native children, the brunt of this problem was felt by the police and the courts. Young Natives who migrated into the cities lacked the prerequisite skills for employment and were unable to cope in a conventional fashion with the demands of urban society. Frustration and unemployment combined with divergent values to produce a style of life that frequently deviated from the social norms and laws enforced in the cities. While greater expenditures on law enforcement increased the numbers of Natives being processed (and reprocessed) in the system, they did not reduce the threat to public order. This simultaneous decrease of effectiveness and increase in costs was underscored by social scientists, who pointed out that nearly half the inmates in provincial jails were Natives.

Acculturating-service organizations were criticized on a different ground. Because Natives as a group were systematically under-certified, exceedingly few Natives enrolled in university, entered unionized occupations, or qualified for credit assistance in purchasing a home or establishing a business. With greater urbanization, Natives became a more visible minority, demonstrably denied access to many of the avenues to success in Canadian society. Native member organizations publicly questioned the legitimacy of training programs and assistance agencies that failed to recruit proportionate numbers of Natives into their publicly funded programs.

Managers of acculturative-service programs were also faced with escalating costs accompanied by decreased effectiveness. Their programs were sporadic, unevenly implemented, and made little attempt to find standardized solutions to Native problems. In addition, they were under pressure to debureaucratize existing, legitimate programs.

Like the public-service organizations, then, the acculturative-service agencies were faced with a legitimacy problem: those Natives most in need of their services were clearly not receiving them. Both in public-

and acculturative-service organizations, middle-level managers, who were responsible for day-to-day internal administration, funding, personnel, and clientele, felt that some action was necessary. Although the issue of legitimacy did not actually threaten their budgets, it did increase public scrutiny of funding and internal administration, reducing managerial discretion and hindering the management of day-to-day operations. However, it is important to point out that this legitimacy crisis *did not* become a political issue.

In order to reach a greater number of Natives, middle-level management in public- and acculturating-service organizations began to fund new projects proposed by accommodating-service organizations.[4] In some cases, existing Native member organizations were co-opted to run these programs. In other cases, funding was provided for the formation of new Native-oriented service organizations. In yet other cases, such as the Native Outreach Program, existing organizations created a new branch to deal with a specific type of client.

Whatever their origins, accommodating-service organizations tended to enhance the legitimacy of existing service organizations. Accommodating-service programs essentially dealt with the problem clients of public-service organizations, and left other operations intact.

By registering, screening, and refering problematic clients, accommodating organizations could forecast or even regulate the flow of such clients into public-service and acculturating programs. Furthermore, as independent organizations, accommodating agencies could tailor specific projects for particular problematic groups. These special programs justified high costs and provided a rationale by which public-service organizations could offer special treatment to, and acculturating-service organizations could relax entry and performance standards for, certain preferred groups such as Natives.

Essentially, by offering a composite program, the middle-level managers of service organizations shifted some of the responsibility for problem clients onto the shoulders of those operating the accommodating organizations.[5] The composite program could accommodate both White and Native values. Moreover, accommodating-service organizations could attract increasing numbers of clients without seriously affecting either the service standards of acculturating organizations or the cost-effectiveness of public organizations.

Ironically, the accommodating organizations inherited the same problems of legitimacy that plagued the public- and acculturating-service organizations. Accommodating organizations are generally small, independent, voluntary associations that undergo major program and staff transformations every few years. Their instability is partly due to the nature of their financial support. Usually, their budget is mostly made up of grants from public-service organizations. These grants are generally earmarked for specific projects designed to last for a limited period of time, often one to three years. As a result, accommodating-service agencies generally offer services for Natives that are far too restricted in focus to adequately address the low qualifications, marginal living standards, low incomes, and high crime rates of Native Canadians.

Accommodating-service organizations are particularly ineffective at placing those clients who no longer need their services. Because the organizations, to some extent, encourage Native values and lifestyles, they do not prepare Natives for White, middle-class society: at best, they produce marginal Natives. Accommodating organizations also face serious problems establishing a permanent source of funding and a clearly defined mandate. In addition, they are aimed at protecting the rights of individual clients, and do not attempt to address the general problems of Natives.

In summary, the accommodating-service organizations have inherited many of the criticisms once aimed at the public-service and acculturative-service organizations. To achieve funding, the accommodating organizations orient their programs towards Native culture to attract Native clients. However, the placement of these clients then becomes problematic. As a result, a large number of Natives enter these accommodating organizations, but few graduate. Because White businesses generally refuse to hire them, Natives become perpetual clients of the agencies and are locked into a limbo between the reserve and the city.

Because the federal and provincial governments desire to provide social services on an equal basis to *individual* members of the general public,[6] they have been unwilling to address the problems of particular groups or communities. The current political climate exacerbates this problem. At the constitutional level, the provincial government has refused to accept sole *legal* responsibility for the social support of status Indians off the reserve. To avoid giving even de facto recognition to the collective rights of Natives, these governments have restricted their support of organizations for Natives to narrow-range, small-scale, temporary projects.[7]

The precarious status of accommodating agencies undermines their effectiveness. Overly specific short-term programs discourage the regular, full-time participation of Natives. Moreover, remedial programs are often too narrow to ensure continued Native participation without a broad range of additional social support to counteract the effects of poverty and unemployment. To obtain this support, accommodating organizations must refer their clients to the system of social services offered by public and acculturating organizations, despite the fact that their own projects often run counter to and are not integrated with these social services. Clearly, whatever the efficiency of accommodating organizations under ideal conditions, the absence of wider social support sabotages their effectiveness and undermines what few gains they manage to achieve.

Notes

1. Some of the material presented has been previously published in *Canadian Public Policy*, 1981.
2. The lengths of time between each step vary and should not be seen as equal. Movement to the next step is not automatic and several starts may be needed before it takes place.
3. This strategy is being implemented by various reserves in Alberta, such as the Blood reserve.
4. At the same time, Natives lacked an elite to promote a rediscovery and resurgence of Native culture. They also lacked service organizations to encourage participation in the larger society. The end result was the creation of a very passive and apathetic population that remained on the reserve or in rural areas. Those Natives who became "active" were generally co-opted and acculturated out of Native culture and into mainstream society.
5. These organizations screen potential clients and sort them into appropriate homogeneous streams before providing services. In essence, accommodating-service programs stream special problems away from the general program. The composite program can accommodate White and Native values, thereby rendering acculturating-service organizations more effective while increasing the clientele of accommodating-service organizations. This new composite organization has allowed an increasing number of Natives to stay in urban areas.
6. Alberta and Quebec are the only two provinces that do not have, or condone, affirmative-action programs.
7. Parts of the preceeding discussion were previously published in *Canadian Public Policy*, 1981.

8

Indian-Inuit
Affairs Program
and Government Policy

Structure of DIAND

The Department of Indian Affairs and Northern Development is responsible for all federal policy and programs concerning Canadian Indians and Inuit; it also administers the Northwest Territories and the Yukon. DIAND administers thirty-six separate *Acts*, including the *Department of Indian Affairs and Northern Development Act*.[1] The Department's mandate includes:

- Initiating, encouraging, and supporting measures to respond to the needs and aspirations of Indians and Inuit people and to improve their social, cultural, and economic well-being.

- Ensuring that lawful obligations to Indians and Inuit are met.

- Encouraging the orderly economic and political development of the Yukon and the Northwest Territories.

- Settling claims related to traditional Native use and occupancy of lands in those areas of Canada where this traditional right has not been extinguished by treaty or superceded by law. (*Annual Report,* DIAND, 1980-81, 9)

Figures 8.1 through 8.7 outline the bureaucratic structure of DIAND. As Figure 8.1 shows, DIAND is comprised of six subsections: Finance and

Management; Northern Affairs; Personnel; Indian Inuit Affairs Program; Corporate Policy; and the Office of Native Claims. Figures 8.2 through 8.7 outline each of these individually. For discussion purposes, Finance and Management, Personnel, and Corporate Policy will be grouped together as Departmental Services.

The assistant-deputy-minister for the Indian Inuit Affairs Program (IIAP) and the executive director for the Office of Native Claims report directly to the deputy minister. The senior assistant-deputy-minister of Finance and Management, the assistant-deputy-minister of Corporate Policy, and the director-general of Personnel also report to the deputy-minister.

Although this chapter will focus upon the IIAP, all six of DIAND's subsections deal directly and indirectly with Native people.[2] A brief statement about the mandate and goals of each of these sections will allow a better understanding of the structure and focus of DIAND as a whole.

INDIAN AND INUIT AFFAIRS[3]

The activities of the Indian and Inuit Affairs Program are directed toward the approximately 303 000 registered Indians in Canada and the 7 550 Inuit who live in northern Quebec, Labrador, and south of the 60th parallel elsewhere in the country.

The program administers the statutory requirements defined in the *Indian Act*, including the registration of Indian people, the deployment of reserve lands and other resources, and the regulation of band elections. It also attempts to ensure that the federal government's lawful obligations to Indians and Inuit under the *Indian Act*, and the treaties are fulfilled.

The stated objective of the Indian and Inuit Affairs Program is to help Indian and Inuit people attain their cultural, economic, and social goals within Canadian society.

NORTHERN AFFAIRS

The Northern Affairs Program assists the social, cultural, political, and economic development of the Yukon and the Northwest Territories, placing particular emphasis on the needs of Northern Natives. The Program operates directly, as well as indirectly, through the governments of the two Territories.

The objectives of the Northern Affairs Program are directed toward:

- Improvement in the quality of Northern life and a higher standard of living for Northern residents.

FIGURE 8.1 *Headquarters summary*

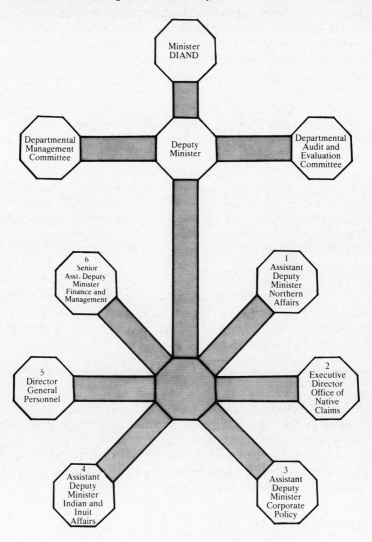

- Equality of opportunity for all Northern residents.

- Protection of the Northern environment as an essential element of Northern economic and social development.

- Encouragement of viable economic development.

- Meaningful progress toward territorial self-government.

The territorial governments, with federal financial support, are now chiefly responsible for providing government services to territorial residents. Therefore, the Northern Affairs Program concentrates on Northern resource development, environmental protection, and political, social, and cultural development. The program also helps to co-ordinate federal government activities in the two territories.

FIGURE 8.2   *Organization: Northern Affairs summary*

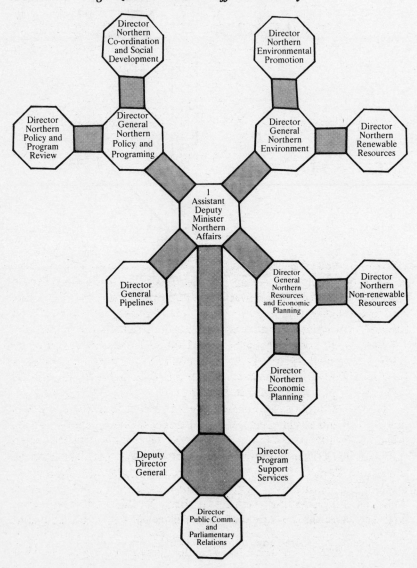

FIGURE 8.3   *Office of Native Claims summary*

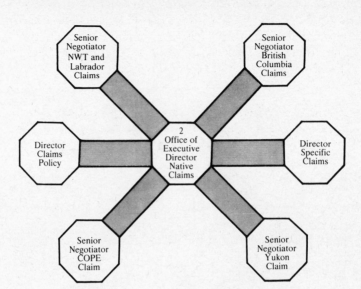

OFFICE OF NATIVE CLAIMS

During the period of colonial rule, successive British governments assumed that Native people had an interest in the land that had to be recognized before White settlement could take place. This assumption was most clearly expressed in the *Royal Proclamation* of 1763, and resulted in a series of formal agreements and treaties dating from the 1780s and adopted by Canada after Confederation. In general, the Natives relinquished large areas of Canada to the Crown in return for benefits including land (reserves), cash annuities, schools, and special hunting, trapping and fishing privileges.

By the 1920s, most of the likely areas of White settlement or development in Canada had been covered by treaties. One exception was the greater part of British Columbia, whose government consistently denied the existence of aboriginal interests. Other regions not dealt with by treaty, the *Royal Proclamation*, or colonial acts included the Yukon, most of the Northwest Territories, northern Quebec, and Labrador. Although little attention was paid to them, Natives in all these areas continued over the years to press for formal settlements through claims submissions, court actions, and political lobbying.

During 1968-69, the federal government conducted a general review

FIGURE 8.4   *Corporate policy summary*

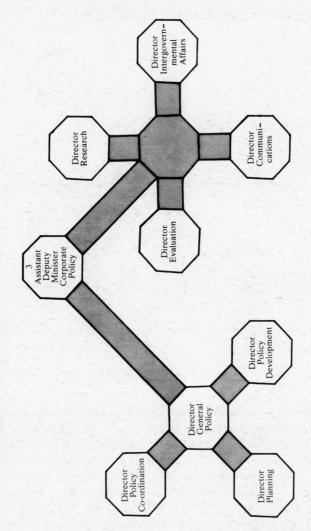

of Native policy. Partly as a result of that review, the government appointed a commissioner in 1969 to research and classify Native claims and to recommend more formal and consistent ways of dealing with them. At the same time, various Native associations began a series of federally funded research studies to determine and establish their treaty and other rights, including aboriginal rights. These associations then pressured the federal government to broaden the jurisdiction of the commissioner to include claims and grievances based on aboriginal rights. In 1971, the government authorized the commissioner to consider any and all Native claims brought before him.

FIGURE 8.5 *Organization: Indian and Inuit Affairs summary*

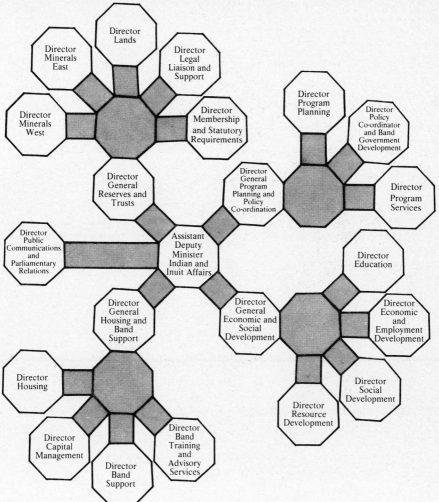

In early 1973, the issue of Native claims, particularly in relation to aboriginal titles, was brought sharply into focus by the Supreme Court of Canada's decision on the Nishga land claim (the *Calder Decision*). Although it rejected the claim on a technicality, the court was split three against three as to whether the Indian aboriginal title to the land continued to exist. This decision led to a policy review by the government. On August 8, 1973, the Minister of DIAND delivered a policy statement that, for the first time, created an Office of Native Claims.

FIGURE 8.6   *Personnel summary*

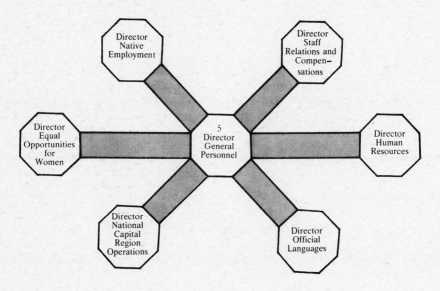

DEPARTMENTAL SERVICES

Departmental Services provides policy direction and central advisory and administrative services to the Indian and Inuit Affairs Program, the Northern Affairs Program, and the Office of Native Claims. It comprises Finance and Professional Services, Personnel, and the Corporate Policy Group.

Finance and Professional Services is responsible for the quality, efficiency, and effectiveness of financial management systems and processes. It is also in charge of the management of physical assets and the administration of all departmental programs and operations. It is headed by the senior-assistant-deputy-minister, Finance and Management.

Personnel's services include: employee classification; staffing and human resources planning; staff training and development; staff relations; Native employment within DIAND; equal opportunities for women and the handicapped within DIAND; official languages; and employee assistance programs. In addition, the director general of Personnel represents the deputy minister with regard to personnel administration matters before the Treasury Board, the Public Service Commission, the Public Service Staff Relations Board, and other federal departments and agencies.

Corporate Policy develops and co-ordinates departmental policy. In

FIGURE 8.7 *Organization: Finance and Professional Services summary*

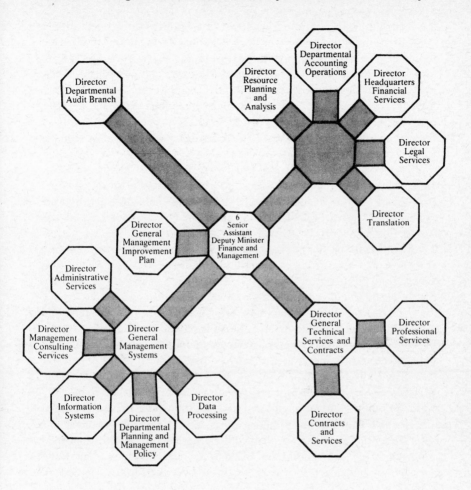

1978, Corporate Policy responsibilities were expanded to include the Parliamentary Relations Division, the Departmental Communications Branch, and the Departmental Secretariat. In January, 1980, the functions of program evaluation, inter-governmental relations, and research, previously located within the Policy, Research, and Evaluation Group in the Indian and Inuit Affairs Program, were also transferred to Corporate Policy. The departmental science advisor, who represents the Department on major inter-departmental scientific committees and advises the Department on science-related matters, also reports to the assistant-deputy-minister of Corporate Policy.

The Indian Inuit-Affairs Program

The bureaucratic structure of IIAP has traditionally been highly centralized in Ottawa. However, with decentralization in the 1970s, each region has become responsible for developing its own new programs. There are nine regional offices across Canada: one in each territory, one for the Atlantic provinces, and one in each of the other provinces. Except for Manitoba, every region contains a number of specific districts, each under the authority of a district manager. These managers have become quite influential, except in Alberta where control is concentrated in the regional office.

About one-fourth of the total employees of IIAP are Natives. However, Natives have not yet gained access to policy-setting positions. Only 2 percent of the Natives employed by IIAP are at the senior and middle-management level. The largest proportion (28 percent) are at the operational level, primarily involved in teaching.

Less than 10 percent of its employees have been with IIAP more than fifteen years. This group is generally called the "old guard" and has almost total control over policy development and implementation. Only one or two of them are Natives.

The IIAP's policies, objectives, priorities, and programs are established by senior executives and then passed down and back up the bureaucratic ladder. Budgets must be developed for each program and approved by Parliament. Most of the budget of the IIAP, 74 percent, is non-discretionary; that is, it is set aside for specific items and non-transferable. As the year proceeds, the IIAP often requests more money.[4] Table 8.1 shows budget components for 1970 through 1979.

In 1967, the IIAP accounted for 1.06 percent of the government's total budget. This figure peaked at 1.74 percent in 1972-73 before it returned to 1.70 percent in 1980. In 1965, IIAP used about one-half of the total DIAND budget. This proportion increased to nearly 75 percent in 1969, but has since steadily declined to a present level of 55 percent. Between 1970 and 1979, actual dollars spent on Natives through DIAND increased threefold. However, during this period, the proportion of total federal expenditures for Natives declined. As Table 8.2 shows, DIAND has experienced a lower expenditure growth rate than other government departments.

Since 1960, considerable shifts have occurred in the distribution of funds among operating expenses, capital costs, and expenditures for grants and contributions. In the early 1960s, over half of the budget was used to meet operating expenses, while the rest was evenly split between the other two categories. In 1980-81, however, operating expenditures only accounted for 37 percent of the budget, while capital expenditures

TABLE 8.1 *Indian-Inuit Affairs Program expenditures, 1970-79 (in millions of dollars)*

	1970-71	*1974-75*	*1975-79*
General program admin. activity	11.5	29.5	47.6
Capital expenditures	0.9	1.9	2.0
Subtotal	12.4	31.4	49.6
Policy and research activity	2.6	4.1	6.5
Economic development activity			
Administration	2.3	2.6	3.7
Development services	4.4	7.2	11.4
Lands	0.9	3.8	8.6
Business services	0.4	8.3	17.0
Arts and Crafts	—	—	0.6
Regional economic planning and development	—	—	2.2
Capital expenditures	2.2	5.8	0.1
Subtotal	10.2	27.7	49.5
Community affairs activity			
Administration	1.0	2.1	4.6
Social services	51.1	87.9	147.2
Band management	6.9	19.9	41.7
Community housing and facilities	6.9	6.4	17.7
Capital expenditures	32.4	47.3	82.2
Subtotal	98.3	163.6	293.0
Education activity			
Administration	3.7	5.0	7.6
Cultural development	—	4.9	5.4
Education in federal schools	18.2	35.6	63.1
Education in non-federal schools	29.8	45.3	94.1
Transportation and maintenance of pupils	11.9	16.7	22.2
Adult education	2.0	3.6	5.9
Vocational education	5.8	9.3	15.0
Employment and relocation	2.1	3.2	6.6
Student residences	13.9	15.4	11.9
Capital expenditures	17.4	25.5	34.1
Subtotal	104.8	164.5	265.8
Total expenditures	228.4	391.0	658.6

SOURCE: Financial Management Reports, DIAND.

TABLE 8.2   *Expenditure growth of various federal departments from 1970-71 to 1978-79 (in 1971 $ dollars)*

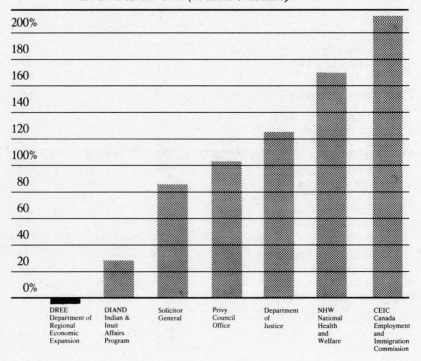

SOURCES: Estimates made for the fiscal years 1970-78, Government of Canada; Estimates made for fiscal year 1978-79, Government of Canada; *Indian Conditions, Survey,* 1980.

on additions and betterments had decreased to 4 percent. Expenditures on grants and contributions had increased substantially and comprised nearly 60 percent of the total budget (*Annual Report,* DIAND, 1980-81). This suggests a wide-scale transfer of the administrative costs of IIAP programs to provincial governments.

The actual spending patterns of the IIAP have not substantially changed over recent years. In the early 1960s, approximately 45 percent of the budget was spent on education. By 1978, this had decreased to 39 percent. Other activities show even smaller changes. Community affairs accounted for 43.1 percent of the budget in 1970 and 43.8 percent in 1978. Economic development, always a low IIAP priority, has ranged from between 6 and 9 percent of the total budget.

Those who determine IIAP policies seldom, if ever, have direct experience of Native issues. Policies are developed by IIAP bureaucrats and amended by bureaucrats from other government areas that are likely to be affected by the policies. As Weaver (1980) points out in her analysis of the 1969 *White Paper*, the Privy Council Office (PCO), the Prime Minister's Office (PMO), the Treasury Board, and the Cabinet wield the most direct influence upon federal policy concerning Natives. In the 1960s, the PCO and PMO were restructured to assert the primacy of the prime minister and Cabinet in the setting of policy and the monitoring of programs. This restructuring has allowed the PCO, PMO, and Cabinet to maintain much closer control of IIAP activities and to evaluate those activities in the context of other government departments (Pross, 1975). The 1960s also saw a major restructuring of the system of standing committees in the House of Commons. This change has permitted members of parliament to interact more directly with the staff of the IIAP, and to expand their roles through a process of open discussion (Weaver,1980).

These two changes removed policy development and implementation from the total control of particular departments and ensured that policies would be evaluated in the context of policies from other departments. Policy advisory councils were created to report to the Cabinet; in effect, these are one step beyond the Cabinet in power. Information from each department is now filtered through the PCO and PMO instead of passed directly from senior bureaucrats to cabinet ministers (Ponting and Gibbins, 1980).

These changes have had a direct effect on organized attempts by Natives to influence policy and program development. There is now another entire set of bureaucrats that must be lobbied. Moreover, they can only be lobbied by an intermediary and within the confines of committees with legitimate powers of inquiry (Pross, 1975). As a result, Native groups must reorganize their efforts if they are to have any influences on the policies that affect them. They must also find a way to use or to counter the increasing input of the PCO and PMO into general policy recommendations (Presthus, 1974).

Government Policy

The federal government has previously maintained that, under Section 91(24) of the *BNA Act*, it has the constitutional obligation to provide funds and services to registered Indians *on reserves*. It argues that off-reserve Indians are a provincial responsibility. At present, there is a serious debate between federal and provincial governments concerning which of them should finance and deliver services to Natives both on and off reserves.

The federal government acknowledges a special relationship between itself and Native Canadians. It agrees that registered Indians and Inuit possess special rights, privileges, and entitlements, whether they live on or off reserves. However, although the federal government acknowledges its responsibility to on- and off-reserve Natives, it claims that they should look to both levels of government for certain services. In addition, the federal government regards its responsibility for off-reserve services in a different light than that for on-reserve services. More specifically, the federal government under Section 91(24) of the *BNA Act*, has accepted responsibility for on-reserve services in more program areas than for off-reserve services.

As Natives move off reserves, they become citizens of a province; as such, they have a basic right to the same services provided by the province to all its other residents. The federal government has a number of direct off-reserve support programs in such areas as housing and post-secondary education. In addition, it provides transfer and block payments to the provinces based on Native population figures under such programs as Established Program Financing and Equalization. These programs are intended to help provide the same services to Natives as are provided to the general provincial population.

The federal government then, maintains that each government has its respective responsibilities based on separate, distinct bonds with Native peoples. Natives who live off reserves are residents of provinces and often contribute to provincial tax revenues; in addition, they have often provided indirectly many other resources now available to the provinces, and are included in the calculation of transfer and block payments to the provinces. The provinces, on the other hand, take the position that Indians are a federal concern and not under the jurisdiction of provincial governments.

The IIAP has been in the process of decentralization since 1964. Originally, DIAND simply stated that Natives were to become a provincial responsibility. This policy was rejected by Native organizations and provincial governments alike. In the mid-1970s, a new policy emerged involving the transfer of federal responsibility to Native bands rather than to the provinces. At the same time, administrative responsibilities were being shifted from Ottawa to the regional and district offices of DIAND. As a result, Natives have gained somewhat greater involvement in the policy formations of IIAP (Ponting and Gibbins, 1980).

The shift of responsibility to band governments is taking place at three levels. First, funds for program management are being transferred from the IIAP to the direct control of the bands. This transfer began in 1968: by 1971, bands were managing about 14 percent of a $260 million budget and, by 1978-79, about 35 percent of a $659 million budget. Second, core funding grants are provided for the basic administrative costs of chiefs, councils, and band managers. In 1978-79, these grants represented 4 percent of the total DIAND budget. Third, band training and support services are supplied to encourage management skills and to provide technical support.

At present, about 50 percent of the total capital and 33 percent of the school budgets are administered by the bands. Approximately 90 percent of the bands are involved in the core funding program. However, these figures show considerable regional disparity. Manitoba bands control a great deal of their operational expenditures, while Yukon bands control very little. As DIAND explains:

> The varying levels of band-administrated funds in each region do not reflect the degree of interest of bands in administering funds but rather:
> - The level of social assistance administered by provincial authorities.
> - The number of Indian children attending provincial schools. (*Survey*, 116)

This new policy of decentralization is apparently designed to promote the autonomy of Native bands. It heralds a shift in federal policy from programs that promote integration and assimilation to those that encourage tribal government and cultural self-sufficiency. Increasingly, band councils are responsible for financial allocations. However, although the IIAP is relinquishing specific control over expenditures, it still retains control of the overall allocation of funds. In effect, the new policy has shifted critical attention away from the IIAP to the local chief, council, and manager.

The new policy has also meant that Natives must be fully involved in discussions on a broad range of program-related and political issues. With the new band autonomy, certain programs can no longer be implemented without first consulting Natives. Moreover, Native associations have been steadily putting pressure on the IIAP, requesting forums for discussion of a range of issues related to federal and provincial policies.

In 1978, a new branch was created within the Policy, Research, and Evaluation Group Corporate Policy to organize tripartite discussions among Native peoples and the federal and provincial governments. The structure of these discussions differs significantly depending on which province is involved, and which issues are considered, and to which degree each party is represented. In general, discussions take place at the request either of Native associations and bands or of provincial governments.

Again, this attempt to provide a forum for Native participation reflects a shift in federal policy from a desire to assimilate Natives toward an increasing emphasis on tribal government. The tripartite discussions partly arose from a belief by Indian Affairs personnel that Natives had developed enough political and leadership skills to articulate their needs. In addition, the provinces became willing to discuss priority issues set forth by Natives, largely to avoid being excluded from any far-reaching negotiations that might take place elsewhere in Canada. However, despite promises to the contrary, Natives are still effectively excluded from much of the negotiation process. Presently, much of the discussion between federal and provincial officials circumvents Native involvement through the use of personal communications, confidential documents, and so on.

In general, the IIAP in the 1960s tried to turn Natives into Whites by integrating them into the capitalist system and encouraging them to shed their Native ways. In the statement at the Federal-Provincial Conference on Poverty in the mid-1960s, the Indian Affairs Department summed up its policy of assimilation as one that enabled Natives "to realize their potential in the economic, social, and cultural sectors of their lives". In the 1970s, this policy shifted to promote the retention of Native culture in accord with a new emphasis on multiculturalism. In addition the policies of the 1970s began to focus on the urban Native population, although, as yet, no coherent strategy with regard to these Natives has been developed.

The origin of DIAND's changing policy goes back to the 1950s. In 1959, Prime Minister Diefenbaker was embarrassed during a foreign tour by strong criticism with regard to Native policy. Upon his return to Canada, he established a Joint Committee of the Senate and the House of Commons to investigate and advise on the administration of Indian Affairs. The context was a favourable one for Native Canadians: Diefenbaker had just won a decisive victory in the 1958 election and Gladstone, a Blood-Indian from Alberta, had just been appointed to the Senate. Due to the Joint Committee's recommendations, the law was changed in 1960 to give Natives the right to vote in federal elections. The Joint Committee also recommended that IIAP should cease to provide special services to Natives and instead should rely on, and share the cost of, the existing services of other agencies including provincial governments.

This position was later echoed by the Alberta *White Paper on Human Resources Development* in 1967, which proposed that the federal and provincial governments should develop a comprehensive program to financially enable provincial and municipal governments to extend all of their services to Natives. Such a program, the *Hunter-Motherwell Agreement*, had recently been terminated due to a breakdown in negotiations. Now, in an attempt to get the jump on the federal government, the Alberta *White Paper* urged the phasing out of federal services and facilities for Natives where provincial and municipal services were already available. Under Alberta's proposals, the federal government was to accept *total* financial responsibility for all programs and services extended to registered, on-reserve Natives; in turn, the provincial government accepted financial responsibility for programs offered to all other Natives. Ten years later, under the *Tripartite Agreements*, this policy, to a limited extent, was adopted.

In 1976, a new mega-policy was introduced by the Minister of DIAND to promote "Indian identity within Canadian society". The definition and evolution of Native identity were to be treated as flexible and dynamic. In general, the policy continues to recognize Native status, treaty rights, and special privileges resulting from land claims settlements. Within Native band and reserve communities, local self-determination and control of Native affairs are to be encouraged. In addition, for the first time, the policy noted that different needs, aspirations, and attitudes among Natives in all parts of Canada rule out a single, uniform strategy. As a result, the policy emphasizes joint participation in program development with organized Native leadership at all levels.

Under the new policy, the federal government takes the initiative in defining the aims and general shape of strategies applied to Native issues. If the government chooses, this process can involve Native representatives at various levels. The major goal of the new policy is to transfer the administration of programs and resources to band governments. The rate of transfer is determined by the desire and ability of each band to assume control of its own affairs, including the implementation of programs. With experience, band administration is becoming more efficient. In 1977, of the nearly $150 million managed by bands, 74 percent was for operating expenses and 26 percent for capital expenses; this is a substantial improvement from 1972 when 90 percent of funds were used as operating expenses and only 10 percent for capital expenses.

At present, the 1976 policy changes are being reconsidered. For example, many critics question the value of programs that encourage a strong cultural identity among Natives without raising their socioeconomic status. However, these reconsiderations have yet to be translated into programs. In Alberta, for example, nearly 75 percent of the service expenditures for off-reserve Natives is spent on community affairs, generally for social assistance; only 14 percent is spent for education and an even smaller percentage for economic development.

Another recent change in philosophy involves the co-ordination of all existing services in a vast program specifically tailored to the needs of Native people. However, so far there is little to suggest that this philosophy is being put into practice. At present, no fully developed model of services for Natives has been developed. Several tentative models have been put forth by IIAP personnel, yet little seems to come of them.

In general, policies at the IIAP are developed internally by middle-level administrative personnel who employ data collected by external consultants. Normally, the IIAP hires ten to fifteen consultants per year to carry out specific research. Although policy development is continuous in the IIAP, it tends to increase dramatically when a government has been defeated or when an election is in progress. This suggests that policy evaluation and development are not systemized but are, instead, a "filler" activity of the Department (Ponting and Gibbins, 1980).

The Latent Functions of IIAP

Like other organizations, the IIAP is a highly structured, rational system that espouses specific policies and pursues specific goals. It has defined Native welfare as its sole concern; overtly, all its activities are geared to improving that welfare. However, also like other organizations, the IIAP pursues certain latent goals that are quite independent of its stated formal goals. As Perrow (1980) and several others have observed, organizations often exist *not* to serve their stated goals, but rather to serve other interests. In fact, some would even argue that the stated policy and goals of an organization largely function only to legitimize its existence. An organization makes its stated goals explicit through its formal policy statements. Its latent goal structure, however, only becomes apparent through an examination of the services that it provides for interest groups other than those that it manifestly serves.

The organizations dealing with Native people all possess a number of latent functions. For the past century, the IIAP and its forerunners have stated their primary manifest goal as the ultimate participation of Natives as equals in Canadian society. The latent goals of these organizations include such self-referential aims as cost-efficiency and freedom from conflict within their own structures. Another latent function is to provide resources for other organizations. Many other institutions make extensive use of the nearly $700 million and 5 000 employees provided to the IIAP at public expense; examples range from Native organizations to educational institutions to businesses.

Although other latent functions could be documented here, none is so extensive as the latent attempt by federal administrators to control the lives of Natives. Throughout its history, the major latent function of the IIAP has been the regulation of Native behaviour. Native people have been lured to cities where their dependent status forces them to conform, or segregated on reserves, concealed from the view of middle-class Canadians. They have been arbitrarily dispersed throughout cities or forcibly bused out of town back to the reserve. Often, the control of Natives has been achieved through the behaviourial requirements attached to various social services. For example, the off-reserve housing program requires applicants to have steady full-time jobs before they are eligible for loans.

Regardless of the technique, the result is that Natives are manipulated and restricted in their actions. To be sure, some Natives are helped in the process: at least sixteen people have received off-reserve housing in one major city over the past 10 years. Many more have obtained educational benefits, training, counselling, and money, but only after conforming to other behaviourial criteria. Thus, the control factor is the central goal of the majority of organizations dealing with Native people.

The insistence of the federal government upon control over its Native "wards" has characterized federal-Native relations since Confederation. As Whiteside points out:

> Perhaps we should recall the various measures the bureaucrats introduced during this period to ensure 'orderly administration': (1) the development of a single piece of legislation in 1876, to govern all the Indian Nations, regardless of varying traditions and history; (2) the systematic destruction of tribal governments and replacement of them with band councils which were really an extension of the Department's (Indian Affairs) structure; (3) the systematic attempt to destroy Indian culture and the outlawing of Indian religious ceremonies; (4) the introduction of compulsory enfranchisement provisions to control bad Indians; (5) the systematic attempts to harness and discredit Indian leaders who attempted to develop or strengthen Indian political organization. (1980:6)

On the reserve, the IIAP is a "total" institution in that it has a monopoly on the delivery of services to a captive clientele. Its organization is characterized by specialization, hierarchy, and regimentation, while its clients are uneducated, unspecialized, and varied. By limiting the choices available to its Native clients, the IIAP shapes and standardizes Native behaviour at minimal cost and risk to itself.

The success of the IIAP is not assessed on the basis of assistance provided to Natives, but rather on the basis of how effectively Native behaviour has been kept under control. The brighter officials at the IIAP know perfectly well that they will not be fired, transferred, or demoted for failing to help Natives receive decent educations, find jobs, mend broken homes, and settle into life in the city. Rather, the officials' assessments will be based on the number of Natives they "handled", and at what cost per person. Programs that fail to meet their announced goals do not result in fired personnel or radical organizational changes. The upper management of the IIAP can simply blame failures on a need for "organizational restructuring", a "lack of adequately trained fieldworkers", a "poorly allocated budget," and so on.

All this is not to suggest that the IIAP does not help Natives. On the contrary, some Natives get bursaries to go to university, some get loans to buy houses in the city, and others get vocational training. Nor is this analysis intended to suggest that IIAP officials deliberately neglect the needs of Native people. Rather, such neglect is the result of internal and structural forces that cause a re-ordering of goal priorities.

Certain internal forces acting upon the IIAP cause it to downplay its stated goal to improve the quality of Native life. Government officials tend to become disproportionately concerned with the number of the employees, the size of the budgets, and the quantity, rather than the quality, of the programs. Because it is difficult, time-consuming, and speculative to assess the effectiveness of an organization, criteria such as these become the indicators of a successful program. Because these indicators measure cost efficiency rather than program effectiveness, they are simple to measure, highly visible, and extremely responsive to changes.

A second internal factor is the emphasis on stability within the IIAP. There is an implicit rule that conflict should not be evident in any federal department. If conflict does exist, it must remain an internal affair. The preoccupation of the IIAP with remaining conflict-free results, once again, in a downplaying of stated goals and objectives.

In all of the organizations that deal with Native issues, officials accept and promote the existing expectations, norms, and morés of a free-enterprise, class-based system. This places severe limitations on the programs offered to Native people. For example, not one organization has suggested that most of the IIAP's budget be given directly to Native people or used to organize Natives into an effective political force. Quite the contrary. One of the better-known attempts to organize Natives politically (CUITA) resulted in the dissolution of one district DIAND office and substantial reassignment of DIAND personnel. A similiar result greeted the ill-fated Community Development Program, which was phased out within a few years of its inception.

Provincial-Indian Relations in Alberta: A Case Study

After the federal government, the provincial government has the most extensive relationship with Native people. Tensions between the federal and provincial governments have been apparent for some time concerning Native issues. The following material documents the relationship between the provincial government of Alberta and the Natives within its borders.

An understanding of the overall political climate of Alberta is essential to comprehend its policies, particularly in relation to the federal government. The most seminal document behind Alberta's policy is *The Case for Alberta* (1938). Even though it is over forty years old, this document is still excerpted in the briefs of the present government. It graphically illustrates Alberta's deep frustration with federal policy. Basically, its theme is that the federal government has consistently failed to heed the social and economic needs of Albertans.

In 1967, Alberta's Premier Manning produced a *White Paper on Human Resource Development* which announced that the development of human resources had become the priority goal of his government. Specifically, he wanted to raise the status of economically and socially deprived Albertans. Manning took the position that all individuals and organizations should have equal access to programs and services, and promised to remove any discriminatory barriers and phase out separate-but-equal programs based on ethnic distinctions. The *White Paper* promised to:

1. Endeavour to persuade the Government of Canada to enter into a comprehensive agreement which will allow the Indian people, under federal jurisdiction, to receive wherever possible the same facilities and services as are available to other residents of the province.

2. Assure to Métis and to Indian people under provincial jurisdiction access to services and development programs on the same basis as all other residents in similar social and economic circumstances and encourage them to become self-determining and responsible residents of Alberta on the same legal basis as other citizens. (1967: 79-80)

The Alberta government was aware that the federal government planned to turn over the financing and delivery of Native services to the provinces. Tentatively this plan had already been mapped out in the short-lived *Hunter-Motherwell Agreement* of 1965-66. Alberta wanted to get the jump on the federal goverment by defining its policy stance before the federal government could develop a long-term organizational structure.

In the late 1960s, Premier Strom hired several lawyers who were specialists in Native affairs to investigate and advise on this issue. At the end of the decade, the Alberta government developed a policy that, while not specifically related to Natives, did have implications for them. This policy stated that the provincial government would recognize ethnic differences but would not direct any program toward specific ethnic groups. Specific programs concerning Natives would be carried out exclusively by the federal government.

During 1977, the Alberta government undertook an extensive analysis of provincial programs and services available to treaty Indians. Traditionally, registered Indians had been reluctant to actively pursue provincial services through fear of eroding their historical relationship with the federal government. The Alberta government wanted to counteract this reluctance, claiming that it wanted to provide *all* Albertans the maximum opportunity for personal, social, and economic advancement (*Policy Statement, Alberta Hansard*, April 25, 1978). As a result, the Alberta government decided to make provincial services and programs officially available to recognized treaty Indians and Native bands on the same basis as to other Alberta residents. Although this policy seems to focus on reserve Natives, its implications for urban Natives are obvious.

The new Alberta policy can be seen as a more current statement of the *Hunter-Motherwell Agreement* of the mid-1960s. Under this old *Agreement* between the federal and provincial governments, registered Indians who entered the city would be classified in one of two ways: unemployable Indians would remain under federal jurisdiction, while employable Indians would move to provincial jurisdiction. All Indians who were off-reserve for more than one year became the responsibility of the provincial government, even though they remained band members. Under this *Agreement*, the province also promised to provide welfare services to all treaty off-reserve Indians. However, the province later changed its mind and returned many financial responsibilities to the federal government.

Under the new policy, Alberta would assume the full cost of delivering services to off-reserve treaty Indians as long as the federal government agrees to redirect its off-reserve expenditures so that on-reserve services can be brought up to provincial standards. The Alberta government also wants to be reimbursed for the on-reserve services it delivers on a 100 percent fee-for-service basis. To date, this policy has not been implemented. Natives have reacted negatively to the policy because they wish to remain under sole federal jurisdiction. The federal government has also been reluctant to meet all of the terms of the policy.

Conclusion

In summary, throughout Canada's history little attention has been paid to developing a long-term policy to deal with Native problems. Moreover, funding of Native programs has always been minimal. Once it became clear that Indians would accept their fate peacefully, the government was allowed to ignore Native issues for more "pressing" concerns, such as building the railroad and effecting White settlement. In the history of Native-White relations, government has only acted on Native issues when forced to. And when government has acted, it has invariably done so in White interests.

Our analysis of the IIAP has shown that its programs have changed considerably over the years and have failed to reflect any long-term consistent policy. In general, however, the IIAP has consistently taken a wardship approach to Natives. Its budget continues to grow in size, partly as a result of its increased bureaucratic structure; other government departments have also increased their budgets to deal with Native issues, but to little effect.

Recently the federal government has tried to involve provincial governments in Native affairs. Generally it has not had much success. Provincial governments, already hard-pressed for funds, have rejected the costs entailed by direct involvement. For their part, Natives have always tended to distrust the participation of provincial governments, fearing a lessening of federal responsibility. Native Canadians are convinced that the federal government must continue to honour its historical agreements with them, and that any transfer of these agreements is unlikely to be in their best interests.

Notes

1. Legislation under DIAND's responsibility includes the following:

NORTHERN AFFAIRS:

Yukon Act
Northwest Territories Act
Territorial Lands Act
Land Titles Act
Public Lands Grants Act
Canada Lands Surveys Act, Part III
Northern Inland Waters Act
Arctic Waters Pollution Prevention Act
Dominion Water Power Act
Oil and Gas Production and Conservation Act
Yukon Placer Mining Act
Yukon Quartz Mining Act
Northern Canada Power Commission Act
Territorial Supreme Courts Act

INDIAN AND INUIT AFFAIRS:

Indian Act
Indian Oil and Gas Act
James Bay and Northern Quebec Native Claims

Settlement Act
Indian Lands (Settlement of Differences) Act
British Columbia Indian Reserves Mineral Resources Act
Caughnawaga Indian Reserve Act
Fort Nelson Indian Reserve Minerals Revenue Sharing Act
New Brunswick Indian Reserves Agreement Act
Nova Scotia Indian Reserves Agreement Act
St. Peters Indian Reserve Act
St. Regis Indian Reservation Act
Songhees Indian Reserve Act
Alberta Natural Resources Act
Manitoba Natural Resources Act
Natural Resources Transfer (School Lands) Amendment
Railway Belt Act
Public Lands Grants Act
Refunds (Natural Resources Act) Act
Saskatchewan Natural Resources Act
Saskatchewan and Alberta Roads Act
Seed Grain Act

2. The following descriptions of DIAND and the summary of each subdepartment's scope and mandate has been taken from the Department's *Annual Report*, 1980-81.
3. Much of the following discussion has been taken from the work of Ponting and Gibbins (1980). Any reader who wishes to investigate either the structure of the IIAP or the personalities within it should consult this work.
4. Ponting and Gibbins (1980) indicate that "the resultant process is a complicated one which must be launched almost two years prior to the *beginning* (April 1) of the fiscal year for which the figures are being prepared."

9

Native Organizations

Introduction

Political organizations have had a long tradition in the culture of Canadian Natives. Unfortunately, little has been written about these organizations and the role they played in the development of Canada.

In the nineteenth century, several efforts were made by Natives to create regional and national political organizations. The demise of these organizations was generally the result of suppression by the federal government and internal discord among the Natives themselves. These problems continued to plague Native political groups well into the twentieth century.

The desire of the federal government to suppress political activity can be seen in Figure 9.1, which illustrates government reaction to a circular, also reproduced here, distributed by Jules Sioui in a 1943 attempt to organize Native chiefs. A far more serious attempt to deny Natives the right to organize and lobby was the *Indian Act* of 1927, which for many years prohibited the political organization of Natives beyond local levels of government.

Early Native organizations were generally tied to specific concerns, such as particular land claims. These organizations had a single focus, were relatively simple in structure, and were limited to particular areas or groups of Natives. Only since the mid-1950s have Native organizations become multifaceted, complex in structure, and representative of Natives from all across Canada (Patterson, 1972).

One of the earliest recorded Native organizations was the Allied

FIGURE 9.1 *Jules Sioui's circular*

PROVINCE ᴰᴱ QUÉBEC ᴼᶠ

CANADA

COMITÉ DE PROTECTION DES DROITS INDIENS

Quartiers généraux au Village Huron de Lorette

Grand chef,

La présente communication vous avise de la tenue, à Ottawa, le 19 octobre prochain, d'une grande convention des chefs de notre nation. Je dois réclamer la présence, à l'hôtel Windsor, de deux ou trois délégués pour chaque tribu indienne.

Les heures graves que nous vivons nous forcent à ébaucher à préciser des projets de réformes sérieuses. Nous devrons établir celles-ci sans retard si nous voulons sauvegarder nos droits, et cela, dans un pays qui est bien le nôtre.

Une réponse affirmative de tous est urgente. Votre aide financière sera aussi bienvenue, car le coût de ces travaux de réorganisation nous sont très onéreux.

Sincèrement,

Head chief:—

This letter advises you that a general meeting of the chiefs of our Nation will take place in Ottawa, on the 19th day of October next. I do claim the presence, at Windsor Hotel, of two or three delegates from each one of our reserves.

The impact of these perilous moments compels us to draw-up serious reforms. We have to establish such reforms in order to put a betterment in the Indian situation, and this, without delay, if we want the maintenance of our rights in our proper country.

An urgent affirmative answer is requested. A financial help will be welcome as this rally and the works to be performed are very expensive and their cost rests rather heavily on our shoulders.

Sincerely,

JULES SIOUI,
chef exécutif du — C.P. — chief executive,
Case postale Loretteville P. O. B.,
Comté de Québec County.

FIGURE 9.2 *The government's reaction to Jules Sioui's circular*

Ottawa, September 23, 1943

G. Swartman, Esq., Indian Agent, Sioux Lookout, Ontario.

Re: Circular letter to Indian Chiefs
from Jules Sioui

I have to thank you for bringing the circular
enclosed with your letter of September 17 to my attention.

For your information I may say that the person who
signed the circular is not a Chief of the Jeune Lorette
Band. He is an agitator and trouble-maker with whom the
Department has had a great deal of difficulty over a
considerable period. Although he is a member of the band
and an Indian under the law, he is physiologically a White
man with no perceptible Indian characteristic. In the
more settled parts of Eastern Canada, there are many of
these legal Indians who retain their status because of the
paternal descent, but who actually have lost all trace of
Indian blood. They are often the most prominent among
the leaders of movements in support of alleged ancient
Indian rights and other claims which form the basis of
agitation. Needless to say their activities in this
respect usually have ulterior motives of self-interest of
one kind or another.

In the present case it is thanks to you that the
circular in question came to my attention and I appreciate
your promptness in advising me of it. I am taking advantage of the information that you have given me to warn the
Indians about the proposed meeting, through their
respective agents. A copy of the circular letter that I
am sending to all Indian Agents on the subject is enclosed
herewith. I sincerely hope that none of the Indians of
your agency will waste their time and money by travelling
to this meeting or becoming involved in the activities of
Mr. Sioui's organization.

Dr. H. W. McGill

Director.

Indian Tribes of British Columbia, formed in 1915-16[1] to lobby for land claims. Because members were almost all from the Northwest Coast of British Columbia, the scope of the group's activities was quite limited. In 1931, the Allied Indian Tribes became the Native Brotherhood of British Columbia. In 1936, a second organization, the Pacific Coast Native Fisherman's Association, was founded. Although the two groups were sometimes in conflict, they merged in 1942, keeping the name of the Native Brotherhood.

The members of the Brotherhood were all Protestants: in 1943, a rival Catholic organization, the North American Indian Brotherhood, was also established in British Columbia. Although the two groups did not clash overtly, ill-feeling and discord between them prevented either from accomplishing much. The federal and provincial governments capitalized on the differences between the two groups using a divide-and-conquer technique. At each hearing, representatives from both Native organizations were asked for briefs. The government representatives then seized on the contradictions between the recommendations of the two groups and used them as an excuse to ignore all the requests of both.

The two Native groups later met with Eastern Canadian Indians and agreed to form a new national organization – the Brotherhood of Canadian Indians. This new organization had no religious bias and consisted solely of non-treaty Indians.[2] In 1946, the Brotherhood attempted to form a coalition with treaty Indians from Saskatchewan. This proved fruitless, partly because of interference by Saskatchewan's CCF government. Later attempts were more successful, but a definite division continues to persist throughout Canada among non-treaty Indians, treaty Indians, and Métis.

While British Columbian Indians have been organized the longest, other Native groups have been active politically since the 1930s. For example, in Saskatchewan, the Saskatchewan Indian Association was formed in 1944, followed a year later by the Protective Association for Indians and Their Treaties. In 1946, these two groups resolved their differences and merged to form the Union of Saskatchewan Indians. Yet another organization, the Queen Victoria Treaty Protective Association, sprang up to oppose the Union: ten years later, it merged with the Union to form the Federation of Saskatchewan Indians. More recently, in 1970, the Saskatchewan Native Alliance was formed, which continues to be active today.

In Alberta, the Indian Association of Alberta (IAA) was established in 1939 and has remained the only really active organization within the province. Others, such as the Catholic Indian League (1962) and the Calgary Urban Indian Treaty Alliance (1972), have played active but short-lived roles in Native issues.

Although the Indian Association of Alberta was formally begun in

1939, it really started in 1919 with the establishment of the League of Indians of Western Canada. For some time, attempts at Native organization had been frustrated by the efforts of RCMP officers and Indian agents. But in 1920, leaders of various tribes got together in Manitoba and successfully established the League of Indians of Western Canada. In the early 1920s, further meetings took place in Saskatchewan, among the Big Iroquois, and in Alberta to expand the organization. In 1930, due to a serious rift between the Alberta and Saskatchewan Natives, the League was subdivided along provincial lines. In 1939, the Alberta League made a number of organizational changes and became the IAA. Throughout the League's history, until 1939, the federal and provincial governments had not recognized its existence or legitimacy and had refused to act upon any of the recommendations it sent to Ottawa.

Organizations in Eastern Canada, particularly since 1960, have not been as vociferous or as organized as their Western counterparts. However, they do have a long history. In 1840, missionaries helped the Ojibeway of Ontario to form the General Council of the Ojibeway Nations of Indians; in 1846, this was renamed the General Council of Indian Chiefs. Although the Council originally included only Christians, in 1882 it expanded its base and became the General Council of Ontario. This organization lasted until 1938 and was the beginning of the present Union of Ontario Indians.

Even though over a quarter of the Indians in Canada live in Ontario, they have not seriously attempted to link up with other provincial or national Native organizations. The independence and aggressiveness of the Iroquois on the Six Nations Reserve have given them a unique position among Indians in Canada.[2] In addition, their American legal status has served to isolate them from other Native organizations in Canada. Other Natives in Eastern Canada, including those in Quebec, are considered non-Indians; as such they are only nominally recognized by federal and provincial governments as legally Indian.

Membership in Native political organizations has generally been determined by ascription: one is born into an organization, rather than choosing to join it. Legal factors also often determine membership; for example, membership in the National Indian Brotherhood is restricted to registered Indians.

Table 9.1 illustrates the number of Native associations that have been active since 1700. As the table shows, the total number of organizations has recently increased considerably.

Table 9.2 illustrates the primary function of a number of voluntary associations active at some point between 1948 and 1978. As stated previously, these organizations have generally emerged in crisis situations to serve a specific need at a specific time; hence, many of them have been very short-lived. However, in addition to solving a specific problem, other Native organizations have expanded their role to assist

TABLE 9.1   Major Native political voluntary associations in Canada, by date of formation

	Prior to 1799	1800-49	1850-99	1900-09	1910-19	1920-29	1930-39	1940-49	1950-59	1960-69	1970-73	Total
National					1		2	1	1	4	6	15
Regional	2	1	1		1	4	1	1		1	1	13
National-Regional Total	2	1	1		2	4	3	2	1	5	7	28
Newfld.-Labrador										1	2	3
Prince Edward Island												
New Brunswick										1	3	4
Nova Scotia								1		2	2	5
Quebec			1		1	2		1		3	5	13
Ontario			1		1	2		2	1	6	7	20
Manitoba								1	1	2	6	10
Saskatchewan						1	1	5	2	1	4	14
Alberta		1				1	2	1	1	4	3	13
British Columbia			1	1	2	1	3	1	4	8	3	24
Northwest Territories							1			3	3	7
Yukon										2	3	5
Provincial Total		1	3	1	4	7	7	12	9	33	41	118
Grand Total												146

SOURCE: Don Whiteside, *Historical Development of Aboriginal Political Associations in Canada*, (Ottawa: National Indian Brotherhood, 1973), 6.

Natives to integrate into Canadian society. In urban centres, these organizations offer relief from the frustrations felt by Natives who have recently left the reserve. Natives with similar backgrounds, values, and experiences can meet to discuss ways of adapting to urban life and to find solutions to specific problems.

Prior to the creation of contemporary Native associations, there were many tribal organizations. These were closely tied to the religious and cultural components of tribal life, and were directed inward, toward members of the group, rather than outward toward society as a whole. Few tribal organizations presently exist and their role for Natives is more symbolic than instrumental; however, in some areas there has been a resurgence of tribal groups, as in the case of pow-wows.

The contemporary organizational structure has largely resulted from increased urbanization. However, although the organizations function within an urban context, their members are generally rural in orientation and are concerned with rural issues. At present there are few organizations run by urban Natives to address urban issues.

A Review of Four Native Organizations

As Table 9.2 shows, most Native organizations play political, social, and cultural roles. These organizations often function in cities to ease the loneliness, frustration, and alienation that Natives encounter when they leave the reserve. Other organizations provide economic assistance, educational support, and centres for urban Natives. The following four organizational types illustrate the diversity and varying degrees of complexity found among Native organizations. Each of them has also had a substantial impact on Native-White relations since the 1960s.

NATIONAL INDIAN BROTHERHOOD

In 1944, attempts were made to establish the North American Indian Brotherhood. The rather loose structure of this organization collapsed in 1950 due to internal discord. In 1954, the National Indian Council was formed and, in 1961, it became the official organization both for status and for non-status Indians. By 1968, the NIC had split into two organizations: The National Indian Brotherhood for status Indians and The Canadian Métis Society for non-status Natives. In 1970, the Métis Society became the Native Council of Canada. Also in 1970, the National Indian Council, composed of middle-class, urban Indians, formally dissolved; this was due to conflicts among its registered, non-registered, and Métis members.

TABLE 9.2   Reasons for the formation of Native Canadian political associations, by time periods[1]

| | Specific: Treaty rights, Land rights, Social issues etc. | | Reason for protest | | | | | |
| | | | General administrative policies | | Other general protests | | Total | |
Year	#	%	#	%	#	%	#	%
I Prior to 1849	4	100	–	–	–	–	4	100
II 1850-1939	10	31	19	59	3	9	32	100
III 1940-65	4	14	18	62	7	24	29	100
IV 1966-73	22	27	30	37	29	36	81	100
Total	40	27	67	46	39	27	146	100

[1]For purposes of this analysis, all national, regional, and provincial associations were counted together. As a result, one could argue that nine "extra" provincial associations are included in the table. (Six in "specific protests," two in "administrative policies," and one in "general protests.") No cell, however, is changed by more than 3 percent because of the inclusion of associations which might be considered as "extras."

SOURCE: Don Whiteside, *Historical Development of Aboriginal Political Associations in Canada.* (Ottawa: National Indian Brotherhood, 1973), 10.

TABLE 9.3   Federally funded off-reserve services provided to Natives, 1980

Location	Friendship Centres	DIAND Offices	Educational/Cultural Centres	Native Newspapers	Native Studies	Native Organizations
Maritimes						
Sydney Mines			x	x	x	x

Province	City						
Quebec	Val D'or	x					x
	Montreal	x	x	x	xx	xxxx	xxxxx
Ontario	Toronto	x	x				x
	Sault Ste. Marie	x	x	x			
	Kenora	x	x		x	x	x
	Sioux Lookout	x	x		x	x	
	London	x	x		xx	xx	
Manitoba	Winnipeg	x	x	x	xxx	x	x
	Brandon	x	x	x	x	x	
	Thompson	x	x		x		
	Flin Flon	x	x				
Sask.	Regina	x	x		xx	xx	x
	Saskatoon	x	x	x	x	x	x
	Prince Albert	x	x	x	x	x	
	North Battleford	x	x		x		
Alberta	Calgary	x	x	x		x	x
	Edmonton	x	x	x	x	x	x
	Lethbridge	x	x		x		
	Ft. McMurray	x	x				
BC	Vancouver	x	x		xxx	xxx	xxx
	Nanaimo	x	x				
	Prince Rupert	x	x		x		x
	Prince George	x	x		x		
	Port Alberni	x			x		
Yukon	Whitehorse	x	x		x	x	xx
NWT	Yellowknife	x	x		x	x	x

SOURCE: *Indian Conditions*, DIAND, 1981, 145.

The National Indian Brotherhood was originally formed to speak for registered Indians on a number of issues and to help them retain their Native values. However, in 1969, a year after it was formed, the federal government's *White Paper* forced the NIB into a position of political leadership that it maintained throughout the next decade (Ponting and Gibbins, 1980). During that decade, the NIB became a national organization with headquarters in Ottawa and about fifty full-time paid staff members.

In 1980, the NIB began to turn away from its unsought leadership position and return some of its decision-making powers to regional organizations and local bands. At present, the NIB only assists local bands and provincial associations when help is requested. It has also taken on the new role of lobbying the federal and provincial governments on behalf of Indians throughout Canada, focusing on influencing the policy decisions of federal officials.

In 1981 and 1982, the NIB directed its efforts toward the entrenching of Native rights in the new Canadian constitution. In this case, the NIB widened its scope to lobby on an international level. Although the NIB's efforts were not totally successful, the new constitution does at least address the issue of aboriginal rights. However, due to the expense of these international lobbying efforts, the NIB has been forced to reduce its staff by nearly 40 percent and to cut back expenditures on other issues. The NIB's position on the constitution has also created some internal ideological divisions among Indians across Canada.

Recent developments suggest that the NIB will soon cease to exist in its present form. The Assembly of First Nations, which met in early 1981, discussed changing the NIB from an association of organizations to an association of chiefs. According to the Assembly, this would properly emphasize the fact that NIB officials have not been elected on a grass-roots basis and do not speak for all Indians.

Registered Indians in Canada are on the brink of choosing a new framework in which to carry out political activities. Three proposals have been advanced. The first two were developed by the Interim Council of Chiefs. The third proposal was presented by a delegation of registered Indians from Manitoba and Alberta.[3]

PROPOSAL NUMBER ONE

Proposal one, predominantly, is a mere juggling of the various governing arms of the NIB, where the first level of authority is the General Assembly (appointed representatives of the various Provincial and Territorial Organizations (PTO's)) followed by both the Interim Council of Chiefs and the Council of Elders. Below this comes the Executive Council (NIB executives, Elders, and PTO presidents and vice-presidents) followed by the NIB executive and staff which acts as the national lobby.

Proposal one replaces the PTO's General Assembly with the Assembly of First Nations as the highest ranking group in the NIB. The Assembly, comprising all 573 Chiefs across Canada, would be responsible for the discussion of national and international issues. Following these discussions, the Assembly would delegate priority work orders to the lower levels of the organization, like the NIB General Assembly does now.

Below this in authority would be the Council of First Nations, composed of 52 chiefs and a 28-member Council of Elders. Representatives would come equally from one of four regions – either north, south, east or west. Seven members of the Council of Elders and 13 members of the chiefs would come from each region. And, each region has the responsibility to choose its representatives.

FIGURE 9.2   *Proposal number one*

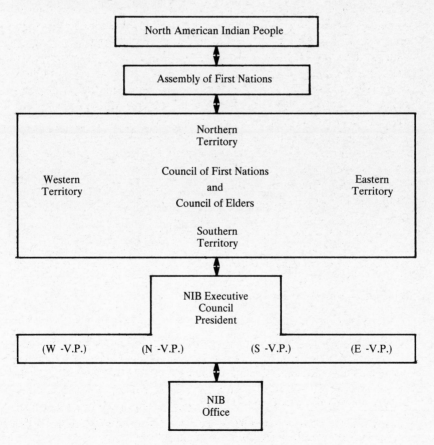

The Council of First Nations would be directly accountable to the Assembly. Along with the tasks of establishing diplomatic relations, nationally and internationally, and establishing "portfolio" committees, this council would be responsible for implementing the Assembly's decisions.

The elders, on the other hand, would fill a spiritual and advisory capacity. They would attend Assembly and Council meetings and evaluate them for spiritual content. The elders would have the added responsibility of monitoring treaty and aboriginal rights negotiations, for the same purpose.

Presumably, since it was never mentioned, the NIB Executive Council and the NIB office would continue as before. The only difference mentioned in the proposal is that the NIB would have four vice-presidents, instead of one. These would come from each of the four areas.

PROPOSAL NUMBER TWO

Again, the only distinction that could be made between proposals one and two is that each has a slightly different structure. Each level of proposal one matches the levels of proposal two. Each council would have the same responsibilities and duties.

As before, the first organizational level would be the Assembly of First Nations. The difference here is that, in proposal two, all 573 chiefs are entitled to membership, plus: the presidents of the PTO's; the NIB executives: the 24 elders of the NIB; and, delegated spokespersons (unidentified).

Membership for both the Elders Council and the 48-member Council of First Nations would, again, be divided on a regional basis – six elders and 12 chiefs from each of the four regions. This time, however, the regions are slightly different.

Area one is composed of British Columbia, the Yukon, and the Northwest Territories; Area two would take in Alberta, Saskatchewan, and Manitoba; Ontario, alone, would comprise Area three; and Quebec and the four Maritime provinces would compose Area four.

The Executive Council, too, would be slightly different. Along with having one chairperson and four vice-chairpersons, the Executive Council would also hold one person from each participating organization. This is in opposition to the straight carbon-copy of the NIB Executive Council proposed in number one.

One structural difference between this proposal and proposal one is that the 24 elders in the Elders Council, would not be a part of the Assembly of First Nations. Instead, the elders would hover in authority slightly below the Assembly, and slightly above the Council of First Nations.

Another structural difference is that the committees, part of the Council of First Nations in proposal one, would be entities unto themselves. They too would hover in their authority, but lower – below the Council of First Nations and above the Executive Council.

Below all this would come the "secretariat", or the NIB.

FIGURE 9.3   *Proposal number two*

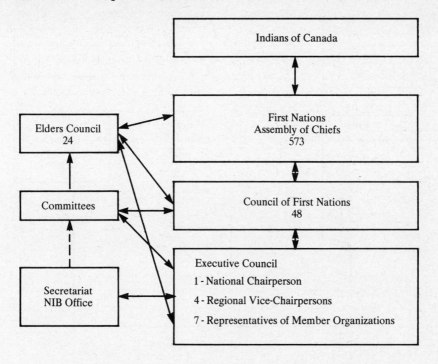

MANITOBA PROPOSAL – OPTION THREE
The structure of the Manitoba proposal is nearly identical to that of proposal two. The primary body would be the Assembly of First Nations, followed closely by what Manitoba calls the "Confederacy of Chiefs" which has the same authority as proposal two's Council of First Nations.

The Council of Elders, as in proposal two, would not be tied to one specific level of authority. Below all these would come the Executive Council of First Nations and its administrative arm, presumably a toned-down NIB. But, the only real difference offered by Manitoba lies in its version of where representation would come from.

The first change in representation occurs in the Assembly of First Nations. Instead of just containing the 573 chiefs of Canada, the Manitoba version of the Assembly would allow headmen of each local Indian government (band) to be members.

The second change comes in the 'Confederacy of Chiefs.' Instead of being represented by PTO members, Canada's Indian people would be represented by chiefs. These chiefs would be allowed membership according to the population of their individual Indian governments.

There are two ways Manitoba suggests this be done: one representative

FIGURE 9.4　*Manitoba proposal – option three*

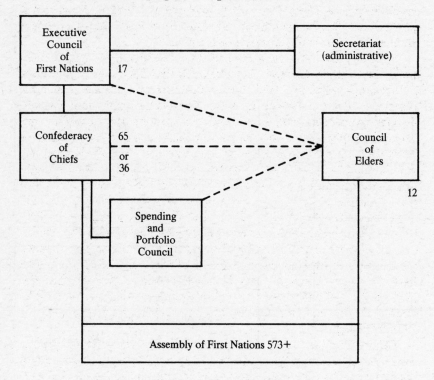

for every 5 000 Indians; or, one representative for every 10 000 Indians. This would mean that the Confederacy would hold either 65 or 36 members.

Structurally, everything else remains the same as in proposal two. Numerically, only the elders will be changed. There will be twelve people on the Elders Council – one for each province or territory.

RED POWER ORGANIZATIONS

Broadly speaking, Red Power addresses the Natives' inability either to separate from or to integrate with the rest of Canada (Franklin, 1969). While Red Power has so far failed to present a clearcut program, its most important focus seems to be on the control of reserve lands.

Red Power advocates are attempting to unite a number of other moderate and militant groups into a network across Canada. Although there are many important differences, some of their major ideological themes have been derived from the Black Power movement in the United States. In general, Red Power promotes self-supporting, self-directing, and commonly-owned Native communities. Red Power members wish to create, develop, and carry out their own political, economic, and social programs. They also want to improve the Native's image on a personal level by changing the negative stereotypes of laziness and drunkenness and by creating a more positive image.

White society often criticizes Natives for being apathetic and unwilling to better their position. Unfortunately, however, one of the most potent forces of colonialism is the way it breaks the spirit and quells the resistance of the colonized minority. Continuing oppression through poverty, poor health conditions, lack of education and job opportunities, stereotyping, and so on, has become ingrained in the very fabric of Native life, and will take more than a few years and a few social programs to overcome. Ironically, when Natives do shake off apathy and, through Red Power groups, try to realistically better their position, they are again criticized, this time on the grounds of stridency and militancy. Confronted with this "catch 22", Red Power advocates have sensibly decided to progress with their own plans and ignore White reactions.

Those pan-American Indians who belong to the League of Nations are generally considered the most radical of the Red Power groups. The League is a very loose inter-tribal organization from which splinter groups, such as the National Alliance for Red Power (NARP), have emerged. More and more militant youths are joining the League or one of its splinter groups.

League members rally under the central issue of treaty and aboriginal rights. They argue that Native tribes must be viewed as nations and want any litigation between Natives and the Canadian government to be referred to the United Nations. The militance of these groups, exemplified by various peaceful and violent demonstrations since 1970, is continuing to grow.

Waubageshig, a League leader, discussing the possibility of violence in Canada, has stated:

> Violence in our communities, both on and off the reservation, is occurring at this very moment. . . . If this does not stop . . . then there is going to be a very angry young Indian population which will say, "What the hell! I have nothing to lose." And we may have political violence. If no one listens to what these young people are saying and nothing is done, then violence will erupt. (1970:167)

Moderate Natives are beginning to view militants like Waubageshig in a far more positive light than they did ten years ago.

Recently, the League's activities have included approaching the United Nations to protest the Canadian federal government's treatment of Indians. Since 1970, the notion of Red Power has been used increasingly by League activists. As Lurie reports:

In many Canadian reserve towns the White population is relatively small but dominates business and commercial interests. All across Canada there have been hostile, even violent "incidents" – so far without fatalities – and many more are threatened. (1971:466)

During the mid-1970s, the American Indian Movement (AIM) gained some support in areas of Canada. AIM views itself as a grass-roots organization in touch with the daily needs of Native people. Its general strategy is based on confrontation politics, coercive threats, and, occasionally, violence. Its fluid membership and loose structure make it difficult to assess its number of members. It is also difficult to determine the impact of this group on younger Natives.

AIM and other militant Red Power groups use techniques that are difficult for bureaucrats to deal with. Many Natives feel that recent changes made by DIAND are a direct result of Red Power activities. However, Red Power is only in its seminal stages and has so far gained support only from a minority of Natives. Like their White counterparts, most Natives are apathetic in their commitment to social change. Even among the activists, there are many traditionalists who spurn the efforts of Red Power advocates.

As Boldt (1980) and Mackie (1974) have pointed out, many Native leaders are beginning to reject White society entirely and are starting to develop the concept of a Native society – a national, and possibly international, Native community. Boldt states that:

This pan-Indian concept and the emergent political and cultural movement with which it is associated is serving to identify new boundaries and to create new over-arching Indian loyalties at the national level. It is a movement to enhance a sense of commonality and group consciousness which goes beyond mere political organizations to include recognition of a shared history of oppression, cultural attitudes, common interests, and hopes for the future. (1980:4)

Boldt (1973) interviewed sixty-nine Indian leaders across Canada to assess the extent of their adherence to militant Red Power ideology. Based on their responses, Boldt was able to identify four basic types of leader: Nationalists, Autonomists, Adapted Departmentalists, and Integrationists. While specific figures are not presented, it seems that nearly half the Natives interviewed held either a Nationalist or an Autonomist position.

Nationalists are committed to complete political independence. They want to create a geographically defined nation-state which would provide residence exclusively for a large number of Natives. Autonomists also want to establish a national Native federation, but within the existing political structure of Canada. They are interested primarily in controlling the processes that regulate their lives, such as education, police activity, and community development. Departmentalists want to retain the political and administrative structures that presently relate to Natives, but with some adjustments to allow for Native input into government decision-making. Finally, Integrationists want to abolish all political structures, such as DIAND, that grant separate status to Natives. They want to eliminate the category of "Indian" and to assimilate all Natives into White society.

The Nationalists see integration as irrelevant. Nationalists are trying to build economic and political institutions that Natives can plan, own, and control. On the other hand, the Autonomists seek integration of Indians into the system, though they want to remain a distinct ethnic group in the socio-political activities of the country. In addition, they agree with the more traditional Native organizations that social change should be achieved through legitimate means. To date, however, most of the Nationalist and Autonomist organizations have chosen to act on local community issues rather than on national issues, which suggests that their impact on the total system has been minimal.

No more than 3 to 5 percent of today's Natives can be considered Red Power advocates. But this does not mean that militant organizations are not important. As research has shown, only a small percentage of a given population ever takes part in riots, revolutions, and urban guerilla warfare. This small group, however, does need moral, economic, and physical support from the wider community, support that Natives increasingly seem willing to give to Red Power activitists. It is not surprising that the RCMP has defined discontent among Natives as one of the most serious threats to Canadian unity.

Red Power supporters have shaken off the White liberal humanism that views violence as the worst possible sin. They argue that violence is inevitable in the struggle to combat racism and achieve control over their lives. Although few Whites can agree, more and more Natives are beginning to do so.

INDIAN-ESKIMO ASSOCIATION

The Indian-Eskimo Association, later called the Canadian Association in Support of the Native People (CASNP), began in 1957 and was dismantled in the early 1980s. The CASNP brought together a largely non-Native group of influential people to act as a lobbying force for Natives. As well, it tried to set up conferences and workshops in which representatives could discuss Native issues with the general public. Although its legitimacy came under attack from Natives several times during its short history, the CSNP did provide the first national organization for Natives and did manage to influence some of the policies that emanated from Ottawa.

Twenty years after its inception, the CASNP is, for all practical purposes, no longer in existence. Other Native organizations, such as the National Indian Brotherhood, the Inuit Tapirisat of Canada, the National Association of Friendship Centres, and the Native Council of Canada (for non-status Indians and Métis) have all come to play more active and forceful roles in Canadian politics.

FRIENDSHIP CENTRES

Prior to 1970, Native organizations were defined as political and therefore ineligible for funding from such government departments as the Secretary of State. When these organizations were redefined as non-political, they began to receive services and support from government departments and agencies. Administrative funding for Native organizations is currently administered through the Secretary of State. As a result of this funding, most urban areas in Canada with a sizeable Native population have Indian Friendship Centres. (See Table 9.3.) At present there are over 70 Centres across Canada, largely because of a $26 million one-time grant by the federal government.

Friendship Centres are designed to act both as drop-in centres and as counselling centres. Ideally, Natives who come to the city can use the facilities to help them adapt to urban life. However, a number of problems have plagued the Centres since their formation. The federal government funds the Centres only on a short-term, year-to-year basis; this prevents long-term planning and development. In addition, the amount of funding is not enough to allow the Centres to effectively play their role and ease the process of urban adaptation.

A third problem is a lack of cohesion among the Native administrators and clientele of the Centres. There are frequent rifts between political factions concerning goals and strategies; in addition, there are time-honoured differences between status and non-status Natives and among diverse linguistic and cultural groups. As a result, a Centre is often dominated by one group to the exclusion of others.

SUMMARY

This short review of four types of Native organizations has demonstrated several points. All these organizations have become important vehicles for meeting the needs of native people. They have all provided forums for the understanding and discussion of Native issues. Each of these organizations has also had to adapt its structure and objectives to existing conditions or quickly lose its membership.

Clearly, the use of formal organizations among Natives is likely to increase. They have discovered that formal organizations carry a sense of legitimacy that can be very effective in persuading governments to act in Native interests. These organizations have also begun to produce the vocal, articulate, and powerful leadership that will be essential to the improvement of Native conditions. Organizations continue to provide opportunities to develop leadership techniques and other political skills for those who choose to move Native issues into the political arena.

Revitalization Movements

There are many other Native organizations that focus on specific political and economic goals. On a more general level, however, there are two influential movements that are attempting to promote a wide-ranging return to Native social and cultural values. These revitalization movements have many implications for Native organizations.

The first of these is the pow-wow movement. The pow-wow is a planned inter-tribal affair usually held on neutral ground. There is dancing and social interaction, ritual healings, and serious discussions on the future of Native life. The young are encouraged to learn Native customs from their elders. It is hoped that, eventually, these pow-wows will build community solidarity among Natives everywhere.

As Corrigan (1970) points out, the pow-wow circuit acts as a communications network to promote the social and cultural integration of many Native groups. Other analysts, such as Howard (1951) and Lurie (1971), have also viewed the pow-wow as the current vehicle for achieving pan-Indianism. In an in-depth analysis, Dyck found that pow-wows "constitute an autonomous achievement which summons a larger community to celebrate the value and the excellence of Indianness in a manner which is both individually rewarding and collectively uncontroversial" (1979:92-93). Furthermore, because pow-wows range over a large geographical area and provide continuity with the past, they can create a community out of various separate reserve communities.

The second form of revitalization movement is the resurgence of prophet religions. A typical prophet religion is that led by Chief Robert Smallboy of Alberta. In 1968, Smallboy and 150 followers left their reserve for the mountains west of Red Deer, Alberta to re-establish their former culture. Life in Smallboy's camp is a mixture of traditional and modern technology. Children are taught in a regular school but also learn woodlore, hunting, and fishing.

In 1972, the federal government revoked Smallboy's permit to remain on a federal forest reserve. A year later, almost half his initial followers left Smallboy and returned to their reserve. However, the movement continually attracts newcomers. Smallboy is presently negotiating with the federal government to remain in a 100-acre area near Jasper Park. Several European environmentalist groups, such as Survival International, are also trying to have Smallboy's case presented to the international Russell Tribunal, which investigates abuses of Native peoples.

Cultural revitalization movements generally arise when colonized people begin to reject their subjugation. Smallboy's camp may be viewed as a nativistic movement although its impact is too recent to analyze fully. However, particularly in the West, several other camps have been established by other leaders who are beginning to attract small followings.

Funding of Native Organizations

How have Native organizations and social movements improved the quality of Native life? Previously, the Native response to White society has been articulatory in that it has incorporated various aspects of White culture (Lurie, 1971). However, with the growth of various organizations and ideological movements, Natives are becoming more politically, socially, and economically aware. Formal organizations have allowed Natives to carry on discussions with the federal government on a legitimized basis. In the past, the government could reject Native claims and recommendations on the grounds that they were conflicting, inconsistent, and did not represent the demands of a clearcut constituency. Today, however, the demands of Native organizations reflect a collectively determined policy and present cogent and coherent arguments.

Although the federal government relaxed its opposition to Native political development after World War II, Native organizations did not really take root until the mid-1960s. Only at that time were Natives able to obtain the funds needed to create formal organizational structures on a regional or national basis. As Whiteside (1980) has shown, money only really became available to Natives around 1966. In 1963, the Centennial Commission provided about $150 000 to Native people to support small projects of their own design. By 1968, the war against poverty was underway, and the Department of Forestry and Rural Development was sending community development workers into reserve areas. As an example, the Federation of Saskatchewan Indians received over $50 000 to help Natives in a variety of ways, including the development of organizations through which they could articulate their needs in a systematic fashion.

The Secretary of State also began to fund Native projects. In 1964, it began to provide a small annual grant to the National Indian Council for holding meetings. By 1970, this had escalated so that the Secretary of State was providing nearly $50 000 to Natives for conferences and sustaining grants. When all sources of funding were combined, Natives in 1970 received nearly $1 million for organizational activities.

DIAND originally reacted negatively to the funding of Natives by other government organizations. It considered these other bodies in direct violation of the principle, maintained since Confederation, that only DIAND could deal with Native issues. DIAND also began to feel pressure as its decisions and authority came under challenge. Moreover, it felt that Natives were receiving funds from other government departments and agencies which could undermine DIAND's policies.

In an attempt to reassert its sole control, DIAND began to provide each provincial Indian Association with a per capita grant of $1 per registered Indian. It also provided 25¢ per registered Indian to the newly formed National Indian Brotherhood. After the federal government released its *White Paper* in 1969, the Privy Council also approved a grant of $500 000 over five years to Native associations for systematic research on various claims and grievances.

By the 1970s, other federal departments and agencies, such as the Central Mortgage and Housing Corporation and the Department of National Health and Welfare, were providing monies to Natives. As Whiteside points out:

> The response of the Department of Indian Affairs to this continued "outside" funding was consistent. They fought back and argued that they alone had the responsibility for Indians and it was both irresponsible and unfair for other departments to interfere with this responsibility. The Department argued further, and rightly so, that the monies were being used by the political associations to force the Department to abandon its existing programs in favour of the ones which the associations demanded.... Some programs in favour from other departments were transferred to Indian Affairs, where they were allowed to either die or become relatively useless. (1980:11-12)

The impact of Native political organizations has been substantial, both for Natives and for government. For Natives, organizations have granted input into the federal and provincial policies that affect them. By so doing, they have provided Natives with instruments by which to bring about social change. But government has also found that dealing with an organization has many benefits. Because the bureaucracies within Native organizations are similar to those in government, both can now interact in an orderly, legitimate fashion. In addition, the government funding of most Native political organizations makes them more vulnerable to government control.

Indians as an Interest Group

The overall aim of Native organizations is to gain sizable input into the government decisions that affect them. In general, Native interest groups have found that appeals to MP's and MLA's are ineffective, except as a last resort. Rather, they have learned to focus on the bureaucratic organizations that affect them most directly, whether at the federal, provincial, or municipal level. Interest groups can also influence government in other ways, such as through annual submissions to the federal cabinet on aspects of federal policy. Local and provincial interest groups may deal directly with the government at any level or may channel their appeal through whatever nationwide organization they possess.

Not all Native organizations are equally effective in their efforts to influence government. The explanation for a group's failure or success seems to lie in its basic organizational structure. Institutional interest groups can be placed at one end of a structural spectrum, and issue-oriented interest groups at the other. In Table 9.4, Pross (1975) delineates the basic differences between the two.

Because of their lack of organizational structure, issue-oriented groups are generally less effective in pursuing and achieving their goals. Moreover, their goals are restricted to a narrow focus and can only be pursued one at a time. The highly structured institutional groups, however, are free to pursue a number of broadly-defined issues simultaneously. Issue-oriented groups have a small membership and a minimal, usually volunteer, staff to handle communications. Institutional groups, meanwhile, can bring extensive financial and human resources to bear on a variety of issues. Clearly, the Native organizations that are more institutional in nature have a greater chance of achieving their goals. Institutional organizations can choose from a variety of persuasive techniques, such as advertising, and can cultivate long-term formal and informal relations with government officials and senior civil servants.

Until very recently, Native organizations have been of the issue-oriented type. Hence they have been unable to generate credibility and carry on sustained wide-scale negotiations. However, Native organizations are presently moving toward the institutional end of the continuum. This shift guarantees that they will become a more potent force in Canadian politics.

TABLE 9.4 *The organizational structure of interest groups*

Institutional	*Issue-oriented*
Possess organizational continuity and cohesion.	Have limited organization and cohesion.
Are knowledgeable about government sectors which affect them.	Possess poor information about government.
Have a stable membership.	Have a fluid membership.
Operational objectives are concrete and immediate.	Show an inability to formulate long-term goals.
Credibility of the organization is important.	Goal achievement is important.

SOURCES: Adapted from P. Tross, ed., *Pressure Group Behaviour in Canadian Politics,* (Toronto: McGraw-Hill, 1975); P. Tross, "Pressure Groups: Talking Chameleons", in M. Whittington and G. Williams, eds., *Canadian Politics in the 1980s,* (Toronto: Methuen, 1981).

Pan-Indianism[5]

As stated earlier, the growth of Native organizations and movements is helping Natives to retain their culture and identity and is reinforcing links among Natives all over Canada. The pan-Indian movement emphasizes the values and beliefs central to the culture of Canadian Natives regardless of local band differences.

There are two different types of pan-Indianism – religious and reform. Religious pan-Indianism has developed in rural areas and urges a style of living that is in harmony with nature. Humanity is viewed simply as one element of nature, always to be respected. In contrast, reform pan-Indianism is largely an urban phenomenon. It not only promotes the traditional values of Native culture, but also tries to facilitate Native involvement in the business and professional life of the city. Its proponents feel that Native culture should be retained as a distinctive jewel in the cultural mosaic of Canadian society (Hertzberg, 1971).

Pan-Indian movements have several ties to White culture. Their emergence coincided with, and was somewhat marginal to, the rise of conservation movements throughout North America. The leaders of pan-Indian movements have extensive contacts with White society: although they all retain a strong affiliation to a Native tribe, they are generally part-White, bilingual, well-educated, and involved in typically White occupations. In addition, pan-Indian movements were and continue to be widely supported by Whites. However, as the movements become more militant in their demands for structural social changes, White supporters are placed in an increasingly embarrassing position.

Pan-Indianism presents a mixture of traditional Native and White values. The emphasis on Native values is all-pervasive, and extends into the decision-making process. Traditionally, Natives feel that, to be valid, discussion of an issue must not be inhibited by rules of order. They also believe that decisions must be reached by consensus, not by majority vote.

Often in past meetings between Native representatives and DIAND, the Ottawa officials have tired of the Natives' seemingly endless dialogue. Believing the Natives incapable of making a decision, DIAND has simply gone ahead and made it for them. Government officials have still not adequately grasped that, for the Natives, all the procedures involved in a dialogue are important in themselves. White officials have also questioned the sincerity of the Natives' consensus approach to group decisions, claiming that, after a consensus decision has been reached, many Natives still talk against it. Again, the accusation of insincerity reflects a shallow understanding of Native culture.

The resurrection of Native humour and its distinctive style of presentation is another aspect of pan-Indianism. Humour has a high priority in Native culture. Unlike Whites, Natives do not tell jokes as such. Instead, they concentrate on stories or anecdotes like the following:

> In a White community several Indians lived nearby. One day an old Indian's horse died. Since it was winter, he pulled it near a creek which provided the town with water. Since spring was nearing, the community was concerned with the dead horse polluting their drinking water. A member of the White community was delegated to talk to the old Indian and ask him to move it. He agreed and three days later the delegate from the community saw the old Indian's son move the horse five feet. This, of course, did not solve the problem. The result was that the White delegate moved the horse. Several weeks later, a second horse of the old Indian also died. He pulled his dead horse onto a hill near a Catholic church. Each day the priest would ask the old man to move it and he would agree, but things kept coming up which prevented him from moving the horse. Each week the stench grew greater, so that after church services one Sunday, the priest and several White men moved it two miles out of town.

Funny? Not to Whites. Yet, when told to a group of British Columbian Indians, the story produced broad smiles and gales of laughter: an old Indian was able to get White men to do his work for him.

Other cultural traits basic to pan-Indianism include an emphasis on sharing and an absence of emotional attachment to personal possessions. As historical potlatches show, considerable status can be achieved through the sharing of worldly goods; a refusal to share is interpreted as selfishness. Other Native characteristics have received less attention from anthropologists, such as an acceptance of the behaviour of others and a deep respect for basic human rights. These attitudes often serve to alienate Natives from the self-serving, manipulative White society that they find when they leave the reserve. As Lurie (1971) has shown, another Native cultural trait is withdrawal from situations that are anxiety-producing.

Although many Natives and Whites see the reserve either as a prison or as a physical and psychological refuge, members of pan-Indian movements regard it as the basis for a viable community. These members are not deterred by the fact that reserves are generally poverty-stricken, isolated, and lacking in essential services.

Limits to the Activities of Native Organizations

Every Native organization and movement, formal or informal, is contributing to Native nationalism and providing Natives with a sense of identity. Increasingly, Natives are confronting the despair and disillusion that accompanies rejection by White society. Natives today are angry people: angry at the treatment they receive when they attempt to integrate and angry at the government's attempts to abolish their reserves.

Native organizational efforts are all limited by a relatively small population size, a lack of access to power, and a dependency on the federal government for funding and resources. Although Native organizations have been able to bring some pressure to bear on private companies and local government agencies, their dependency on the federal government is still the most significant limitation to their activities.

As Dosman (1972) has shown, when Natives in Saskatoon organized the Indian and Métis Development Society to be completely independent of the Department of Indian Affairs, it was deliberately discredited and eventually destroyed by DIAND. An even worse example of DIAND interference was its reaction to the Indian Association of Alberta (IAA) in the mid-1970s. When it became evident that the IAA's leader, Harold Cardinal, was moving away from standard DIAND policies, Indian Affairs charged the Association with improperly spending federally allocated money and with failing to account for nearly half of its expenditures.

Most Canadians were aware of the incident but few know of the subsequent events. The Association produced documents to show that it had spent the money as directed, with written approval from DIAND and the Secretary of State Department. Then documents were also produced to show that both federal departments had improperly requested that sizable portions of the IAA grant be spent on programs for which money was not allocated. Finally, and crucially, the IAA was denied a hearing at the standing committee on Indian Affairs in which to publicly clear itself and prove that all money had been spent in accordance with the initial terms of its funding.

Because he felt that personalities were clouding the issue, Cardinal resigned as president of the Association. From the time of the initial charges until Cardinal resigned, all federal support for the Association had been cut off. Within weeks of Cardinal's resignation, however, the remainder of the grant was paid to the IAA as well as additional money not requested. Despite these events, Cardinal was re-elected president of the IAA a year later.

While forcing the resignation of controversial leaders through financial sanctions may solve problems in the short term, such government actions unwittingly contribute to the growth of Native nationalism. Nonetheless, the federal government continues to exert control over Native organizations by a variety of means. It can offer or withold information that is essential for effective planning and operations. It can co-opt the loyalties of Native leaders or define an organization as radical to reduce the chances of private financing and support.

The growth of pan-Indianism is facilitated by the spreading of information and values relevant to Natives. Until recently, this process was hindered by primitive communication processes, a lack of literacy, and linguistic diversity among the Native population. However, as English becomes the working language of Natives, as literacy levels rise, and as greater funding is provided, Native groups are increasingly gaining access to news media. Table 9.5 shows the distribution of various Native publications in the eight regions of Canada. In 1978, there were sixty-seven Native periodicals, as compared to thirty-seven in 1971.

Native periodicals tend to be rural in orientation, although over half are published in cities (Price, 1978). As Price (1972) points out, the growth of Native periodicals in a city reflects the increasing development of other institutions. Periodicals also provide information to many Natives throughout Canada and reinforce Native values.

Most Native periodicals aim to develop political awareness and Native identity, as well as to promote action on particular issues. In an analysis of three major Indian papers, *The Calumet, Native People,* and *The Drum,* Price (1972) found that policies differed quite widely. The Northern newspaper favoured the assimilation of Natives, while in Eastern Canada, the paper aimed for integration. The newspaper for Western Natives, however, maintained a basic liberationist, or separatist, ideology. Nevertheless, the three papers did share several themes. For example, each argued that the Indian problem was really a White problem. Other shared topics included the superiority of traditional Native culture, the inability of Whites to understand Natives, and the need for Natives to develop their own resources.

TABLE 9.5   *Native periodicals by area in Canada*¹

	Number	Periodicals	Proportion of Status Indians	Associations
Number		67	260 000	407
Maritimes	2	3%	4%	5%
Quebec	4	6%	11%	5%
Ontario	19	28%	22%	18%
Manitoba	8	12%	14%	15%
Saskatchewan	10	15%	14%	13%
Alberta	4	6%	12%	16%
BC	9	13%	19%	21%
Territories	11	17%	4%	7%
Total	67	100%	100%	100%

¹Some periodicals are unilingual (in one language, either French, English, or a Native dialect) while others are bilingual.
SOURCE: J. Price, *Native Studies* (Toronto: McGraw-Hill Ryerson, 1978), 186.

In the North, radio programs in Native dialects not only disseminate information but also provide a platform for Native issues. However, the government still attempts to censor these programs before they are aired. At present, moreover, most programs are controlled by Whites and originate in the South. Recently, the CBC rejected a Native proposal to give Native broadcasters some access to the new Northern satellite system.

Recent Political Activities

When the federal government published its *White Paper* in 1969, a number of Native organizations began to play a leadership role in Native-White relations. They adopted offensive strategies and abandoned their previous defensive positions. The *White Paper* produced a loose coalition of Natives who had previously belonged to separate groups with diverse goals.

The formal briefs presented to the federal government in opposition to the *White Paper* were separate but similar in content; these included the *Brown Paper* by British Columbian Natives, the *Red Paper (Citizens Plus)* by Alberta Natives, and *Wahbung* by Manitoba Natives. Those Natives who did not submit formal briefs appeared to be in basic agreement with those who did. The coalition that resulted from the *White Paper* was an important milestone in Native political organization. Natives had previously been unable to form strong coalitions against earlier bills, such as *Bill C-130* (1963), which provided for the disposition of Native claims.

The 1969 *White Paper* to some extent reflected the basic sentiments of White Canada. It assumed that if Canadian Natives were to become fully integrated into Canadian society, they must change radically. It argued that the separate legal status of Natives kept them from fully participating in the larger society. Therefore, the *White Paper* proposed the following changes, to take place over approximately five years.

- Repeal the *Indian Act* to enable Natives to control their lands and acquire title to them.
- Have the provincial governments assume responsibility for Natives as they have for other citizens in their provinces.
- Make substantial funds available for Native economic development as an interim measure.
- Phase out the Department of Indian Affairs and Northern Development which deals with Native affairs.
- Appoint a commissioner to consult with Natives and to study and recommend acceptable procedures for the adjudication of claims (*Indian Policy*, 1969:6).

Supporters of the *White Paper* argued that the creation of reserves and, subsequently, of the *Indian Act* had prevented Natives from participating in the development of Canadian society. They felt that Natives had been legally and administratively discriminated against and therefore had not been given an equal chance of success.

In general, the opponents of the *White Paper* saw it as a disguised program of cultural extermination (Cardinal, 1969). Opposition particularly focused on the Natives' right to maintain their ethnic identity. Critics felt that Natives should remain legally, administratively, and socially separate if they so chose. The Hawthorn Report (1966-67), a sort of Royal Commission on the "Indian problem", recommended that Natives be granted special status as "citizens plus" to ensure the preservation of their separate identity.

Opponents of the *White Paper* also argued that it would make all outstanding legal suits against the government, specifically concerning land claims, redundant. They also viewed skeptically the government's promise to "make substantial funds available for Indian economic development".

The Minister of Indian Affairs claimed that the *White Paper* was a response to Native recommendations. Critics have responded that either the Minister acted dishonestly on behalf of White economic interest groups or entirely misinterpreted Native attitudes. Whatever the answer, Natives claim they were not consulted before the drafting of the *White Paper.*[6]

Opponents to the government position want Natives to remain a distinct ethnic group, free to control their own affairs without undue interference by provincial or federal governments. They want to develop Native autonomy through the establishment of inter-provincial Native organizations and the restructuring of present Native social institutions. In other words, they want political organizations to be created by Natives, for Natives, and under the control of Natives.

All three Native briefs presented several arguments against the implementation of the *White Paper,* along with their own positions and recommendations. Natives have often been criticized for failing to make constructive proposals of their own. However, the *Brown Paper,* the *Red Paper,* and *Wahbung* each presented several concrete proposals and specific strategies to solve Native issues. The following summaries outline the major recommendations in those Native briefs.

The *Red Paper* is the best known of the briefs and was the most specific in its proposals concerning education and economic development. The *Red Paper* argued that the *Indian Act* must be reviewed and amended, but not repealed. This argument was echoed by the other briefs, particularly *Wahbung,* which recommended specific changes in such areas as wills, health services, and elections of chiefs and councils.

All of the briefs discussed the Department of Indian Affairs. They rejected the *White Paper*'s proposal to abolish it, arguing that it should become a smaller structure more attuned to local and regional Native needs. All the briefs argued that local tribal or band councils must be given more decision-making powers by Indian Affairs so that they can take the initiative in the social, political, and economic development needed to tap previously ignored reserve resources. However, only the *Brown Paper* stated that Indian Affairs personnel should be exclusively Native.

Because treaties have not been established with most British Columbian Natives, land rights are still paramount for them; therefore the *Brown Paper* explored the land issue in considerable depth. The other two briefs also allude to land rights but did not discuss them in detail.

The *Brown Paper* was the least comprehensive in its treatment of economic development, while the *Red Paper* was very explicit. The *Red Paper* proposed that an Alberta Indian Development System (AIDS) be created to upgrade Native socio-economic status through community economic development. Through AIDS, Natives would arrange to do work needed in the community, and industry-related jobs would be developed. AIDS would be controlled by a dual corporate structure formed by Native and non-Native leaders. Natives would set the goals and priorities of all projects and non-Natives would advise and assist in the development of these goals. A capital fund of $50 million would be needed, $30 million to come from the federal government, $10 million from the Alberta government, and $8.7 million from private industry. Alberta Natives would also invest an initial $1.3 million.

The *Red Paper* also presented the most extensive recommendations with regard to education. It proposed the creation of an Indian Education Centre (IEC) to be located in the centre of Alberta to provide equal access for all Alberta Natives. The IEC would teach Native children how to successfully adapt Native skills and values to life in the larger Canadian context. It would also teach them modern skills to help them achieve success in the job market. In essence, the IEC would be run by Natives to assure them a secure place in Canadian society.

The federal government initially approved the IEC in principle. In 1971, the Department of the Secretary of State initiated the funding of an educational concept referred to as Cultural Education Centres. These centres were to provide alternatives to existing middle-class White schools. They were designed to render education meaningful to Natives and to stimulate self-worth and self-confidence among Native students. The Department of Indian Affairs opposed the Secretary of State and fought the creation and financing of these centres, ultimately gaining control of most of the funding. Whiteside comments on DIAND's power play:

> In a short time the Department gained control over almost the entire program. Once they controlled the funds, they convinced the existing centres to adopt a very narrow view of education, and to emphasize Indian culture. At the same time, the Department created many small centres which spread the limited funds across more and more centres. Thus, by encouraging small centres and giving the funds to the band councils to do with as they wished, the Deparement ensured that large centres had to close because of lack of funds. (1980:12)

Theoretically, Cultural Education Centres were to be replaced by Native Studies Programs attached to existing post-secondary institutions. In the end, one Native Studies Program was implemented in Lethbridge and Native Counselling Services were approved for Alberta's two major universities.

In *Wahbung,* the Manitoba Indian Brotherhood recommended that a joint committee of the Brotherhood and the regional office of DIAND be established with an equal number of Natives and Whites to handle Native issues. From this committee, several joint boards and commissions covering local government, economic development, welfare, education, and policing could be established. *Wahbung* also recommended that a cabinet committee be formed consisting of Native leaders to advise on cabinet policy decisions concerning Natives.

In 1974, in response to this recommendation, a joint committee of NIB and DIAND was created. Although it did not take the recommended form, a special cabinet committee was created for the first time to deal specifically with Native concerns. The overall structure consisted of the NIB executive council and federal cabinet ministers. Within this, there was also a joint sub-committee and a joint working group. However, in 1978, the NIB withdrew from the committee and it died a quite death.

All the briefs argued for immediate recognition of treaty and aboriginal rights, and the establishment of a commission to interpret the government's treaty obligations. The *Brown Paper* and *Wahbung* did not make specific recommendations on Native claims. They did, however, recommend a Claims Commission be established through consultation with Natives and that it be *able to make binding judgments.* The *Red Paper* quite explicitly rejected the concept of a claims commissioner. It argued for a full-time Minister of Indian Affairs and the creation of a permanent standing committee of the House of Commons and Senate to deal only with registered Indians.

A claims commissioner was established in the late 1960s and an Office of Native Claims was established in 1973. The commission is only advisory, although, with the approval of the Department of Justice, it will investigate and take action both on comprehensive and on specific claims.

The Native briefs also urged Native control over reserve finances, taxation, reconciliation of injustices, housing, and health services.

Although the proposals contained in the three briefs were developed independently, there were very few contradictions. The proposals did, however, reflect each group's special needs: for example, British Columbian Natives were concerned with land, and focused on treaties, aboriginal rights, and the land issue. However, all the briefs agreed on major issues such as economic development, education, and the *Indian Act.*

Over a decade after the briefs, little has changed. Some minor recommendations have been implemented in watered-down versions, but basic structural and philosophical changes have not taken place in the government's Native policy.

The basic thrust of the *White Paper* was to eliminate reserves. An examination of the reservation termination policy that was implemented in the United States sheds considerable light on this issue. Between 1953 and 1960, over sixty reserves were eliminated in the United States. By 1960, the results were clearly so disastrous that the scheme was halted.

In 1954, the Klamath Indian reservation of Oregon began to be phased out and, in 1958, termination was completed. Prior to termination, the Indians had developed a thriving business based on reserve forest products. From this resource alone, the average income for each person was about $800 a year and the average family income was $3 000 to $4 000. Many Indians worked at other jobs on and off the reserve, raising the average income per family to nearly $6 000; by 1954 standards, this placed the Indians in about the ninetieth percentile of the American population. By 1958, when the termination was complete, many Klamaths were on welfare and had suffered as a result of extreme social disorganization. Family stability had decayed sharply, crimes of all kinds had risen acutely, and the community social network had broken down. By 1960, nearly a third of the Klamath Indians were on welfare or in mental or penal institutions throughout Oregon. Through termination on White terms, a thriving, self-sustaining community had deteriorated into a social disaster area.

Theoretically, the Klamaths should have succeeded in their transition. As Spencer and Jennings (1965) noted, the Klamaths were much more individualistic than other Indian tribes, and therefore had more in common with White society. If the results were so disastrous for the Klamaths, then they are bound to be worse for other Natives.

Other terminations of American reserves have produced similar results. However, these findings are consistently ignored by those who favour the phasing out of reserves in Canada.

Conclusion

The supporters of the *White Paper* proposals are in essence advocating cultural genocide. They seek the removal of the "citizen's plus" policy that grants special status to Natives, arguing that Natives cannot be truly integrated into White society unless special status is removed. Yet, as the charter group of Canada, British Canadians have always claimed special status, as have French Canadians, with their entrenched language and religious rights.

Increasingly, Natives are viewed as a threat to the unity of Canada. Ottawa has learned well from its experiences with Quebec the problems that will arise if Natives gain in power as a distinct cultural group. One solution is to refuse to recognize them as distinct, regardless of the problems they would face as a result. If Natives could be legally defined out of existence, the money now spent on them could be diverted to other, more cost-effective, areas.

Removal of the legal status of Natives would not lessen discrimination against them. Natives would occupy the same depressed economic position as now, but without any group identification. They would become fully marginal. Moreover, this marginality would not be wiped out in a generation: the stigma of Native birth is not only cultural but physiological. Because intermarriage between Natives and Whites is decreasing in Canada, the marginal Native would haunt Canadian society for many decades.[7]

Those who want to end the special status of Natives implicitly adhere to the myth of equality. This myth claims that, since everyone is equal, no one should be discriminated for or against. It is easy enough to stop the discrimination that favours Natives, by eliminating economic incentives, affirmative action programs, educational advantages, and so on. However, out of political expediency and other reasons, few efforts are made to stop discrimination against Natives.

In a nation that advocates cultural pluralism, the *White Paper* proposals seem incongruous. Clearly the proposals continue to be supported as a response to the recent growth of Native political and economic organizations. If these organizations are allowed to control reserve policies and funds, they will become formidable pressure groups by 1990. The harsh sanctions imposed by the Minister of Indian Affairs on the Indian Association of Alberta suggest what Native organizations can expect if they continue to challenge DIAND's authority.

At present, over $1 million a year is spent on Native organizations, with limited results. One problem is simply that Natives are still in the process of developing the skills that most Whites take for granted. Far more serious, however, is the fact that Native organizations only have impact at the paper level: federal approval is needed before any money can actually be spent on programs. Moreover, the federal government seldom agrees with Native organizations on spending priorities. The government is constantly changing its long-range plans and shuffling its bureaucratic slots for allocating monies. Even when an allotment can be clearly perceived as unrealistic at the local level, however, it cannot be changed. If DIAND allocates several thousand dollars to be spent on a given project, then no amount of counterargument by local Native organizations can divert any of this money into another project.

Although substantial amounts of money are given annually to DIAND for Indians, very little of it is spent on meaningful programs that can activate long-range social change. For example, in 1971-72 DIAND gave about $1.2 million to Indian associations for service contracts; less than $20 000 of this was allocated to economic-development projects. Of DIAND's total budget, 43 percent is consumed by salaries and staff support for its White bureaucrats and never reaches the reserve. If these salaries alone were given to reserve Indians, a sizeable capital base could be established to promote further economic development.

Political ability is vital to the survival of any group of people. In Canada, the cultural awakening of Native people has been preceded and outpaced by the growth of their political awareness. Natives are becoming increasingly sophisticated in their use of organizations to further their goals. This new knowledge will make itself felt more and more in Canada as we move further into the 1980s.

Notes

1. For a more complete discussion of the history of BC Native organizations, the reader should consult Drucker, 1958.
2. The Six Nations community is attempting to separate politically from Canada. This may account for their lack of militancy.
3. By mid 1982, the NIB was phased out of existence and replaced by the Assembly of First Nations.
4. The following material is from *Indian News,* June, 1981, Indian and Inuit Affairs Program, 1-5.
5. The term "pan-Indian" is not used by Indians but was invented and is used now by social scientists.
6. See, for example, the work of S. Weaver, *The Hidden Agenda: Indian Policy and the Trudeau Government,*, 1980.
7. In 1961, the endogamous rate of Native marriages — Natives marrying Natives — was one of the highest in Canadian history. In fact, it increased from 91 percent in 1951 to over 93 percent in 1961.

10
The Métis

Introduction

The Métis are a unique people in Canadian society. Originally they grew out of the symbiotic relationship that existed between Natives and the European immigrants to the New World. Yet it was the later government implementation of a complex set of social and political acts that ultimately determined their status as a separate ethnic group. Figure 10.1 locates the major belts of Métis and non-status Indians in Canada.

Estimates of the number of Métis range from less than 500 000 to over 1 000 000, depending on the source. Because the census no longer identifies the Métis as a separate ethnic category, not even the federal government has accurate statistics. Only Alberta keeps official records and only for its Métis colonies. In 1980, approximately 4 000 Métis resided on those colonies; estimates of Alberta's off-colony Métis population range from 8 000 to 15 000.

Although the Métis form only a small segment of Canadian society, they are well worth studying for a number of reasons. They emerged out of a unique set of social and political conditions and played a major role in the political development of the West. At present, they are becoming an important force in the development of Native-White relations in Canada.

The Métis have argued for many years that, as a special people, they are entitled to aboriginal rights. The federal government has maintained that those Métis whose ancestors signed treaties or received scrip and land have had their aboriginal rights extinguished (Cumming, 1973). Presumably, others have not.

267

FIGURE 10.1   *Major population belts of Métis and non-status Indians*

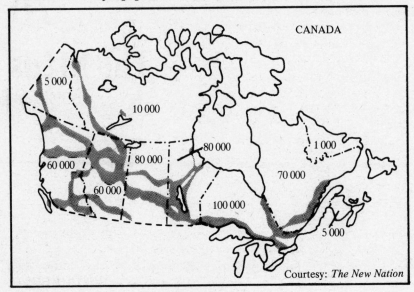

CANADA

5 000

10 000

80 000

60 000

80 000

1 000

60 000

70 000

100 000

5 000

Courtesy: *The New Nation*

SOURCE: *Indian Record,* Vol. 43, No 1 (winter, 1980), 7.

Over the years, the federal government has often recognized the existence of Métis claims. Under the *Dominion Act* and the *Manitoba Act*, the government provided scrip and land to Métis to extinguish their aboriginal rights. The 1889 Treaty Commission was instructed to treaty with the Indians and to investigate and extinguish any half-breed titles (Cumming,1973). In the 1930s, the Ewing (Halfbreed) Commission asserted the existence of Métis claims. As late as 1969, the Indian Claims Commissioner also argued for the aboriginal rights of Métis, stating that these are well established in Canadian law. According to the Commissioner, various actions of the federal government, such as scrip allocation in Western Canada and the Adhesions to Treaty No. 3, have granted special status to the Métis, both morally and legally.

Even while recognizing Métis claims, the federal and provincial governments have tried to wish them away. The rights of Métis in the Northwest Territories were ignored until rebellion was threatened in 1885. In the 1940s, the federal government deleted Métis from the census as a separate ethnic category. In 1944, Indian Affairs removed the names of nearly 1 000 Indians from the roll, arguing that they were really Métis. Although a subsequent judicial inquiry forced it to replace most of the names, clearly the federal government was hoping that the Métis would simply assimilate into White society and disappear, along with their claims.

In their attempts to retain their ethnic status and to receive compensation for aboriginal rights, the Métis, like the Indians and Inuit, have created complex and highly political organizations. The Métis argue that those of them whose ancestors did not take treaty or receive scrip or land still have aboriginal rights. At present, the relationship between the Métis and the federal and provincial governments varies from province to province.[1]

In the Northwest Territories and the Yukon, the Métis are working alongside status Indians and Inuit to negotiate an agreement with the federal government. In British Columbia, on the other hand, the provincial government has consistently refused to recognize the special rights of any aboriginal people in the province, including the Métis.

In Alberta, the provincial government's *Métis Betterment Act* outlines its relationship with the Métis. The Alberta government does not acknowledge the legal existence of Métis off the colonies. Therefore, all Métis individuals who do not reside on the colony are considered regular Albertans with no aboriginal or special rights. Like Alberta, Saskatchewan excludes Métis from any land claim registration now taking place with status Indians. In Saskatchewan, farms have been established for Métis, with land bases of less than four square kilometers. Although Manitoba has historically recognized the Métis, it has recently refused to acknowledge their existence. The few monies that the Métis Association had been receiving from the provincial government for special education and cultural activities have been cut off.

In Ontario, the Métis are recognized and are eligible to receive funds from a Native Community Branch. However, the Ontario government is reviewing this policy because of its high cost. Although Quebec claims to define Métis and non-status Indians as Indians, it refuses to fund or implement programs for these special groups. In order to be officially recognized by the Quebec government, the Métis would have to reject the *Indian Act* and accept new terms outlined by the Quebec government.

In the Atlantic provinces, most governments simply refuse to acknowledge the existence of the Métis. Although Prince Edward Island recognizes the Métis, it has no special policy because there are so few of them.

At the federal level, the Métis have received no formal legal or constitutional recognition except that established in the *Manitoba Act* of 1870. The Métis argue that, under this *Act*, they were recognized as a separate people with certain rights. Furthermore, because the *Act* cannot be changed without Britain's consent, which hasn't been given, the Métis

and non-status Indians continue to have legal status. The federal government has established a cabinet committee on Métis and non-status Indians
to investigate more fully the claims and issues put forward by them.

Because of the different problems they face, the Métis of each
province have formed their own political structures; these include such
diverse groups as the Saskatchewan Association of Métis and the Métis
Association of the Northwest Territories. The Native Council of Canada
represents Métis and non-status Indians at the federal level and acts as
an umbrella organization linking each of the provincial groups.

The Métis have based their conflicts with the federal and provincial
governments on three issues. First, they claim that the distribution of
land and scrip, particularly under the *Manitoba Act*, was unjust and
inefficient. Second, they claim that the compensation their ancestors
received was insufficient to extinguish Métis aboriginal land titles; indeed,
Western and Northern Métis were never compensated at all. Third, the
Métis argue that they are Indians under the terms of the *British North
America Act* and therefore entitled to special consideration from the
federal government (Barber, 1977).

These claims take different forms according to particular regional
factors. In Manitoba, the Métis Association wants compensation for the
loss of 1.4 million acres of land that they claim Louis Riel negotiated
with Ottawa in 1870. They also want outright ownership of large tracts
of land and compensation for land lost to settlers. In Ontario, the Métis
and Non-status Indian Association, which claims a membership of
200 000, is trying to obtain a free trade zone from the government to
settle its aboriginal land claims without costing taxpayers any real money.
A free trade zone is a parcel of land near an international port of entry
where goods can be assembled or brought in from other countries without
being subject to customs duty while they remain there. Customs duties
apply only if the goods are moved out of the zone into Canadian Customs
territory.

Until very recently, the federal government has responded negatively to these claims. Since the Indian Land Commissioner has lately
given credence to some Métis claims, however, the government has
decided to honour those it deems legitimate. Nonetheless, the federal
government remains fully committed to the extinguishing of Métis as an
ethnic category. While compensation may be made in the form of money
or land, no concessions will be made in the area of political control.

In the following pages, Dr. Olmsted outlines the origins of the Métis
in Canada. He demonstrates the process by which an ethnic group
emerged, sustained itself, and entered into a continuing struggle to
survive. The material focuses particularly on the social and environmental complexes affecting the Métis in Canada and acknowledges the
experience of Mixed Bloods elsewhere in North America.

The Mixed Bloods in Western Canada:
An Ecological Approach²

Whenever the myth of blood has been used to identify separate races of human beings that are in contact with one another, there have been social categories of individuals referred to as Mixed Bloods. According to the myth of blood, racially pure members of a society are superior to those of mixed blood (Montagu, 1943).

Canada is no exception to this rule. Members of one such group, the Métis, identify their origins as occurring "nine months after the first White man set foot in Canada" (Sealey and Lussier, 1975:1). Several hundred years later, and several thousand miles to the north and west, Justice Berger (1977:209) defined as Métis, "Native people who describe themselves as having a distinct history and culture, as well as aspirations and goals that differ from those of the Dené."

This essay will consider the development of several distinct categories of Mixed Bloods in Western Canada. Mixed Bloods have previously been discussed using racial, moral, political, and psychological frames of reference. An *ecological* approach is used here as a particularly useful tool for discussing a people who emerged over a few generations as an adaptation to a drastically changing physical and social environment.

THE ECOLOGICAL APPROACH

Several concepts are central to any ecological analysis. The first of these is adaptation, which may simply be defined as "the process whereby beneficial organism-environment relationships are established" (Hardesty, 1977, 21). For humans, the most obvious, and apparently successful, form of this is behavioural adaptation, which can be measured through changes in a culture's technology, organization, and ideology. In cultural ecological studies, these changes have usually been studied by examining isolated, subsistence-oriented groups that have little interaction with external social organizations (Bennet, 1969).

By definition, however, Mixed Bloods are not isolated from either Native or dominant social and cultural organizations; nor have they confined their social and material resources to the immediate environment. Historically, Canadian Mixed Bloods have relied upon co-operation with organizations such as fur companies and governments, and successful competition with other groups such as European settlers and Indians. Therefore, a study of the processes of co-operation and competition cannot be restricted to relations among the Mixed Bloods themselves or between the Mixed Bloods and local competitors. Mixed Bloods must be considered in the context of the larger social environment, as well as the physical environment.

Frequently, the discussion of human competition and adaptation has been couched in the same terms as the ecological analysis of any biological population and its environment. However, in human ecology, when an invading population from a relatively advanced culture is exploiting resources in a less-developed area, ecologists and geographers commonly refer to the metropolis-hinterland relationship.

The *metropolis* generally refers to a relatively powerful urban and industrialized organization that extracts primary or partially processed resources from a *hinterland* that it controls;[3] socio-economic stratification is inherent in this relationship. Several of these powerful organizations entered and competed within Western Canada, with direct implications for several Mixed-Blood groups.

First, from France and Montreal via the Great Lakes system, came the free traders and eventually the North-West Company (NWC). This organization provided the social environment for the Red River Métis and the Bois-Brulé, also called Hivernants or Western Métis. Initially, these groups were concentrated in a region bounded by Pembina, Winnipeg, and Cypress Hills, Edmonton, and Prince Albert.

Next, from England and Scotland, through York Factory on Hudson's Bay, came the Hudson's Bay Company (HBC). Initially, it was limited to the Arctic and the forests of the Precambrian Shield, but it quickly established the Red River Colony and parkland trading posts in direct competition with the North-West Company and the free traders. Associated with the Hudson's Bay Company were the Home Guard Cree, the Country-born, and the "English" half-breeds.

Less organized, and with less impact, were the American free traders from New York and Boston who entered the Prairies along the 49th parallel. Their interaction was primarily with the Plains Indians, the Red River Métis, and the Bois-Brulé[4].

Although the Mixed Bloods were not isolated groups, the concepts of physical distance and social distance played a strong part in their history. Those of mixed blood who assimilated to the Indian culture received little power or status and radically distanced themselves, socially and physically, from the dominant metropolitan society. Those of the same social mixture who were educated in Eastern Canada or Europe were often completely assimilated into the dominant society and lost their Mixed-Blood identities altogether; they experienced no social or physical distance from the metropolis at all. For example, James Grant remained in Scotland after his education, while his brother Cuthbert returned to Canada and became a Métis leader (McLeod and Morton, 1974).

The physical environment was an important influence on the interactions of Indians, Mixed Bloods, and Europeans. Because the environment substantially influenced the activities both of Indians and of Whites, it largely determined the cultural traits available for the Mixed Bloods. In addition, the control of environmental resources was a continuing concern for Mixed Bloods. In the West as elsewhere, resources and their control have influenced the development of human co-operation and competition.

According to Berry, members of reserves in the Eastern United States "are Indians by whatever criteria you choose to apply – except biological" (1963:15). Whiteside and Whiteside (1979) maintain the same for Eastern Canada. In Canada and the United States, many Mixed Bloods became Indians by taking treaty. Apparently, Indian status was frequently based upon lifestyle and self-identification.

In Eastern Canada, and probably in British Columbia, no clear category for Mixed Bloods existed until the mid-1900s. As Brown (1978) points out, although many Mixed Bloods were involved with the major fur companies by the late 1700s, they were not described as such in the fur-company records. Culturally, Mixed Bloods in Eastern Canada were either Indian or White until about 1850. At that time, factors such as the pressure for land, the emergence of educated Mixed-Blood leaders, and rumours of Riel's activities in the West all put pressure on colonial administrators to separate Indians and Mixed Bloods. Similar pressures may presently be occurring in the Northwest Territories.

In Ontario, individuals were socially labelled on legal, not biological, grounds. Although Eastern Mixed Bloods did not really develop as social groups, the labels that described them became the basis for the labelling of Mixed Blood groups in Western Canada. In the fur trade records before the 1821 HBC and NWC merger, the HBC classified persons as "Indians," "Natives" (Mixed Bloods), or English. The NWC, with its English-Canadian management and French-Canadian workforce, used "Indian" for Indians, "Halfbreed," "Métis," and "Brules" for Mixed Bloods, and "Scotch" and "Canadian" for Whites (Brown, 1978). As Brown asks, "Would Charles Isham . . . or Cuthbert Grant's offspring react to being called Métis, Halfbreed, Indian, or Country-born with puzzlement, anger, acceptance, or pleasure?" (1978:158)

As Brown (1978) also points out, usage of the seventeenth and eighteenth centuries explicitly associated the term "half-bred" with mongrelization and inferiority. The derived term "halfbreed", then, although widely used in North America, is a derogatory word for a subordinate group. Mixed Bloods who use it indicate acceptance of their subordinate position, and low self-worth. For the balance of this chapter, the term will appear only in quotations, as it is neither academically nor historically useful. The remaining terms will be examined to see whether they actually reflect different ecological adaptations.

THE WESTERN MIXED-BLOOD EXPERIENCE

The Western movement of French, British, and American explorers and traders indicates that Mixed Bloods originated in the West in the late seventeenth and early eighteenth centuries. Groups of Mixed Bloods may have formed as early as 1740-50 (Pritchett, 1942). A Prairie Métis population and a Mixed-Blood population in the Hudson's Bay area are claimed by 1775 (Sawchuck, 1978). In the southern plains, which later became American territory, the lack of permanent trading posts, wintering traders, and company trappers probably prevented the early concentration of Mixed-Blood populations.

Sawchuck (1978) and Pelletier (1974) agree that by 1835 many of the Canadian voyageurs of the North-West Company were Mixed Bloods from New France. When members of this group retired from the fur trade, they remained in the Northwest with their Indian wives and Mixed-Blood children. They were generally referred to as "freemen" and appear to have remained loyally dependent on the NWC. From the freemen were eventually descended the Red River Métis and the Bois Brulé.

Although the HBC initially discouraged mixed marriages, liaisons inevitably occurred. By the 1770s, a journal noted that at each HBC post there was "a breed of people easily distinguished from the real Indians by their lighter coloured hair" (Brown, 1977:39). This group was often referred to as the "Home Guard Cree" (Foster, 1976:74) and occupied an intermediate position between the Indians and Whites in the HBC similar to that of the freemen in the NWC. In 1835, the HBC changed its policy to officially permit intermarriage and local settlement. The HBC's need for local skilled labour was largely responsible for the adaptations that produced the group of Mixed Bloods labelled "Country-born" by Foster (1976, 1978).

THE RED RIVER MÉTIS

The lifestyle of the Red River Métis (or simply Métis) was active and adventurous, with a strong emphasis on hunting, travelling, and trading. Although their ideology spurned sedentary activities, they often received Roman Catholic educations at Red River or elsewhere.

In the 1900s, the Métis occupied an area bounded in the north by Fort Edmonton on the North Saskatchewan River and Prince Albert on the Saskatchewan River. In general, the Cypress Hills were the southwest limit and the Missouri River the southern boundary. Fort Garry and the Red River settlement acted as the entry and focal points for the entire region. Métis territory was largely prairie grassland, dominated by the presence of the buffalo.

Because the Métis were initially involved in the transportation and trade of furs throughout this area, they developed a comprehensive knowledge of plains geography. From their Indian connections, they developed a vast knowledge of the plants and animals necessary for survival. The Red River hunt of the Métis shows a unique and successful blend of Indian and European skills combined with their own thorough geographic awareness. Because Métis society was largely organized around the hunt, we will describe it in some detail.

Belcourt (1944) and Ross (1972) have provided two of the most often-used and detailed accounts of the Métis hunt. The general elements of the hunt can be outlined as follows:

1. Assembling of horses, Red River carts, equipment, and general supplies.
2. Election of captain and council, and setting of the rules for the hunt.
3. Travelling to the hunting grounds.
4. The hunt.
5. Return to settlement and disposition of meat.
6. Dispersal to the river lots where, between hunts and journeys, "the Métis sustained themselves in a variety of ways such as fishing, trapping for furs, practising small-scale agriculture, and working as wage labourers for the Hudson's Bay Company . . . " (Sprenger, 1972:158).

In assembling their hunt, the Métis responded with great ingenuity to the demands of adaptation and competition. For the hunt to succeed, two categories of animal were necessary: hunters and draft animals.

The concept of the buffalo-running horse, trained to chase buffalo, came from the Indians and gave the Métis a competitive advantage over European hunters. There is also evidence that the Métis had better horses than their Indian competitors. Throughout historical descriptions of the Métis, reference is made to the buffalo-runners as their prized possessions. In addition, the Métis aggressively pressed claims against other settlers for the hay rights supposedly associated with their river lots. The HBC also attempted to upgrade Red River livestock by importing blood sires from England and the United States (MacEwan, 1952). Finally, the Indians faced difficulties that the Métis did not in wintering their horses (Roe, 1955).

The Métis also mastered the use of draft animals, whether light horses or oxen, through the development of the Red River cart. Resembling the two-wheeled carts of Scotland, France, and Quebec, but made entirely of native wood and rawhide, the Red River cart introduced the wheel to the Prairies. In a day, the Métis could transport 500 pounds of buffalo meat for 50 miles with a cart and horse or 1 000 pounds for 20 miles with an ox (Sealey, 1978). With their travois and pack saddles, Indian meat-traders simply could not deal in the same volumes as could the Métis.

The Métis had to take a considerable amount of food, clothing, and equipment on the hunt. In general, woollen clothes and blankets, guns, pots, tea, and tobacco were purchased on credit from the Hudson's Bay Company. The Métis buffalo hunters had good credit ratings, much better than the Selkirk settlers during the agricultural difficulties of the 1800s. Again, this gave the Métis a competitive edge: the Plains Indians were not as well equipped, and often received goods second-hand from the Métis and the Cree (Ray, 1974). The Métis were further benefited by considerable trading, borrowing, and sharing among themselves. Often referred to as a Métis trait, this form of co-operation is one of the oldest human adaptations, and one of the most successful.

European observers of the hunt were often surprised by its democratic but strict and functional organization (Ross, 1972). Probably as a result of cultural diffusion, the Métis hunt was very similar in organization to that of the Plains Indians.

As Oliver (1962) states, the organization of the hunt was a fundamental adaptation to environmental factors, namely the buffalo and the plains. Although not truly migratory, the buffalo moved around considerably, often from day to day. For most of the year, they were scattered into small herds; during this time, both the Métis and the Indians operated in small, independent groups, similar to most hunters and gatherers. However, in late summer and fall during the breeding season, the buffalo gathered into large herds. For the Indians, this became a time for tribal groupings and a communal hunt. The Métis, although they had no tribal structure, also participated in a large-scale communal or corporate hunt.

The organization and success of the communal hunts depended on effective leadership and accurate environmental knowledge. As Hardesty has shown, for the Indians,

> ... strong leadership was necessary to maintain control within the tribal aggregation and, more important, to police the hunt itself to make sure that no individual threatened the success of the group hunt. (1977:25)

Here again, the Métis' social organization was similar to that of the Plains Indians. Among hunting peoples, leadership is often based on knowledge, wealth, and hunting skills. On the Prairies, those individuals who were best at locating buffalo, water, grass, and competing hunters were often elected as hunt leaders.

Another major qualification for leadership was the ability to manipulate information networks. Although the Métis were not noted for such large yearly gatherings as the Shoshone fandango of the various Sun Dances, gatherings did take place on seasonal holidays such as Christmas and Easter. As Thomas (1972) points out, these gatherings allowed various subgroups to pool their environmental and social information.

Throughout the rest of the year, individual Métis frequently visited one another and exchanged information.

The Métis are noted historically as great gossips and visitors (Ross, 1972), and view themselves as very sociable (Alta Fed. of Métis Settlement Assoc., 1978). In some regions, a "bush telegraph" continues to exist in which messages are carried from settlement to settlement by travellers. This process, which involves visiting, travelling, gossiping and story-telling, created networks extending from Northern Saskatchewan to Whitehorse in the Yukon, and Fairbanks, Alaska (Slobodin, 1966). In order to milk these information networks, individuals had to develop reputations for hospitality, strength, and wealth. In return for information, a Métis leader would have to provide resources such as food, tea, tobacco, and music.

Buffalo-running among Indians and Métis has been described by many authors (Ross, 1972; Belcourt, 1944). It was a communal form of hunting, in which large numbers of people provided support for the individual skills of a relatively small number of hunters. After the animals were killed, the wives and children of the hunters adeptly prepared preservable robes, skins, dried meat, pemmican, fat, and marrow.

Although the Métis did not depend on the buffalo quite as extensively as did the Indians, they, unlike the Indians, were able to initiate large-scale production of pemmican and "grease", producing a cash crop from a previously subsistence item. A successful hunt was cause for great celebration on return to the settlement. Between 1839 and 1841, more cash was produced by the Red River hunt than by the entire Red River colony (Ross, 1972).

The between-hunt stage of Métis life is often omitted in discussions, but ecologically and socially it formed an integral part of the Métis cycle. This between-hunt stage permitted the Métis to diversify their skills through *occupational pluralism*, an economic adaptation still used by marginal people, including the Métis (Clarke, 1972).

The sedentary life of the Métis between hunts is difficult to describe for several reasons. First, hunting is a more glamourous pursuit than gathering or subsistence agriculture, and was therefore recorded more widely. Second, gathering and subsistence agriculture are generally performed by women, children, the aged, and infirm, who were seldom objects of interest for the travellers, historians, and authors who produced accounts of Métis life. Finally, prejudice and discrimination against the Métis have distorted the historical records: the often-inept efforts of the Selkirk settlers, who represented the ideal behavioural norm, were praised, while the successful adaptations of the Métis were condemned as "savage". For all these reasons, the valuable social histories presented by authors such as Ross must be interpreted through a corrective screen. Fortunately, recent books by Campbell (1973), Carpenter (1977), and

Van Kirk (1980) are providing additional information on the contributions of Mixed-Blood women to social and physical adaptations.

The river bank was central to the sedentary life of the Métis. The use of river banks ranged from short-term fishing, hunting, trapping, and trading, to association with trading posts and missions, to the permanent river lots of New France founded at Red River, Grantown, Batoche, and Pahan (Victoriaville) near Edmonton.

The success of Métis settlements was generally determined by environmental, economic, and social factors. Obviously, successful hunters and traders with large families and strong community ties could maintain their homes all year round. They could then create the visible improvements, such as plowed land and a large house, which would eventually lead to a firm claim on the land, better economic conditions, social acceptance, and probable assimilation.

Occupational pluralism among the Métis took other forms besides the great hunt and the sedentary season at Red River; the Métis also harvested or produced wild rice, cabins, Red River carts, clothing, lime and limestone, maple sugar, salt, and seneca root. They also used their hunting skills to make war, when so directed by their leaders. Occupational pluralism exemplified the unique Métis adaptation of European and Indian behaviour. It produced the export products – pemmican, grease, and furs – that gave the Métis financial freedom. This freedom, in turn, at least symbolically encouraged a *core ethnic* of Métis, transforming them into a "people who possess and act out the cultural stuff of their origins a fair percentage of the time" (Stymeist, 1975:54).

From approximately 1850 to 1885, the adaptations of the Métis allowed them to emerge as a distinct group that could successfully compete economically with the Canadian and American governments, the Hudson's Bay Company, and the Plains Indians. At this point, the Métis' description of themselves as the "New Nation" contained very little exaggeration. In addition to their melding of Native and European social organization and technology, the Métis' ideology and culture was strongly enhanced by the development of distinctive legends, styles of dress, music, and poetry. These cultural adaptations further strengthened the Métis' position as the most prominent of the Western Mixed Bloods.

THE COUNTRY-BORN

Commonly in Western Canada, people of mixed blood who did not have French surnames were dismissed with the derogatory term "half-breed". Yet, after the establishment of the Red River Settlement and the 1821 merger of the fur companies, English and French "half-breeds" were reported in nearly equal numbers. Given this equal start, and the subsequent English colonization of the West, why are the Mixed Bloods still associated almost exclusively with the "French half-breeds"?

In the absence of European women, the Hudson's Bay Company's early prohibition of mixed marriages was less than effective. By the mid-1700s, groups of Mixed Bloods, distinguishable in appearance from Indians, began to appear around HBC posts. These Mixed Bloods were often referred to as "Home Guard Cree", because of their physical and cultural attachment to HBC trading posts; the term "half breed" did not emerge until the nineteenth century (Brown, 1977). The social adaptations of the Home Guard Cree have been called "the cultural fount from which the Country-born originated" (Foster, 1976).

In a succinct comparison of the North-West Company and the Hudson's Bay Company, Brown (1980) points out that, while the British managed the North-West Company, their labourers were generally French Canadians, Scots, Americans, Métis, and eastern Indians such as the Iroquois. The Hudson's Bay Company, in contrast, was much more a product of the European class and power structure of its time: it tended to recruit both management and labour from appropriate areas of England and Scotland. This policy proved difficult to maintain, however. If economic conditions were good in Britain, recruits were difficult to obtain. Moreover, British workers were not well adapted to life on the Bay (Brown, 1980). By 1800, craftsmen of the Hudson's Bay Company found openings for their Mixed-Blood sons, and Native women and children performed many of the household tasks around the posts. (Brown, 1977A).

At this point, the ecological adaptations of the Country-born and the Métis began to diverge rapidly. By 1821, with the merging of the two trading companies and a concentration of population at Red River, a discernable Country-born ideology had emerged. Oriented to the British social environment, this ideology promoted the "urban" skills of the trading post, rather than the rural skills of the forests and prairies.

John E. Foster explains the emergence of the term "Country-born" to describe "English half-breeds":

When the Mixed Bloods, conscious of their "British" and "Protestant" ways, wished to distinguish themselves from the Métis and from the British-born segment of the population, they used the rather vague phrase "my countrymen". This phrase, however, lends support for an infrequently used term found in documents originating with British-born Anglican missionaries. The term "Country-born",[5] no doubt a polite affectation, was used to designate those Mixed Bloods whose cultural ways were not those of the Métis.... The Country-born did not use this term themselves. (1976:72-73)

According to many historians, the ultimate goal of the Country-born was the life of the highly ranked, upper-class, British fur-trader. To achieve this life, one must be literate, Anglican, and suitably schooled in the appropriate manners.[6] However, due to discrimination, not many Country-borns could attain these heights. Those who failed often found roles as clerks, craftsmen, and farmers.

Just as in nineteenth century Europe, the position and influence of the father determined the placement of his children in the social hierarchy (Foster, 1976; Pannekoek, 1976). Indeed, the organization of the Country-born was very much the social organization of the preindustrial England metropolis. Patriarchal, Anglican, and monarchist, Country-born values encouraged hard work, sobriety, and obedience. Middle-class crafts, clerical, and agricultural occupations were highly sought after.

Although the technology of the Métis and the Country-born did not vary significantly, it was applied in a very different manner. The Country-born employed horses, guns, boats, canoes, and country-adapted clothing on farms, trading posts, and factories for the good of the Company and the Empire. The Métis used these same articles to become a radical New Nation.

A comparison of two well-known Mixed Bloods emphasizes this crucial difference. The Honourable James McKay of Deer Lodge, a Country-born, was described by the Earl of Southesk as "a Scotsman though with Indian blood on the mother's side, . . . born and bred in the Saskatchewan country" (Southesk, 1968:8). McKay's biography documents considerable physical and social skills applied within approved British institutions from the Hudson's Bay Company to the Canadian Pacific Railway (Goosen, 1978). In appearance, occupation, and skills, McKay had much in common with another Mixed Blood of great repute, Gabriel Dumont (Woodcock, 1975). However, Dumont applied his expertise to the ideology of the New Nation, to the buffalo hunt, and to the riverbank settlement, much to the chagrin of the British establishment.

Many famous Mixed Bloods, such as Grant, Ross, Brady, Isbister, and Pangman were ideologically aligned with the Country-born, but were actually Métis. Nonetheless, although the Country-born represented a distinctive cultural adaptation, and were equal in population to other Mixed-Blood groups, they did not develop an ethnic core. Indeed, the very fact that they were successful in their adaptation made it easier for them to assimilate into the increasingly Protestant, literate, and agriculturally-oriented Western Canada that emerged after 1870.

THE BOIS BRULE

The antique literary term Bois Brulé (burnt-wood people) describes a unique social, ecological, and economic category of Mixed Bloods. The

Bois Brulé population was probably quite large, but not very visible due to its physical and social distance from more publicized groups. The Bois-Brulé were the poorest of the Mixed Bloods. This relative poverty was largely due to the ideology of the early Bois-Brulé, who attempted to maintain the independent subsistence lifestyle of the Plains or the Forest Indians.

Also called "Western Métis", the Bois Brulés were sometimes called the Hivernants, as the following description by Giraud shows:

> There figured among these "Hivernants" several groups: Métis who had definitely abandoned the Red River with a desire to devote themselves exclusively to the hunting life; *Western Métis who had never known any other existence*; a few elements who had become detached from the settlements of the Prairies or Park Land and returned there less and less often and for increasingly short visits; and finally the true "Hivernants" who would periodically follow their old custom of cold weather peregrinations away from the Red River or the Assiniboine. (1954:12, italics added)

Researchers have found a similar mixture of backgrounds in present day Métis settlements.

Deliberately avoiding agriculture, education, and religion, the Bois Brulé ideology attempted to maintain the subsistence lifestyle of the Prairies and Parkland. With the closing of the Prairies, the Bois-Brulé were forced north and west from the agricultural lands, and have adopted more and more of the values and behaviours of the northern Indians, with whom they are associated. Economically, socially, and ecologically, the Bois Brulé have virtually assimilated into the lifestyle and culture of northern Natives. Environmental destruction, social distance, and the lack of a strong cultural identity have maintained the poor social position of the Bois-Brulé, who now account for a large portion of the Métis population.

The Bois-Brulé are organized according to kinship groupings, and their technology has followed that of the larger society, though on a marginal, subsistence level.

THE NORTHERN MÉTIS

This category of Mixed Bloods in the Northwest Territories was established by Slobodin:

> The original Indian- or Eskimo-European unions in very few cases date back as far as a century. Non-aboriginal ancestry is much more varied than it is for the Southern Métis, including a noticeable minority of non-European (Polynesian, Micronesian, American and African Negro). However, the non-aboriginal nationality most heavily represented in northern Mackenzie genealogies is Scottish . . . . A majority of the Northern "mixed" families are

Protestant. Another contrast with the Métis proper is that these people do not look to common traditions larger than intra-familial .... There is no term for the more northerly population which is at once generally employed and is acceptable to the people themselves. (1966:13)

The environment and culture of the Northern Métis is distinct from that of the Southern, Plains, or Red River Métis. The Northern Métis have become increasingly visible as resource development has moved northward.

THE METIS AND THE METROPOLIS

The Métis and the Country-born were physically and socially the hinterland children of metropolitan France and England. And, over the years, various metropolitan processes transformed the Métis into a destitute social group in Western Canada.

The first step in this process was the conquest of Canada by England in 1759. A brief period of free trade ensued, which was good for Western Canada but less so for Britain. French and English traders in Montreal formed the North-West Company, which entered into direct competition with the Hudson's Bay Company. In 1812, the Selkirk settlement was founded to give the Hudon's Bay Company an advantage by cutting off the main trade route from the West to Montreal. In 1816, the North-West Company responded by using Métis,under Cuthbert Grant, to cut off supplies to the Red River and evict the Selkirk settlers. After the Seven Oaks massacre, Alexander Selkirk made arrangements to defend the settlement and, in 1821, the Hudson's Bay Company absorbed the North-West Company in a business transaction. Thus, in short order, the Métis lost the support of France, Montreal, and the North-West Company, and incurred the hostility of Britain.

Although some of the French-speaking, Catholic Métis went to work for the Hudon's Bay Company, they were at a competitive disadvantage against the English-speaking, Protestant, Country-born who already worked there. After 1821, the Métis increasingly centred their activities around the Red River settlement. To support themselves, they turned to the buffalo hunt and the free fur trade with the Indians, which, though discouraged by the HBC, was supported by a new metropolitan power, the United States.

Eventually the Métis lost their freedom to trade in the United States and, in 1867, Manitoba became a province under Confederation. Canada then replaced England as the major metropolitan influence on the Métis; in 1869, by purchasing Rupert's Land, Canada also replaced the Hudson's Bay Company.

Unfortunately for the Métis, Louis Riel's attempts to create a New Nation, or at least entrench the laws and customs of the Métis in the province, were failures (Stanley, 1971; Howard, 1952). Metropolitan support for Riel never materialized in the United States and, more importantly, no direct support developed in Quebec. Although French Canada was outraged in 1869 and 1885, it simply did not provide enough French-speaking immigrants to offset those from Ontario and America (Silver, 1976).

The Country-born who joined Riel also assumed the minority status of the French-speaking, Catholic Métis. After 1870, Riel's followers left Red River for the West, and began to adopt the lifestyle of the Bois Brulé. In 1885, under Dumont and Riel, they attempted an uprising against Canada and lost. After this loss, all Mixed Bloods were left open to minority persecution, as no sector of the metropolis was left to support them. At the same time, the Métis way of life came under heavy attack by government and economic interests.

THE MÉTIS AND THE ENVIRONMENT

Although it is pleasant to discuss the emergence of a successful ecological adaptation, it is difficult to achieve the thoroughness and exactitude that science demands. Due to more substantial documentation, and perhaps more practice, it seems much easier to describe the destruction of an ecosystem.

For the Métis, the collapse of their environment began with the placing of restrictions on "commons", or common property resources. Previously,

> ... most of the population depended for its basic subsistence on the natural products of the country over which they roamed and hunted. These products were open to use by the Indian bands that claimed the territory as their hunting grounds and by anyone else who could gain access to that territory. (Spry, 1976:21)

The first resource of the plains to vanish was the buffalo. Under the combined onslaught of Indians, Métis, traders, settlers, missionaries, hide hunters, and adventurers, the buffalo moved further from the settlements and became increasingly scarce. In approximately 1880, the buffalo stopped being a free common resource, and became, for all purposes, extinct (Spry, 1976; Nelson, 1973; Roe, 1951). The commercial and cultural mainstay of the Métis had vanished, leaving behind only bones to be picked and sold to industry.

At the same time, but less observably, the Métis were also being deprived of two other common resources, land and water. Métis adaptations, both social and environmental, involved part-time, nomadic use of land and water. In order to receive a title to land under the 999-year leases of the Hudson's Bay Company, the land had to be paid for, trade had to be licensed, and at least one tenth of the land had to be plowed. Although many Métis claimed land under these leases, few proved title. As a result, many of the Red River Métis were squatters.

After Rupert's Land was transferred to Canada, Natives began to lose their land rights. The Plains Indians signed treaties, moved onto reservations, and completely surrendered their nomadic lifestyle. Apparently, many Mixed Bloods, probably Bois-Brulé, also took treaty and officially became Indians at this time. The Métis, in exchange for their land rights, were issued with scrip which entitled them to claim land. "Money scrip" was also used that could be converted to land or to cash.[7]

Three major factors resulted in the government's failure to persuade the Métis to permanently settle on individually owned land. First, because of their nomadic lifestyle, few Métis regarded one piece of land as home for all seasons, in all years. Second, scrip grants took place after the 1870 and 1885 uprisings, when Métis were unpopular in the West (Pelletier, 1975). To escape prejudice and re-establish their old way of life, many Métis decided to cash in their land scrip and follow the buffalo further west (Carpenter, 1977). After the 1885 uprising around Batoche, many Métis appear to have taken scrip around Edmonton. Again they used the cash to move north and west, off the Prairies entirely, in search of an opportunity to practise their old lifestyle.

The third factor was competition against the Métis for choice land claims. Corporate land ownership arrived in Western Canada as quickly as the buffalo had vanished. The federal government, the railways, and the Hudson's Bay Company controlled vast areas. In the southwestern Prairies, virtually all the land was under ranch-grazing lease by 1885. Although speculators and claim jumpers preyed on all land claimants, the Métis scrip holders were highly visible and frequent victims. Métis without scrip had little chance of finding any land at all, as the following passage suggests:

> (At Ft. Qu'Appelle) Treaty No. 4 had been negotiated in 1874 nd here the Cree and Saulteux Indians expected to camp each year when they received their treaty payments.... Meanwhile, however, the buffalo were becoming very scarce and a number of Half-breed hunters began to look for land to settle on. They came to the Qu'Appelle Valley and the Indians... applied to the Indian agent for an assurance that they would always have their treaty money paid at this point.... The Half-breeds were headed off, but all except a small portion of the 1 000 acres at issue... had already been applied for by a Mr. Smith representing the "honourable Mr. Bowen of Winnipeg." (Spry, 1976:34-35)

The competition for land was particularly concentrated around areas like Fort Qu'Appelle and its Fishing Lakes, as the commons of water, wood, and fish became consumed or restricted. Settlers, steamboats, and sawmills used up increasing amounts of wood; in Manitoba, by 1862, "exaggerated cuts by speculators had upset the Métis whose lands would be of little use if all the wood had gone" (Spry, 1976:31). From Lake Winnipeg to the North Saskatchewan, commercial fishing and pollution made subsistence increasingly difficult:

> It was not so much local individuals fishing for their own use that was the cause of the trouble, but fishing for sale to make a profit, especially when more efficient – and so more destructive – gear was used. (Spry, 1976:31)

In semi-arid areas, those who control the water also control the land. To solve this problem, the Crown traditionally reserves shoreline ownership. In the West, however, the shorelines were often controlled by private, or corporate owners: as people of the commons, the Métis could not gain access to many lakes and rivers except illegally. For example, traditional Métis fishing in the Qu'Appelle river and lakes violated ownership and game laws.

The Métis also lost other common resources. Pelletier has carefully described the Manitoba Métis' use of buffalo, fish, maple sugar, lime and limestone, wild rice, seneca root, and salt as common resources. In each case, industrialization destroyed Métis techniques and often the resource base itself.

In areas such as the Red River and Batoche, where the Métis retained their river-lot claims, the land could not adequately support the Métis lifestyle. Moreover, the river lot also proved unsuited to commercial or industrial farming.

> As commercial farming developed after 1920 and more bush from the rear of the lots was cleared, it became apparent that the long river lot held serious disadvantages . . . . The main disadvantage related mainly to the lot's length and the time taken to return to the farmstead by the river. Since the advent of tractors and powered field machinery in 1947 . . . more fieldwork has been undertaken therefore along the length of the lot. This has contributed to serious soil erosion problems on some of the lots. (Ironside and Tomasky, 1976:15)

Previously, Métis prosperity had depended "on the people's knowledge of the country and on their skill, endurance, and pertinacity as travellers, hunters, fishermen, and foragers" (Spry, 1976:23). These qualities had provided subsistence for the Métis, produced articles for trade, and had helped them find employment as guides, hunters, soldiers, traders, boatmen, and freighters. Between 1870 and 1890, however, Métis

products were replaced by the cloth, wagons, and boats of the metropolis and Métis travelling skills were made redundant by the railroad
and the steamboat. White society, having segregated the Indians on
reserves, no longer needed the Métis to act as defending soldiers,
middlemen, or traders. The historical niches of the Métis in the Prairie
ecosystem had vanished.

After failing in the Red River, Qu'Appelle, Batoche, and other
Prairie river environments, some Métis made one last attempt to gain
land under official tenure. Moving into the "bush" country of the Parkland, they took land under the *Homestead Act*. Unfortunately, the land
clearance and improvements needed to prove title were difficult to
apply without expensive technology and capital:

> Gradually the homesteads were reclaimed by the authorities and offered
> to the immigrants. The Halfbreeds then became squatters on their land and
> were eventually run off by the new owners. One by one they drifted back to
> the road lines and Crown lands where they built cabins and barns and from
> then on were known as "road-allowance people". (Road allowances are
> Crown lands on either side of road lines and roads.) (Campbell, 1973:13)

Often, when its resource base is destroyed, a species is also destroyed.
Although the Métis have been forced continually northward into increasingly marginal environments, they still survive as a group (Slobodin,
1966; Berger, 1977). Before commencing on this survival, we must
consider the Métis' relationship to their social environment. For human
groups, the social environment is often more crucial to survival than the
physical environment.

THE MÉTIS AND THE SOCIAL ENVIRONMENT

A people strong enough in 1870 to form a government in a vacuum
among such giants as the British Empire, the Hudson's Bay Company,
and the United States of America must surely have proven the success
of its adaptation to Prairie life. Nonetheless, the strength of the Métis
never raised the social rank of Mixed Bloods in Western Canada. Ultimately, the processes of prejudice and discrimination contributed
significantly to the Métis' decline.

Over the centuries, four justifications have arisen for discrimination
and prejudice against the Métis. The first was the war between France
and England that extended to Eastern Canada and resulted in the subordination of French interests. The second was the Protestant-Catholic
conflict in Europe, whereby Protestantism became associated with British
interests through such organizations as the Orangemen and the Masons
(Howard, 1952). The third was the colonial ideology that branded indig-

enous peoples as savage, childlike, and inferior. Finally, the rise of urbanism and mechanized agriculture in the West resulted in a lack of tolerance toward those who stood in the way of progress. The Métis, as French, non-White, rural, non-farm Catholics, have been targets for prejudice on all four fronts.

By 1900, physical and social changes in Western Canada had reduced the Métis to marginal people in marginal environments. Scrip fraud, debt, and competition from agriculturalists had pushed many Métis from the plains. Some migrated to the United States or took treaty as Indians. Others clustered around towns and reservations. Misery and destitution were paramount.

Between 1896 and 1909, an attempt was made in Alberta to settle Métis farmers in an area that was a combination of a reserve and a homestead. This "Métis reserve" called St. Paul des Métis, eventually failed through lack of interest, lack of capital, contested land titles, and the introduction of French-Canadian settlers (Stanley, 1978).

From 1900 to 1929, little literature on the Métis is available. Presumably, during this time, they continued their occupational pluralism and eked out a living from wage labour, hunting, trapping, fishing, and subsistence agriculture. Health care, education, and housing remained at nineteenth century levels, while actual and relative income and living standards declined with the loss of the fur trade and the hunt. Meanwhile, the rest of Canada was enjoying an economic boom, increasing the relative deprivation of the Métis.

In 1929, industrial collapse was accompanied by severe drought and related environmental damage throughout Western Canada (Gray, 1966;1967). The result was a severe economic depression. Prairie-dwellers were driven from their farms in great numbers, either leaving the region entirely, migrating to the city, or moving into the northern bush. Those who entered the bush competed with the Métis for already insufficient environmental resources.

During the Depression of the 1930s, a group of Métis approached the Alberta government to seek assistance for their people. The Ewing, or Halfbreed, Commission was created to examine the Métis' social conditions (Ewing Commission, 1935). The key word used by the Commission to describe Métis life was "destitution". As a result, Alberta passed a *Métis Betterment Act* to set aside six areas for Métis settlement.The Métis farmed eight colonies on this land. As Hatt reports:

> Requirements for becoming a member of a settlement include fulfilling the legal definition of a Métis, plus those requirements set down by each colony. On the Beaver Métis Colony, the local council accepts applications from Métis for settlement, and then the council votes on the acceptance or rejection of each particular family. (1969:21)

Except for the Ewing Commission, there is virtually no literary, academic, or legislative information available on the Métis between 1930 and 1955. However, two bitter accounts of Métis childhood during this period indicate a continuing social, economic, and cultural deterioration as well as continued or increasing prejudice and discrimination from others (Campbell, 1973; Adams, 1975).

In the mid-1950s, social scientists produced a torrent of government-sponsored studies of the North. These studies, as summarized by F. Hatt (1971), concluded that the Métis, along with other Native groups, were discriminated against with respect to health care, housing, education, and economic opportunities. Métis culture was fragmented and its relation to the larger industrial society inadequate. When Natives migrated to urban areas, they were unlikely to succeed due to lack of job experience, poor education, and discrimination. Continuing prejudice and discrimination against Métis, and their resulting marginal ecological position, made it particularly difficult for them to maintain and adapt their culture as other ethnic groups had done in Western Canada.

In 1974, studying the relationship among stereotypes, prejudice, and behaviour, Mackie asked a sample of Albertans to describe Native people:

> The perception of the Indians . . . is an overwhelmingly negative image of an ostracized group that neither shares the work or success values of the surrounding society nor receives its material rewards. The open-ended descriptions also emphasized their lack of commitment to striving, their poverty, low level of education, and rejection by outsiders. (1974:42)

Although the Natives are no longer accused of savagery, this view is identical to complaints found in the historical accounts of the Red River settlement. Mackie also finds that Natives are "correctly described as differentially poor, rural, prolific, and uneducated" (1974:44). Mackie devised a social distance scale on which Anglo-Canadians were ranked as 1, with zero social distance: her sample ranked North American Indians as twenty-second and Métis as twenty-third out of twenty-four categories.

An examination of Native participation in the larger society finds very low levels of achievement and reward (Frideres, 1974). In northern Ontario, Stymeist finds that Indians are virtually excluded from the social life of the town: "Indian people as a whole are not a part of that complex system of ethnic categories that so characterizes non-Native ethnicity in Crow Lake" (1975:73). The degree of social distance from, and perceived lack of shared values with, White Albertans similarly excludes Indians and Métis from the Alberta mosaic.

Physical distance also influences the social and economic position of the Métis. A recent study of Nova Scotian Blacks describes the effects of physical distance from a metropolitan centre on the social and economic characteristics of a minority group. The authors divided their subjects into Halifax Mid-City, Urban Fringe, and Rural Non-Farm (Guysborough) Blacks. They conclude that:

> ... in contrast with city and urban-fringe Blacks, who are themselves a poor group, the Guysborough Blacks have a larger dependency ratio, larger household size, bigger families, more complicated household structure, considerably smaller incomes, more unskilled workers, and poorer educational achievement .... Guysborough County is, itself, the poorest county in Nova Scotia .... The Guysborough Blacks ... can be considered among the poorest of the poor. (Clairmont and Magill, 1977:284)

If a distribution map of the Métis were available for Western Canada and the Northwest Territories, a majority would be found in similarly marginal, rural, non-farm environments.

In his discussion of non-Native ethnic groups, Stymeist developed an "ethnic gradient" that distinguishes among core, peripheral, and name ethnics.

> "Core ethnics ... possess and act out the cultural stuff of their origins a fair percentage of the time. Most core ethnics are older people. Next there are the "peripheral" ethnics, those who may be familiar with the language and customs of an ethnic category, but seldom use them .... Finally, there are the "name" ethnics, people who are regarded as having an ethnic dimension simply because their ancestors are or are assumed to have been "ethnics". (1975:54)

The name ethnics would appear to be typical of culturally marginal people, like the Northern Métis. With no distinctive culture of their own, the Métis gain no cultural advantage from their ethnic designation and are at the same time denied access to the dominant culture.

The vestiges of culture available to peripheral Métis, such as those at Red River, are those traits which continually exacerbate the hostility of the dominant culture. Negative stereotypes are reinforced by Métis who speak French or an Indian language, who refuse to take demeaning jobs seriously, who support large and often irregular households, and who prefer immediate to deferred gratification.

Currently, the Métis are faced with a crucial need for a core culture on which to focus their identity. The Red River Métis and the Northern Métis had only perhaps a century to evolve a separate dialect and unique customs and values. Before and after that period, and probably during it, the Métis' physical and social environment worked against the development of a Métis culture.

All contemporary examinations of Métis life reveal Métis confusion as to personal and group identity. The following anecdote demonstrates this confusion.

> One violent French Métis nationalist, with an English family name, was aghast when shown incontestible proof that his great-great-grandfather had originated from Derbyshire. He acidly remarked, "So you tell me I am an Englishman. Sapristi, I go jump off that Diefenbaker bridge." (Davis et al., 1965:566)

Beyond limited family and community support, Métis self-identity has either been ignored or attacked. However, a recent growth in historical and political awareness may help the Métis to revive their culture and overcome the fragmentation caused by territorial dispersion.

The painful and destructive effects of racial and ethnic discrimination against the Métis have been observed by many authors (Campbell, 1973; Adams, 1975; Pelletier, 1974; Stewart, 1974). Non-White, French-speaking, rural, and Roman Catholic, the Métis are not only a minority group, but possibly even a "pariah" group. As Barth states,

> (T)he boundaries of pariah groups are most strongly maintained by the excluding host population . . . .Where pariah groups attempt to pass into the larger society, the culture of the host population is generally well known; thus the problem is reduced to a question of escaping the stigmata of disability by disassociating with the pariah community and faking another origin. (1961:31)

Throughout Canada's history, the host, or dominant, societies have rigorously maintained the boundary between themselves and the Métis. In the Prairies, the social boundaries have been maintained by the "myth of blood" (Montagu 1943:15-19). Regardless of their own failures, "full-blooded" Indians and Whites can both claim, by virtue of their racial purity, intellectual and moral superiority to the "Halfbreed".

The social and legal structures governing agriculture in Western Canada have dutifully supported this view. From village lots through giant ranches and vast timber and mineral leases, the White presence in Western Canada has made itself known through the ownership and exploitation of land. As full wards of the state, treaty Indians were protected from land competition and granted reasonably inalienable land-reserves. The Métis, however, lacking land hunger and unprotected by the state, were exploited through land scrip fraud or pushed north into unorganized Crown land. When land was owned by Métis, it was often too small for hunting and trapping, and unsuitable for grain farming.

The boundary for Métis identity does not rest on cultural differences between Métis and Whites or status Indians, but on the social and legal exclusion of the Métis from these two groups.

Conclusion

As members of the Métis pariah group move into the larger society, various trends are likely to develop. The name-ethnic Métis can probably assimilate by leaving communities in which they are identified as Métis and adopting the occupations and lifestyles favoured by the host society. However, the achievements of these assimilated Métis will do nothing to increase the status of Métis generally. Moreover, the assimilation process throws into relief an identifiable group of peripheral Métis who contribute to the maintenance of racial stereotypes. The core Métis culture, meanwhile, with no practical value for the host society and no longer relevant to its social and physical environment, will continue to decline as older generations die. As the core Métis disappear, the peripheral Métis will become further exposed to hostility and rejection by White society. Through physical distance from urban centres, local discrimination, and poor facilities, the Métis will remain the poorest of the poor, pariahs.

Since 1970, some changes favourable to the Métis have emerged. Although resource development has again increased in the North, developers have been forced to take Native land rights, social conditions, and environmental repercussions into account. Resulting studies have done little to improve social conditions, but have at least stirred an interest in Native lifestyles and rights. In addition, territorial, provincial, and national Métis voluntary associations have emerged. These groups are active at every level, and range from friendship centres to land-claims advisors and criminal advocates.

Western Canadian academics, writers, and artists are increasingly focusing on the plight of the Métis in Western Canada. Whether White, Métis, or Indian, these historians, social scientists, novelists, painters, and playwrights are publicizing Métis issues and culture. Many of them are quoted or cited in this article; others are viewed on television, heard on radio, and read in newspapers and magazines. Perhaps, through their various media, they will help the Métis to become proud of their heritage and assist the non-Métis to understand that heritage.

Currently, the relationship between the Métis and White society is one of confrontation rather than retreat. Although legal battles have replaced militant confrontations at Seven Oaks or Batoche, they at least suggest that nearly a century of apathy and neglect may soon be over.

Notes

1. For a more thorough statement of the status of the Métis, the reader should consult "Native Rights: Policy and Practices," *Perception,* Vol. 4, 2. (Nov.-Dec., 1981). Much of the information from pages 269 to 270 comes from this article.
2. As written for this volume by Dr. A. Olmsted, University of Calgary, Calgary, Alberta.
3. For a more detailed discussion of these concepts, and their relationship to Western Canada, see Davis, 1971.
4. Detailed descriptions of these environmental complexes are available in most social geography texts. See, for example, Harris and Warkentin, 1974.
5. In a relevant parallel, the term "Country-born" is recognized in Ireland as a "polite affectation" in reference to the Anglo-Irish, the Protestant offspring of the unions between the English and the Irish "Natives".
6. The mechanisms used to try to attain this "ultimate respectability" are analyzed by Brown (1977A and 1978).
7. For details of the *Manitoba Case*, see Pelletier, 1975.
8. From *Halfbreed,* by Maria Campbell, reprinted by permission of The Canadian Publishers, McClelland and Stewart Limited, Toronto.

PART III

The following section presents a theoretical perspective by which Native-White relations in Canada can be explained. This perspective focuses on the White dominant group's use of power, including force, to maintain its strong position.

As Myers (1914) and Ryerson (1960) have shown, Canada's development can be seen as a series of conflicts between contending groups, beginning with that between European colonizers and Native peoples. This conflict culminated in the suppression of Native peoples. As Ossenberg (1980) succinctly states:

> The ascendency of a merchant class through the fur trade was associated with the rapid decline in the power of the Native peoples . . . as the fur trade was replaced by the wheat economy, the labour of Native peoples became virtually superfluous. (1980:19)

Since their defeat, Native people have been suspended in a state of perpetual dependency.

Recently, however, Natives have begun to organize and to acquire the skills needed to create meaningful social and structural changes in their lives. While each Native organization is individual in focus, collectively they may be able to exercise a moral influence if not actual political power (Elliot, 1980). To the extent that such Native issues as ecology coincide with the concerns of the larger society, a facilitation of Native goals may be realized.

Ultimately, many Native groups would like to achieve *sovereignty of Native government*. Certainly, in the near future, Native organizations will continue to press for additional power and to intensify their efforts to gain more control over their lives.

The following section explores the issues involved in obtaining this control. It also examines the possible consequences for Canada if Native needs continue to be ignored and Native demands are left unanswered.

11

A New Perspective on an Old Problem: The Macro-Model

A Theoretical Model: Colonialism

Clearly, the Native population must develop economically to gain control of its destiny. However, the mechanisms to achieve this remain unclear. The White dominant group's efforts to resolve Native-White relations have ranged from the annihilation of Natives to acculturation and assimilation. These efforts have, in general, created more problems than they have solved.

The solution to a problem often depends on how the problem is perceived. The nature of the analytical framework through which Native-White relations are viewed largely determines what solutions can be put forward. Social scientists have generally viewed Native-White relations through a micro-model. Because micro-models are based exclusively on individual relationships, they can only perceive discrimination and prejudice on an individual, not structural, basis. Not surprisingly, the solutions that result from this model promote individual advancement and entrepreneurship. In this chapter, however, a macro-perspective will be presented; different solutions will arise as a result.

The analytical model presented here has as its forerunners those offered by Cummings (1967), Carstens (1971), and Patterson (1972).

Drawing heavily on these authors, the macro-model used here presents the Indian reserve as an internal colony that is exploited by the dominant White group in Canada. White Canadians are seen as the colonizing people while Natives are considered the colonized people.

By conceptualizing the reserve as an internal colony of a larger nation, it is possible to see beyond the individual factors involved in inter-group behaviour. While the individualized approach has offered much to the study of Native-White relations, it has not really produced any cogent explanation of those relations. Nor has it produced any meaningful improvement in the Native's position in our society. If anything, that position has worsened.

Many social scientists have rejected the colonial analysis as misleading, claiming that our social and political patterns are significantly different from those in, for example, Africa or India. Although there have certainly been differences, however, these do not obscure the fact that the indigenous peoples of Canada were unquestionably colonized and that their position in Canada today is a direct result of the colonization process.

Tabb has described conditions in a typical underdeveloped country as follows:

> ... low per capita income; high birth rate; a small, weak middle class; low rates of increase in labour productivity, capital formation, and domestic savings; and a small monetized market. The economy of such a country is heavily dependent on external markets where its few basic exports face an inelastic demand (that is, demand is relatively constant regardless of price, and so expanding total output may not mean higher earnings). The international demonstration effect (the desire to consume the products enjoyed in wealthier nations) works to increase the quantity of foreign goods imported, putting pressure on the balance of payments as the value of imports exceeds the value of exports. Much of the small modern sector of the economy is owned by outsiders. Local entrepreneurship is limited, and in the absence of inter-governmental transfers, things might be still worse for the residents of these areas. (1970:22)

This is a relatively accurate description of a reserve in Canada today.[1]

The colonization process can be considered in seven parts (Kennedy, 1945; Blauner, 1969). The first concerns the incursion of the colonizing group into a geographical area. Usually, this takes the form of forced-voluntary entry; acting in its strong interests, the colonizing group forces its way into an area. In Canada, both French and English settlement followed this pattern. At present, many Northern Natives argue that forced-voluntary colonization is occurring in the North.

The second attribute of colonization is its destructive effect on the social and cultural structures of the indigenous group. In Canada's case, White colonizers destroyed the Natives' political, economic, kinship, and, in most cases, religious systems. The values and norms of Native people were either ignored or violated. For example, after the War of 1812, when a large number of White settlers arrived, the colonial government decided that Natives should be forced to surrender their nomadic lifestyles. Official programs were developed and, between 1830 and 1875, legislation was enacted to carry out this destructive policy (Surtees, 1969).

The third and fourth aspects of colonization are the interrelated processes of external political control and Native economic dependence. In the standard practice of colonization, the mother country sends out representatives through which it indirectly rules the newly conquered land. In our model, the representative ruler is DIAND. Until 1940, Indian Affairs decided which Natives could and couldn't leave reserve lands. Native self-government has been effectively prevented. Until recently, band funds could not be used by Natives to develop social and political organizations of their own (Whiteside, 1972). In some cases, Natives have been allowed their own chiefs and band councils, but these are advisory only, with no real power. Council recommendations continue to be subject to acceptance or rejection by DIAND.

The Minister of DIAND can suspend almost any right set forth in the *Indian Act*. For example, Section 80 of the *Indian Act* authorizes band councils to pass by-laws for public health and traffic regulation. However, to date, the Minister has granted fewer than two-thirds of band councils permission to do so.

Acting through the governor-in-council, DIAND can also veto any decisions of band councils. Section 82 of the *Indian Act* allows a band to enact money by-laws. However, first the governor-in-council must find that the band has reached a "high state of development". At present, fewer than fifty bands have been so defined, and these have mostly used their powers to build sewers, wells, and so on. Section 68 of the *Act* allows a band to "control, manage, and expand in whole or in part its revenue moneys". No band was actually permitted to do so until 1959, and to date fewer than 20 percent have received permission. Section 60 allows a band "the right to exercise such control and management over lands in the reserve occupied by that band as the governor-in-council considers desirable". To date, the governor-in-council has found this desirable for less than ten reserves.

Section 35 of the *Act* explicitly states that reserve land can be expropriated by the federal government at any time. In 1971, the National Indian Brotherhood announced that the federal government had redrawn treaty maps and stripped titles to a number of land parcels claimed by Natives. Natives were not consulted before or during the redrawing of the maps. Significantly, the federal government did not refute the accusations. Moreover, the NIB uncovered a classified government memo ordering that all copies of previous treaty maps be destroyed.

In the initial stages of colonization, the colonized people generally accept their fate. Only later do they reject their powerless position. Native leaders on reserves today tend to be considerably more militant than those who initially signed treaties. But even if Natives no longer accept their subordinate status, there is little they can do to change it. Although, as Boldt (1980) has shown, many Native leaders are currently viewing extra-legal activity as a viable method of pressing their claims, other Natives have surrendered to a general apathy and dispiritedness. The process of acculturation and the demise of indigenous Native tribal associations have eroded Native self-identification. Communal bonds have broken down among individual Natives and among bands, contributing to the continued failure of Native organizations. Leadership responsibilities on the reserves have become further divided and poorly defined, exacerbating the disorganization of Native groups. The success rate for Native organizations is very low; most are dissolved soon after they are created.

In the political arena, Natives have been ineffectual for several reasons. Most importantly, they have been prevented from voting or running for office until recently. Except for in Nova Scotia, Natives did not receive the right to vote in provincial elections until after World War II. They did not receive the federal franchise until 1960. Needless to say, this severely restricted their ability to make political demands. Those with no voice in the political structure that governs their lives have no means of influencing or sanctioning the policies that affect them.

After receiving the vote, Natives were initially skeptical of their new rights and failed to exercise them to any great extent. This attitude is changing however. For example, in the 1968 federal election, nearly 90 percent of the Native population that voted in a Saskatchewan riding cast their vote for a Red Power candidate. In the 1982 provincial election, an Aboriginal Party was established in Saskatchewan.

Natives remain economically dependent on White society because their reserves are treated as geographical and social hinterlands for White exploitation. White-controlled businesses exploit non-renewable primary resources such as oil, minerals, water, and forest products, and ship them to urban industrial centres for processing. This practice has two important results for reserve Natives: the development of Native-owned industries is pre-empted and Native occupational activities remain at a primary level. As the treaties and the *Indian Act* show, federal policy has always tried to orient Native occupations toward agriculture and primary industries.

In the colonization process, a two-level system develops in which the White colonizers own, direct, and profit from industries that depend upon exploitation of colonized Natives who provide an unskilled, seasonal work force. On the reserves, the long-term result has been a Native population that lives at subsistence level, working at unskilled, seasonal jobs in primary industries and practising subsistence agriculture to survive. Although the profits from raw material production are based on reserve resources and cheap Native labour, they disappear from the reserve into the pockets of White entrepreneurs.

Reserve hinterlands are at a low level of economic development. Economic development is not the same as economic growth. Economic growth refers to an increase in the productive capacity of an area's economy, while economic development reflects a change in the structure of an area's economy, such as a movement from primary extractive or agricultural industries to secondary or processing industries. For example, Alberta reserves and Métis colonies have experienced considerable short-term economic growth due to oil and mineral discoveries but no real economic development.

As Boldt points out, this lack of economic development has a profound effect on Native leadership and political organization:

> Most striking is the statistic relative to leaders who derive their influence from the economic sector. Not a single Indian leader could be classified as exercising his influence in the economic sector. This provides evidence of the degree to which Indians generally have been excluded from the Canadian economic sector and hence the power structure. (1980)

The federal government has effectively discouraged the economic development of reserves, as the *Income Tax Act* and the *Indian Act* show. Fields and Stanbury find that:

> If Indians choose to undertake economic development of their reserves utilizing the form of a limited company, then they lose the benefit of exemption from taxation as individuals or as a band. Income earned by a corporation wholly owned by Indians is subject to taxation the same as any corporation – even if the income is derived solely from activities on a reserve. (1975:203)

The structural complexities involved in the payment of property taxes on reserve lands also prevent Natives from profitably leasing their lands. To exemplify this, Fields and Stanbury posit an example in which a developer decides to build a warehouse on a piece of rented property. Two similarly suitable locations are available; one is on an Indian reserve, the other is not. The firm discovers that it can rent either the reserve or the off-reserve land for $3 000 per year. When it approaches the band, however, it finds that it must agree to pay taxes to the municipality assessed at $1 500 per year, as though it owned the land. In order then, to compete with the owner of the off-reserve land, the band must reduce its rent to $1 500 per year to absorb the taxes. As Fields and Stanbury point out, by leasing its land instead of developing and occupying it itself, the band incurs an opportunity cost of $1 500.

A fifth characteristic of colonization is the provision of low-quality social services for the colonized Natives in such areas as health and education. A 1980 survey by DIAND confirms a desperate need for adequate social services. For example, the report points out:

- Life expectancy, a reflection of health standards, is still ten years less than that for the national population.

- In 1964, an estimated 36 percent of the Indian population received social assistance; by 1977-78, between 50 and 70 percent received social assistance.

- One in three families lives in crowded conditions. 11 000 new houses are required and 9 000 need repair. Less than 50 percent of Indian houses are properly serviced, compared to a national level of over 90 percent. (1980:3)

Although Native living conditions have improved in some material ways, social problems, including alcohol abuse and welfare dependency, have increased.

The last two aspects of colonization relate to social interactions between Natives and Whites and refer to racism and the establishment of a colour-line. Racism is a belief in the genetic superiority of the colonizing Whites and the inferiority of the colonized Natives. With a colour-line, indicators such as skin pigmentation and body structure are established to become the basis for determining superiority and inferiority. Interaction then goes on only among members of the same group: Whites interact with Whites and Natives with Natives. In Canada, for example, Indians have the highest rate of marriage within their own ethnic group – 93.6 percent.

The ultimate consequence of colonization is to weaken the resistance of the colonized Natives to the point at which they can be controlled. Whether the motives for colonization are religious, economic, or political, the rewards are clearly economic. White Canada has gained far more than it has lost in colonizing its Natives. Although Wuttnee (1972) claims that the federal government has spent $2 billion on Natives over the past century, he fails to point out that it has profited by about $60 billion. For example, the federal government spends $530 per treaty-Native per year and $740 per non-Native. From that source alone, the result is a saving of $210 per Native per year or a total of $52 million per year (Fidler, 1970).

Currently, Métis in Alberta are suing the federal government over non-payment of royalties on the extraction of natural resources from Métis colonies. The Métis began a legal battle to win the mineral rights to their land in 1938. They estimate that the royalties on the 200 producing oil and gas wells on their land amount to $60 million.

Proposing Solutions

Like any model, the colonization approach has certain limitations. The world is complex: people, social structures, and cultures change with time. Of necessity, however, a model is frozen in time, a static recreation of what occurs around us. In order to construct a portrait that corresponds closely to the real world, we select and incorporate certain variables, discard others as unimportant, and make assumptions about how people behave.

If the resulting model produces accurate explanations and predictions, it can be considered successful. It may then become a useful tool in finding solutions to social problems and in developing social-action programs. If, however, a model proves incapable of providing accurate predictions or explanations, it must be revised or discarded.

Economic Development

To break the pattern of colonization, Native Canadians must reject the notion of individual entrepreneurship or individual capitalism. Instead of seeking personal economic development, they should aim at achieving community ownership and control of reserve economies (Dubois, 1940).

In general, the federal government has retained control of development schemes by only allowing Natives to implement projects rather than plan them (Hatt, 1969). Moreover, as Hatt has shown, Native programs tend to be short-term experimental or pilot projects, which can be terminated quickly with few problems. According to Hatt, these programs have "therapeutic" value only; because they defuse protest and do not seriously disrupt the status quo, they perform effectively as social control mechanisms. In short, federal programs make little effort to truly address the problems of Native people.

Despite federal resistance, Native people must somehow create viable economic units within the reserve and control them as a community. This view has been expressed by Deprez and Sigurdson:

There can be no question that it is imperative for Canada's Native population to become involved in more productive economic activities. In strictly economic terms, the continuous dependence of the Indian on government assistance constitutes a serious drain on the financial resources of Canada. Even more significant is the fact that these people comprise a very significant potential labour force and a potential that today is not being utilized. But by far the most important dimension to the employment problem of the Indians is the humanitarian one, because participation in a viable economic activity is essential if the Indian is to maintain his sense of self-respect. (1969:11)

Several basic assumptions underline the need for community development and control, assumptions which the federal government is unwilling to accept. First, all people fundamentally desire to better themselves. When their attempts to do so are blocked, the social and psychological damage is considerable. Second, the major obstacle to improvement is a lack of resources, such as funds, skills, equipment, and education. Third, given resources and opportunity, people find their own effective ways to meet their needs and improve their lives. In the past, Natives have been forced to try to solve problems by White methods; procedures foreign to White culture have been attacked and rejected. Fourth, a change in only one component of a group's behaviour seldom produces meaningful, lasting results. A simple influx of money does not solve very much; the social behaviour of humanity has many facets. Each component of behaviour stands in a relationship to another. This must be considered when attempts at change are made (Lagasse, 1962).

This structural approach to social change necessitates a historical perspective on Native-White relations, along with an understanding of the institutional structures that influence Native life. Rather than focusing on the individual as the unit of analysis, such an approach examines the socio-economic role of internal Native institutions and their external relationships (Girvan, 1973). For too long, theorists have viewed Native-White relations as a "Native problem" rather than as a "White problem", and failed to take external factors into account.

Clearly, the "Native problem" has been created by the economic, cultural, and political structure of Canada. Contrary to previous explanations, the position of Native people in Canada is not totally the result of cultural isolation or particular psychological tendencies. Nor do racial and cultural discrimination provide a sufficient explanation for the low socio-economic position of Natives in Canada. While discrimination may have retarded socio-economic upward mobility, it has not eliminated it. Sunkel (1973) has shown that a totally marginal group is "deprived of all means of access to a source of income of reasonable level and stability" (1973:141); clearly this is not the case for Natives in Canada.

The marginal position of Natives in Canada can only be explained when various types of discrimination against Natives are considered along with their limited sources of income and their lack of control of the means of production. The manner in which resources are deployed, whether human, capital, or technological, determines the level of employment, the extent of industrialization, and the distribution of income. As Mariategui (1934) pointed out fifty years ago, the roots of the Native problem are economic and lie in the system of land owner-ship. This clearly implies that the economy is not embedded in social relations, but rather, that social relations are structured within society's economic institutions (Polanyi, 1974).

The federal government argues against the creation of industries and jobs within the reserve. It contends that the reserve is basically a residential area and cannot be converted to industrial or commercial use. For example, recommendation 3 of the *Hawthorn Report* states:

> The main emphasis on economic development should be on education, vocational training, and techniques of mobility to enable Indians to take employment in wage and salaried jobs. Development of locally available resources should be viewed as playing a secondary role for those who do not choose to seek outside employment.

At the same time, the federal government is trying to force the Native population off the reserves and into the cities. The result is devastating. The most capable and aspiring Natives leave the reserve which is then managed by a residue of non-skilled, low-aspiring individuals. As a result, the reserves are becoming less able to provide their residents with the living standards minimal to survival.

A far more realistic alternative is to upgrade existing Native indus-tries and create new ones. The creation of new jobs for Natives would also boost reserve profits, upgrade individual income standards, and provide invaluable experience for the development of Native leaders in community and business affairs. Clearly, Natives themselves want to create and control economically viable ventures on reserves. As Peters has stated:

> We want access to development resources which means the right to partic-ipate in provincial development activity and the right to direct access to all federal departments without intervention of the Department of Indian Affairs. The Indian Affairs Department is playing a "gate-keeper" role in opening up these outside resources to Indian communities. There is a tend-ency for the Department to do all it can on its own and turn over what it chooses to the provinces or other federal departments. In this way, the branch ensures its own future, but, in so doing, is failing to help the Indians to find their place in the provincial and national community. (1968:6)

Historical Perspective

Before comparing the advantages of individual entrepreneurship and community-controlled development, a brief socio-historical review is needed of Native-White relations.

Initially, Natives were regarded as non-human savages to be exterminated or ignored. They were also regarded as lazy, filthy, uninhibited, and uncivilized. During the nineteenth century, the Natives fell victim to conscious and unconscious genocide: the expansion of Western civilization that produced this result was viewed as a manifestation of Christianity. White settlers embodied the Protestant ethic of thrift and willingness to work hard. Because Natives did not share this ethic, they were rejected as pagan savages, with no claim to Christian charity (Hunt, 1940).

Eventually, through the proselytizing efforts of various churches, the Natives became Christians (Trigger, 1965). As Christians, they came under the rubric of Christian ethics and could no longer be so blatantly exploited. Because prejudice and discrimination were by then solidly entrenched in Canadian society, an ideology of inherent White superiority was introduced to justify White dominance and exploitation. White superiority and dominance was attributed to processes of natural selection reflecting the Social Darwinism prevalent in the late nineteenth century.[2] By the laws of nature, then, White exploitation and westward expansion were inevitable. As Willhelm has argued:

> In the thoughts of the light-skinned people of early America, no White man ever commands because he "chooses" to do so; it is not by his choice, but by the will of God or the act of Nature that he rises to the fore at the expense of inferior races. To rule is really to submit, in the first instance, as an obedient believer of God's command and, in the second instance, as a helpless pawn abiding by Nature's laws governing the races of men. The White races, in the final analysis, never felt superior in an absolute sense since they yielded to the Christian Bible and to Nature's demand in commanding inferior races. When the Indian and Negro were in the animalistic state, they were heathens; Whites fulfilled obligations to the Almighty in defending racists' feelings against the non-believers and would suffer no sense of loss should they even exterminate the non-White. Indeed, failure to fulfill Christian precepts exposes the right to question Christian descent; to be judged by a God on the basis of diligent hard work makes it only proper for man himself to judge others by the identical standard. Consequently, Whites merely carried forth their Christian duty to let out extermination and enslavement to non-Christians. (1969:3-4).

The sciences, particularly biology, were perhaps the greatest unwitting contributors to racism in North America. Biologists in the late-nineteenth century claimed inferior species could be physiologically distinguished from superior species. Racial attributes were labelled and attributed to various groups to account for their behaviour. The scientists claimed, in fact, that the genetic, racial make-up of individuals caused their social behaviour; the evidence suggests that most White Canadians believed them.

According to racist theory, no amount of effort by Natives or assistance from Whites could compensate for the Natives' natural inferiority. This conviction is evident in the government's decision to establish Native reservations. The reserves were to act as holding-pens for worthless people, inferior children, wards of the nation. In the treaties, when "concessions" were made to Native interests, they generally co-incided with White interests (Green, 1969). The Riel Rebellion of 1885, as well as the subsequent execution of Riel, was both the final extension and the climax of Native-White relations in Canada, and established the pattern of subjugation that continues to persist today.

Present-day White Canadians have a new strategy in their relationship with Natives – the myth of equality (Willhelm, 1969). The myth's basic premise is that all humans are equal no matter how diverse they appear to be. This acts as a rationale for denying special privileges and affirmative action programs to various minority groups.[3] The federal government's *White Paper*, which recommended that reserves be terminated and special status revoked, exemplifies this myth. Current legislation also reflects a growing adherence to the myth of equality. Proponents argue that the laws which now express the equality of ethnic groups are sufficient, regardless of the impact of centuries of entrenched discrimination.

Finally, another rationale for racism involves a view of Canada's resources as limited. More for Natives translates as less for Whites. As Dixon has noted with regard to Black-White relations:

> If I am pro-Black, then I must be anti-White. If I am pro-White, then I must be anti-Black. Another way of stating the either-or concept is the two-person, zero-sum game. According to the strategy of this game, if, for example, a sum of 100 units of some commodity is to be distributed between two people, then any change in a given distribution means that increasing one side causes a corresponding decrease in the other. Similarly, in the context of . . . race relations, any gain for Black is viewed as a loss for White and vice versa. (1971:29)

As Mills (1961) argues in *The Sociological Imagination*, a historical perspective is essential when examining inter-group behaviour so that the changing relationships between the structural components of society can be understood. Others have also argued that a knowledge of a nation's history is indispensable to an understanding of its contemporary issues. Certainly, a non-historical point of view has no means of evaluating social change. Society is not static. In order to understand the dynamics of change in a social system, its long-range developments must be apparent. As Mills (1961) has suggested, to have meaning, a social analysis must examine the mechanics behind social trends. In other words, we must ask how the structure of society is changing.

Factors Necessary for Community Control

Data presented earlier showed that Natives possess the lowest economic status in Canada. Those data also suggested that Natives currently serve as a secondary labour pool to provide cheap labour when the supply is scarce and to be quickly laid off when the supply increases.

Consequently, Native workers are very useful to White society. Because they ensure that the labour supply consistently meets industry's needs, they keep labour costs, and hence prices, at a minimum. At the same time, they enable White employment to be maintained at a constant level.

As Piore (1968) demonstrates, every nation has a dual labour market. The first market consists of jobs that pay well, offer stable, long-term employment, provide good working conditions, and include chances of advancement. In the second market, the reverse applies. Research carried out by Buckley, Kew, and Hawley (1963) shows that this dual market operates within the economic structure of Canada. In his study of urban Natives, Nagler found that

> ... there are also seasonal commuters (Indian) who come to the city when employment levels are high. These workers usually stay in cities while employment is available in construction and related industries and then return home during the slack periods to which many of these industries are subject. (1971:12)

In 1970, a Special Senate Committee Hearing on Poverty cited a large mining firm in northern Manitoba which employed Natives exclusively on a casual basis. Casual workers do not get all the fringe benefits of full-time workers. According to the Committee's report, even Natives who had worked at the mine for twenty years were still on the casual payroll. Similarly, La Rusic (1965) showed that no Natives working for mining-exploration companies had ever been on the full-time payroll. Even though these workers were highly skilled, they were denied equal working conditions with Whites. After twelve years, Cree workers were still employed as casual workers and restricted to menial activities.

In a capitalist system, economic development occurs in a series of stages; "pre-capitalism" gives way to a series of capitalist refinements. As the system develops, it creates certain market forces that effect other regions. "Spread effects" result when growth in one area creates development in other areas, and "backwash effects" occur when growth in one area drains resources out of a hinterland (Dunn, 1975). When urban centres develop, backwash effects create obstacles to development in such peripheral regions as Native reserves.

The early colonizers were primarily interested in Native people as military allies, as a potential market for their manufacturing industries, or as a source of labour for primary industries such as trapping and logging. Natives produced raw materials for White society but did not participate in any industrial growth. As the colonizers began to bring in capital, technology, and skilled labour from Britain and Europe, the Natives were increasingly isolated from the mainstream Canadian economy and restricted to employment patterns that were marginal in every respect. Consequently, Natives became increasingly dependent on trade goods and on the capital of foreign-owned companies. This economic cleavage, combined with racial and cultural differences, served to isolate Natives from all aspects of White culture – technological, social, and ideological.

The Native economic world today is not totally isolated; some commercial links do exist with the larger economic structure. However, in terms of total national or even regional productivity, Native production is small and most of it is consumed internally. For example, Native craft sales can be divided into internal and external sales. In 1961, of the $407 606 earned through craft sales, $276 354, or over two-thirds, was spent by other Natives. By 1970, the total value of sales was $1 491 662 of which $383 647, or just over one-fourth, was spent by other Natives; while this is an improvement, it still represents a significant amount of total production. These economic patterns maintain Natives in a perpetual dependency relationship with White society (Stavenhagen, 1963).

It is generally assumed that, as the rate of investment increases in a nation, the production output and the employment opportunities also increase. However, this assumption ignores the distinction between a modern and a primitive technology. As investments increase in the modern technological sector, automation accelerates; this means that employment opportunities are actually reduced. Therefore, an increase in the rate of investment leads to further under-development of the total employment field and ensures that those in the primitive technology sector (agriculture) will remain unemployed (Sunkel, 1973).

Natives are economically dependent in that they cannot manipulate the operative elements of their economic system (Brewster, 1971). Put another way, Natives are unable to function as an independent economic entity. Because the marginal economy of the reserve is dependent on outside credit, savings are rendered virtually impossible. And, due to the legal prohibitions of the *Indian Act* and the incursion of capitalist values that encourage entrepreneurship and discourage community ownership, the specialized, dependent economy that has managed to grow on the reserve is controlled by a small group of Native elites (Dosman, 1972). As a direct result of these factors, Native people have consistently lacked the human and financial capital needed to develop the reserve economy.

White Canada continues to encourage individual entrepreneurship rather than community control on the reserves. If Natives establish communally controlled, independent, economic enterprises, they will no longer provide a cheap seasonal labour supply for the larger corporate structure. If Natives are no longer unemployed on the reserve, they will have to be paid higher wages and offered more security to leave.

At present, the economic outlook for Natives does not appear very bright. Nonetheless, the potential for successful development does exist. The metropolis-hinterland relationship that maintains reserves at a subsistence level can be changed through community development and ownership of reserve industries. Given land, capital, natural resources, and a skilled labour force, Native autonomy could become a reality. The first three factors will be discussed in the following pages. As for skilled labour, it is enough to state that, though Natives currently have very few technical skills that can be used to further economic development, this can be quickly changed.

LAND

Reserve lands are essential to any plan for economic viability. However, because opportunities vary from region to region, the amount of assistance required also varies. For example, 65 bands with slightly over 40 000 members hold lands strategically located near major expanding urban centres. There is a great deal of undeveloped potential in these lands for urban, commercial, industrial, and recreational use. Considerable opportunities also exist for these band members in the labour force of the nearby cities.

The federal and provincial governments have consistently encouraged the agricultural development of reserve lands, with poor results. The use of reserves for farming was implicit in all treaties. Most recently, Alberta has created a program to further agricultural lands on reserves, claiming that, in 1980, only about 15 percent of agricultural potential was tapped, mostly under the control of non-Natives. Yet evidence clearly shows that agricultural development is not a viable strategy for economic growth.[4] Indeed, agricultural development can be viewed as a social control mechanism imposed by White society.

Across Canada, fewer than 1 000 000 hectares of reserve lands are potentially arable and only about 500 000 hectares could be used for grazing (DIAND, 1980). The remaining lands can support neither crops nor animals. If all potential arable and grazing land was fully developed, it would still only support a maximum of 4 000 farms. Given that each farm could support 10 people, roughly 40 000 Natives could be sustained. But what about the other 200 000 reserve Natives? Moreover, although the total area of reserve lands per capita has remained constant for the past twenty years (DIAND, 1980), recent increases in the Native population mean that by 1990 the hectares per capita will decrease substantially.

Other factors also inhibit Native control over reserve lands. Section 20 of the *Indian Act* prohibits Natives from buying land on their own reserves without the approval of the Minister. Bands also require special authority to purchase off-reserve lands. For some provinces, Section 32(1) of the *Act* only permits products grown on reserves to be sold to other band members, and even this requires written approval from the superintendent. Other economic controls include the *Farm Credit Act* established by the federal government to help Native farmers. In an astounding bureaucratic paradox, the *Act* gives a Native farmer long-term credit but only after a first mortgage has been taken on the farm. However, because the Crown owns all farms on the reserve, Natives cannot get first mortgages; the *Act* is totally useless to them.

NATURAL RESOURCES

According to DIAND, the mineral potential, both short- and long-term, of reserve lands is substantial, particularly for hydrocarbons. Between 1970 and 1980, Native revenues from mineral development increased over tenfold. From oil and gas alone, reserve revenues may well exceed $4 billion over the next twenty-five years.

Although oil and gas are generally confined to Alberta, other valuable mineral resources exist on the reserves of other provinces. As Figure 11.1 clearly shows, a sizable percentage of reserves in most provinces have "good-to-excellent" potential for the development of metallic, non-metallic, or structural resources. In the past few years, many economic feasibility studies have shown that these resources could be developed by Natives to improve conditions on their reserves.

Resources such as timber, tourism, and water are also valuable and untapped; these will be very important within the next few years.

FIGURE 11.1   *Mineral inventory: percentage of reserves in each province with good-to-excellent mineral potential*

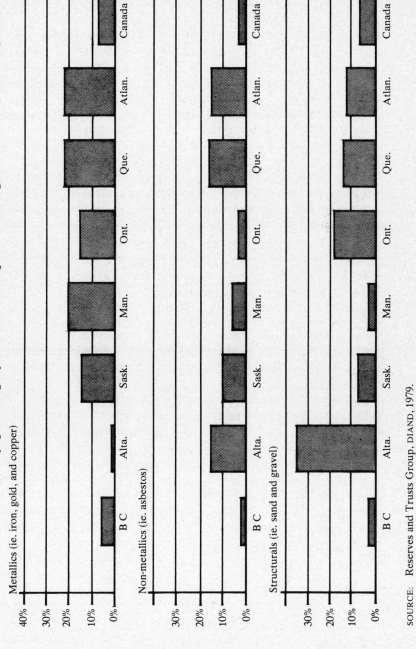

SOURCE: Reserves and Trusts Group, DIAND, 1979.

Fort Alexander, for instance, has a considerable amount of timber that could be milled at low cost. Well over 2 million pounds of fish were caught commercially by Natives in 1969. Forest products from reserves in 1967 included 90 million feet of timber, 65 000 cords of pulp wood, 1 million fence posts, and nearly 1 million Christmas trees (Canada Year Book, 1967:205). Further development has taken place since this time. Tourism, which may be regarded as a type of natural resource, has been under-exploited but could, in certain cases, become an important source of reserve revenue.

Reserve natural resources continue to be either undeveloped or controlled by White corporations with the official approval of DIAND. When potential mineral resources are found on a reserve, they are explored and developed by oil and mining companies under the provisions of the *Indian Act*. Oil and gas rights are offered by public tender and are granted to the company offering the highest cash bonus. Recently, the Alberta government has changed its tax structure so that companies exploring for gas and oil on reserve lands are ineligible for the tax benefits they would receive for off-reserve exploration. The possibility of Native development of these resources is never considered, and Natives remain a colonized people.

AVAILABILITY OF CAPITAL

Although the *Hawthorn Report* shows little correlation between the amount of capital income per band and the level of economic development, this finding is somewhat misleading. Few bands are allowed to control their own money. As a result, when a band does manage to increase its per capita income, the money is not re-invested in the reserve or in the band. Under federal direction, accumulated finances enter what is commonly called the "trust-fund", are invested in government bonds, or are used to fund one of several welfare projects on the reserve. Although the money that accumulates is substantial, it is kept out of Native control; during the 1970 fiscal year, DIAND administered band trust-funds totalling $30 million. Natives can be forgiven if they appear suspicious of this process: an investigation is still underway to ascertain how a Western band's trust-fund of $2.5 million diminished to less than $500 000 between 1968 and 1972.

Native groups or individuals who request money from DIAND are generally turned down. Each request must go through a series of bureaucratic procedures and be approved by the federal government. It generally takes from one to five years for a grant or loan request to be approved or rejected. Moreover, the final terms are never the same as those originally sought: they are modified at each step along the bureaucratic path. Jean Chretien, one-time Minister of DIAND, vividly detailed the problems in a Toronto speech:

> First the band council decides that they want to do something constructive and reasonable with a piece of their land as many of them do. They pass a council resolution which they hand over to the Department's agency office. It is sent from there to the regional office. The regional people, anticipating that their superiors in Ottawa will ask questions, ask questions themselves. Back it goes to the agency and back to the band. The band gets another meeting organized. They answer the questions and put the proposal back into the mill. It goes to the agency, to the region, and it finally reaches the head office where the lawyers get at it. They ask more questions that the region had not thought of. Back it goes. Eventually all the quesions are answered and it comes to me. (1969:8)

The loans and grants allocated by Indian Affairs are never enough to adequately finance a developmental scheme. Generally, the maximum is $10 000 to be repaid within five years. In 1965, the average grant was $100. In 1967, less than $500 000 was allocated to Natives in 115 grants, for an average of slightly over $4 000. In 1972, the loan fund was increased to over $3 million, but there continue to be restrictions on amounts and repayments. The Special Senate Committee Hearing on Poverty has noted that:

> ... though this fund has been of great assistance to Indians, it is still too small .... (T)o effect major economic change, more technical and managerial support must be made available. (1970:89)

Since 1960, several economic-development programs have emerged. Between 1960 and 1970, the main source of funding for economic development was the Indian Revolving Fund, a loan fund available to small businesses. This plan was narrow in focus, unambitious, ineffective, and could only offer several limited amounts of money. In 1970, the Indian Economic Development Fund (IEDF) was introduced for Native commercial and industrial development. Altogether, the (IEDF) made available $70 million in direct loans, $30 million in guaranteed loans, and approximately $10 million in non-repayable contributions; direct loans were obtained through DIAND, and guaranteed loans through private banks or lending institutions with security supplied by DIAND. By 1979, almost $100 million had been loaned to Natives through the IEDF, a considerable advance over DIAND's past record.[5] However, although the average size of DIAND's disbursements increased dramatically from the early- to the mid-1970s, the IEDF began to give priority to small, independent economic ventures in 1977.

While the IEDF is the major single supporter of Native economic development, other government departments have also contributed. Table 11.1 shows which departments have been involved and how much each has contributed in the five-year period between 1974 and 1979.

TABLE 11.1 *Economic development programs: federal expenditures on Indians ($thousands)*

	1974-75	1975-76	1976-77	1977-78	1978-79
CEIC					
Canada Works	—	—	—	21 442	21 581
Young Canada Works	—	—	—	2 232	2 511
LEAP	—	843	1 024	1 277	—
CMTP	9 018	11 398	15 088	16 716	10 333
CMITP	—	886	2 651	2 759	1 280
Outreach	282	476	902	1 009	754
Summer Youth Employment	496	871	1 357	5 034	4 705
Treasury Board					
FLIP	—	750	9 843	4 338	727
DREE					
Special ARDA	2 000	3 640	3 150	3 140	—
ARDA III	740	260	30	—	—
Other	—	20	100	100	—
Fisheries and Oceans	—	—	—	365	456
DIAND	27 668	34 002	44 591	42 647	43 481
Total	40 204	53 146	78 794	101 059	85 828

SOURCE: *Indian Conditions, Survey,* DIAND, 1980.

Community Development and Control

La Violette (1961) argues that for any ethnic group to survive it must be able to assert control over its fate. Essentially, the struggle for survival is a struggle for identity. The group must view its past positively and maintain strong links with traditional customs and beliefs. It must also achieve political equality and look forward to a promising future. These processes can only be set in motion at the grass-roots level. If Natives are going to control their destiny, they must implement community control immediately.

At present, reserves are not controlled by Natives. White Canadians occupy virtually all the powerful positions on the reserve, whether as RCMP officers, postal workers, store-owners, missionaries, teachers, or federal employees. An Indian Affairs survey in 1971 found that slightly over 7 000 non-Natives lived on reserves; of these, nearly 5 000 belonged to self-supporting families. The first step, then, is to remove non-Native teachers, police officers, federal officials, and so on, and to replace them with stable, local, resident Natives.

At present, governments are encouraging Natives to develop small businesses on an individual basis. By promoting individual entrepreneurs, White society maintains an indirect control of the reserve. When local businesses are owned by individual Natives, the larger White-dominated economic structure remains intact and White control is achieved in two ways. First, White society wins the loyalties of the Native businessmen, who are potentially important community leaders. Second, the visible ownership of local business by Natives defuses anti-White feelings and reduces the likelihood of violent demonstrations. The community becomes more stable, the leadership potential of White-affiliated Native businessmen is enhanced, and the White domination of the community economy, though less direct, remains intact. In addition, discontent is defused through acceptable channels (Tabb, 1970). Clearly, the strategy of individual entrepreneurship will not change the economic position of Natives substantially in the future.

Although community development must be encouraged, it must *not* be financed by the corporate sector of Canadian society. The federal government must not allow the corporate sector to interfere with or influence the development of Native communities. Native economic development is not in the corporations' interests. So far, through close ties with the political elite, corporations have successfully blocked the federal financing that would permit Native development. If Natives are allowed to develop and control the reserves, they will eliminate corporate contracts for reserve projects and drain off the unskilled-labour surplus for primary industries.

If the corporate sector were allowed to initiate economic development on reserves, franchising would result. Under a franchise system, a corporation advances money to an individual Native who then manages a store which sells the corporation's product exclusively. The corporation also provides certain services and trains staff to ensure proper marketing techniques. In return for setting up the store, providing the loan, and training the staff, the company reaps several benefits, including a large percentage of the profits and access to the reserve and nearby communities. Franchising is an efficient and inexpensive way to guarantee White corporate control of the reserve. Again, the presence of a Native staff defuses anti-White sentiments and prevents the organization of cohesive revolt. Moreover, the development of the reserve by outsiders allows for external control over the speed, extent, and nature of that development (Tabb, 1970:58).

Although White institutions are promoting individual entrepreneurship, many Natives have begun to recognize that the result of this policy will be continued subordination. Increasingly, cogent arguments like the following are being put forward in support of Native community control and development:

To accomplish this task, four sets of recommendations are proposed: (i) The establishment of economically viable reserves controlled by the Indians with sufficient natural resources to ensure adequate incomes for the residents. The key element in this recommendation is that the natural resources of expanded Indian lands should be firmly placed in the control of the community and its representative leaders. (ii) The establishment of an Indian corporation which can receive direct grants and long-term low-interest loans, to promote economic development on the reserve, to improve and initiate village services, and to in other ways enable Indians to better utilize their natural and economic resources. (iii) A major revamping of the educational system so as to reduce discontinuities in learning, sustain affective ties with parents, strengthen the student's self-image as Indian, and maintain his self-esteem, as well as prepare him to be economically and socially competent in dealing with the institutions of the larger Canadian society. (iv) The establishment of an Indian social-development program, funded by the federal and/or provincial governments, which can assist in providing the mechanism for the emergence of new Indian leaders, increase communication with other Indian and non-Indian groups, and promote local and regional community, social, and political infra-structures. (Chance, 1970:33-35)

To ensure success, Native economic development should follow a balanced approach. Just as a balanced diet includes a variety of foods, a balanced approach requires that several different industries be created simultaneously. If Native investment is diversified over a broad range of industries and economic sectors, these components will eventually become mutually supporting. Adherents of an unbalanced approach, meanwhile, advocate the development of one central industry that is likely to cause new and different industries to also be built. Its supporters feel that once the key industry is set up, the social overhead capital will continue to rise without a need for much long-range planning. In my opinion, the unbalanced approach lacks foresight and would not be suited to reserve economics.[6]

Proposals for Indian Advancement

Native people have all the basic resources needed to make the reserve economically viable. The following proposal would allow Native peoples to control their lives, uphold their identities, and become integrated into Canadian society on their own terms. These are not new proposals. Groups such as the Manitoba Indian Brotherhood in its *Wahbung* and the Indian Association of Alberta in its *Red Paper* have made similar recommendations. However, this section ties these ideas together in a single recipe for meaningful social change.[7]

1. *The full title of reserve lands must be given to Natives.* Under the *Indian Act*, the Minister of DIAND has absolute control over the lands established by earlier treaties. This control must be wrested from Ottawa bureaucrats and returned to the reserve communities. Natives need guarantees that, as they improve their land, they will not be encroached on by large cities, and that as they discover valuable minerals, they will not lose ownership of their land and resources. At the same time, the rights and obligations of both status and non-status Natives must be recognized by the federal government.

2. *Natives must be compensated for lands taken by White settlers.* The ancestors of fewer than half the Natives in Canada made treaties with the Canadian government. In addition, treaties were generally used as a quasi-legal weapon against the Natives.[8] By setting up reserves, the government was able to make prime land available to White settlers and to exploit natural resources without Native interference. As Morris states:

> In consequence of the discovery of minerals, on the shores of Lakes Huron and Superior, the government of the late Province of Canada, deemed it desirable, to extinguish the Indian title, and in order to that end, in the year 1850, entrusted the duty to the late Honourable William B. Robinson, who discharged his duties with great tact and judgement, succeeding in making two treaties. (1880:42)

Reserve grants to Indians were disproportionately small. For example, in Manitoba, 7.45 million acres were given to the Hudson's Bay Company, 1.9 million acres to the railroad, 1.4 million acres to the Métis, and fewer than 400 000 acres to the Indians. On a per capita basis, land grants given to White settlers at the time were about double those for Indians.

Native land claims fall into three categories: unfulfilled treaty commitments; lands taken from Native ownership through non-treaty processes; and comprehensive claims, illustrated in Figure 11.2. Unfulfilled treaty commitments formed the basis of claims filed by the Indians of Treaty No. 7; in 1977, the Supreme Court awarded these Indians $8 million in reparation for the government's long-term failure to distribute ammunition as specified by the treaty. Illegally seized lands formed the basis of the 1973 Wagmatcook band claim in Nova Scotia. According to the band, some 1 500 hectares of land had been severed from their reserve prior to and following Confederation. Although the federal government refused to accept responsibility for lands alienated in the late 1800s, it must pay the band $1 192 000 for later land seizures; however, over $200 000 has been deducted to pay back a federal loan for the band's research and legal expenses.

A further basis for Native claims, not yet established in law, rests on the outrageously misleading explanations given to Natives concerning the amount of land they were about to lose. Consider, for example, the terms used in the Selkirk Treaty (Treaty No. 1):

> The Indians then inhabiting the region were described as being of the Chippawa, of Saulteux and Illistine or Cree nations. They were made to comprehend the depth of the land they were surrendering, by being told, that it was the greatest distance, at which a horse on the level prairie could be seen or daylight seen under his belly between his legs. The consideration for the surrender, was, payment of 100 pounds of good merchantable tobacco, to each nation annually.[9] (Morris, 1880:15)

The actual areas involved here amounted to about 17 000 square miles.

Natives should also be compensated for the fact that they were not allowed to choose the land that formed their reserves. The Natives were only offered land considered inappropriate for White settlers. As is fully documented by White statements of the time, the territories offered to Natives were only considered fit for Crown land if turned down.

3. *The* IIAP *must be turned over to Natives.* Indian Affairs should be placed under the control of Natives with little or no outside interference. Under these conditions, DIAND could become as effective a lobbying force for the Natives as it has been against them in the past.

TABLE 11.2 *Economic activity summary, 1974-75, for Canadian Indians on reserves*[1]

Activity	Operations	Indians employed	Income total
Agriculture	1 191	1 637	2 487 374
Fishing	490	696	398 478
Forestry	203	913	898 008
Arts & crafts	1 455	2 603	303 984
Tourist outfitting and guiding	175	323	164 092
Commercial recreation	42	203	208 247
Industrial commercial, and real estate	610	1 900	2 743 456
Mineral	17	18	—
Wildlife	1 687	1 816	514 535
Other activities	—	6 446	—
Employment-Total	—	16 555	7 718 174

[1]These data are based upon 211 bands, including 377 reserves.

SOURCE: Departmental Statistics Division and Economic Program Development Division, DIAND, 1976.

As controllers of the IIAP, Natives would be able to allot budget expenditures as they saw fit. Currently, over 40 percent of DIAND's budget is spent on community-affairs programs, predominantly for welfare payments. Less than 10 percent is invested directly into community development, and less than 5 percent into economic development, the one area that would allow Natives to regain social and economic independence.

As Hatt has observed, Natives are not currently involved in the planning and development of government projects on the reserve. For instance, at a Manitoba reserve, timber land is being leased to a White-controlled corporation. In Ontario, the government has denied an Indian band the finances to develop its mining resources, but has given money to a White corporation for the same purpose. Clearly Indian Affairs, which claims to represent Native interests, supports a system in which Natives can only participate in industry at a marginal level as workers, and never as owners, planners, or directors.

4. *Natives must gain control of their trust funds in Ottawa.* Natives must have immediate access to these trust funds as well as complete control over spending them. Since 1960, Natives have gained some control over the funds through such reforms as the 1969 removal of Indian agents from reserves. The funds administered by the bands have also

increased, rising from $34.9 million in 1971-72 to $227.2 million in 1978-79. However, even DIAND has recognized that this process is much too slow:

> Although there has been a significant increase in local administration by Indians, the fact that bands are not yet fully self-administering communities may reflect both the difficulties of adopting to new forms of government and lingering obstacles in the *Indian Act* and/or government relations with Indian bands. (1980:88)

At present, the federal government apparently does not envisage full Native control in the near future over income generated from land, mineral resources, and Native investments. In lieu of Native control over trust funds, the federal government has tried to establish a number of alternative funds, loans, and grants. These alternative programs, however, are short-term, narrow in focus, and generally under-funded.

Most of the money in the trust funds comes from land, oil, and gas leases, and from the sale of natural resources such as timber and minerals. Before 1959, the trust-fund money was invested in commercial securities, but since then the federal government has assumed responsibility for handling it. Money from the funds must be used "in the interests of the band", interests which are determined by Ottawa. At present, Native projects must be approved by government before any money is released (Dunning, 1971).

Heilbrun and Wellisz (1969) have proposed that the federal government use the International Bank for Reconstruction and Development, the International Finance Corporation, and the International Development Authority as models. These organizations make loans to under-developed countries for various projects and provide equity for economic development. Programs adapted from these models would be of enormous benefit to reserve economies. First, because project workers would not be subject to an annual review for continued funds, they would not have to fear losing their support at the end of the second or third year. Second, projects could be developed that progressed slowly but steadily toward a cumulative goal. Finally, qualified staff would be attracted to the projects by the security that would accompany elimination of the annual funding review.

Table 11.2 shows the present commercial and industrial development of Indian reserves. There is a notable absence of any secondary, or processing, industry on the reserves. Additional data reveal that over 33 percent of the commercial businesses on reserves are controlled by Whites and that the total of nearly 900 commercial businesses employ just over 1 000 Natives, or just over 1 Native per business. These figures support claims that individual entrepreneurship is contrary to Native interests.

5. *Treaty rights originally guaranteed by the federal and provincial governments must be upheld.* The treaties completed the surrender of traditional Native lands from the borders of Ontario to the borders of British Columbia. In essence, these were peace and friendship treaties. The government agreed to provide reserve lands in trust for Natives to occupy and to grant Natives hunting, fishing and trapping rights on unoccupied Crown lands. If Natives lived adjacent to the White settlers in peace, they would receive rations, annuities, ammunition, agricultural implements, seeds, and cattle in varying amounts.

These agreements today pose a number of problems. For example, no settlements were made regarding the exploitation of natural resources on reserve lands: currently, only dividends for oil and gas discoveries accrue to Natives. Moreover, the land-base of the reserves was calculated by population at the time of settlement and without regard to future generations.

Disputes today between Native bands and the government focus on the failure of government to maintain many of its commitments, such as the distribution of tobacco, ammunition, and farm implements. Rights that were guaranteed to Natives and have since been denied include water rights, rights under the *Customs Act* to bring duty-free goods into the country, hunting rights under the *Migratory Birds Convention Act*, and fishing rights under the *Fisheries Act*. All of these are crucial attempts by Natives to upgrade their economic status and develop their reserve communities.

None of these suggestions are likely to find popularity among White Canadians. However, as MacGregor (1961) argues, creative development of any type will not emerge on the reserve until all conscious and unconscious forces opposing the Native administration of reserve lands are significantly reduced. Natives must be given authority to enact social changes without fear of reprisals from federal and provincial governments.

On Native reserves today, most economic development reflects minimal government support, short-term financing, and an unbalanced single-industry approach; in short, the antithesis of Sorenson's and Wolfson's (1969) recommended strategy for economic independence. By rejecting government support, Natives could keep profits within the reserve. With these savings, industries could be created that employed only Natives. Unfortunately, however, this process would be extremely slow. Instead, Natives should force governments to supplement local savings with capital grants and low-interest credit. This would eliminate the need for White-controlled middle-men and a dependence on outside credit.

Native people have to make a crucial decision. Can they allow selected outside interests to invest money in reserve development in exchange for various considerations? Or can they go it alone? Like the newly emerging nations, Natives must balance a desire for economic independence with a need for quick capital; so far, emerging nations have found that, although outside entrepreneurs and corporations stimulate economic activity in the short run, long-term economic development actually decreases and the per capita income is subsequently depressed.

Clearly, internal capital development is the answer. A self-contained, Native sub-economy could trade with the surrounding White population without having to drain capital by duplicating any existing services, such as highways and hydro-electricity. As a result, the sub-economy would have an important "external trade" advantage. The sub-economy would be composed of straightforward corporations owned and controlled by the Native community. These corporations would supply products to White-controlled industries but would not purchase goods in return (Sorenson and Wolfson, 1969). As Natives became self-sustaining and integrated with the larger economy, their modified sub-economy would survive and expand.

Conclusion

In relations between any minority group and dominant group, the minority group will attempt to change its position in the system by making demands. The dominant group must react to these demands either positively or negatively. In general, the dominant group will respond positively up to the critical point at which the status quo is seriously endangered (Lightbody, 1969).

Up to the critical point, the minority group continues to work within the system. As the critical point is approached, however, tension increases. Eventually, as the minority group is forced to press its demands further, overt conflict begins. As Lightbody explains,

> ... beyond (this critical point) the state must realign its institutional structures about a new ethnic configuration by either physically attempting to suppress the dissident elements into grudging assimilation into the culture, or through accepting the creation of the new political nationality and moving itself toward being an ethnically homogeneous national group. (1969:334)

At the critical point, the confict moves outside existing laws and results either in a change to those laws or in civil disobedience and revolt.

Willingness to pass the critical point into violence varies with the minority group. Certainly, Native Canadians have approached the point reluctantly, after long centuries of subjugation. Despite all they have endured, very little violence has taken place. However, with the upsurge of Red Power, Natives are demonstrating a determination to move outside the law if conditions do not soon improve.

Currently, Native Canadians find themselves isolated from White society and confronted by discrimination on a daily basis. To counter this position, they have recently begun the long, arduous task of defining their group identity and clarifying their future goals. The recent growth of Native organizations and periodicals shows that Natives are strengthening their political and cultural position. And, as Boldt has shown, they are increasingly willing to engage in "extra-legal" politics:

> Enlightened Indian leaders reject White society's comfortable notions of slow and steady progress toward the achievement of basic human rights for their people and most are inclined not only to approve of extra-legal activity as a justifiable means for achieving their conception of the "good society", but are also willing to participate and, if necessary, suffer the consequences of such actions for their cause. (1980:33)

Natives have learned over time that externally-directed conflict tends to enhance group solidarity. Group boundaries come into sharp focus as in-group members are differentiated from out-group members. As conflict emerges, the group is also forced to explicitly define its aims and goals. As grievances are defined, adversaries emerge and are identified. In the case of Native groups, the adversaries are White: relations between the two have become a zero-sum game.

In a zero-sum game, one player always gains precisely what the other player loses, and vice versa. In other words, relations between the two sides are always competitive and antagonistic. Identification with one's "side" pervades the daily life of each group member. Each participant finds a particular role in the collective action and receives internal and social rewards for behaviour that reinforces group aims. Identification with the group grows, as do linkages with other members. As Pettigrew describes:

> Recruits willingly and eagerly devote themselves to the group's goals. And they find themselves systematically rewarded (by the group) . . . . They are expected to evince strong racial pride, to assert their full rights as citizens, to face jail and police brutality unhesitatingly for the cause. Note that these expected and rewarded actions all publicly commit the member to the group and its aim. (1964:195-96)

And, as Himes states, out of organized group conflict grows a strong group identity:

> In the interactive process of organized group conflict, self-involvement is the opposite side of the coin of overt action. Actors become absorbed by

ego and emotion into the group and the group is projected through their actions. This linkage of individual and group in ego and action is the substance of identity. (1966:10)

With the emergence of Red Power, the sense of alienation experienced by many Natives has been dispelled by a new sense of significance and purpose. The personal ethnic identity of Natives is stronger now than it has been for many decades. As Pitts (1974) points out, ethnic identity is a social product, a result of actions and interpretations in a social context (Paige, 1971). As Brown argues:

A race conscious group . . . is a social unit struggling for status in society. It is thus a conflict group and race consciousness itself is a result of conflict. The race of the group, though not intrinsically significant, becomes an identifying symbol, serving to intensify the sense of solidarity. (1935)

Native identification is a mixture of internal dynamics and external pressures. At present, that identification is being translated into what Enloe (1981) calls ethnic mobilization – the mobilization of an ethnic group's resources and manpower to better its position. White Canada is bound to respond with such contemporary demobilization techniques as the *White Paper* to remain in a controlling position. Native mobililization in turn will increase, and the accelerating spiral of conflict will be set in motion.

Meaningful changes are desperately needed in the political, social, and economic position of Native Canadians. Acting from frustration and helplessness, Native leaders are increasingly abandoning the legal means to effect those changes. If White Canadians do not act quickly and respond effectively to Native demands, the future of Native-White relations in this country may well be written in blood.

Notes

1. Carstens (1971) uses a "peasantry model," although he agrees that the reserves can be viewed as little colonies within the dominant group.
2. In the middle of the nineteenth century, Charles Darwin published his *Origin of the Species*. His theoretical perspective centred on concepts such as evolution, natural selection, and survival of the fittest. It was an easy step for the layman and the social scientist to apply these biological concepts as evidence that Whites were somehow "more fit" than the groups they had defeated. Similarly, as long as a group continued to successfully exploit and make war on other nations, it proved itself further evolved.

3. Recommendation 7 of the *Hawthorn Report* says that Natives should be regarded as "citizens plus" because they possess certain additional rights as charter members of the Canadian community.

4. Recommendation 24 of the *Hawthorn Report* says that "in all but a minority of cases, no attempt should be made to train, encourage, and finance any large number of Indians to engage in commercial farming . . . ".

5. Compare this figure with the $131 000 loaned to Natives between 1938 and 1948.

6. For a more thorough discussion on the relative merits of the "unbalanced" versus the "balanced" approach, see Rosenstein-Roda, 1943; Nurske, 1953; Scitovsky, 1954; Hirschman, 1958; Lewis, 1956; Perroux, 1953; and Fellner, 1956. The first four authors advocate the balanced approach; the remainder support the unbalanced approach.

7. Others, such as Walsh and the Native Alliance for Red Power, have also suggested removal of legislative and constitutional bases of discrimination, recognition of the unique contribution of Native culture to Canadian society, provision by government agencies of certain services and programs for all Canadians, and more developed social services for Natives (Walsh, 1971:162-65).

8. A commission set up to investigate the provisions of Treaty 8 and Treaty 11 recommended in a 1959 report that money be paid to Natives to set up a reserve system. So far, nothing has been done.

9. In some cases, Indian commissioners were paid 10 percent of the money made from the sale of Indian lands.

BIBLIOGRAPHY

ABLON, JOAN. "American Indian Relocation: Problems of Dependency and Management in the City." In *Phylon,* 26 (Winter, 1965): 362-71.

ADAMS, HOWARD. *Prison of Grass.* Toronto: New Press, 1975.

THE ALBERTA FEDERATION OF MÉTIS SETTLEMENT ASSOCIATIONS. *The Métis People of Canada: A History.* Calgary: Gage Publishing Ltd., 1978.

ALLAN, D.J. "Indian Land Problems in Canada." In *The North American Indian Today,* edited by C.T. Loram and T.F. McIlwrath. Toronto: University of Toronto Press, 1943.

ANDERSON, A. "Linguistic Trends among Saskatchewan Ethnic Groups." In *Ethnic Canadians,* edited by M. Kovacs. Regina: University of Regina, 1978.

ANDERSON, DAVID, and ROBERT WRIGHT. *The Dark and Tangled Path.* Boston: Houghton Mifflin Co., 1971.

ANDRIST, RALPH. *The Long Death.* New York: Macmillan Publishing Co. Inc., 1964.

BARBER, LLOYD. *Commissioner on Indian Claims: A Report: Statements and Submissions.* Ottawa: Supply and Services Canada, 1977.

BARNETT, M.L., and D.A. BAERREIS. "Some Problems Involved in the Changing Status of the American Indian." In *The Indian in Modern America,* edited by D.A. Baerreis. Wisconsin State Historical Society (1965): 50-70.

BARTH, FREDERIK, editor. *Ethnic Groups and Boundaries: The Social Organization of Culture Difference.* Boston: Little, Brown and Co., 1969.

BARTLETT, R. *Indian Act of Canada.* Saskatoon: Native Law Centre, University of Saskatchewan, 1980.

BEAR ROBE, ANDREW. *A Study Tour of Canadian Friendship Centres,* Vols. 1 & 2. Ottawa: Steering Committee for the National Association of Friendship Centres, 1970.

BELCOURT, G.A. "Buffalo Hunt", translated by J.A. Burgess. In *The Beaver,* (December 1944): 13-17.

BENDIX, R. *Native Building and Citizenship.* New York: John Wiley, 1964.

BENNET, JOHN W. *Northern Plainsmen.* Chicago and New York: Aldine-Atherton, 1969.

BERGER, THOMAS. *Fragile Freedoms: Human Rights and Dissent in Canada.* Toronto: Clarke, Irwin & Co. Ltd., 1981.

BERGER, THOMAS R. *Northern Frontier, Northern Homeland — The Report of the MacKenzie Valley Pipeline Inquiry,* Vol. 1. Ottawa: Minister of Supply and Services Canada, 1977.

BERRY, BREWTON. *Almost White.* New York and London: Macmillan Publishing Co. Inc., 1963.

BLAUNNER, ROBERT. "Internal Colonialism and Ghetto Revolt." In *Social Problems,* 16 (Spring 1969): 393-408.

BIENVENUE, RITA, and A.H. LATIF. "Arrests, Dispositions and Recidivism: Comparison of Indians and Whites." In *Canadian Journal of Criminology and Corrections,* 16 (1974): 105-16.

____. "The Incidence of Arrests among Canadians of Indian Ancestry." Paper presented at Canadian Sociology & Anthropology meetings in Kingston, Ont., 1975.

BOEK, W.E.,. and J.K. BOEK. "The People of Indian Ancestry in Greater Winnipeg. Appendix 1: A Study of the Population of Indian Ancestry Living in Manitoba." Manitoba Department of Agriculture and Immigration, 1959.

BOLDT, M. "Canadian Native Leadership: Context and Composition." In *Canadian Ethnic Studies,* 12, 1(1980): 15-33.

____. "Indian Leaders in Canada: Attitudes toward Equality, Identity, and Political Status." Ph.D. dissertation. New Haven: Yale University Press, 1973.

____. "Philosophy, Politics, and Extralegal Action: Native Indian Leaders in Canada." In *Ethnic and Racial Studies,* 4, 2(1981): 205-21.

BOWLES, R. "Charter Group or Capitalist Class: An Analysis of Faces Shaping Canadian Ethnic Structures." Mimeographed. Peterborough: Trent University, 1979.

BOYCE, G.A. "New Goals for People of Indian Heritage." In *Sixth Annual Conference on Indians and Métis.* Winnipeg: Welfare Council for Greater Winnipeg, 1960.

BRAROE, N. *Indians and Whites: Self-Image and Interaction in a Canadian Plains Community.* Stanford: Stanford University Press, 1975.

BREWSTER, H. "Economic Dependence." Mimeographed. London: University of London, Institute of Commonwealth Studies, 1971.

BROWN, DEE. *Bury My Heart at Wounded Knee.* New York: Holt, Rinehart & Winston Inc., 1971.

BROWN, JENNIFER S.H. "A Colony of Very Useful Hands." In *The Beaver,* (Spring 1977): 39-45.

____. "Linguistics, Solitudes, and Changing Social Categories." In *Old Trails and New Directions: Papers of the Third North American Fur Trade Conference,* edited by Carol M. Judd and Arthur J. Ray. Toronto: University of Toronto Press, 1980.

____. *Strangers in Blood.* Vancouver: University of British Columbia Press, 1980a.

____. "Ultimate Respectability: Fur Trade Children in the 'Civilized World'." (Part One of two parts.) In *The Beaver,* (Winter 1977a): 4-10.

____. "Ultimate Respectability: Fur Trade Children in the 'Civilized World'." (Part Two of two parts.) In *The Beaver,* (Spring 1978): 48-55.

BROWN, W.C. "Racial Conflict among South African Natives." In *American Journal of Sociology,* 40: 569-681.

BUCKLEY, HELEN J. KEW, and F. HAWLEY. "The Indians and Métis of Northern Saskatchewan." Saskatoon: Saskatoon Centre for Community Studies, University of Saskatchewan, 1963.

CALDWELL, GEORGE. "Indian Residential Schools." Ottawa: Department of Indian Affairs and Northern Development, 1967.

CAMPBELL, MARIA. *Halfbreed.* Toronto: McClelland and Stewart Ltd., 1973.

CANADA, GOVERNMENT OF. *Annual Report 1966-67; 1967-68; 1968-69; 1969-70.* Department of Indian Affairs and Northern Development. Ottawa: Queen's Printer, 1966-70.

_____. "Canadian Committee on Corrections Report (Ouimet Report)." Ottawa: Queen's Printer, 1969.

_____. "Committee to Inquire into the Principles and Procedures Followed in the Remission Service of the Department of Justice of Canada Report (Fauteux Report)." Ottawa: Queen's Printer, 1956.

_____. "Evaluation of the RCMP Indian Special Constable Program (Option 3B)." Ottawa: IIAP, Evaluation Branch, Department of Indian Affairs and Northern Development, March 1978.

_____. *In All Fairness: A Native Claims Policy.* Ottawa: Minister of Supply and Services, 1981.

_____. "Indian Affairs and Northern Development Business Loan Fund: Indian Economic Development Direct Loan Order Policy and Guidelines." Ottawa: Department of Indian Affairs and Northern Development, Loan Fund Division, 1978b.

_____. *Indian Conditions, A Survey.* Ottawa: Department of Indian Affairs and Northern Development, 1980.

_____. *Indian News,* Vol. 22, 10 (January 1982). Ottawa: Department of Indian Affairs and Northern Development.

_____. *Perspective Canada I.* Ottawa: Information Canada, 1974.

_____. *Perspective Canada II.* Ottawa: Statistics Canada, Supply and Services, 1977.

_____. *Perspectives Canada III.* Ottawa: Statistics Canada, Supply and Services, 1979.

_____. "A Recommended Plan for Evaluation in Indian Education." Ottawa IIAP. Department of Indian Affairs and Northern Development, Program Evaluation Branch, 1978.

_____. "Report of Task Force: Policing on Reserves." Edmonton: Department of Indian and Northern Affairs, 1973.

_____. "Social Assistance and Related Social Development Programs of the Department of Indian and Northern Affairs." Ottawa: IIAP, Department of Indian Affairs and Northern Development, 1979.

_____. *Statement of the Government of Canada on Policy, 1969. (White Paper).* Ottawa: Queen's Printer, 1969.

THE CANADIAN SUPERINTENDENT. *The Education of Indian Children in Canada.* Toronto: Ryerson Press, 1965.

CARDINAL, H. *The Unjust Society.* Edmonton: Hurtig Publishers, 1969.

CARPENTER, JOCK. *Fifty Dollar Bride.* Sidney, BC: Gray's Publishing Ltd., 1977.

CARSTENS, PETER. *"Coercion and Change."* In *Canadian Society,* edited by Richard Ossenberg. Scarborough, Ont: Prentice-Hall of Canada, Ltd., 1971.

CASTELLANO, MARLENE. "Vocation or Identity: The Dilemma of Indian Youth." In *The Only Good Indian,* edited by Waubageshig. Toronto: New Press, 1970.

CHANCE, NORMAN. "Development Change among the Cree Indians of Quebec." Ottawa: Summary Report, ARDA Project 34002 (Reprint 1970), Department of Regional Economic Expansion, 1970.

CHASE-DUNN, CHRISTOPHER. "The Effects of International Economic Dependence and Inequality: A Cross-National Study." In *American Sociological Review,* 40 (1975): 720-38.

CHRETIEN, J. "Indian Policy . . . Where Does It Stand?" Speech at Empire Club, Toronto, Oct 16, 1969.

CLAIRMONT, DONALD H., and DENNIS W. MAGILL. "Nova Scotia Blacks: Marginality in a Depressed Region." In *Canada: A Sociological Profile,* 2nd ed., edited by W.E. Mann. Toronto: Copp Clark Pitman, 1979.

CLARKE, ROGER. "In Them Days: The Breakdown of A Traditional Fishing Economy in an English Village on the Gaspé Coast." Ph.D. dissertation. Montreal: McGill University Press, 1972.

COLVIN, E. "Legal Process and the Resolution of Indian Claims." In *Studies in Aboriginal Rights,* 3. Saskatoon: Native Law Centre, University of Saskatchewan, 1980.

CORRIGAN, S. "The Plains Indian Pow-wow: Cultural Integration in Manitoba and Saskatchewan." In *Anthropologica,* 12, 2 (1970): 253-71.

CUMMING, G. GRAHAM. "The Health of the Original Canadians 1867-1967." In *Medical Service Journal,* 13 (February, 1967): 115-66.

CUMMINGS, P. "Indian Rights—A Century of Oppression." Mimeographed. Toronto: Indian-Eskimo Association of Canada, 1969.

_____ . "Our Land—Our People: Native Rights, North of 60", In *Arctic Alternatives,* edited by D. Pimlott, K. Vincent, and C. McKnight. Ottawa: Canadian Arctic Resources Committee, 1973.

CUMMINGS, P., and N. MICKENBERG. *Native Rights in Canada,* 2nd ed. Toronto: Indian-Eskimo Association of Canada, 1972.

DANIEL, R. *A History of Native Claims and Processes in Canada.* Ottawa: Department of Indian Affairs and Northern Development, 1980.

DARROCH, A.G. "Another Look at Ethnicity, Stratification, and Social Mobility in Canada." In *Ethnicity and Ethnic Relations in Canada,* edited by J. Goldstein and P. Bienvenue. Scarborough, Ont.: Butterworth and Co. (Canada) Ltd., 1980.

DAVIS, A.D. "Canadian Society and History as Hinterland versus Metropolis." In *Canadian Society,* edited by Richard J. Ossenberg. Scarborough, Ont.: Prentice-Hall of Canada, Ltd., 1971.

DAVIS, ARTHUR K., CECIL L. FRENCH, WILLIAM D. KNILL and HENRY ZENTER. *A Northern Dilemma: Reference Papers.,* Vol. 2. Calgary and Bellingham, Wash.: Western Washington State College, 1965.

DAVIS, ARTHUR. "Urban Indians in Western Canada: Implications for Social Theory and Social Policy." In *Transactions of the Royal Society of Canada*, 6, 4 (1968): 217-28.

DENTON, T. "Migration from a Canadian Indian Reserve." In *Journal of Canadian Studies*, 7 (1972): 54-62.

DEPREZ, PAUL, and GLENN SIGURDSON. "Economic Status of the Canadian Indian: A Re-Examination." Winnipeg: Centre for Settlement Studies, University of Manitoba, 1969.

DIXON, VERNON. "Two Approaches to Black-White Relations." In *Beyond Black or White: An Alternative America,* edited by Vernon Dixon and Badmer Foster. Boston: Little, Brown and Co., 1971.

DOSMAN, EDGAR. *Indians: The Urban Dilemma.* Toronto: McClelland and Stewart Ltd., 1972.

DRIBEN, PAUL. "We Are Métis." Ph.D. dissertation. Minneapolis: University of Minnesota, 1975.

DRUCKER, P. "The Native Brotherhoods: Modern Intertribal Organizations on the Northwest Coast." Bureau of American Ethnology, 168. Washington, DC: Smithsonian Institute, 1958.

DUBOIS, W. *Dusk of Dawn.* New York: Harcourt, Brace and Co., 1940.

DUNNING, R. "Ethnic Relations and the Marginal Man in Canada." In *Human Organization,* 18, 3 (1959): 117-22.

———. "The Indian Situation: A Canadian Government & Dilemma." In *International Journal of Comparative Sociology,* 12 (June, 1971): 128-34.

DYCK, N. "Indian, Métis, Native: Some Implications of Special Status." In *Canadian Ethnic Studies,* 12, 1 (1980): 34-36.

———. "The Politics of Special Status: Indian Associations and the Administration of Indian Affairs." In *Ethnicity and Politics in Canada,* edited by J. Dahlie and T. Fernando. Agincourt, Ont.: Methuen Publications, 1981.

———. "Pow-wow and the Expression of Community in Westeren Canada." In *Ethnos,* 1-2 (1979): 78-79.

EDMONTON, CITY OF. "Native Adjustment to the Urban Environment: A Report on the Problems Encountered by Newly Arrived Natives in Edmonton." Edmonton: Social Services Department, Social Planning Division, 1976.

ELIAS, D. "Indian Politics in the Canadian Political System." In *The Patterns of "Amerindian" Identiy,* edited by Marc-Adelard Tremblay. Québec: Les Presses de L'Universite Laval, 1976, 35-64.

ELLIOT, J. *Educational and Occupational Aspirations and Expectations: A Comparative Study of Indian and Non-Indian Youth.* Antigonish: St. Francis Xavier University, 1970.

———. *Minority Canadians: Native Peoples.* Scarborough, Ont.: Prentice-Hall of Canada, Ltd., 1971.

———. "Native People, Power and Politics." In *Multiculturalism, 3, 3 (1980): 10-74.*

ENLOE, C. "The Growth of the State and Ethnic Mobilization: The American Experience." In *Ethnic and Racial Studies,* 4, 2 (1981): 123-36.

EWING COMMISSION REPORT. *Royal Commission on the Conditions of the Half-Breed Population of the Province of Alberta Report, 1935.* Sessional Paper No. 72, 1935.

FEDERATION OF SASKATCHEWAN INDIANS. "Off-Band Members in Saskatchewan." Mimeographed. Saskatoon: 1978.

FIDLER, DICK. *Red Power in Canada.* Toronto: Vanguard Publications, 1970.

FIELDS D., and W. STANBURY. *The Economic Impact of the Public Sector upon the Indian of British Columbia.* Vancouver: University of British Columbia Press, 1975.

FISHER, A.D. "White Rites versus Indian Rights." In *Transaction,* 7 (November 1969): 29-33.

FISHER, R. *Contact and Conflict: Indian-European Relations in British Columbia, 1774-1890.* Vancouver: University of British Columbia Press, 1977.

FOSTER, JOHN E. "The Métis, the People and the Term." In *Prairie Forum,* 3, 1 (Spring, 1978): 79-91.

_____. "Mixed Bloods in Western Canada: An Ecological Approach." "The Origins of the Mixed Bloods in the Canadian West." In *Essays on Western History,* edited by Lewis H. Thomas. Edmonton: The University of Alberta Press, 1976.

FITZGERALD, P.K. "Introduction" to *The Indian in Modern America,* edited by D.A. Baerreis. Wisconsin State Historical Society, 1956.

FRANK, ANDRÉ GUNDER. *Capitalism and Underdevelopment in Latin America.* New York: Monthly Review Press, 1967.

FRANKLIN, RAYMOND. "The Political Economy of Black Power." In *Social Problems,* 16 (Winter, 1969): 286-301.

FRENCH, B.F. *Historical Collections of Louisiana,* Dublin: Part 3, Arbers Annals, 1851.

FRIDERES, J.S. *Canada's Indians: Contemporary Conflicts.* Scarborough, Ont.: Prentice-Hall of Canada, Ltd., 1974.

_____. "Indians and Education: A Canadian Failure." In *Manitoba Journal of Education,* 7 (June, 1972): 27-30.

FRIDERES, J., and J. RYAN. "Program Evaluation of the Calgary Native Outreach Office." Unpublished report. Calgary: University of Calgary, 1980.

FUCHS, ESTELLE. "Time to Redeem an Old Promise." In *Saturday Review,* January 24, 1970: 53-58.

GAMSON, W. *Power and Discontent.* Illinois: Dorsey Press, 1969.

GERBER, L. "Community Characteristics and Out-migration from Indian Communities: Regional Trends." Paper presented at Department of Indian Affairs and Northern Development, Ottawa, Nov. 9, 1977.

_____. "The Development of Canadian Indian Communities: A Two-dimensional Typology Reflecting Strategies of Adaptation to the Modern World." In *The Canadian Review of Sociology and Anthropology,* 16 (1979): 4.

GIRAUD, MARCEL. "Métis Settlement in the Northwest Territories." In *Saskatchewan History,* VII, 1 (Winter, 1954) 49-53.

GIRVAN, N. "The Development of Dependency Economics in the Caribbean and Latin America." In *Social and Economic Studies,* 22 (1973): 1-33.

GOOSSEN, JAYNE N. "A Wearer of Moccasins." In *The Beaver,* (Autumn, 1978).

GRAY, JAMES H. *Men Against the Desert.* Saskatoon: Western Producer Book Service, 1967.

_____. *The Winter Years.* Toronto: MacMillan of Canada, 1966.

GREEN, JEROME. "When Moral Prophecy Fails." In *Catalyst,* 4 (Spring, 1969): 63-79.

HAGAN, J. "Criminal Justice and Native People: A Study of Incarceration in a Canadian Province." In *Canadian Review of Sociology and Anthropology.* Special issue, (August, 1974): 220-36.

HARDESTY, DONALD L. *Ecological Anthropology.* New York: John Wiley & Sons Inc., 1977.

HARPER, A. "Canadian Indian Administration: The Treaty System." In *America Indigena,* 7, 2 (1947): 129-40.

HARRIS, R. COLE, and JOHN WARKENTIN. *Canada before Confederation.* New York: Oxford University Press, 1974.

HARRISON, G.S. "The Alaska Native Claims Settlement Act: 1971." In *Arctic,* 25, 3 (1972): 232-33.

HATT, FRED K. "The Canadian Métis: Recent Interpretations." In *Canadian Ethnic Studies,* 3, 1 (1971): 23-26.

_____. "The Métis and Community Development in Northeastern Alberta." In *Perspectives on Regions and Regionalism and Other Papers,* edited by B.Y. Card. Edmonton: University of Alberta, 1969, 111-19.

HAWTHORN, H.B. *A Survey of the Contemporary Indians of Canada,* 2 Vols. Indian Affairs Branch. Ottawa: Queen's Printer, 1966-67. Excerpts reproduced by permission of Information Canada.

HAWTHORN, H.B., ET AL. *The Indians of British Columbia.* Toronto: University of Toronto Press, 1958.

HEILBURN, JAMES, and STANISLAW WELLISZ. "An Economic Program for the Ghetto." In *Urban Riots,* edited by Robert Conner. New York: Random House Inc., 1969.

HERTZBERG, HAZEL. *Search for an American Indian Identity: Modern Pan-Indian Movements.* Syracuse, NY: Syracuse University Press, 1971.

HIMES, J. "The Functions of Racial Conflict." In *Social Forces,* 45 (1966): 1-10.

HIRSCHMANN, ALBERTA. *The Strategy of Economic Development.* New Haven: Yale University Press, 1958.

HODGETTS, J.E. *Pioneer Public Service—An Administrative History of the United Canadas, 1841-1867.* Toronto: University of Toronto Press, 1955.

HOEBEL, E.A. "To End Their Status." In *The Indian in Modern America,* edited by D.A. Baerreis. Madison: The Wisconsin State Historical Society, 1956, 1-15.

HONIGMAN, JOHN. *Personality in Culture.* New York: Harper and Row Pubs. Inc., 1967.

HOWARD, J. "Notes on the Dakota Grass Dance." In *Southwestern Journal of Anthropology,* 7 (1951): 82-85.

HOWARD, JOHN KINSEY. *Strange Empire.* Toronto: Swan Publishing Co. Ltd., 1952.

HUNT, GEORGE. *The Wars of the Iroquois: A Study in Intertribal Trade Relations.* Madison: University of Wisconsin Press, 1940.

INDIAN ASSOCIATION OF ALBERTA. *The Native People.* Edmonton, 1971.

INDIAN TRIBES OF MANITOBA. *Wahbung (Our Tomorrows).* Winnipeg: Manitoba Indian Brotherhood, 1971.

INNIS, HAROLD A. *The Fur Trade in Canada.* Toronto and Buffalo: University of Toronto Press, 1970.

IRONSIDE, R.G., and E. TOMASKY. "Agriculture and River Lot Settlement in Western Canada: The Case of Pakan." In *Prairie Forum* I, 1 (April, 1976): 3-18.

JACK, HENRY. "Native Alliance for Red Power." In *The Only Good Indian,* edited by Waubageshig. Toronto: New Press, 1970.

JAMES, BERNARD. "Social-Psychological Dimensions of Ojibwa Acculturation." In *American Anthropologist,* 63 (August, 1961): 728-44.

JENNESS, DIAMOND. "The Indian Background of Canadian History." Bulletin No. 86, Anthropological Series No. 21. Ottawa: Department of Mines and Resources. 1937.

_____. *Indians of Canada,* 7th ed. Ottawa: Queen's Printer, 1967.

JOHNSON, S. *Migrating Native Peoples Program.* Ottawa: National Association of Friendship Centres, 1976.

JONES, FRANK and WALLACE LAMBERT. "Some Situational Influences on Attitudes toward Immigrants." In *British Journal of Sociology,* 18 (March, 1967): 408-24.

KAEGI, GERDA. *The Comprehensive View of Indian Education.* Toronto: Indian-Eskimo Association of Canada, 1972.

KARDINER, ABRAHAM, and LIONEL OVESEY. *The Mark of Oppression.* New York: W.W. Norton & Co., 1951.

KENNEDY, RAYMOND. "The Colonial Crisis and the Future." In *The Science of Man in the World Crisis,* edited by Ralph Linton. New York: Columbia University Press, 1945.

KING, CECIL. "Sociological Implications of the Jeannette Corbiere Lavell Case." In *The Northian,* 8 (March, 1972): 45-55.

KWAN, K.M., and TAMOTSU SHIBUTANI. *Ethnic Stratification.* Toronto: Macmillan Co. of Can. Ltd., 1965.

LAGASSE, JEAN. "Community Development in Manitoba." *Human Organization,* 20 (Winter, 1962): 232-37.

_____. *A Study of the Population of Indian Ancestry Living in Manitoba.* Winnipeg: Department of Agriculture and Immigration, 1959.

LAING, A. *Indians and the Law.* Ottawa: Queen's Printer, 1967.

LARUSTIC, IGNATIUS. "Hunter to Proletarian." Research paper for Cree Development Change Project, 1968.

LUSSIER, ANTOINE S. and D. BRUCE SEALEY, eds. *The Other Natives the—les Métis,* Winnipeg: Manitoba Métis Federation Press, 1978.

LA VIOLETTE, F.E. *The Struggle for Survival.* Toronto: The University of Toronto Press, 1961.

LESLIE, J. and R. MAGUIRE. *The Historical Development of the Indian Act, Treaties, and Historical Research Centres.* Ottawa: Department of Indian Affairs and Northern Development, PRE Group, 1978.

LIGHTBODY, J. "A Note on the Theory of Nationalism as a Function of Ethnic Demands." In *Canadian Journal of Political Science,* 2 (1969): 327-37.

LINDENSMITH A., and A. STRAUSS. *Social Psychology.* New York: Holt, Rinehart and Winston, 1968.

LOWER, A. *Colony to Nation: A History of Canada.* Toronto: Longman, Green & Co., 1957.

LURIE, N. "The Contemporary American Indian Scene." In *North American Indians in Historical Perspective,* edited by E. Leacock and N. Lurie. New York: Random House Inc., 1971.

LYON, L., J. FRIESEN, W.R. UNRUH, and R. HERTOZ. *Intercultural Education.* Calgary: Faculty of Education, University of Calgary, 1970.

MACKIE, MARLENE. "Ethnic Stereotypes and Prejudice: Alberta Indians, Hutterites, and Ukrainians." In *Canadian Ethnic Studies,* 6, 1-2 (1974): 39-53.

MANUEL, G., and M. POSLUMS. *The Fourth World: An Indian Reality.* Toronto: Collier-Macmillan Canada Ltd., 1974.

MARIATEGUI, J.C. *Siete ensayos de interpretacion de la sealidad peruana,* 2nd ed. Lima: Editorial Libreria Peruana, 1934.

MARULE, M.S. "The Canadian Government's Termination Policy: From 1969 to the Present Day." In *One Century Later,* edited by J. Getty and D. Smith. Vancouver: University of British Columbia Press, 1977.

McCASKILL, D. "The Urbanization of Indians in Winnipeg, Toronto, Edmonton, and Vancouver: A Comparative Analysis." In *Culture,* 1 (1981): 82-89.

McCULLUM, H., and K. McCULLUM. *This Land is not For Sale.* Toronto: Anglican Book Centre, 1975.

McEWAN, GRANT. *Between the Red and the Rockies.* Toronto and Buffalo: University of Toronto Press, 1952.

McINNIS, E. *Canada: A Political and Social History.* New York: Holt, Rinehart and Winston Inc., 1959.

McLEOD, MARGARET and W.L. MORTEN. *Cuthbert Grant of Grantown.* Toronto: McClelland and Stewart Ltd., 1974.

McNAMARA, ROBERT. "The Ethics of Violent Dissent." In *Urban Riots,* edited by Robert Connery. New York: Random House Inc., 1969.

MELLING, J. "Recent Developments in Official Policy towards Canadian Indians and Eskimos." In *Race,* 7 (1966): 382-89.

MÉTIS AND NON-STATUS INDIAN CRIME AND JUSTICE COMMISSION. *Report.* Serpent River Reserve, Cutler, Ont.: Woodland Studio, 1977.

MICKENBERG, NEIL. "Aboriginal Rights in Canada and the United States." In *Osgoode Hall Law Journal,* 9 (1971): 154.

MILLS, C.W. *The Sociological Imagination.* New York: Oxford University Press, 1961.

MONTAGU, ASHLEY. "The Myth of Blood." In *Race, Individual, and Collective Behaviour,* edited by Edgar T. Thompson and Everett R. Hughes. Glencoe, Ont.: The Free Press, 1943.

MOORE, R. "The Historical Development of the Indian Act." Draft manuscript. Ottawa: Department of Indian Affairs and Northern Development, 1978.

MORRIS, ALEXANDER. *The Treaties of Canada with the Indians of Manitoba and the North West Territories.* Toronto: Belfords, Clarke & Co., 1880.

MORTON, W.L. "The Historical Phenomenon of Minorities: The Canadian Experience." In *Canadian Ethnic Studies,* 13, 3 (1981): 1-39.

_____. *The Kingdom of Canada: A General History from Earliest Times.* Toronto: McClelland and Stewart Ltd., 1963.

MYERS, G. *A History of Canadian Wealth.* Chicago: University of Chicago Press, 1914.

MYRDAL, G. *Rich Lands and Poor.* New York: Harper and Row Pubs. Inc., 1957.

NAGLER, MARK. *Indians in the City.* Ottawa: Canadian Research Centre for Anthropology, St. Paul University, 1971.

NAMMACK, GEORGINA. *Fraud, Politics, and the Dispossession of the Indians.* Norman, Okla.: University of Oklahoma Press, 1969.

NEILS, ELAINE. *Reservations to City.* Chicago: University of Chicago Press, 1971.

NELSON, J.G. *The Last Refuge.* Montreal: Harvest House Ltd., 1973.

NURKSE, RAGNAR. *Problems of Capital Formation in Underdeveloped Countries.* New York: Oxford University Press, 1953.

OLIVER, S.C. "Ecology and Cultural Continuity as Contributing Factors in the Social Reorganizations of the Plains Indians." In *University of California Publications in American Archeology and Ethnology,* 48, 1 (1962): 123-35.

OSSENBERG, R., editor. *Power and Change in Canada.* Toronto: McClelland and Stewart Ltd., 1980.

PAIGE, J. "Political Orientation and Riot Participation." In *American Sociological Review,* 36 (1971): 810-19.

PANNEKOEK, F. "The Anglican Church and the Disintegration of Red River Society, 1818-1870." In *The West and the Nation,* edited by C. Berger and R. Cook. Toronto: McClelland and Stewart Ltd., 1976.

PATTERSON, E. PALMER. *The Canadian Indians: A History Since 1500.* Don Mills, Ont.: Collier-MacMillan Canada Ltd., 1972.

PELLETIER, EMILE. *A Social History of the Manitoba Métis.* Winnipeg: Manitoba Métis Federation Press, 1974.

_____. *Exploitation of Métis Lands.* Winnipeg: Manitoba Métis Federation Press, 1975.

PELLETIER, W. *Two Articles.* Toronto: Neewin Publishing Co., 1970.

PETERS, OMAR. "Canada's Indians and Eskimos and Human Rights." Paper presented to the Thinkers' Conference on Cultural Rights, 1968.

PETTIGREW, T. *A Profile of the Negro American.* Princeton: D. Van Nostrand Co., 1964.

PIORE, MICHAEL. *Public and Private Responsibility in On-the-Job Training of Disadvantaged Workers.* Department of Economics Working Paper. Massachussetts: MIT Press, 1968.

PITTS, J. "The Study of Race Consciousness: Comments on New Directions." In *American Journal of Sociology,* 80 (1975): 665-87.

POLANYI, KARL. *The Great Transformation.* Boston: Beacon Press Inc., 1974.

PONTING, J.R., and R. GIBBINS. *Out of Irrelevance: A Socio-political Introduction to Indian Affairs of Canada.* Toronto: Butterworth & Co. (Canada) Ltd., 1980.

PRESTHUS, R. *Elites in the Policy Process.* London: Cambridge University Press, 1974.

PRICE, J. "Historical Theory and the Applied Anthropology of U.S. and Canadian Indians." In *Human Organization,* 41, 2 (1982): 43-53.

____. *Indians of Canada: Cultural Dynamics.* Scarborough, Ont.: Prentice-Hall of Canada, Ltd., 1979.

____. *Native Studies.* Toronto: McGraw-Hill Ryerson Ltd., 1978.

____. "U.S. and Canadian Indian Periodicals." In *Canadian Review of Sociology and Anthropology,* 9 (May, 1972): 150-62.

____. "The Viability of Indian Languages in Canada." In *Canadian Journal of Native Studies,* 1, 2 (1981): 349-61.

PRICE, R., ed. *The Spirit of the Alberta Indian Treaties.* Montreal: Institute for Research on Public Policy, 1979.

PRITCHETT, J.P. *The Red River Valley, 1811-1849: A Regional Study.* Toronto: Ryerson Press, 1942.

PROSS, P. *Pressure Group Behaviour in Canadian Politics.* Scarborough, Ont.: McGraw-Hill Ryerson Inc., 1975.

RAY, ARTHUR J. *Indians in the Fur Trade.* Toronto and Buffalo: University of Toronto Press, 1974.

REEVES, W., and J. FRIDERES. "Government Policy and Indian Urbanization: The Alberta Case." In *Canadian Public Policy,* VII, 4 (Autumn, 1981): 584-95.

REPORT ON THE AFFAIRS OF THE INDIANS IN CANADA. "History of the Relations between the Government and the Indians." In *Journals,* Section 1. Ottawa: Queen's Printer, 1844.

RICHARDSON, B. *James Bay.* San Francisco: Sierra Club, 1972.

ROE, GILBERT FRANK, *The North American Buffalo.* Toronto and Buffalo: University of Toronto Press, 1951.

ROMANUIK, A., and V. PICHE. "Natality Estimates for the Canadian Indians by Stable Population Models, 1900-1969." In *The Canadian Review of Sociology and Anthropology,* 9, 1 (1972): 1-20.

ROSENSTEIN-RODAN, P.N. "Problems of Industrialization of Eastern and Southeastern Europe." In *Economic Journal,* 53 (June-September, 1943): 128-56.

ROSS, ALEXANDER. *The Red River Settlement.* Edmonton: Hurtig Publishers, 1972.

RYERSON, S. *The Founding of Canada: Beginning to 1815.* Toronto: McClelland and Stewart Ltd., 1960.

RYAN, J. *Wall of Words: The Betrayal of the Urban Indian.* Toronto: Peter Martin Associates, 1978.

SAWCHUCK, JOE. *The Métis of Manitoba: Reformulation of an Ethnic Identity.* Toronto: Peter Martin Associates, 1978.

SCHMEISER, D. *The Native Offender and the Law.* Ottawa: Information Canada, 1974.

SEALEY, D. BRUCE. "One Plus One Equals One." In *The Other Natives: the Métis.* edited by Antoine S. Lussier and D. Bruce Sealey. Winnipeg: Manitoba Métis Federation Press, 1978.

SEALEY, D. BRUCE, and ANTOINE S. LUSSIER, *The Métis — Canada's Forgotten People.* Winnipeg: Manitoba Métis Federation Press, 1975.

SHEA, I.G. *Charlevoix's History of New France.* New York: Colonial Documents, Vol. 2, 1879.

SIGGNER, A. "A Socio-demographic Profile of Indians in Canada." In *Out of Irrelevance,* Chapter 2, edited by J.R. Ponting and R. Gibbins. Toronto: Butterworth & Co. (Canada) Ltd., 1980.

SIGGNER, A., and C. LOCATELLI. *Regional Population Projections by Age, Sex, and Residence for Canada's Registered Indian Population, 1976-1991.* Ottawa: Research Branch, Department of Indian Affairs and Northern Development, 1980.

SILVER, ARTHUR. "French Québec and the Métis question, 1869-1885." In *The West and the Nation,* edited by Carl Berger and Ramsay Cook. Toronto: McClelland and Stewart Ltd., 1976.

SLOBODIN, RICHARD. *Métis of the Mackenzie District.* Ottawa: Research Centre for Anthropology, St. Paul University, 1966.

SORENSON, GARY, and MURRAY WOLFSON. "Black Economic Independence: Some Preliminary Thoughts." In *The Annals of Regional Science,* 3 (December, 1969): 168-78.

SOUTHESK, THE EARL OF. *Saskatchewan and the Rocky Mountains.* Edmonton: Hurtig Publishers, 1968.

SPECIAL SENATE COMMITTEE HEARING ON POVERTY. *Proceedings,* Vols. 13-14. Ottawa: Supply and Services Canada, 1978.

SPENCER, R. and J. JENNINGS. *The Native Americans.* New York: Harper and Row Pubs. Inc., 1965.

SPRENGER, G. HERMAN. "The Métis Nation: Buffalo Hunting versus Agriculture in the Red River Settlement." In *Western Canadian Journal of Anthropology,* III, 1 (1972): 158-78.

SPRY, IRENE. "The Great Transformation: The Disappearance of the Commons in Western Canada." In *Man and Nature on the Prairies,* edited by Richard Allen. Regina: Canadian Plains Research Center, 1976.

STANBURY, W., and J. SIEGAL. *Success and Failure: Indians in Urban Society.* Vancouver: University of British Columbia Press, 1975.

STANLEY, GEORGE. "The Indian Background of Canadian History." In *Canadian Historical Association Annual Report.* Canadian Historical Society, 1952.

STANLEY, GEORGE F.G. *The Birth of Western Canada: A History of the Riel Rebellions.* New York: Longman, Green and Co., 1961.

STAVENHAGEN, R. "Seven Fallacies about Latin America." In *Latin America: Reform or Revolution?,* edited by J. Petras and M. Zeitling. New York: Greenwich Press, 1963.

STEWART, WALTER. "Red Power." In *Canada's Indians: Contemporary Conflicts,* edited by J.S. Frideres. Scarborough, Ont.: Prentice-Hall of Canada Ltd., 1974.

STYMEIST, DAVID H. *Ethnics and Indians: Social Relations in a Northwestern Ontario Town.* Toronto: Peter Martin Associates, 1975.

SUNKEL, OSWALDO. "Transitional Capitalism and National Disintegration in Latin America." In *Social and Economic Studies,* 22 (1973): 132-76.

SURTEES, R.J. "The Development of an Indian Reserve Policy in Canada." In *Ontario History,* LCI, 2 (June, 1969): 87-98.

SYMONS, T.H.B. "The Obligations of History: A Review of Native Rights in Canada." In *Indian-Eskimo Association of Canada Bulletin,* 2, 3 (1970): 5-7.

TABB, WILLIAM. *The Political Economy of the Black Ghetto.* New York: W.W. Norton and Co., 1970.

THOMAS, CYRUS. "Indian Land Cessions in the United States." In *18th Annual Report of the Bureau of American Ethnology,* Vol. 2. Washington DC: Smithsonian Institute, 1896.

THOMAS, D.H. "Western Shoshoni Ecology Settlement Patterns and Beyond." In *Great Basin Cultural Ecology: A Symposium,* edited by D.D. Fowler. Desert Research Institute, Publications in the Social Sciences, 8, 1972.

TOBIAS, J. "Protection, Civilization, Assimilation: An Outline of Canada's Indian Policy." In *Western Canadian Journal of Anthropology,* 6, 2 (1976): 13-30.

TRIGGER, BRUCE. "The Jesuits and the Fur Trade." In *Ethnohistory,* 12 (Winter, 1965): 30-53.

TRUDEL, MARCEL, and GENEVIEVE JAIN. "Canadian History Textbooks." In *Studies of the Royal Commission on Bilingualism and Biculturalism,* No. 5. Ottawa: Queen's Printer, 1970.

VALENTINE, V. "Canadian Indians." In *Ethnicity, Language, and the Cohesion of Canadian Society,* edited by R. Breton, J. Reitz, and V. Valentine. Montreal: Institute for Research in Public Policy, 1978.

VANDERBURGH, R. "The Canadian Indians in Ontario's School Texts: A Study of Social Studies Textbooks, Grades 1 through 8." Report prepared for the University Women's Club of Port Credit, Ont., 1968.

VAN KIRK, SYLVIA. *Many Tender Ties.* Winnipeg: Watson & Dwyer Publishing Ltd., 1980.

VERDUN-JONES, S., and G. MUIRHEAD. "Natives in the Criminal Justice System: An Overview." In *Crime and Justice,* 7/8, 1 (1979-80): 3-21.

VINCENT, DAVID. *An Evaluation of the Indian-Métis Urban Problem.* Winnipeg: University of Winnipeg Press, 1970.

WADDELL, JACK, and O.M. WATSON. *The American Indian in Urban Society.* Boston: Little, Brown and Co., 1971.

WALKER, JAMES. "The Indians in Canadian Historical Writing." Paper delivered at Canadian Historical Association meetings, 1971.

WALSH, GERALD. *Indians in Transition.* Toronto: McClelland and Stewart Ltd., 1971.

WASHBURN, WILCOMB. "Indian Removal Policy: Administrative, Historical, and Moral Criteria for Judging Its Success or Failure." In *Ethno-History,* 12 (Winter, 1965): 274-78.

WAUBAGESHIG. *The Only Good Indian.* Toronto: New Press, 1970.

WEAVER, S. *The Hidden Agenda.* Unpublished manuscript. Waterloo, Ont.: University of Waterloo, 1980.

WHITESIDE, D. "Bullets, Bibles, Bureaucrats, and Businessmen: Indian Administration in Upper Canada, 1746-1980." Address to the Indian Historical Conference, Walpole Island Reserve, November 15, 1980.

_____. "A Good Blanket Has Four Corners: An Initial Comparison of the Colonial Administration of Aboriginals in Canada and the United States." Paper presented at the Western Association of Sociology and Anthropology, Calgary, Alta., 1972.

_____. "Historical Development of Aboriginal Political Associations in Canada: Documentation." Ottawa: National Indian Brotherhood, 1973.

WHITESIDE, DON (sin a paw), and SCOTT DOUGLAS WHITESIDE. "Indians in Upper Canada through 1845, with special reference to half-breed Indians." In *The Circle being Threatened.* Ottawa: Aboriginal Institute of Canada, 1979.

WILLHELM, SIDNEY, M. "Red Man, Black Man, and White America: The Constitutional Approach to Genocide." In *Catalyst,* 4 (Spring, 1969): 3-4.

WOODCOCK, GEORGE. *Gabriel Dumont: The Métis Chief and His Lost World.* Edmonton: Hurtig Publishers, 1975.

WUTTNEE, W. *Ruffled Feathers.* Calgary: Bell Books Ltd., 1972.

Index